FIRE ON THE MOUNTAIN

** THE WHOLE TOMATO **
Edition

Copyright © 2007 by Roger Sachs

Freedom Crusade,
1810 N. Tanya Court, Suite 201,
Santa Maria, CA 93454
E-mail address: freedomcrusade8@gmail.com

All rights reserved. No part of this publication may be reproduced, stored in a retrieval system or transmitted, in any form, or by any means, electronic, mechanical, recorded, photocopied, or otherwise, without the prior permission of the copyright owner, except by a reviewer who may quote brief passages in a review.

Printed in the United States of America

ISBN 10: 0-9785433-0-0
ISBN 13: 978-0-9785433-0-3

www.freedomcrusade.info

CONTENTS

PREFACE 7

PART I
"THE ROAD TO OBLIVION"

1	"FIRE ON THE MOUNTAIN"	11
2	"FREMONT FARMERS"	22
3	"EAST SIDE KIDS"	29
4	"MISERY, AGONY & HEARTBREAK"	45
5	"DEUTSCHLAND"	51
6	"CHRISTMAS BELLS IN VIENNA"	60
7	"ELVIS" AND THE "EM CLUB"	66
8	"CLIFF"	71
9	"ORLEANS, FRANCE"	77
10	"A BRICK OF HASH"	83
11	"WESTWARD HO"	91
12	"LA 1968"	97
13	"KINGS AND SILVERS"	109
14	"PAY TO PLAY"	120
15	"THE WHITE HOUSE"	128
16	"BARBARIAN"	141
17	"SIX KILOS & A HEARTACHE"	152
18	"IT'S JUST A BOWL OF CHERRIES"	163
19	"I GOT A PLAN"	173

PART II
"LA MESA"

20	"ALONE IN T.J"	183
21	"THE STREETS OF SAN DIEGO"	196
22	"O.B. TO BOULDER"	208
23	"MIKE"	216
24	"WHAT A TRIP"	225
25	"RICH MAN'S SPEED"	235
26	"A MONKEY NAMED ROSE"	245
27	"THE BLACK JEW"	257
28	"TEN SECONDS"	272
29	"LA OCHO"	282
30	"LA MESA"	288
31	"LIKE A YO-YO"	294
32	"PARTNERS"	303
33	"CHOCOLATE MESCALIN"	309
34	"THEATER OF THE MACABRE"	319
35	"ABSTRACT CROSSES"	329

PART III
"CUSTOM PLATES"

36	"THE MEADOW"	339
37	"TOPANGA DAYS"	350
38	"KIMO JO"	356
39	"TREE RENT"	361
40	"SIGN AFTER SIGN"	370
41	"A SECURITY BREACH"	382
42	"THE MIDNIGHT HOUR"	387
43	"IF THERE'S ANY TRUTH"	394
44	"REV"	402
45	"UPSIDE DOWN WORLD"	411

46	"THE DREAM"	417
47	"THUNDER IN THE SKY"	422
48	"AMAZING"	431
49	"THE VINEYARD"	439
50	"CITY OF REFUGE"	445
51	"REAL MEXICAN PANCHOS"	450
52	"AN APACHE AND A MISSION"	457
53	"TROUBLE IN PARADISE"	461
54	"THE FBI LIED"	472
55	"ANIMAL"	479
56	"SECOND CHANCES"	487
57	" REBEL WITH A CAUSE "	496
58	"TO OPRAH FROM LONNIE "	504
59	"CUSTOM PLATES "	509

Postscript 522
Acknowledgements 526

*Dedicated to my Apache Indian friend Henry Garcia
and his wife Anita
(and to all those who help along the path)*

They often say that good things take a long time "a coming". Maybe this story will qualify. I started it in 1975 ... and it's definitely been a long time coming. This is 1997 and counting.

I see this gigantic branch reaching out over the Grand Canyon ... with me getting ready to walk ... like an almost grown up Huckleberry Finn with bare feet. It gets narrow out there. Can you visualize hanging by a twig over the Grand Canyon? I can. That's about how qualified I feel to undertake this task ... but hey ... this is America. Who knows, it might be a rush hanging by a prayer in space.

I've been learning about timing and being in tune. Well, I feel the timing is right for this story. It's a true account with more than a few twists. The path intersected and intertwined with several radical characters. One they called ... "The Phantom". Another one was simply labeled ... "Animal" ... and then there was Lonnie Frisbee. What a trip! It might even take two or three short books to complete one long story. We'll see. (Ten year update ... another decade has shot past. That was quick. I'm putting the entire story together and calling this initial printing "The Whole Tomato".) I've also changed several names to protect people's privacy. Nevertheless, to the very best of my ability I'll make sure that every detail is just the way it happened. That's a tall order. Be it as it may ... this is the truth ... so help me God!

ROGER SACHS

Sometimes it takes a little poison to make a cure.
—Lonnie Frisbee

PART I

"THE ROAD TO OBLIVION"

CHAPTER ONE

"FIRE ON THE MOUNTAIN"

I looked up into the starlit June sky through the branches. My mind was racing a million miles an hour. It was a super dark night in 1975. Suddenly, I thought of my Grandpa Ira. A wave of anger and grief hit me like a truck.

"He is dead!! You son of a _____! I grabbed a 2 x 4 and ripped it loose. The combination of Angel Dust, cocaine, and alcohol blasted through my body with incredible power. I grabbed another 2 x 4 and continued to destroy my tree house.

I started to cry as I glared back into the sky and screamed at the top of my voice … "Kill me you mother _____er! Take me out! Get me off this piece of crap!"

Time stood still. Forever I cursed God and called him every name I could hurl into the darkness.
"Why Grandpa Ira you heartless bastard? Why him? Why not one of the millions of ___holes everywhere???"
I was crying so hard I was stumbling around. Convulsions of rage. Would he kill me? Who cares?
"____ you! Do it!
My brain was like an amplifier. Every emotion, every thought, intensified a million times. The tree house evaporated. I was in a force field of grief and unreality. I became bolts of anger. I was tripping big time. A thousand years of eternity passed. A million years of eternity.

Confusion and helplessness stabbed me in the back. My lungs were collapsing. I never stopped crying.

I **screamed,** "Somebody help me! Please help me!"

Finally, after forever, a tiny little voice came out of a long tunnel. It was Debbie, and I was temporarily back in Topanga Canyon. Back in the treehouse. I dropped to my knees and cried like a baby. I looked straight at my girlfriend through a flood of tears, and screamed ... "Help me Debbie!"

She was a shadow. She sounded scared ... "I'll help you Roger ... please ... what can I do?"

Another voice came from below ... down in the meadow ..."Are you all right Debbie?"

I jumped up and screamed with everything left in me ... "Get the ____ away from my tree Satan!"

The voice below hesitated and said ... "I'm not Satan ... I'm Spike ... Debbie, are you all right?"

"I'm OK. I'll be all right ... Really, Spike it's OK."
That's the last I remember.

• • •

Ira Anderson McDonald was my grandfather. I loved him very much. My family doesn't really know much about his early life. In fact, I could kick myself for not asking Aunt Nig more about him a few years back. She was my grandmother's sister. One of the Everett clan ... and might have known a lot about his early years. But now, she is dead also.

The little bit I do know about Grandpa's childhood is this ... he was born in either Maryland or Virginia on May 16th, 1906. His mother, my great-grandmother, was named Anna Davies McDonald. She had red hair and died when Grandpa was about two or three years old. He lost both his parents as a child, and was then passed from relative to relative, and to different friends as they had need for farm help. He had three brothers, George, Earl, and Joe. We don't know one thing about his father, except that his name was John, and that he died and left the four boys orphaned. Grandpa Ira might have been paired up with Joe after his parents died, because as adults Grandpa used to drive to West

Virginia to visit his brother a lot. They were real close. We don't know about my great uncle George or Earl, or whatever became of them.

GRANDPA IRA MC DONALD

Somehow or other Grandpa ended up in West Virginia in the 1920's, a young man working as a farm hand. From that point we know quite a bit, because it was the violent, but interesting, and often sad beginnings of our family on my mom's side. As a matter of fact, one night in the mid-sixties I asked Grandpa Ira how he met my grandmother, and was successful in getting lots of stories out of him. I was home on leave from the Army, and he was visiting at my parent's home in Ohio. My Aunt Cathryn, his youngest daughter had dropped in also. He had us all cracking up because he was a great storyteller.

We were drinking beer at my mom's kitchen table, and having a good time picking Grandpa's brain. I wasn't smart enough to ask about his childhood or a million other questions that I now have. However, I had enough on the ball to go grab some paper and take notes. At the time as a teen-age soldier, I was mostly interested in his first hand version of different escapades that I'd heard about, especially concerning his radical Scotch Irish temper. Grandpa was kind-hearted, generous, and soft spoken ... but he loved a good barroom brawl if there was half a reason.

Grandpa answered my question about meeting Grandma and said, "I was hired on at the Stonebreaker farm down in West Virginia, and one day Stonebreaker happened to catch me with his wife, Sadie. We were in the barn, and well, we had kind of a fight."

I was surprised ... "You mean Sadie ... like our Grandma Sadie?"

I knew Grandma was married before, and that my Aunt Wade was from her previous marriage ... but this was some new detail.

Somebody at the table asked, "What did Stonebreaker do to you?"

"He didn't do anything to me. I knocked the ever living snott out of him right there in the barn, where he jumped me," Grandpa replied. "Later Stonebreaker beat Sadie, and ran her off. She took Wade, and moved back in with the Everett's. I used to check on her from time to time back up in the hills. I felt bad for her. I wasn't in love at the time, but felt guilty for all the trouble I caused.

I really felt sorry for her to be living back at home with her father. Let me tell you about Old Man Wade Everett. He'd be your great-grandfather. He was probably the meanest son-of-gun that you could find. Everybody hated him. His wife hated him. All his kids hated him ... and he had a bunch of them. He beat them all. Everybody in town hated him too. When he went into a bar he'd always yell out ... 'Fire on the mountain, snake in the grass, the old man died with a rag in his _ _ _.' People would say... 'Here comes 'Fire on the Mountain', but they all hated his guts. He fought with everybody."

Old Man Everett

Grandpa continued ... "One day I went up to the Everett place and found everything all busted up, and Sadie and her mother beat real bad. Old Man Everett had left and gone into town. I told the whole family to pack everything they could, and get in my car. We crammed 13 people, mostly kids and babies into my Model T Ford. We headed out for Ohio, where I knew of a couple factories that were hiring. That dirty old fool came home to an empty house. When he found out that I took his family ... he swore he'd kill me if it was the last thing that he ever did."

Back at the kitchen table, my dad who liked to pick on Grandpa Ira because of all his superstitions asked ... "Did any black cats run across the road on your way to Ohio?" It was funny to us because Grandpa had so many superstitions, and one of them really annoyed my dad. You see, Grandpa would never leave a building by any other door than the one he entered. It was real bad luck. Also, when you get out of a rocking chair, you never let it keep rocking. That's bad luck too. A bird in the house means a death in the family. He had tons of them.

Well, every once in awhile he would come over to our house, and the garage door would be wide open. He'd come in that way. The garage was also my dad's warehouse for his Frito-Lay distributorship. Later in the evening after a meal, and after the garage was all locked up ... with my dad snoring in his recliner, someone would wake my dad up and say ..."You have to let Grandpa out through the garage". My dad would mumble, and grumble, and shuffle half asleep out into the cold garage to unlock everything ... and let Ira out. No way in the world would Grandpa go out the front door five steps away.

Grandpa answered my dad, "In Pennsylvania a black cat ran right across the road in front of us. It took us most of a day to find a way around that spot. We figure we drove about an extra 180 miles."

My dad just shook his head back and forth, like only he can do with that critical half smirk on his face.

Grandpa Ira went on to tell us how that when they arrived in Fremont, Ohio the youngest baby had died from the trip. He found the family a place to stay, and then drove back to West Virginia to bury the baby. It was illegal to bury a body anywhere, except in a cemetery in Ohio or Pennsylvania. They didn't have any money to buy a plot, so Grandpa drove back with a dead baby in the rear seat. You could bury your dead anywhere at that time in West Virginia. By the time he returned to Ohio another child had died, and he was forced to turn immediately around, and drive another dead baby to a lonely West Virginia hole in the ground.

He felt responsible for the family, but still didn't want to marry Sadie. Nevertheless, over the next few years they managed to have two children. Grandpa also confessed to marrying another gal in a nearby town about this same period. However, they were only together a short time. After a major disruption he left her.

Finally, he decided to marry my Grandmother, and Sadie Everett became Sadie McDonald. Altogether, my Grandma had 10 children, one from her previous marriage, and nine with Grandpa Ira. However, Junior, the firstborn of my grandparents, died of pneumonia at 6 months, and two other babies were stillborn. The surviving children were Wade, Earl, Pauline, Faye Rose, Polly (my mother), Cathryn, and Dwight, my favorite uncle, who is nicknamed Sonny.

Although my Grandpa caroused extensively in his youth, and liked to hunt and fish, gamble, drink, and fight ... he was also a very hard worker. With virtually no education, he worked his way up through the factories until he became plant manager of Wahl Refractories Corporation. Over the years he often held two jobs at the same time, and was well respected. He bought a two-story house on Cottage Street, where my mom and most of his children grew up. My Aunt Pauline and Uncle Jim still live in that house till this day.

Uncle Paul and friend (Acting Up)

As a little girl my mom can remember Grandpa Ira coming home with Uncle Paul on the weekends after the bars closed. They'd be drunk with bloody knuckles and torn clothes from the latest bar room battle. They'd be laughing and drinking some more, and maybe do a blow by blow instant replay of the night's activities. Uncle Paul Everett was one of Grandma's brothers, and he was great friends with Ira McDonald. They called each other Jake.

My dad, who has never been in a fist fight in his entire life, told me that it would take several men to pull Grandpa Ira off someone in one of his skirmishes. He would go into an absolute rage. Ira never got whipped. Those were some of the stories I was anxious to hear directly from Grandpa … mainly because I'd been in lots of fights in High School, and in the army. It seems to be a Buckeye thing, or maybe a mid-western thing, (or maybe an Irish thing).

Grandpa Ira continued … "One day Old Man Wade Everett showed up here in Fremont. He came in the house, and tried to kill me with a knife. Let me tell you, I did some pretty darn fast-talking, and talked him out of it. Then, when he put his knife down, I grabbed a butcher knife from the kitchen, and was able to pin the old fool. I stuck my knife right to his neck, and made him swear an oath that he would **never-ever** try to kill me again."

"Did he swear one," I asked.

"You bet your sweet ___ he did."

"Would you have really killed him if he didn't swear an oath?" I asked again.

"I'd have cut that son-of-a-you-know-who from ear to ear if he hadn't," Grandpa answered.

It's really not funny to find out that your grandfather almost murdered your great-grandfather and so on ... however, the way he put things, along with his low gravely voice ... and especially after a few brews, he had us laughing so hard we were choking for breath a couple times.

"Then," he said ... "the old fart came and lived with us! We got along all right after that."

Grandpa continued, "As a matter of fact, since you was asking about a good fight, the old man got his tail beat real bad one night down at The Greeks. It's Bucks now by State Street Bridge and the river ... but back then everybody called it, 'The Bloody Bucket'.

Your Uncle Floyd came and told me about Old Man Everett getting busted up, right after it happened the same night ... and also about this bunch of brothers who like to run things down there. It was one of them who got to the old man. I had a broken leg at the time, and Floyd took me down there. Earl who was about 14 wanted to come along. I made him wait in the car, and Floyd and I went in the tavern. We ordered a drink, and I had Floyd point out the brother. I wanted to make sure I got him first.

A group of them were sitting at a table, and I went up and asked this particular fellow for a light. As he was getting some matches out, I said ... Are you the smart son-of-gun messing with Old Man Everett ... and then I started knocking people down with my crutch. I busted up that whole bar with that crutch, and got every single one of them brothers real good. Let me tell you, that place was one heck of a mess ... and then the cops pulled up in front. I snuck out the back door, and hid on the floor of the car with your Uncle Earl. We were on the floorboards of that old car for over an hour hiding. There was some more fighting inside, and the cops hauled off practically the whole bar to jail."

He told us a few more war stories, and how he and Uncle Page and Uncle Paul used to bust into bars and yell out ... "Hey, any of you son-of-a _____s think you can whip us???" Some of his stories were really a crack up. He had a crippled little finger from busting a co-worker in the teeth after he refused to re-pay a loan. The guy repeatedly told Grandpa,

"I'll pay you next Friday Ira, I promise." About the tenth time he said that … he swallowed a couple teeth … and Grandpa permanently mangled his little finger.

I never saw my Grandpa's Irish temper, or his sucker punching abilities, because that was before my time. To me, he was always a big, gentle, generous man, who loved kids, and liked to get us laughing. My grandparents divorced when I was in grade school, and Grandpa lived with Deloris for over 20 years after that.

Maybe Old Man Wade Everett was called "Fire on the Mountain", but to me the real fire on the mountain … was Grandpa Ira. I'll let someone else figure out … who the dead old man with the rag in his "tail" was. Hopefully when the angels lit the rag he shot off in the right direction.

Grandpa Ira & me

CHAPTER 2

"FREMONT FARMERS"

Carl Sachs Sr. & Sisters (Lula & Fern)

Fremont, Ohio is my hometown. To me it was a terrific place to grow up in America. It's located in the northwestern part of the Buckeye state. The surrounding countryside is mostly flat and gently rolling fertile farmland. Different sized forests, large creeks, rivers, and literally hundreds of miles of small streams then cut up the local geography. I love it. Port Clinton, which is on Lake Erie, one of the Great Lakes, is a short trip up the meandering Sandusky River from Fremont. A swift boat ride from Port Clinton can get you into Canadian waters in a matter of minutes, not hours. Ohio has some of the best of what the mid-west has to offer. I even love the extremes of the four seasons ... cold sub-zero winters, beautiful springs, and hot muggy summers with wonderful thunder and lightning storms. My favorite time is the cool nippy fall days revealing every shade of autumn color imaginable ... and it's time to clean your 12-gauge, and pin on a plastic hunting tag.

One of the local claims to fame is an old black canon, named Old Betsy that sits in front of Birchard Public Library in the middle of Fremont. If I can remember some of my grade school history, my American forefathers built a fort on the banks of the Sandusky River, somewhere in the late 1700s or early 1800s. The fort was named Fort Stephenson, and was less than twenty miles upstream from Lake Erie. The settlement that grew around the fort was named Lower Sandusky, and then much later became Fremont. Anyway, in the War of 1812 the British attacked the fort with an overwhelming force of hundreds of soldiers and thousands of Indians. But, with less than 200 men and a single canon the Americans ran from position to position (with the canon) ... so fast, that they won the battle. They forced the British to retreat ... thinking that the fort was too well defended. It was thanks to good old ... "Old Betsy".

• • •

In contrast to my mom's somewhat rowdy family, my dad was the youngest son of a well-respected farming family. I don't want to bore anyone with an extensive genealogy, but if we power through a little bit of background history from my father's side, it will shed some light indirectly on this story. The Sachs family had settled in Ohio just outside Fremont, several generations back. They are German, hard working, church-going farmers. My grandfather, Carl Sachs Sr., married Hazel

Hubert, who taught school in one of the old time, one-room country schools. Many students never had another teacher besides my grandmother. Grandpa Sachs was a devout Lutheran, and **never-ever** worked on Sunday ... not even at harvest time, regardless of the weather. He also never drank a drop of alcohol in his life. My grandparents were both in their upper thirties when they got married, and from that late start produced four sons and one daughter. They are Bill, Howard, Don, Marion, and my father, Carl M. Sachs Jr. ... the baby of the family.

I always wondered about my farming ancestors. How many generations back did they immigrate to America? Where exactly did they come from in Europe? Things like that. I hear one of my ancestors, Hans Sachs, was one of Napoleon Bonaparte's bodyguards. How did a German relative of mine become the French Emperor's bodyguard? I have no idea. He is buried in McGormley Cemetery outside of Fremont. But, I had lots of other questions.

My grandpa Sachs' younger sister was Lula B. Sachs. She was my Great Aunt, and a big influence in my life. I loved her very much. When she died in 1976, I ended up with a box full of her papers and personal items. For years I've carted that box around, only glancing at its contents a couple times. It's a miracle I still have it. Recently I read through everything, and was amazed. It was filled with family history, a personal diary, birth notices, death notices, and even an unfinished book that Aunt Lula had worked on. To me it was a great discovery.

A family tree can sound a little confusing real quick, but briefly I discovered that Henry Sachs emigrated from Germany four generations back. He would be my Great Great Grandfather. From a portrait that his granddaughter, (my Great Grandma) showed me, he had a big old beard. He married Barbara Faber from Bohemia, Germany. They immigrated to America buying a farm in Ohio in the early 1800's way before the Civil War. Farmers were released from military service if they gave a horse to the Union army, and my distant Grandfather gave them a horse. Smart move or I probably wouldn't be here. (It is reported that more Americans were killed in the Civil War than in World War I, World War II, the Korean War, Vietnam, Afghanistan, and Iraq put together.)

My European ancestors, Henry and Barbara Sachs had six children. One of the younger children was my Great Grandfather, William. He was born on December 10th, 1866 right after the Civil War. He died four years before I was born, so I never knew him. He married Clara Cora, Catherine Martin. I knew my Great Grandma real well as a little kid. She died at age 90 on August 3, 1956. I was almost nine years old when she died. I have lots of memories of spending weekends at her house, next to the main farm outside of Fremont.

My Great Grandparents, William & Clara had only three children, my Grandpa Carl and Aunt Fern, who were twins, and also my Aunt Lulu Sachs. ("Lulu" is pronounced with an "a" on the end instead of a "u"). They finally bought a farm of their own. I think it was originally 80 acres. Their only son, my Grandpa Carl Sachs grew up, and farmed that land his entire life. During World War I he was heading for France when the war ended. He lucked out, came home to the farm, and married my Grandma Hazel. Together they raised their family of 5 kids on the Ballville farm. My dad was born on that family farm, and as a kid plowed the fields with big old workhorses. He can still remember when they bought their first tractor.

Hazel Sachs was also the gentlest, and most loving grandmother you could imagine. I remember she always had fresh baked oatmeal cookies in a container on top of the refrigerator. When all us grandkids would be tearing through the house, she would redirect our energy, but never lose her temper. I never once heard her yell at anyone.

"Cloe" and Grandpa Sachs, Randy & Grandma Sachs, Cousin Patty & me

Grandpa Carl Sachs & Roger Karl

She told me one day when I was about ten years old ... "When you were born, and I found out that your mom and dad named you Roger, I was more than a little upset! One of my students was named Roger, and mercy sakes that boy caused me so much trouble! He caused me more grief over the years than all the other students combined. I honestly thought he would never amount to anything."

My grandma continued ... "But a couple years ago I had a knock on the door, and lo and behold a well-dressed man greeted me. It was my student Roger. After all the years he came back to thank me. And do you know, he's the only one. He showed me pictures of his family, and he now has a professional career. We had such a nice visit. Since I've retired he has been my only student to come look me up. I would have never imagined it in a million years. It is a wonderful blessing to me!"

CHAPTER 3

"EAST SIDE KIDS"

On September 28th, 1964, just four short days after I turned 17 years old, I was inducted into the United States Army. My parents reluctantly signed the papers allowing a minor to volunteer for military service. I'm sure signing those documents was also accompanied by a considerable sigh of relief. I had been a nice little kid all my life, until I hit my teenage years ... and then, as in many cases, all hell broke loose. I really put my parents through a few things.

Let me back up a little. My father met my mother on a crowded country school bus one morning. He was fifteen years old. There were no seats left by the time the bus stopped for the Cottage Street crew. My mom's sister, Pauline, was in one of my dad's classes, and said to the skinny young farm boy ..."Come on Carl, be a gentleman, and give us your seat!"

My mom reflects back ..."Do you think he'd get up? He just laughed, and sat there. I should have known something right then and there, don't you think?"

Nevertheless, my dad got a hold of a snapshot of my mother, and has carried that photo in his wallet for over 50 years now. The picture is all weathered and dog-eared, but you can still distinguish the three pretty, and shapely teenagers in hula skirts. My mom is on the right, with Pauline on the left, and my future Aunt Margaret in the middle. Shortly after World War II ended, my dad ran off with young Polly Marie McDonald. At the time they ran off and got married, they were still both in high school. Grandpa Ira threw a fit, and wanted to get the marriage annulled, but my Aunt Lula Sachs talked him into giving the kids a chance … for the sake of the baby, which was discovered to be on the way.

I was born on September 24th, 1947, eight months and two weeks after the wedding. My mom would later complain to me …"Couldn't you have just waited another 2 weeks to stop all the wagging tongues?" She had really run off to escape the turbulent home-scene … like most of her sisters and brothers ended up doing. Even my favorite uncle, Uncle Sonny lied about his age, and joined the Air Force at sixteen years old during the Korean War. My teenage dad took his teenage bride, and started our family on an old abandoned farm … out in the country, **way** back down a dirt lane, on the way to Green Springs, Ohio. They rented the farm for half the crops.

Probably the first memory I have in my entire life … is pressing my nose to the farmhouse window, and looking outside. I was about 2 years old. It was night, and the only thing I could see in the darkness was a small rectangle of yard at the base of a big tree. The inside house lights behind me lit up the small patch of yard like a rectangular spotlight. In the middle of the illuminated rectangle was a little field mouse, which I was watching with great intent. Suddenly, a shadow swooped down out of nowhere. By the time I blinked, a huge owl had replaced the mouse in the center of the frame. For just an instant the silent predator looked right at my window with beautiful, perfectly round, yellow eyes. Those eyes were forever shocked into my memory. And then there was nothing but grass.

The farm was an incredibly hard life, especially for my mom. By the time she was 21 she had three boys, Roger, Randy, and Ricky, but still didn't have running water, or an inside toilet, or a dryer. The farmhouse had sat empty for who knows how long and was falling apart. To make things tougher she is a little bit of a perfectionist, and always had to have a spotless home, with us kids dressed in neat clean clothes. Try that ... when you have to put pots and pans out to catch rainwater leaking through the roof, or when the clothes you hang out to dry ... continually turn to ice. She would bring in the stiff clothes, and iron them to get them dry. Maybe the worst thing was that my dad would take the car at night, and work at the Sugar Beat Company, leaving her all alone in the country with three little kids. My mom caved in, and had a complete physical and emotional breakdown on that farm.

She told me ... "One day I laid down on the couch for a while. Pretty soon I heard one of you boys crying in the bedroom. I tried to get up but couldn't. The crying went on forever. I heard your Uncle Howard, I think it was him, come in the house and talk to me, but he sounded like an echo. I couldn't understand anything he said. Then, I was in a hospital hallway. I saw a woman near me strapped in a wheelchair and a straight jacket. She was screaming and screaming continuously! She had terror in her eyes. I looked at her and understood completely. I **knew** I was an inch away from being that woman. Your Grandma Sachs had said to me one time, 'Where's your faith girl?' I cried out to God, 'Please don't let me be that woman! Please God!' All I could do was say over and over and over in my mind "Jesus" — "Jesus" — "Jesus". I'm not kidding, it's the only thing that kept my sanity." They gave my mom shock treatments.

Eventually my dad gave up farming, and was probably the first Sachs to move into "town". My youngest brother Robby was born a bonified city boy. We took a lot of crap about being the four "Rs". But anyway, I wouldn't trade being raised on Oaklawn Avenue for anything. My parents bought a tiny 3-bedroom house, which lucky for us kids, was on the edge of town, and still had a touch of country.

It bordered right on a huge forest on the east side of Fremont with a meandering creek and nearby fields. There was a set of Railroad tracks that went on forever in both directions. Way behind the tracks was the "Second Woods". It was a kid's paradise, and I had lots of eastside neighborhood friends to help me invade it. There was Gary Ohms and his brother Rich, Denny Atkins, Rod Burkett, Tom Beckley, Dick Beazel, David Russell, Nancy Jacobson, Mary Wilson, Pee Wee Noviski, Dennis Eberly, and on and on.

I went to a brand new school named Atkinson Elementary School. I got all A's and B's, and was kind of shy in the public scene. All the teachers, except maybe one, thought I was a sweet little kid. I was really into the outdoors, practically living down at the creek. I was born with a wet foot, and always had snakes, and frogs, and salamanders. I ran a trap line for muskrat, and also captured a young great horned owl, with those beautiful yellow eyes. I kept it for quite awhile. My Cub Scout teacher, Mrs. Russell told my mother that I had artistic talent ... and to this day consider myself about half an artist.

In keeping with the Sachs tradition, my parents dressed us up like tiny saints in little suits, and hauled us off to St. Marks Lutheran Church. I hated Sunday school, and butch haircuts, and bow ties. I mean, I loved my dad's family, especially Grandma Sachs and my Grandfather's younger sister, Aunt Lula. However, I have to be honest, and say that I thought most of them were way too serious, and no fun at all.

Aunt Lula was a big exception. She planted some real good seeds into my young life. One turned out to be a serious traveling bug. **I love to travel.** I think I was one of her favorite nephews … maybe because she helped to save me from the adoption board.

Aunt Lula

It was right up her alley, because she did social work in several big cities. As a single career woman, she did things like pay my way to Pittsburgh, Pennsylvania on a bus ... by myself, to spend a couple weeks with her. I was twelve years old.

It was a huge adventure for a small town kid. I can still vividly remember the highlights of my trip to Pittsburgh. I think it was 1958, and John Kennedy was running for President. On the bus to Pennsylvania a group of pretty girls about nineteen or twenty years old befriended me. I kept them laughing with silly stuff. They all hoped that Kennedy would win the election because he was "cute".

In Pittsburgh my aunt took me to Carnegie Museum and to a Planetarium. We ate in nice restaurants. I couldn't believe that people left all kinds of money just lying on the table after they ate. We went up the steep inclines, and made a trip to Kennywood Park, which to me was better than Disneyland. Aunt Lula's apartment was right across the street from the huge major league baseball stadium. We went to see the Pittsburgh Pirates play. Hank Aaron crashed into the outfield wall right below where I was sitting, and made an incredible catch. He was hurt. I went to work with my aunt, and she had me draw a simple little drawing for the quarterly publication that her agency put out.

She told me ... "save a copy of this, because it is the first thing you ever got published." (I hope it's not the last.) I think I still have a copy somewhere. The quarterly was called "Tid Bits". It was a great a trip to Pittsburgh ... an eye-opening trip ... a challenging trip ... and a loving trip.

Jesse Ohms

Even though I loved my aunt, and appreciated the things she did for me, I still hated church. There was one exception. Our Sunday school director was a pretty lady named Jesse Ohms. She organized a youth bowling league, and actually taught most of the kids including me how to bowl. I got pretty good, and bowling has been a love of mine ever since. I carried a 178 average in a league a few years back. However back then as a kid, I was happy to break a hundred. When my mother had her second major nervous breakdown, and another series of shock treatments ... Mrs. Ohms absolutely took over for my mom ... with meals, and cleaning the house, and looking after the four of us boys. My mom and Jesse eventually became best friends for life. Jesse moved to California, and started a school for the severely handicapped. I thought to my young self ... "If there is such a thing as a 'saint' on this earth ... then Jesse Ohms is definitely one!"

Most other Christians seemed to be total boring hypocrites. I asked my Grandpa Ira McDonald if he ever went to church, and he said ... "When I was a kid we used to hide in the bushes on Sunday, and then jump out, and beat the living snott out of the kids going to church. That's about as close as I got."

For some reason I thought that was real funny. I always identified more with my mom's side of the family. Nevertheless, we were forced to go to church every Sunday until I was about 13 years old. I went all through catechism classes, was an altar boy, confirmed into the church ... and then totally quit.

JOHN LEWIS

When I hit my teenage years I began to rebel. By this time my father was doing quite well in his business ... but my parents were having real problems in their marriage. My dad had been inducted into the "good old boys" club with a clique of wealthy local businessmen. He stayed out until all hours ... night after night ... coming home drunk as a skunk, and saying ..."Polly, so help me God, I'll never do it again."

But then my mom would start in ... "How could you do this to me again Carl ... over and over and over ... you heartless (blankety-blank)!!!" ... and then we'd hear the glass breaking, and the doors slamming, and the crying. It happened a thousand times. I started hating my father.

I also decided that I hated school. I discovered pool halls, and smoking cigarettes, playing hooky, and of course girls. My reputation at school started to slowly change from being a nice, college prep type of kid ... to a rowdy delinquent. I ended up having a unique cross section of friends, but basically I was changing fast. One thing for sure ... I totally rejected church, and religion, and hypocritical Christian morality. It was the early 60s. The Beatles were singing ... "with a love like that ... you know you can't go wrong... yea ... yea ... yea!!"

One day when I was about 14 years old, Pee Wee Noviski, said, "Lets go down to John Lewis' house."

I had gone through grade school with Pee Wee. We had played on the Jaycees Little League team together ... and now we were finally in the famous Fremont Ross High School. We were actually in Jr. High, but this was before they built the new High School. The hundred year old, three story High School still housed both Jr. and Sr. High, as well as the feared Little Giants.

I asked, "Who is John Lewis?"

"He's this old black bootlegger that lives down by the river. He's kind of scary, but he's all right. He knows me because a friend took me down there a couple times. He'll sell beer to kids if he knows their cool. He only charges a quarter for a beer. Do you want to go down there with me?" Pee Wee asked.

"I don't care," I replied, and we were off. We were supposed to stay at a school basketball game, but instead we took off, and walked a mile or so over to Bidwell Avenue, and then down along the river where all the black people live behind downtown. My adrenalin was pumping a little extra as the lights from downtown became dimmer and dimmer. There were absolutely no streetlights on Bidwell. Pretty soon there was nothing but starlight. The old houses that lined both sides of the street were like shadow houses.

Kenny, (that's Pee Wee's real name), was saying, "It's pretty scary back here, especially at John's house. His house is probably the oldest one. The porch sags in the middle, and all that ... but don't worry about it. OK? Do you want to keep going?"

Inside I was totally paranoid ... but I told Pee Wee ..."Hey, don't talk so loud. We've come this far, so we might as well go all the way. How much farther is it?"

"It's not far ... it's right over there."

It was so black where Pee Wee was pointing that I couldn't see anything until we practically bumped into the house. Bidwell came to a dead end at the railroad embankment, which was probably 20 feet high. The embankment extended to the left probably 200 feet where it met the old RR trestle that crossed the river. John Lewis' house was the last house on the left, nestled back against the river, and the embankment.

We crunched down the stone driveway to the rear of the house, and onto the sagging wood porch. It was 2 steps up, and extended completely across the back of the old house. It was classic, everything creaked, and the house was completely dark and dead silent. Pee Wee knocked softly on the door a couple times. A minute later we heard a loud drawn out … "Whooo dhar". I could hear someone getting out of bed.

"It's Pee Wee, John. Can we buy a beer?"

Pretty soon a light went on inside, and this tall big black man appeared at the back door in his trousers.

"Is that you Nooooviski? Now whoooo in the heck is that thar with you? Maaan, don't you know I don't want a bunch of punk ____ing kids cooooming around here? Anyway, whooo the blazes are you boy?"

He was waiting for an answer.

"My name is Roger Sachs."

"Sachs … well I'll be a mother ____er ! Would you be Howard's boy, or Bill Sachs or which one of them Sachs' are you little Sachs?"

"Carl is my dad," I answered. We were still standing on the back porch, and I was shocked that this silhouette of a black stranger knew my family. I could instantly tell he was some kind of character like no one I had ever known. At the same time, I wasn't afraid any more.

I see yer old man all the time … he be the potato chip man. Is that right? Noooow, tell me this, little Sachs … was it your old man that up and married one of them McDonald girls?"

"Yeah that's right. How do you know so much about my family?" I asked.

He let out this huge laugh that echoed clear down Bidwell, and said, "Well kiss my black ___. Can't you see I got eyes in my head? Why, I've been sitting down at the railroad crossing every morning at the state street bridge … from 6 o'clock in the morning till 9, maybe 9:30 every day … for more years than you know how to count. Don't you know that absolutely nothing happens in this town unless it crosses State Street Bridge. Why, I see your daddy drive that big fat Frito truck back and forth, back and forth, across the river like a chicken with it's ___ing head cut off. Wat the heck you people be doing with aaaalll that money?"

Before I could say a word, old John Lewis continued … "Maaan, I know dang near everybody … and everything that goes on in this town. Why your grandddaddy McDonald brought a little tractor down here years and years ago, and plowed up that garden right therre behind you. You can't see it in the dark, but that garden goes all the way down to the Sandusky River. He did up 2 or 3 places right here on this very same street, and did one heck of a good job!

Noviski, maybe this white boy is all right. You boys come inside, and I'll get you a beer. Whooo da ___ gots da money?"

Well, that was the first bootleg joint I ever went to. As a matter of fact, John Lewis was the first grown up black man I ever personally met. I knew Willie Walker from my Little League team, but that was about it. As a young teenager ... I decided that "Black is beautiful" from hanging out at John Lewis'. I was one of the few whites that were totally accepted by the constant flow of John Lewis' clientele. I got drunk with them, I gambled with them, I made life long friends with young and old. My neighborhood buddies and I used to shoot rabbits at night with a spotlight, and sell them to John Lewis. He would sell them to his neighbors. John Lewis also owned about 10 old houses in Fremont. He was a businessman. I used to steal cases of potato chips, slim-jims, and beer nuts, from my dad, and sell them to John Lewis. I was almost like a local hero with my black friends. Over the next couple years I was also tagged a nigger lover more than once in Fremont ... but always behind my back.

What would my Grandma Hazel think of me hanging out at a bootlegger's place down by the river? She had died when I was still in grade school. I don't think she would be down on black people ... but I know she would be greatly disappointed in her rebellious young grandson. "I miss you Grandma!"

"MARK MY WORDS"

I bought a Mo-Ped when I was fourteen from the savings off my country newspaper route. When I was 16, I bought a really neat 1957 Ford for $300. It was the Custom model and had been sooped up by the previous owner with a dash mounted tachometer and Hollywood mufflers. It sounded like 20 speedway cars roaring out of hell. My dad made me change the mufflers, but the new glass packs sounded almost as good. It was my very first car. Back in the late 50s and early 60s Fremont was just like a town out of "Happy Days". Every day kids would drag race all the way through town ... right down Rt. 20. The cops looked the other way for the most part. Fonzie was named Denny Miller. He was one of my heroes until he ripped me off.

I had quite a few girlfriends in Jr. high and high school, and fell madly in love with most of them. Judy Steins, Connie McCoy, Cheri Schey, Nancy Young, Linda Beckley and several others. For over two years I went steady with Linda McCloy, a girl from St. Joes, the Catholic high school. She wore angora around my class ring, and wrote a love letter in ink on the driver's seat of my car. Our first child was going to be a girl, and we decided to name her Veronica. I took Linda down to John Lewis' one time and she was the hot topic with all my black friends for months. They would say ... "How you be coming up with such a mean looking broad anyway ... now that is one F I N E long-coat (white girl). Man ... you done got yourself a movie star or something there ... listen here Saxie... that mama might be more than you can handle ... so don't be forgetting your friends now ... Ya hear!!!" Then the whole place would roar with laughter, as someone paid John Lewis to buy me a shot of Seagrams.

About the worst thing a rebel can do is get mobile. Just ask James Dean. As things got worse between my parents, I became more and more uncontrollable. In my sophomore year, we had a girlfriend who worked in the principal's office. When my buddies and I wanted to skip school, she would mark M/C, meaning "mother called", next to our names. After missing over 60 days of school, the assistant principal called my house to find out what kind of chronic illness I had. I got in all kinds of trouble for that. Another time, I ran away in the middle of the night in my 57 Ford with two good friends, Gary Ohms and Rod Burkett. I literally drug them out of bed, and we were off for California ... headlights ablaze. This was in the aftermath of a fight, and one of the several breakups with Veronica's mother. We got caught in Chicago after running out of gas and money.

In my junior year the school counselor called me in to his office claiming that a certain female student was pregnant by me. This particular girl had developed a real bad reputation in Fremont. Her father came to school, and was in the office confronting me along with the counselor. It was pretty intense. The next day around 10 guys from Ross High agreed to sign a list, that they also were involved in pregnant making activities, with her, and with her consent, at approximately the same time as me. And that was the truth. It also turned out to be a false alarm. Months later at a wild party she apologized with smiles for picking me out of the lineup when she thought she was pregnant. Thanks for the vote of confidence. It was crazy.

My parents had to come to the police station several times to pick me up. One time for fist fighting after school. Another time, I got so drunk with some friends at a party that no one would ride with me in my car. I wouldn't let anyone else drive either, so they all piled into another car. I was trying to get home, but was literally seeing double of everything. Double headlights coming at me ... double center-dividing lines, double everything. I knew I had to pull over or I was going to die.

The next thing I know it was daylight outside, and I was shocked to hear a cop knocking on my car window. He made me roll the window down and said, "What are you doing? Turn your car off. Look where you are under the back of that truck. Get out of the car!"

After getting out in the crisp cold air, all stiff and still half drunk, the officer said, "A lady called the station, and said she woke up hearing a car running practically all night. This morning she said she saw your car roll a block down the street, and smash into the back of this flatbed truck that your car is under. Look at your car! What have you been drinking boy?"

I told him I only had a couple beers at a party, but when I was driving home I got so tired that I was falling asleep. I pulled over because I was too sleepy to drive. I left the car running cause it was cold, etc. etc. He didn't buy my "teenager sleeps through crash" theory ... and again my parents had to make a trip to the police station.

The real reason I decided to enlist in the Army, was because Linda had broke up with me again, and started dating an old rival of mine. I had already broken my X-friend's nose in a much-publicized fight over another girlfriend two years previous. Only that time it was a reverse situation. Cheri Shey, who wasn't shy at all, broke up with Tony, and started going steady with me. Anyway, that turned out to be a couple month long puppy love thing. This was different ... this was two years of my life ... this was my movie star ... the mother of my future daughter ... and I was going to break his neck.

I found Tony at the pool hall, and drove him in my car out in the country. He swore to me that he wasn't interested in Linda, and that he didn't want to fight me again. He said it wasn't his fault that she broke up with me. He added ... "I only talked to her on the phone a couple times, because Becky said Linda wanted to talk to me." I found out later that he lied about everything, except not wanting to fight.

The very next night I got totally drunk at John Lewis' place. When he wouldn't sell me any more to drink, I stole one of his giant two gallon bottles of whiskey. In my smoking brain I devised a plan of action. I drank a couple more shots, drove to Linda's house in the middle of the night, and squeezed into the kitchen through a **tiny** milk door. It took about an hour, because I could only get my head and one shoulder through the opening. I went upstairs one-step at a time, hardly breathing, past her parent's bedroom, and into Linda's room. We broke up about two weeks before. I whispered for her to wake up a couple times. Finally, Linda woke up ... and whispered back in the dark ... "Is that you Tony?"

I went ballistic. When she realized it was me, she told me to get out, or she was going to call her dad. I told her I didn't give a ____. I grabbed her arms. She broke away, and ran out the door and down the hall with me right behind her. I can't remember if I pushed her down the stairs, or if she tripped ... but the next thing I know, I was body slammed from behind, and went headlong down the steps with a powerful man on my back. It was her father, Art.

We ended up down on a landing where the staircase made a right turn. He literally picked me up, and threw me against a wall. He used his forearm in my neck to keep me pinned there.

"What is going on here Roger?" He was pumped ... "What are you doing busting in my house, and messing with my daughter? You're lucky I didn't blow your head off you dang fool kid! I could kick your ___ right now! Do you want to find out if I can?"

I told him, "No, I believe you. Linda broke up with me. I know I'm wrong." That was about all I could say with half my windpipe cut off.

He stared at me for a while, and then said ... "Look, I'm going to take you down to the kitchen and get some coffee in you, and then we'll talk. Linda, you go upstairs and get back to bed."

For a couple years I had spent more time with this family than my own ... by a million miles. They were so close, loving, expressive, and outgoing. I very much wanted that, and loved every minute of our time together. I was crazy about Linda.

"Look", Art said ... "I'm real sorry about you and Linda breaking up. Of all the boyfriends that she ever had, Barbara and I both have liked you the most. You kids have gone together a long time, and who knows what will happen down the road. You broke up, and went back together before. Women are impossible to figure out sometimes. Half the time we can't live with them … but believe me, we can't live without them. Linda knows how we feel about you, but we can't make her choices. One thing for sure Roger, you can't solve anything by getting totally blind drunk, and then busting into peoples houses!"

Art was like my father. We talked until the wee hours. I told him I was going to join the Army as soon as I turned seventeen. He had done exactly the same thing … enlisted when he was 17. He said it was one huge mistake. He tried his best to talk me out of it. **"Don't do it Roger, you'll be sorry! Mark my words!"**

I loved and respected Art more than I can express … but I had made up my mind … teenage fool that I was. "Good-by Linda. Hope you have a nice life with __ hole Tony. I'm heading for Germany!"

CHAPTER 4

"MISERY, AGONY & HEARTBREAK"

At Fort Knox Kentucky, there are three steep hills that the GI's have nicknamed Misery, Agony, & Heartbreak. They are really little mountains, and during "basic training", we had to climb each of them in full battle gear. It was a trip. At night we crawled, combat style, on our elbows, with M-14s in hand, through fields and ditches, and under rolls of barbwire. Above our heads tracer bullets from 50 caliber machine guns were zinging like crazy, and foxholes were blowing up all around us. It was my favorite part of basic ... not that I wanted to be Rambo or anything. Besides, who is that? ? ? This was 1964, and we never even heard of Vietnam.

I think every American soldier is a hopeless romantic. I know I was. All I could think of was Linda. Mail call was the absolutely most important event imaginable. If you don't get a letter from somebody, mom, or Uncle Jerry, or Aunt Lula, or somebody ... it's total rejection, and then the disappointment turns to anger. It's ... "Uncle Sam sucks, along with every one of these loud-mouthed, puffed-up, ridiculous drill sergeants." Of course, to add to the despair, there came the occasional letter from my high school friends, bringing me up to date on all the latest parties, and all the latest happenings around Fremont and Port Clinton ... in addition to who was going with who. It was murder hearing all that. I was homesick, lovesick, bald, and pissed off.

"Art ... why didn't I listen to you! O-God, I must be a total idiot to get stuck in here for 3 years!!!"

After Linda and I broke up, I had licked my wounds, and started going out with this girl from Clyde, Ohio for a couple months. I had actually dated her younger sister a couple times, but when big sister broke up with a longtime boyfriend, I started going with her. She was very pretty and really a sweet girl. The two sisters were only a year apart. I invited her to my upcoming Junior Prom. She got so excited when I asked her, that it actually embarrassed me.

In the meantime, I got this phone call one evening from Barbara, Linda's mother, saying ..."Roger, I don't mean to bother you, but could you do me a huge favor? Linda thinks you hate her. She's been mooping around here for weeks. She can't study. She hardly eats, and I don't know what to do with her. Could you **please** just call her, and talk to her, and tell her you don't hate her?"

Barbara went on in her cleaver, but charming way, to let me know that Linda had had a change of heart, and the thing with Tony was nothing, etc. etc. With a little hesitation, I went for it ... hook, line, and sinker. Linda and I got back together. I procrastinated in calling the other girl up, to break our prom date ... and then never did. She got totally stood up. I still have guilt feelings about that.

I didn't go to the prom either. However, Linda and I went to a couple parties afterwards up at the Lake. We stayed out until almost 4AM. We were madly in love again. But lo and behold, shortly before I enlisted Linda and her entire family moved out of state to Oklahoma. I went ahead and joined the Army for a 3-year hitch.

"Mail call" ... came at Ft. Knox, but Linda didn't write ... and "here we go round the mulberry bush". Soon, I heard through the grape vine, that she met someone in her new hometown. Life was kicking my butt over this chick. I did get a special letter from Vicki, her ten-year-old little sister. She wrote that I was her favorite person ever ... and that she loves me "more than the Beatles" ... and when can I come see her ??? ... cause she cries a lot when people talk about me. I kept that letter on me for many, many years until it wore out and got lost.

For eight straight weeks during basic training we were restricted to the barracks completely. However, one Sunday we found out that we could be released for Chapel service. Oh well. Several of us went just to get free for a while. It was a Sunday evening. This little chapel was full with probably 200 or more soldiers. The service was completely different than the formal Lutheran format that I had been exposed to. The Chaplain was real animated, and sincere sounding. He kept talking about how God wanted to fill all the empty places in our heart and lives, and kept talking about Jesus. I felt real funny.

He asked people to come forward if they wanted to have a brand new life, and forgiveness, and go to heaven. Dozens of soldiers got up, and went to the front of the Chapel. I felt a powerful urge to join them. But, I forced myself to stay put. I thought to myself ... "this guy is playing on our emotions. He's one smooth talker, and knows we're a bunch of homesick GIs. He's trying to cram religion down our throats while we're down. I'm getting the heck out of here!"

After basic training they sent me to Ft. Jackson, South Carolina. I had been guaranteed Europe as my enlistment option, but first I had to complete another 8 weeks of AIT (Advanced Individual Training).

Christmas came up, and I was granted a leave to go home. I took the longest bus ride of my life ... from Columbia, S. Carolina, to Fremont, Ohio. I hate cross-country bus rides. In my boredom I read a newspaper article about some U. S. military advisors who had been killed in Cambodia. They were the first casualties in Southeast Asia. The article talked about Vietnam also. I didn't think much about it ... I never even heard of Vietnam before ... I was just so glad to get away from the Army for a while.

I think the first thing I did after visiting my family, was to go down to John Lewis' and drink about 10 beers on a Saturday morning. Within the first couple days I also discovered that my girlfriend was back in town, with her family for the Christmas holidays. Like magnets we were back together, along with renewed vows of undying love. She never wanted to be apart from me again, and Linda said ... "maybe my parents will let us get married now."

The answer was, "No" ... " Linda is still 16, and needs to finish another year and a half of high school. When she graduates, and if you kids still feel the same ... it will be a different story."

And then before I knew it, I'm back at Ft. Jackson ... even more homesick, and more lovesick. But this time the mail clerk was being good to me. I was also going broke calling Oklahoma via glassed in phone booths. Nevertheless, the Army was becoming somewhat bearable. I wanted to be a paratrooper. They stuck me in typing school, and made me a "clerk typist". They said I scored high in language, and composition on my aptitude tests, so it was 8 hours of typing per day for two months. They needed clerical personnel. It was kind of fun though. I got up to about 68 words a minute with 2 or less mistakes. My mentality was, "Let's just make the most out of a bad military situation."

A couple weeks before I finished my AIT, I received an urgent phone call from Barbara in Oklahoma. She said, "Roger, I have some rather shocking news. Linda is going to have your baby, and she wants to marry you. Would you still like to marry her?"

I told her ... "Yes I would."

Barbara continued ... "Well, Art and I didn't want it to work out exactly this way, but anyway that's water under the bridge. I talked to your company commander, and we've arranged for you to get a 10-day emergency leave, starting next week. They are sending you to Germany after that. I also talked to your mom in Ohio. We are going to fly you to Oklahoma. Then we're going to drive to Texas for the actual wedding ceremony, because there is no waiting period in Texas. Is all this OK with you? Anyway, I'm going to put Linda on the phone now."

I must admit that after the phone call, I was reeling with a slight case, of big-time shock. Was this the Twilight Zone? My brain was having trouble tracking ... it was coming so fast. But whatever ... I was totally zapped and excited ... and happy as a lark. Touchdown Veronica!!!

A few days before I was scheduled to leave for Oklahoma, I heard my name announced over the barracks intercom ... "Private Sachs report immediately to Company Headquarters." I was quickly ushered into a Captain's office, and told to ... "stand at ease". He said ..."Well, private, it seems like your little ___ing woman had a false pregnancy ... so there's no wedding ... no babies ... and absolutely no leave! We have cut you a new set of orders, and you are to immediately roll up, and have your ___ here tomorrow morning at 0600 HRS, for transport to Brooklyn Harbor and Europe. Here is a copy of your orders. You are also ordered not to contact this girl, or any of her family members. Is that understood? Dismissed."

How quickly a person's life can be completely changed forever. A new direction by cold-blooded decree. Thousands of miles of opposite direction, with oceans of ominous years and separation looming overhead. I was helpless to do anything about it. I didn't even have any fight left in me. I was numb. It felt like the end of the world. I had nothing ... except $1.80 in my pocket.

They flew me in a big old prop driven aircraft to Fort Gordon, Georgia ... my first airplane ride ever, where we transferred to another military transport plane. We arrived in New York, and were bussed to Brooklyn Harbor like cattle in the freezing February gloom. The huge USSN Buckner was casually waiting to gobble 1500 of us up. We were faceless plastic toy soldiers with duffel bags. This was the final voyage of the aging troop transport ship. For eleven days on the angry Atlantic Ocean ... I added seasick ... to homesick and lovesick.

Maybe I was living out some sick script ... it couldn't get any worse. But then, of course, there stood the most manicured, spit-shined black dude I ever saw. He elevated himself above the crowd, revealing his Godlike stripes, and barked out, "Listen up girls ... I need ten volunteers for night KP ... and I volunteer you ... and you ... and you"... and naturally, amongst hundreds of bodies, he aimed that pretty black finger right at me ... "and you ... and you ... and you" ... until we were ten.

"Hey blood, it's me ... Sachs ... what's wrong with you?"

For eleven days I didn't see the sunshine. We slept during the day in bunks stacked 5 high, and reported to the galley at 1830 HRS. We were relieved from duty when we finished peeling and scrubbing 2000 pounds of potatoes, 500 pounds of radishes, hundreds of pounds of onions, etc. etc. This is while the stainless steel room went side-to-side, up and down, backward and forward, all in one continuous sickening motion. My life was definitely all about ... Misery ... Agony ... and Heartbreak.

CHAPTER 5

"DEUTSCHLAND"

Europe was a trip. Our ship landed at South Hampton, England and stayed one day. We were not allowed to leave the ship, but at least our eyes saw a tiny glimpse of the U.K. Then, we were back in rough seas, and crossed the English Channel. The USSN Buckner docked in Hamburg, Germany. It was so weird walking down the gangplank, and touching solid ground for the first time in a couple weeks. From there, we were put on different civilian trains heading into the heart of Germany. Europe is so different than America. I absolutely love to travel … and Germany was exactly the way I envisioned it … except that I was shocked to still see so many bombed out buildings and war rubble.

It had been twenty years since World War II ended, but the evidence was still everywhere in pockets. How many baby-faced American soldiers like me had stepped on this same soil, only to be riddled by Nazi bullets? It was hard to imagine, what it really must have been like, two decades earlier. I figured I was pretty lucky to be here now, instead of then … and realized that thousands of soldiers had faced bigger problems … than a shattered love life at the ripe old age of 17. I decided to get my lip off the ground and "get with the program". Not necessarily the Army program … but how about … a "one-each-type European Adventure" program. Besides, as the train whizzed down the tracks, I couldn't help but notice quite a few great looking German girls mixed into the landscape.

My final destination was Mannheim, Germany. I was assigned to Headquarters Company, 102nd Signal Battalion, located at Coleman Barracks. So, I reported in, and immediately was absorbed into my permanent German duty station. They assigned me to the typing pool. Every day ten or twelve of us would type up orders, correspondence, and every kind of boring form that you could imagine. I was the newest arrival ... a Private E-2 ... and absolutely the lowest you can go on the local chain of command. That means that every job, and every duty, or any task, that even slightly resembled ca-ca ... was mine.

About the first fellow GI that talked to me after duty hours, came up with a big smile and said ..."When's your ETS anyway?"

(That's when you rotate back to the states for discharge.)

I said ... "September of 67."

He started laughing and hooting, and came back with ... "Let me see, that's somewhere around 950 days ... of this **insanity**! You know, there are definitely a few short-timers running around Mannheim ... but ask me how short I am private!"

With half a smile I replied, "I'll play ... how short are you?"

"Two days ... two lousy stinking days ... I'm so short, I'm inside my shoes. I'm there. I'm back in the world. I'm so short a little ant could step on me. But hold on ... what did I just figure ... nine hundred something or other ... was that what we came up with? Man, if I had a hundred days left ... that's forever... I'd be so depressed! I think I'd cut my ____ ing throat if I had **nine hundred**!" Then he walked away shaking his head and laughing.

There were a bunch of guys present for his little performance. Of course, they all laughed along with him ... at my expense. Anyway, I took it in good spirits. His message was a sorry truth that I didn't want to think about. I mean in six months, which is a **long** time, I'd still have 770 days left. After two full years, I'll still have 220 days left. Idealistic stupid kids like me, deciding to run off and join the military for 3 or 4 years ... have no comprehension of how incredibly long it really is ... when lived out day-by-day, month-by-month, and year-by-year.

The very first weekend in Mannheim I was invited to go downtown with a bunch of guys. It was great ... I love Germany. The people were really friendly. I didn't feel any antagonistic "defeated enemy" attitude at all. Everyone I met seemed to enjoy Americans, and respected our presence there. It seemed to be an atmosphere of freedom, and liberation from the past. Hitler and all that was an old nightmare. Nevertheless, Mannheim itself still had large sections of town that were rubble ... entire city blocks. But then again there was also new construction everywhere. The autobahns with absolutely no speed limits ... were great.

I immediately got hooked on Wienersnitzel, and "brockhurst mit cheese", but most of all ... Germany makes the best beer in the world. It is so smooth and good tasting that you can drink a barrel of it ... but look out, because it's night and day compared to American beer. Some of the soldiers would get so drunk that they didn't even know their own name, or unit, or anything. The MPs would have to search them to find ID. One guy in our unit came up missing in the dark on the way back to the barracks. Two hours later they found him lying in a ditch telling his life history to a multi-ton iron tank. He was cussing, and saying, "You don't know what I've been through you cold piece of garbage! ____ you!! Take that big gun of yours, and shove it up your ____". The guys who found him came back laughing and cracking up.

I didn't know what a hangover was until I invested some leisure time at a local Guest Haus, Germany's version of a pub. You wake up in the morning feeling like yeast is in your mouth. I'd run to join the line to the coke machine before breakfast, and be sick to my stomach until mid-afternoon. My head would be absolutely splitting in two. I'd swear ..."that's enough of that crap" ... but by nightfall it was party time again.

Linda never wrote me. I heard through the grapevine that her whole family moved from Oklahoma to Colorado. Apparently, Art was transferred. He was an electrical engineer who worked for the government. I felt like I still loved Linda, and always would, but as the months wore on the fire started to die down. I also started counting how many times in my young life, that this gal had totally messed with my brain. I don't think she really tried ... it was just our chemical destiny or something. Maybe I was better off to be about ten thousand miles away.

I made several good friends at the 102nd Signal Battalion. A Pvt. Kramer and myself decided to hitchhike to Denmark. He was from Bemidji, Minnesota ... the former "ice box" of the USA ... that is, before Alaska became a state. We took a 14-day leave from Uncle Sam, and proceeded to stick our thumbs out on the autobahn. It was slow, tough going, but we finally made it to Frankfurt, about 50 miles away. We decided at the rate we were going, it would take forever to reach Denmark ... so in Frankfurt we bought train tickets to Copenhagen ... and boarded a crowded German train. The train was briefly waiting for passengers inside the old and massive Frankfurt train station. Before boarding I needed to make a quick pit-stop, and was mildly shocked when a middle-aged woman was inside the men's public "toilet"... sitting on a chair right across from the urinals. She had a container, and was collecting a few phennings from each dribbling patron. Europe was definitely different.

The train ride north was one of the highlights of my whole time in Europe. We had our own little compartments seating 6 people each. Everyone was real friendly. Kramer and I became exceptionally merry toasting our temporary freedom with our hidden stash of Canadian Club ... and I met a beautiful young student from Düsseldorf. She could hardly speak any English, but joined us in several of our toasts to international peace and good will. She was totally fun and innocent, and we ended up "necking" for about the last hundred miles, before her stop in Düsseldorf came up. I almost got off the train with her, but she just laughed, and waved saying "aviedersien". I was so drunk I even forgot to get her address or anything ... but she lives in my heart forever.

At one point of our continuing journey, we noticed that the train seemed to be doing strange things. It was behaving very similar to the USSN Buckner ... and we soon discovered that we were not stopped at another station at all, but the train was actually inside an ocean going ferry. It was a bigger shock than the urinal lady. I guess I must have slept through European geography in school. I had no concept that we would be crossing a sea to get to Denmark. Our ignorance made us laugh like crazy, as we rode our train, inside a ship, across the Baltic Sea. It was a great occasion for another toast "on deck".

We finally reached our destination ... Copenhagen, which is the capital of Denmark. It was the spring of 1965. Over the next few days we spent most of our time in a place called "The Tivoli". It was the original site of the first World's Fair back in the twenties or something like that. Now, it's like a huge amusement park, and we had a great time. I saw the first real longhaired guys in my life at the Tivoli. The Beatles mop-cut hair was about as radical as I'd seen up to then.

We took a guided tour of the canals one day. We saw the famous Little Mermaid sitting on her rock, and the royal palace, and old cathedrals, along with numerous other places of interest. It was great ... I enjoyed impersonating a tourist. We passed through most of the city as we sailed up and down all the different canals. It was educational. I wondered if Aunt Lula knew that Denmark was about 90% Lutheran. That's what the guide told us. I sent home lots of post cards.

One late evening we went into a crowded bar down by the waterfront. It was filled with Danish sailors, and all kinds of rough looking characters. It was scary. All of them were giving us rude and dirty looks. I ended up getting into a fight when a man pushed me. Almost instantly, as people pulled us apart, the police came in, and hauled Kramer and I off in the back of a real-life European patty wagon. I thought we were headed for jail, but the van stopped a couple miles down the road. The cops with the funny looking uniforms released us ... with a stern Danish warning ... to stay away from the waterfront taverns. After a considerable sigh of relief ... I told Kramer ... "DANG!"

On the way back to Mannheim, we spent a couple days in Hamburg, Germany. Somehow, we again managed to find ourselves deep in a radical section of another city. There, we discovered a whole bunch of German girls who were **not even** as innocent as my pretty frauline from Düsseldorf. Prostitutes were sitting in nearly every window of the buildings displaying themselves, and luring in potential customers. The narrow curving streets were packed with people. It was just like Canal Street in Amsterdam, which is a favorite spot for soldiers and tourists. One girl in this red light district, looked just like Ann Margaret. I kid not. I went inside, but couldn't get into paying Ann for sex. It was too weird. In a sleazy bar the next day, a dolled up hustler successfully extracted all of Kramer's money, every single penny. Afterwards he was totally sick about paying her everything he had. I had a few dollars left, and we survived on Bavarian salami and bread for the remainder of our trip. It was fun though.

Back in Mannheim, in the firm grip of the military machine, time started dragging on. The few days of leave, and the very few weekend passes that I ever got approved, were nothing compared to the incredible asinine drudgery of everyday Army life. I hated it with a passion. I was accused of having a bad attitude, and a chip on my shoulder, and being a punk kid, and things like that. For the most part, it was all true. The First Sergeant, who basically ran everything, openly hated my guts ... and I hated him more. The only problem was, that he could make my life hell on earth, with his God-like authority over us ... and all I could do in return was to silently hate him with a passion. I was 20 minutes late for bed check once, and given an Article 21, which is non-judicial punishment. My sentence was 30 days of weekend KP, and 90 days restricted to the post. I additionally had special orders to scrub every filthy, smelly, food-caked, grease-dripping, metal garbage can at the mess hall, with steel wool ... "until you can see your sorry ___ face". As time crept on in this ... "dog eat dog ... butt kissing Army", I began to understand how somebody could actually be driven to murder.

Now, in the same way that First Sergeant Walcott could make your life totally miserable ... if he wanted to ... he could also make things absolutely peaches and cream ... for those willing enough, or maybe even fortunate enough, to get their noses real creamy brown. His company pet was Specialist Walker. Naturally Walker had the best job in Company Headquarter ... which was mail clerk. He also had his own private jeep, because he had to daily drive 30 miles to Heidelberg to pick up our mail, and bring it back to our Unit. And of course, he was exempt from all normal duty rosters. He got promoted the second there was an allocation, and seemed to get every perk available, etc. etc. In spite of all that, I still kinda liked him, because he was a lanky, mellow, kickback, quiet, type of guy.

One day Kramer mentioned that Walker had announced, in my absence, that he didn't like me, and would like to kick my butt. He had said this the previous night to a small group of his friends while they were downtown drinking. It really hurt my feelings. I didn't say anything for about a month. Walker himself never said anything like that to me. Then one weekend a bunch of us were drinking in my quarters. There are four bunks to each large room, and sometimes we'd have some great bull-sessions. We had bottles of booze lined up like a liquor store. Everyone was getting blasted including me. Anyway, Walker was there and said something sarcastic to me, to which I replied ... "Hey Walker, I hear you don't like me, and would like to kick my tail. Is that true? ... Well, here I am. Why don't you get up, and let's go behind the barracks."

He was lying back on his elbows, and just smiled at me ... not saying a word. I taunted him several times, but he just kept the condescending grin pasted on his face, and wouldn't budge. That really got my Irish going ... "Look crap for brains, don't just sit there and grin. You seem to enjoy going around behind my back badmouthing me. So, get the _____ up ... cause I'm telling you to your **face** in front of everybody, that you're an butt-kissing coward. If you don't get off that bunk, I'm going to pull you off."

Walker said, "I'm not going anywhere with you."

With that, I grabbed his fatigue shirt, and we started fighting right in the room. Somehow we ended up by the door, which was closed. I managed to hit him in his mouth so hard that it knocked him backward over a footlocker, and onto another bunk. As he fell backwards, his combat boot made a black streak in an arc across the white door. He kept fighting, but I got him in a headlock, and was uncontrollably pounding his face with my free hand. I slammed him into a metal wall locker as a room full of people pulled us apart.

After they separated us, I was shocked when I saw Walker's face. Actually, I was a little scared. His entire face, hair, and clothes were solid blood. They had to take him to the infirmary in Heidelberg, because he needed stitches in his lower lip. It was cut completely in two, which is where most of the blood had come from. The duty NCO made me clean all the blood, which was everywhere, as well as to scrub the black shoe polish steak off the white door. I figured I was really in for it now ... messing up the First Sergeant's number one boy.

Everyone knew about the fight, but to my surprise Walker filled out an official written report saying that he tripped getting into his jeep, and had busted his lip on the frame of the vehicle. Again, I was shocked, and really truly appreciated that. We never became friends or anything, but didn't have any more problems either. However, the First Sergeant called me into his office on Monday morning, and ranted and raved, cussed, and let me know that he knew the real score. He said ... "You think your tough or something ? ? ? I could take you right now out behind the bunker, and kick your ___ with one hand tied behind my back! Heck ... I have a 17-year-old kid that could kick your rear end!"

I said ... "I'm only 17."

The First Sergeant with his blockhead, and big red alcoholic nose looked surprised. He stared back at me ... "Is that right? Is that all the older you are?" He paused quite awhile, and said, "That explains a lot of things. I could never figure you out, Sachs. I thought you were older, but dang, you're just a little punk kid. Get the ____ out of my sight!"

Man ... life in the Army ... for a rebellious teenager is the pits. If anybody reads this, please don't go into the service until you're at least nineteen or twenty years old. Nevertheless ... after that, the First Sergeant seemed to lighten up on me a little bit. He even came to my defense one time when I had a scrape with the civil authorities. He actually got me off a big hook.

But, my troubles were not over. For example, the Army kept me a Private E-2 for as long as legally possible. Years later, my brother Randy made Staff Sergeant E-6 in less time than it took me to make PFC ... although that was during the heat of Viet Nam. But, literally everyone on our post seemed to get promoted before me. Even soldiers who had been in ten times as much trouble ... got promoted. I eventually found out that there was a regulation that the Army must discharge me, if I wasn't promoted after 14 months in grade as an E-2 ... that is, unless I had a court martial, or some bad time on my record, which I didn't. Like clockwork they promoted me to PFC during my 14th month ... right on the deadline. Even my promotion was a punishment.

Another problem I had was a run in with a black friend. He was a Spec 4, and had discovered that I'm not prejudice. He was married, and showed me photos of his wife and daughters back in Chicago. We got to be pretty tight. For quite a few months we went off post drinking, and exploring Germany together. Then, one evening he tells me in a very tender, and sincere way, that he's in love with me, and wants to give me a blowjob. We were both drunk, and I thought he was kidding. But he wasn't ... and he kept coming on.

I told him ... "Look Willie, we've been friends for quite awhile. I've **really** enjoyed hanging out with you. Let's just forget this conversation totally. We can still be friends and everything ... but drop this other crap. I've been hit on before several times back in Ohio as a little kid, and had a few things happen, but never expected it from you. It's not where I'm at Willie ... it's not my cup of tea ... so that's all I want to hear about any of this. Can you dig it?"

Willy was looking at me with big sad eyes ... and said ... "I can't help how I feel, but I respect where you're coming from Rog. I'll be good and won't mention it again. OK?"

But he did, and the next time he "sweet talked" me, (and that's exactly what it was like ... sweet talk), I got mean, and ordered him to stay clear of me. I **absolutely** never told anyone a thing. As far as I know, no one knew he was gay. Over the next six months I had two more brushes with homosexuals who were in my unit. One of them was in the very next bunk to me in my room. This time it was a white guy who had just re-enlisted for 6

Fire On the Mountain

years, and had received a $6000 bonus. I never suspected he was gay either, but one night he offered me $50 to masturbate him. I couldn't believe it. I had a lot less sympathy for him, because he wasn't even a friend. I told him if he ever mentioned anything like that again, I was going to knock his teeth out. But again, I never told a single person about him either.

Then, a friend of mine told me that this particular roommate was telling people that I had made homosexual advances toward him. I blew a fuse, and when I came back to the barracks that night he was in bed sleeping. I turned the bright overhead lights on, and woke everyone up … and called this guy out.

"Hey MR. LIFER … get up! I want everyone here to know that you're a lying son-of-a-_____, and a queer on top of that. What did you say to me that one night? Listen everyone … this creep offered me fifty bucks to beat him off. I told him to get lost … and I never said a word to anyone about it. But now this jerk is going around accusing me. So what do you have to say you ___ing faggot? If I'm lying, get out of bed and do something about it."

He said, "I'm not going to fight with you Sachs, because you would probably kick my tail … but remember this … one of these nights you're going to go to sleep, and in the morning you're going to get up and look in the mirror … **but won't recognize yourself!**"

I ran over and tried to grab him, but everyone broke it up. The next day I went to the Company Commander, who was a Captain, and let him know that I didn't want to bunk in the same room as this guy any more. I told him the whole story, and especially about the threat to attack me in my sleep. I continued my silence about my former black friend, and the other homosexual in our unit, because I thought those incidents were ancient history … but this recent scenario was way out of hand.

Germany was great … however, this Army experience left much to be desired. I especially didn't like the idea of some paranoid pervert rearranging my face in my sleep. I tried to press charges when nothing was being done, but they transferred Specialist So-and-So completely out of Mannheim. Seemed to me, like the Army protects its lifers, regardless of sexual preferences or stated policies. Nevertheless, after he left … I slept much better in Deutschland.

CHAPTER 6

"CHRISTMAS BELLS IN VIENNA"

My first Christmas in Europe was coming up, and I took a 10-day leave with a soldier friend named Yanos Sovari. He was originally from Hungary. His family had escaped from behind the Iron Curtain in 1955, and immigrated to the U.S.A. I had turned 18 in September, and he was less than a year older than me. Yanos was different than anybody in our company. He was real smart and handsome, and was taking a heavy load of college courses at an extension of the University of Maryland, which the Army offered. Instead of blowing all his money on Lowenbrau, and chasing fraulines, he bought a nifty little VW bug. But, nobody really liked him … except I did. He was a loner, and very sensitive, and acted a little arrogant … but I felt it was just a smokescreen for feeling out of place and left out. My mother always accused me of being drawn to the misfits, and the down and outers. Maybe it takes one to know one.

Yanos inspired me to take some college courses … and he explained that I could take a test and get a high-school GED, since I had dropped out of school at the end of my junior year. I got a hold of a few books, and managed to pass the test. Actually, I had my high school diploma before any of my old friends … but I would have given my right arm to be back at Fremont Ross High. Shortly thereafter I was accepted at the European branch of the University of Maryland. I only took 2 or 3 courses while in Germany … but I pulled above average grades, and felt real good about "higher education". Yanos even got me reading "Thus Spake Zarathustra" by Friedrich Nietzsche. The amazing thing was that I understood it … demented as it is. Friedrich was definitely another down-and-outer that needed a friend.

Anyway, during Christmas season 1965, Sovari and I took off from Mannheim in his little bug, and headed south through Germany. I had gone north last time, so it was time to see what's happening down south. If I knew what was awaiting me ... I wouldn't have been so gung-ho about this trip. However, southern Germany was beautiful, and by the time we hit the Austrian Alps I couldn't believe my eyes. No photograph or post-card could match what I was seeing. I'm a northern Ohio, flat as a pancake, endless cornfields, raised boy. Here in every direction were massive, towering snow capped mountains, covered with forests and huge cliffs, and incredible rock formations. The sky was bluer than blue, and crystal clear, with picture-perfect billowing clouds. Winding between the mountains were rivers and waterfalls, and meandering shorelines along deep silver-blue lakes. Every so often there would be a quaint little village in the distance with thatched roof houses, and smoke curling up from several of the chimneys. It looked so beautiful, and so peaceful, that I just wanted to jump out of Sovari's bug and live there forever. It felt like fairytaleland. All I needed to do was find Gretchen with long blond braids. We'd raise little blue-eyed kids and billy goats ... and live happily ever after.

Sovari and I eventually reached an ancient city named Salzburg, and spent the night. I had never seen so many statues, and castles, and works of art in my life. It was definitely inspirational. We drove around the city before it got dark, but then the whole town closed up at about 6:30 PM. Absolutely nothing was open. It was weird ... so we slept and split. Our southern destination was Vienna, Austria. I enjoyed traveling with Sovari, although I embarrassed him in a couple restaurants by refusing to eat with my fork in my left hand. Fat old ladies with brown velvet hats looking down their noses at an uncultured American didn't really bother me. So what if I was born with a fork in my right hand ... but Yanos obviously wanted to exhibit proper European culinary refinement. I drank my first cup of Espresso at his invitation. It was terrible, and so strong that I almost choked. But we had fun ... or at least I did.

Finally we arrived in Vienna. On the drive down Yanos had explained that some friends and relatives from his home in Budapest, Hungary were in Vienna. They had planned a get-together with Yanos on Christmas Eve. He was **real** careful to explain that it would probably be better if he went alone. He said they didn't speak any English, etc, and I'd probably be bored. I figured it was my table manners, but anyway I wasn't offended. We got a room in a hotel that felt like, and probably was, several hundred years old. The ceiling in our narrow rectangular room was at least 20 feet high. There was a huge wooden bowl of water to wash up with. Even the key to the room looked like it belonged to Count Dracula.

Yanos was determined to introduce me to some culture, and asked if I had ever attended an opera. Fremont was a little short on Opera houses, so I humbly confessed that I never had. He proceeded to give me an education on Vienna's world famous reputation as a centuries old artistic hub. It sounded good to me ... so we were off to see the Opera ... the wonderful Opera of Aus. I liked it. So did little Mikey, (of TV commercial fame). It had everything. Fat ladies with horned helmets, beautiful damsels, and sword wielding baritone dudes jumping around in leotards. It really didn't matter that I couldn't understand one single word. It flowed real nice ... and I felt elevated.

Well, Christmas Eve came and I made plans to explore Vienna on my own. I myself had noticed a world famous symbol ... a couple rabbit ears prominently displayed above a nightclub called The Playboy Club. It was about a mile from our hotel room, so I figured I'd check it out. After a brisk walk, they wanted some outrageous cover charge to get in, so forget that. However, right next door was another nightclub named, "The Teen Club". It was a first-class nightclub with a big dance floor, full bar, and live rock-and-roll bands. The place was packed to the gills. It had been **real** cold and snowy the last few days, so I had broke down and purchased my first full length, continental-style wool coat the day before. Inside the club they had a regular coat check, so I turned in my one and only, self -purchased Christmas present, in return for a little ticket-stub.

I ordered a drink, and checked the place out. As the night progressed I asked this beautiful brunet to dance. Then I asked her again. Her name was Heidi, and she spoke great English. She asked if I was by myself ... to which I told her my Sovari story. She then asked if I would like to join her table with the friends she came with. So within a couple hours of exploring Vienna on my own, I was having a real Austrian experience with the locals. We spent several hours talking and drinking, mixed together with a couple slow dances. I tried to talk Heidi into splitting, but she was going to a mid-night mass with her parents, and of course the following day, Christmas, was totally consumed with her family.

Heidi's friends were a young married couple. The husband had just been released from 12 months in the Austrian army. We compared notes on life in the military, and he bought me several mixed drinks. We had a great time. He got paid something like $12 a month while he was laying his life on the line for the motherland. I thought my $78 a month as a new recruit was bad. Another couple joined us at our table, the drinks kept flowing, and everyone was picking my brain about America. In the midst of it, I managed to get Heidi's phone number. This definitely beat the Opera.

But then like they say ... all good things must come to an end. Heidi had to split about 11:15 and the other 2 couples had to go also. My comrade had spent about 3 months salary on drinks for everyone. It was expensive, and as my new friends were all saying goodbye ... with vice-grip tight, hearty, handshakes ... they told me to finish a couple nearly full drinks ... and then they were gone. There I was all alone at the table, with a huge buzz, trying to decide if I should head back to my room, or hang out a little longer. The place was still packed, the music was loud, and I decided The Teen Club was better than looking at a wooden bowl full of water in an empty room.

About the time I finished my drink, a waiter came up, and said something in German or Austrian or whatever. I thought he was complaining that I was about to start on one of the leftover drinks on the table. I proceeded to try to explain that my friends had told me to finish them off ... but of course he didn't understand any of my English. Then, he grabbed my arm, and tried to pull me out of my seat. I jerked my arm away from him, and out of nowhere there appeared about four or five waiters.

The first one grabbed me again, and pulled me into the aisle. All of them started firing punches at me at once. I never experienced anything quite like this ... but instantly everything went into slow motion. I couldn't believe this was happening. All I could do was try to duck the blows by bending down. Two of them probably could have done a better job on me than five ... because there was hardly any room to move in the isle between the tables. I bent over trying to cover my head, and strangely noticed details of the floor. Like distant thundering bombs, I could feel blows hitting the back of my head, and the side of my head, and then the top of my head ... "this really isn't happening!" Then, this huge fist appears right out of thin air. It slowly swoops up, bigger than a large screen TV, and BAM ... smashes into my mouth and nose. It was 3-D without glasses. Blood shot out of my face all over. Fists kept coming and coming. Somehow, I was able to stay in my covered up, rope-a-dope cocoon ... and I instinctively reached into my pocket ... still in slow motion. I could feel my little knife. I slid it out cupped in my hand. It took both hands to open the blade, and they kept beating me, and beating me, but they didn't see the knife.

Someone hit the play button ... and bingo we were in live action speed again. I took the knife in my right hand, and with all my strength slashed it straight up through the maze of bodies and fists coming at me. Blood was all over ... I couldn't see ... and it was an act of total desperation. Miraculously, the blade of the knife missed everyone. When my arm reached it's highest trajectory ... there was immediately half a dozen hands grasping it, and trying to get the knife out of my hand. I was by now crying, and screaming, and desperately trying to stab my attackers ... with everything I had.

They couldn't get the knife away from me, and the next thing I knew, I was entirely lifted up by all of them. They carried me, like pallbearers, feet first past the crowded tables, and down some steps, while I continued to try to strike down with my single fang. My face was level with the face of one guy carrying me. He punched me so hard that I jerked my head in the other direction, only to have the guy on the other side ... also punch me square in the face. I totally freaked ... and frantically renewed my efforts to stab them. They quickly carried me to a huge wooden post, and started beating my hand against it, to dislodge the knife. After several smashes I couldn't hold it anymore.

I was crying and screaming, and really thought they were going to kill me. But, to my complete and utter amazement, they continued carrying me straight out the front entrance to the street, and with a heave literally threw me on top of a parked Volkswagen. As I slid off the side of the car onto the icy cold sidewalk, the waiters all turned around, and went back inside the club.

I couldn't believe it was over. I just lay there for a few minutes in a complete bloody daze ... but I knew I had to get up, and get the heck out of there. Forget my brand new coat … I was thinking cops, and charges like attempted murder, or assault with a deadly weapon. I couldn't believe they just let me go. I got up and started to run for about a couple blocks. When I stopped running the cold really hit me. I had on one of those pale blue dress shirts, like a white shirt … only this one was completely blood soaked down the front. There were still a few people walking down the streets. As I passed them they were all staring at me. My face and mouth were caked with blood, and already swollen to ugly proportions. I felt **exactly** like the Hunchback of Notre Dame.

Then as I continued to the hotel, I had probably the loneliest feeling of my entire life … it's the reason for this whole chapter. It affected me. I never felt so alone, or so unknown, or so unwanted. I was now on a dark street that was completely deserted in a strange city, thousands of miles from home, beaten to a pulp on Christmas Eve. It began snowing … and was absolutely beautiful … but so cold. Then, just like in some novel … all the church bells in Vienna started ringing. I couldn't believe it! It sounded like hundreds of them for miles around. They rang and rang and rang.

"Something else … it must be midnight … Merry Christmas Roger". I started crying again, and hurried up my step to try to stay warm.

CHAPTER 7

"ELVIS" AND THE "EM CLUB"

I returned to Germany and eventually the black eyes, grotesque lips, and other distortions from my beating in Vienna began to subside. I had several visions of walking into the Teen Club with a fully automatic weapon. Stupid thoughts … but then, I'd shove those fantasies aside, and tell myself … "Listen …You need to flow with the blows."

By now Vietnam was going strong. But, I was continuing to have my own little battles within the peacetime occupational ranks of Germany. I was getting real tired of it … super tired of it. I even considered volunteering for Vietnam. Over there, I was sure that the "chain of command" had to have a little more human decency, and basic respect for people. Otherwise, they would get their heads blown off. I heard stories from rotating soldiers about gung-ho, manipulating, political, jerk-type leaders, who "accidentally" got killed by friendly fire. I don't know if it was true … but I can definitely visualize it. ("Maybe First Sergeant Walcott and I could volunteer on the 'buddy plan'!") However, I was informed that I was ineligible. At that time, the Army would not accept volunteers under 19 years old for Vietnam. By the time I would turn 19, there wouldn't be enough time left for me to complete a mandatory 13-month combat tour. I was stuck right where I was in the 102d Signal Battalion.

Dave Setchel and Dusseldorf sister

I did eventually manage to get a four-day weekend pass to go to Munich. I made the trip with a friend named Dave Setchel, who I had met in Basic Training. He was from Bettsville, Ohio, which is only about 14 miles from Fremont. He got stationed in Stuttgart or something, but we stayed in touch, and met in Munich for our weekend getaway. Off we went to the Hofbrahaus ... the famous 3-story tavern where Hitler made some early Nazi speeches during his rise to power. A stein of beer, which was about 20 ounces, cost 1.25 Marks, a little more than a quarter. The exchange rate at the time was 4 Marks per US dollar. So, for a buck you could get blasted. We made the rounds, and eventually met two sisters from Düsseldorf at a bus stop, and spent the whole day touring Munich with them. It seems like all the girls from Düsseldorf are sweet and pretty. We took a bunch of pictures. Munich definitely has a party atmosphere. During the annual Oktoberfest it is something like the Mardi Gras in New Orleans.

On our last day in Munich I met another German girl who really liked me. Why couldn't it have been a day earlier? She was with me our entire last day, and even took a bus with us to the train station to see me off. She gave me her address, and I wrote out mine. Setchel boarded the train, and was yelling from the platform of the very end car to hurry up, because the train was leaving. He was right ... and it immediately started to take off. I was about 20 yards away, and gave my new girlfriend a quick kiss, and started running.

About a week later I got a letter from Munich. She wrote ... "It was the most romantic moment of my life. When you run to catch the train, I didn't think you could do it. But then you jump on with suitcase, and your friend trying to help. It was just like a movie."

Well, back in Mannheim the movie was becoming more like a horror flick. I had fallen asleep on the train after Setchel got off, and went about two hundred miles past Mannheim. I didn't have any money left, and the conductor kicked me off the train. I finally contacted a nearby army base, by phone, which sent a couple MPs after me. They in turn, called my unit. Ten hours later a jeep arrived to take the AWOL soldier back. Here we go again ... I was restricted to the base, etc, etc.

Coleman Barracks was a pretty big base, and wasn't without a few redeeming qualities. For one thing, it had a neat Rod and Gun Club... with the coldest beer in Dodge. There was also a full-blown gym and recreation center. The PX sold clothes, and German cameras, and cigarettes for $1.50 a carton. What a deal. But for me, Coleman Barracks' most legitimate claim to fame was its history with Elvis Presley. This was the military base where Uncle Sam housed "The King of Rock and Roll" on his newsworthy tour of duty. It was right here in Germany where Elvis courted his beautiful teenage Army brat ... and all this was only 8 or so years prior.

I have always been an Elvis fan. When I was in the 6th grade back on Oaklawn Avenue I started collecting little 45 records. The first 3 records I bought were "Good Golly Miss Molly" by Little Richard, "Great Balls of Fire" by Jerry Lee Lewis, and "Jail House Rock" by Elvis Presley. I was watching Ed Sullivan in glorious black and white when he first introduced Elvis to the masses. Elvis inspires my imagination ... and Coleman Barracks was my contact point with royalty.

His presence was still lingering in the Vegas style, EM Club ... which Elvis built for his fellow GIs' at Coleman Barracks. To have an "enlisted man's club" which outclassed the "officer's club" was **special**. It conjures up love ... along with a deep appreciation for higher human expression. The club had a full bar, a huge dining area, with a large raised stage, and a dance floor. It also had a casino area with slot machines, and featured live entertainment on weekends. It was really cool, and packed most every night.

I never went out with the total intention of getting drunk. Getting inebriated usually happened as a natural by-product of looking for some excitement. But one Saturday morning, in the midst of this most recent military restriction, I told Kramer ... "Let's go to the EM Club. I feel like getting totally wasted. You want to come along?"

It was only about 9:30 AM and Kramer wasn't game. So I walked the 20-minute walk to the EM Club by myself. When I got there a bartender was just opening the place up, and I was his first customer in the empty club. I sat on a lonely barstool, but within 45 minutes a couple alcoholic looking sergeants joined us. Payday had just happened ... so God bless America ... "and you too, Elvis". By noonish the bar section was almost full, and I was eating peanuts, drinking German beer, and giving my money to a row of one-armed bandits. Kramer showed up about two o'clock in the afternoon, and I was already flying like a kite. I don't even remember too much from mid-afternoon until a band started playing in the packed out hall that evening.

I was so drunk it was a crying shame. I do remember Kramer and I, and another guy were sitting at a table while a band was playing. By now I had graduated to mixed drinks. Then, here comes my old black friend Willie. He pulled up a chair. Previously, he had been sitting at a nearby table with several other black dudes. I looked at him, and said with a snarl ... "Willie, get off my table."

"That's not very polite of you Roger. I just want to see how you guys are doing," he replied with a hurt voice.

"I don't give a ____ what you want. Just get out of here right now ... and I'm not kidding you."

But he wouldn't leave, and the other guys at my table started getting on my case. Willie just sat there with those sad brown eyes. I wanted him out of my sight, and off my table, and I didn't feel like telling anybody why ... "Just take your sorry ____ away from here! I told you before to stay clear of me."

I continued to scorch him with more cursing and verbal abuse. Willie's black friends were starting to tune in on what was happening at our table. As one of them headed our way, Willie jumped up and intercepted him. They argued for a while, and went back to their table. I figured I was about to get my face altered again, but ... "____ Willie

… _____ the Army … _____ all the slimy faggots in the world … _____ everything!!!"

The remainder of the night is a fog with huge blank spots. I must have stayed late at the club mumbling to Elvis or something. I think my friends abandoned me. I do remember someone staggering around with me on the way back to the barracks. I don't know who it was. I also remember falling in gravel and getting sick. They found one of my boots by the motor pool, and the other one a quarter of a mile away. When I got to my unit I clearly remember the duty officer. He came out of the office to see what all the commotion was about.

That particular night the duty officer was a stocky, well-groomed, quiet, Mexican American staff sergeant, who had never said one cross word to me ever. I always thought he was the nicest NCO in our unit. But the instant I saw him I screamed obscenities at him calling him all kinds of names. Two or three guys tried to drag me up a flight of steps toward my room, but I continued to scream at this sergeant at the top of my lungs. Then I puked all over the steps. When I got to the top of the steps, I heaved some more, and all the way down the hall. The poor NCO called the Battalion Commander, who was a Colonel, and he held the phone up so the Colonel could hear the continuous screaming. It echoed down the halls all the way from my room on the top floor of the building. The last thing I remember is barfing some more out of my second story window.

The next day I woke up so sick, and so messed up that I couldn't believe it. I felt like dying … but instead, was promptly ushered in before the authorities. They were going to Court-Martial me all the way. But first I had a whole lot of puke to clean up. It was even streaked down the outside walls and windows.

Oh God, Oh God, Oh God … "What a ____-up I am."

CHAPTER 8

"CLIFF"

It was clear that I was in deep trouble. My superiors were talking insubordination, drunk and disorderly, and other charges along those lines. This is while I was already on restriction for being AWOL ... as the result of my slumber party through Germany. Someone in my unit suggested that I go see the Base Chaplain. Maybe he could help. For one thing he was a high-ranking Colonel. So, I immediately went in to see him.

I spent around three hours in his office. He was a kind man, and easy to talk to. I gave him a run down on my whole life history up to, and especially including, my present predicament. Several times he tried to suggest that I allow God to work in my life by becoming a committed Christian.

I responded by saying ... "Sir, I know I'm in a lot of trouble, and that I'm probably my own worst enemy by some of my behavior ... but as far as religion goes, I can't buy it, even though I hope God is real. There must be something going on out there, but I'm not going to be a hypocrite by claiming that I know what it is. You seem really sincere. I wish I could be as convinced as you are, but what I need right now is some advise on what to do about this mess I'm in at my Company.

The chaplain continued to patiently listen to my troubled life, asking a question or two from time to time. There were quite a few entanglements involving people that I don't want to hurt by writing about them ... but I told him everything. I needed help. In the end, he shocked me by saying ... "You're a man of fifty years old, in many of your life experiences. You have a choice. You can use all that, as a foundation to build a better life, or you can allow your past to destroy you. I still want you to consider the claims of Jesus Christ. I believe He is the answer to all our problems including each man's final destination in heaven or hell. I am going to give a call to your Company Commander, and see if I can be of some help in this present situation. Thank you for honestly sharing with me all that you shared today."

What a neat man. I wondered if he could really help me over at the 102nd Signal Battalion. Even if he couldn't, it felt so good to get everything off my chest. It also felt like he cared, and maybe even understood me a little bit. That means a lot too. Well, a couple days later, I saw him in our hallway coming out of our Company Commander's office. It felt real funny. I wondered what was going on ... but knew inside that it must be about me. I had this humbling feeling of appreciation come over me. The reality hit me that this Colonel had personally come to my unit to defend me. I was positive that's what he did.

The next day I was called into the office, and informed that I was being given a new duty assignment. Many units at Coleman Barracks were required to supply personnel for a variety of positions, which kept the overall post functioning. Positions like Gate Guards, and workers for the PX etc. My new job was working in the Post Gymnasium. So, effective immediately, I was to get my personal things out of the typing pool, and report to the gym. Could this be true?

I was informed by my Company Commander that he had talked to the Post Chaplain. It was their consenting feeling that a change of scenery might do some good in my situation instead of a Court-Martial ... and I was to take the opportunity, and demonstrate that they had made a good decision. I couldn't believe it! **Mercy in the military!** "Thank you Chaplain ... even though I never went back and personally thanked you ... you greatly rekindled my hope in humanity, and hope in myself. God bless you!"

Working at the gym was even a better job than mail clerk. I was taken off all duty rosters ... KP, flag detail, morning mustering, and everything ... because my hours at the gym constantly changed. There were four of us, and so every four days one of us had to keep the gym open until 10 PM. But it was such a gravy assignment. All we did was check out basketballs, and weights, and once a day dust mop and oil the hardwood basketball court. We had a little office ... and in between handing out basketballs we perpetuated a long-standing card game. The Sergeant in charge was a mellow, easygoing, black, buck-sergeant (E-5). They taught me to play Tonk, which is a modification of pinochle and euchre. We played for money, and kept track of the standings on a big calendar. A couple officers and high-ranking sergeants came in regularly to join in the game. It was a blast.

With some of my free time, I was working on a pencil drawing of the Heidelberg Bridge and castle. I put a lot of hours into it. One of the guys thought it was pretty good and asked if I had ever met the artist downstairs. "Downstairs where?" … was my question, because I had never seen any evidence of a lower floor to the gymnasium.

My friend replied … "Oh yeah, there's a really neat bomb shelter way down under the far corner of the building, and this artist guy, named Cliff, has made it into a regular art studio. He's really good, and does all kinds of artwork for the brass. He also paints peoples portraits, and sells crazy sweatshirts, with little monsters driving hot rods, and all kinds of stuff. He's really cool. You should show him your drawing."

A couple days later I followed my friend down some concrete steps, into a vaulted area with a large circular metal door. The door looked just like a submarine door with a big round valve handle right in the middle. We cranked the valve open, unlatched the door, and stepped through into the neatest underground art studio I had ever seen. My friend called out to Cliff who yelled back at us from another room … "Come on in".

A tall lanky soldier holding a paintbrush emerged from another room to our left. My friend introduced us, and Cliff took me on a brief tour of his studio. He had paintings all over, and a huge homemade work area, with custom easels, and a large glass palate. Of course, the place had no windows being a bomb shelter, but Cliff had rigged up all kinds of makeshift creative lighting. He was obviously not one of these slob type artists with dried up brushes and paint everywhere. The place was clean, and orderly, and I could feel creativity and production in the air. I spent a couple hours watching Cliff work on a painting. Unlike me, it didn't bother him at all for people to look over his shoulder while he worked. It was the beginning of one of the most lasting, and interesting friendships of my life.

The next day I took some of my drawings to show Cliff. He really liked them, and wanted to know if I had ever worked with oils or acrylic. Not really … and Cliff told me I could come work in his studio any time. He had plenty of room, and several work areas. What a joy over the coming months ... the countless hours I spent in that studio, talking, watching, painting, and drawing in that special subterranean retreat.

Cliff taught me how to use an airbrush. He had been painting all kinds of custom pictures on sweatshirts for the soldiers, and making lots of money. He could whip out these incredibly realistic looking little monsters, driving hot rods with smoke coming off the tires, and flames shooting out of the engines ... and stuff like that. The GIs were eating it up. He used fabric paint, and the paintings lasted as long as the sweatshirts. I got the hang of it, and Cliff took me in as a partner when he got this one big order. I bought my own compressor, and a brand new German airbrush. We had a blast.

I was down in the studio during almost all my off-duty time. Cliff would often stay late at night, and we'd talk and talk and talk, as we worked on this or that project. He was quite a character. His full name is Clifford Davidson. He is from Douglas, Arizona and was an adopted son in a large family. His favorite subjects were Hawaii, and surfing, and sex. He was about 24 years old when we met, and I had just turned 18. He spent several years in Hawaii, and one night I asked him how he decided to move to Hawaii.

"Gee Rog, when I graduated from school I got a job for a while, and saved up some money. Douglas, Arizona was pretty boring, and I always wanted to go to Hawaii. So, a buddy and me put together a little nest egg, and hopped on a plane to Honolulu. When we got there I almost went crazy! There were all these gorgeous chicks running around everywhere. The air was warm and moist ... and the water was crystal clear, and warm as heck ... even at 3 A.M. It's just like paradise ... no lie!

Anyway, Scott and I went out and rented a nice apartment, and bought a used car. That almost completely wiped out all our money right away. Plus, we cruised all the clubs, spent a lot of money on cover charges, and mixed drinks, and went to the famous beaches ... all trying to score a couple of the chicks, who were absolutely driving me bananas. But dang ... it was like we had the plague or something. We couldn't even get a good conversation going. Neither one of us got laid ... not even once for the first three months in Hawaii. It was sorry.

Then we met this local who told us ... 'Hey you guys are doing it all wrong. Get rid of that silly apartment, and find some shack down by the beach. Anything, as long as it's near the water. Then, get rid of that car

Fire On the Mountain

too. Buy an old clunker, throw a couple surf boards in the back … and watch what happens.'

Gee Rog … that's exactly what we did. I found this old house about a block from the beach. It was up this steep hill, but it had a fantastic view. We sold our car, and bought this 48 Studebaker. It wouldn't even make it up the hill to our pad … except in reverse. Every single time we went home, we had to back up the darn hill. It was a riot! We stuck a couple surfboards out the window, and hit the beaches.

It was like magic … absolute magic. We got righteously into the surf scene, and threw a few parties … and pretty soon it was "jackpot" with the chicks. I had locals, and gorgeous tourists from all over the world sleeping with me and falling madly in love. It was hog heaven. I worked part time delivering cars for a car lot. A couple chicks would even come down and get naked, right there, on my lunch break in one of the cars. It was totally far out."

Cliff had a couple big photo albums of his adventures in Hawaii … with a story behind each picture, and each girl. He almost married a rich girl from Australia, and I saw lots of pictures of her. He also had a post card from Waikiki Beach, in which he was in the picture, on the post card riding a wave … on his 10-foot plus board. (This was the early days of surfing in the late 50s). I just loved killing time in Germany, listening to Cliff tell story after story … about the time he lived out his fantasies as a playboy surf bum in tropical Hawaii.

After a couple years in Hawaii, Cliff went home to Arizona, and ended up marrying a hometown girlfriend, and getting drafted into the Army. According to him, he had a terrible marriage, because his wife had had something awful happen to her as a little girl … and she was terrified of sex. How ironic, Cliff the sex maniac, marries a gal who is unable to have sex. Cliff said they made love once on their honeymoon, and she got pregnant. They had a baby girl. Since then she practically wouldn't let him touch her. He brought his wife overseas with him, but I only met her once in Germany while visiting their off-post housing. With all his art earnings Cliff bought a brand new Triumph TR7 sports car. It was really sharp. Nevertheless, I really felt sorry for Cliff and his wife both … because of their sad marriage.

Cliff was scheduled to get discharged from the Army about one year before me. We made plans to go to Los Angeles, California … and start an art studio together. We talked about it all the time. He also wanted to attend an art college in LA, and be near the ocean. I told him … "Surfs up Cliff … It's a deal!"

CHAPTER 9

"ORLEANS, FRANCE"

Just like so many times before ... when everything is going great guns ... then BAM, something happens, and deja-vu ... all good things must come to an end. I loved working at the gym on Coleman Barracks, and playing Tonk every day with a bunch of neat guys. I loved spending all my free time in an underground, World War II bomb shelter ... art studio. Cliff was like my big brother, art teacher, and best friend, all wrapped into one. We became super good friends in spite of our age and rank difference. He was a buck sergeant ... three stripes. I was a PFC ... one stripe. But then came the bad news ... my entire unit, the 102nd Signal Battalion, was being transferred out of Germany to Orleans, France. "You gotta be kidding!" My neat little world came crumbling down.

In early April of 1966, I drove a duce and a half truck, in a caravan of vehicles through Germany, through a section of Switzerland, and then part way through France, to our destination in Orleans. The first thing I noticed about France was the lousy roads ... compared to the new autobahns throughout Germany. Also, there was twice as much war rubble. Everything looked so dirty, and gloomy, and untidy. Even the sky seemed to be continuously overcast all the time. The whole place was depressing. Not only that, but the French people seemed to despise Americans. Something's wrong with this picture. Our defeated German enemies love us ... and our liberated French allies despise us. I was also curious ... where are all the famous beautiful French girls? Every one I saw seemed to have hairy legs, a long hooknose, and a big black forest growing under their armpits. Maybe I just missed Germany, and had an attitude.

Not only did France not agree with me, but I also had a new First Sergeant who was worse than First Sergeant Walcott. I was on a collision course with him, and guess who usually won. Not me. There were a couple highlights though. The local officers found out that I was artistic, and had me paint a big picture, and make banners and signs, for some high and mighty party they were having. I chose to paint a picture of the Joan of Arc statue that was in the center of downtown Orleans. It was a huge warhorse with Joan of Arc in full armor pointing a victorious sword. The 1st Lieutenant, who had me do the work, came back later, and said that my painting was the hit of the party. He told me, "If I'd have had 75 of them, I could have sold every single one."

I tried to keep the painting, but they used it at another party, and someone swiped it. One of my fellow enlisted men commissioned me to paint him the same picture for $25, but I didn't like it as much as the first one. Nevertheless, he seemed to be happy, and I was twenty-five bucks richer. It was my very first sale, unless you count sweatshirts.

The same lieutenant had me work on a battalion newspaper with him. I was the assistant editor, illustrator, paste-up man, and typist. A couple months later, both the lieutenant and I received an official letter directly from the Pentagon, which was weird, commending our latest Battalion newspaper, and stating that a copy of the commendation was to go into our permanent military file. Then, a General from another unit across town "borrowed" me to make official charts with sophisticated drafting equipment, which I had never used before. That was fun too, but all this made the First Sergeant hate me more, because I was getting out of quite a few extra duties, and out from under his hideous thumb.

I always swore that while I was in Europe I wasn't going to waste my leave time, and my money by going home to the States. Who knows when I'd ever get back here? But, after about two and a half months in France, I was so homesick, and so sick of the mental gymnastics that the Army, and the First Sergeant was laying on me, that I put in for a 30-day leave to the States. I had to get away. My leave was scheduled for June.

A couple days before I was to fly home I received a letter from Colorado. It was from Barbara, my old girlfriend's mom. I was totally surprised. She wrote … "Roger, I hope everything is going well for you. It's been a long time, and a lot has changed, but I want you to know that Linda has never gotten over you. And now we have a real crisis on our hands, because Linda heard from a friend in Fremont that you are coming home in June. She wanted us to let her go see you, but it wasn't a good time with all that is happening in our lives at the present. But now, Linda has run away, and for two days we have been worried sick about her. She might have taken a bus. We're not sure. The authorities from Colorado to Ohio have all been alerted. Somehow, in my heart I believe she is going to make it through to you, and if she does, would you please have her call us immediately so we know she's all right. We all miss you Roger, and I hope you have a great time back at home. Please, please, please, let us know the minute you hear anything from Linda. Love, Barbara

What a trip! I handed the letter to one of my buddies. He looked up and said ... "Man, I wish I'd get a letter like that." I think I even saw a little tear in his eye.

Well, before you know I was flying across the Atlantic Ocean in an old noisy four-engine prop airplane. I had hoped to fly in my first jet ... but no big deal. Anything beat two weeks on a ship. I was shocked to hear them announce we were flying over Iceland. I guess we went up and over. Somehow, I connected to the Detroit airport ... and there was mom, and the old man, and my youngest brother Rob. God Bless America, and Coke-a-Cola, and big wide streets, and real disc jockeys. It was like Alice in Wonderland. I never thought I'd miss cornfields ... but they were absolutely perfectly beautiful.

As we drove into Fremont it looked about half the size that I remembered it. It's amazing how we perceive things differently from one vantage point to the next. There was State Street Bridge where I caught stringers full of white bass. "I wonder how old John Lewis is doing?"

A day or two after I got home, I received a phone call from Colorado. It was Linda. She got caught in Illinois or something. We talked for a long time. In a way it seemed really strange talking to her, like I didn't even know her. I couldn't put my finger on it. Maybe I wasn't ready for round 17. She said her parents were going to let her come see me in a couple weeks if I wanted her to. I told her that would be great ... and I meant it.

People in Fremont had really changed in a year and a half ... especially my brothers and schoolmates. Everyone had grown up so much. The class that was behind me in high school was graduating in a couple days. I made the rounds, visiting friends and relatives. While I was at my Aunt Pauline's house, my cousin Janie and I were looking through her school annual. Janie is one of my favorite cousins, and was graduating that week. I saw a picture of an old girlfriend, and told Jane ..."Hey, there's Nancy Young. I used to go steady with her when I was in the 9th grade."

Before I even met Linda I had a short fling with Nancy. She was real sweet, and super popular ... and successfully ripped my heart out on her birthday. While we were going steady, I bought her (almost) the whole top ten for her birthday, and then hid the records down the street from her house in some bushes. My plan was to walk her to the park dance at Roger Young Park ... pretend to get something from the bushes ... and surprise her with my thoughtful, loving present.

When I got to her house, her sister Bobby came to the screen door, and with a real sad face handed me my ring saying ... "I'm sorry but my sister wants to give this back to you. She won't come to the door because she's in the back crying ... I think she's going steady with Gary Ohms now. Sorry."

Gary Ohms had practically been my best friend all my life ... what a rotten deal! I walked back to the bushes, and smashed "Party Lights", and all the other records into a hundred pieces on the sidewalk. Anyway, I forgave Gary because she broke up with him too in about a week, and went back with her old boyfriend, Pat Hoffman. He was a junior at St Joe's, and Nancy was in the eighth grade. She went steady with him the rest of the way through school ... almost five years. Janie told me Pat recently gave her a diamond ring, and they were going to get married after she graduated.

Janie said ... "I'll see her tomorrow night at the graduation ceremony. Do you want me to say anything to her?"

"Sure ... tell her I said Hi."

I was enjoying my homecoming immensely. In Europe, it was really hard to meet decent girls. The couple girls I met on leave were neat, but it was impossible to keep anything going from hundreds of miles away. I wrote a letter or two to my girlfriend in Munich, but never made it back down there, and we stopped writing. Around the base GIs had a bad reputation, and the only girls seemed to be barmaids and hard looking whores. All they wanted was money. But in Fremont I felt like a celebrity. My buddies and I were partying night and day. Everybody was real glad to see me again ... and I was running into new girlfriends and old. It was great.

One day my mother told me that some girl had called for me about a dozen times. I asked who it was, but my mom said she wouldn't leave her name.

"If she calls again … tell her to leave her number and her name or else stop calling."

The next day when I came home my mom said, "That girl called again today. It's Nancy Young and she's working as a telephone operator. That probably explains things. She must call every time she gets a break, or a breath of fresh air. Anyway, she left a number for you to call her back. So … p l e a s e … call her."

I was totally shocked, "Your kidding … she's engaged to Pat Hoffman!"

I called Nancy, and a week and a half later … we decided to get married. It was crazy. Pat Hoffman freaked out. My brain freaked out. Everybody freaked out. I called up Colorado … and didn't know what to say to Linda, but finally blurted out … "I need to tell you something, I'm getting married." There was total silence on the phone. I felt horrible, and finally Linda asked … "To who?" I told her, and said I was really sorry things hadn't worked out for us, and wished her a good life. I couldn't believe what I just said to her … but it was definitely me … I heard me myself.

Nancy told me that she was secretly in love with me all through high school, but thought I hated her after the time she had broke up with me. She said I would always avoid her in the halls, and never would speak to her. I didn't remember doing that, but for sure I never suspected that she had a crush on me. I thought she was exclusively Pat Hoffman's property. She knew I went with Linda for years … so we kind of had something in common in that regard. Years with someone else, and now fate throws us together again.

Only fate was named Jane Brink. I found out later from Nancy, that instead of relaying my message of "Hi" at the graduation ceremony, Jane went up to Nancy and said … "Do you remember my cousin Roger Sachs. He said he used to go steady with you. Well, he's home on leave from Germany, and would like to see you!"

Life is so full of twists and turns.

My main rational for getting married so quickly … was to get out of

France. I figured we would **almost positively** get married anyway ... so why not get married now. If you're married your maximum tour of duty in Europe is 24 months. I already had 16 months in Europe, so if we got married now my rotatation date back to the states would be in 8 months. Otherwise, I would be stuck for another 15 months in the stinking 102nd Signal Battalion. Plus, Nancy could join me overseas, and we could live together off base. Maybe France could be romantic after all. It sounded a whole lot better than sleeping in a 20-man snoring bay ... and waking up to an egotistical First Sergeant screaming at everyone.

So, after a small wedding at my old St. Marks Lutheran Church, and after a short honeymoon in Port Clinton, Ohio in a cabin by the lake ... I was off flying in my first jet ... heading for Orly Field in Paris, France ... married at the mature old age of 18. Nancy joined me three months later, and we lived in an upstairs corner of an ancient château with a classic gated courtyard, on the outskirts of Orleans, France.

CHAPTER 10

"A BRICK OF HASH"

When I returned to France, they had already initiated a Court Martial against me. Soldiers in my unit were taking bets … if I'd ever come back or not. The First Sergeant must have thought he was definitely in the money, when I was a "no-show", and an extra week slipped past my return date. However, back in Fremont I had obtained an emergency 10-day extension on my leave through our local recruiting office. The First Sergeant's countenance actually fell, when I handed him my approved paperwork granting me the extension.

The First Sergeant was even more ticked, when a Major from Mason Fort requested that I be temporarily assigned to his office. Mason Fort was a small Army base about 15 miles from our even smaller compound. It meant that I was "issued" my own jeep, which I drove daily … through a really neat section of French countryside. I loved that drive with its windy little narrow roads, and peasant-looking farmers intently watching me go by. What a different way of life people have in different parts of the world.

The Major made me an illustrator, and my job was to produce these fancy briefing charts for more high-level meetings. It was similar to what I did for the General's office, but with more art work. It was interesting to get the inside track on a bunch of political happenings, because De Gaul was kicking the American Army out of France. I was making charts of how the US military was going to transfer huge communication systems over to the French government, in mapped-out phases … and stuff like that. It was a neat job. Driving back and forth to Mason Fort also meant that I was temporarily exempt from the infamous duty rosters. But believe me, before it was all over, I got more than my share of each and every extra duty. We even had "all night" patrol duty, where we had to walk around the compound with our weapon all night long. It was incredibly hard to stay awake.

Some soldiers were having a much harder time adjusting to the military than me. I saw, and heard of, numerous examples of young soldiers going AWOL, cracking up emotionally, getting medical discharges, and even getting locked up, and dishonorably discharged for all kinds of violations. The stockade for all of Europe was at our very own Coleman Barracks. My unit back in Germany ate lunch with the prison guards in a common mess hall. One guard told me about a nineteen-year-old soldier who couldn't handle the Army, and went AWOL a couple times. His unit court-martialled him, and gave him six months in the stockade. While he was being transported, he jumped out of a vehicle and took off running. According to our mess hall friend, there was absolutely no where for the AWOL kid to get away ... but one of the guards fired a round in the air, and a second round hit him square in the back of the head. Dead forever at nineteen-years old. What a bummer.

Well, when I first went to work at Mason Fort there was quite a stir going on there also. A distraught young soldier had recently climbed a tall electrical tower at the post. He intentionally grabbed a hold of a multi-thousand volt high-tension line and killed himself. It fried him to a crisp. I talked to an eyewitness who said he was really a mess. The rumor was that this kid's family was forcing an investigation, and that the military machine was super uptight about the entire thing. I personally never got suicidal in the Army, or even considered going AWOL ... and for that matter, I was actually surprised that my fellow soldiers were taking bets on me. However, the Army did definitely teach me how to hate real good. If pushed hard enough, under the right or wrong circumstances, I might have been capable of killing a First Sergeant or two in a combat zone ... but hopefully not.

On the brighter side ... a major victory in my win column was when Nancy showed up three months later. **We missed Paris in the springtime** ... but made it several times in the fall. Paris was only a quick 60-mile train ride away. We even celebrated New Years Eve 1967 in front of the Arc de Triumphe. At midnight everybody ran around the overflowing streets kissing everybody in sight. In the heat of that moment was about the only time the French unwittingly liked me ... a true red-blooded American! I do have to admit; there were a few pretty girls in Paris. And then, of course … a couple young French Casanovas were really getting into kissing Nancy. Like a fool I let it go on for quite awhile … but finally had to convince a couple of them, that enough was enough. We were all about half looped. "Happy New Year!"

The upstairs apartment inside the old chateau we rented was really neat. It was furnished with OK things, and had a big living room, kitchen, and all the essentials. Of course the ceilings were a mile high. Out back were a couple green houses and fields. The only thing that really freaked me out … was that it had huge spiders. I killed about six of them … and the granddaddy of them all was about 4" in diameter, including his big hairy legs. A French family owned and lived in the rest of chateau, and they were cordial enough. They had a seventeen or eighteen year old daughter, named Jessica, who liked to hang out with us. She spoke good English, and was really nice.

Nancy would have to walk about three quarters of a mile to the main road to catch a bus. When she went grocery shopping, and came home with multiple heavy bags, she would work her way to the chateau in stages. She'd leave a couple bags beside the road, and carry the rest a couple hundred feet, set those down, and go back to get the other groceries … all the way, back and forth. The street was real narrow, and had old homes sparsely scattered along the street we lived on.

"A BELI LUGOSI CEMETERY"

Part way down our street on the left was an old, old, old cemetery. I doubt if Columbus had even discovered America when those people died. Maybe the Indians hadn't discovered America. It was ancient looking with a big wall around it, and a heavy metal wrought iron gate. At night when Nancy and I would walk past it … it would spook the heck out of us. There were no streetlights at all, and it would be pitch black most of the time on that street … unless there was a full moon. Sometimes I would make weird noises to scare Nancy and get her mad, but a couple times that cemetery definitely got my heart pumping a little faster. I guess I watched too many late night horror movies as a kid with Linda Lee … my neat babysitting cousin.

One night Nancy and I went out on the town to some French tavern, and I got smashed. On the walk home we came up to our Beli Lugosi cemetery. It was a totally black night. With my drunken courage, I decided that I was **absolutely sick and tired** of that graveyard scaring the heck out of me … so I pushed open the huge creaky gate. I walked in. The gravestones looked like giant shadowy chess pieces. Some of them were 10 or 12 feet tall. Nancy yelled at me to get out of there. I absorbed the total silence for a while, and then challenged every ancient corpse in the place, to come on out and fight like a human. I stumbled around, drunk as a skunk, and started yelling … "Hey you creepy son-of-a-____s, you finally got me! Here I am … so ____you all!!!"

Nancy was now begging me from the street … "Roger … get out of there, you're crazy! "

I climbed up on top of a gravestone, and continued yelling … "What's taking so long. **See what you've done now** … you even got me in trouble with my wife … so get your bony ____s out here where I can see you … Right now!!!"

I probably would have had a heart attack if a mouse had moved, but there was nothing but total silence. About every other ancient tombstone had a statue or a cross on top of it. Nancy left me behind, and was waiting down the street. I walked over to another massive tombstone, and hopped on top. She was **insistently** yelling at me some more … to get going. I was flashing on the place, and waited a long time in the morbid silence. Anyway it seemed like a long time. Finally, I yelled out … "OK … You bunch of cowards … until we meet again … kiss my ____… and have a nice nap!"

As I walked out of the gate, I looked back inside the cemetery, and one of the trees looked like it had the face of the devil engraved right on it … horns and all. I kept looking at it, because I had never noticed that before. Then it seemed like my eyes were playing tricks on me in the darkness with all the shadows … cause it looked like the face moved a little! "I better get out of here!!!"

On normal nights our chateau apartment became the party spot for a few of us. One time two of my friends, Fields and Christopher, were over when the landlord's daughter was there. Young Jessica was one of the pretty French girls. Jim Fields asked her if she ever played "spin the bottle", so after a little explaining … we all ended up playing. Seems like every time I turned around some guy was kissing my wife, but we had a blast.

Both Fields and Christopher were what they call … PKs … meaning, "preacher's kids". Fields dad was a Pentecostal preacher, and Christopher's was a Methodist or Presbyterian minister. I had bought this big reel-to-reel tape recorder from the PX in Germany. One night we all got drunk, and Fields grabbed the microphone. I snapped on the tape player, and we began taping our own wild and tipsy "revival meeting". He started walking back and forth throwing his arms around, and screaming things … "In the naaaaaame of Jesus!" He had me laughing so hard I thought I'd die.

"Brothers and sisters … get your sorry little rears down this sawdust trail, and REPENT!!!! You need the LORD … HALLELUJAH, and you need him right NOW … before GOD ALMIGHTY fries your little hot dog, and che-ches off in HELLS FIRE … FOREVER …

And then Christopher would jump up, and start tag preaching … Thank you Reverend Fields! That was inspirational … but Brother before you preach to these filthy sinners here in this house of ill-repute … why don't you stop screwing all them whores down in Pigalle yourself. Come on! Come on now!!! It's here for you too Brother … HONALULU … HANG TEN!!!

The two of them went back and forth. They had Nancy laughing so hard she was doubled up on the floor. She was a non-practicing Jehovah's Witness, and neither one of us had ever heard that kind of preaching … especially with the salt and pepper these guys put on it. It was hilarious. We carried on so much that the next day the landlord came up complaining, because we had knocked some plaster off the ceiling beneath us in the house below. What a trip.

About a month after our revival meeting, my same two PK buddies came over, and had a little something they wanted to share with us. Fields was all excited, and started explaining to Nancy and I … "Hey, you know, back in El Paso, Texas where I'm from they have a lot of pot that comes across the border from Mexico. I was always taught that pot, which is really marijuana, is just like one of the hard-core narcotics like heroin. Did you ever see the movie, 'Reefer Madness'?"

"Yea … they showed that movie to us in Jr. High".

"Well … that is a bunch of baloney. Really! They make out like if you smoke one marijuana cigarette, you'll be totally addicted, and get sick, and go through withdrawals, and all that. That will happen if you use heroin or something, but they're lying about pot. All kinds of kids are smoking it back in the States now. I've tried it a whole bunch of times, and believe me, it's safer than drinking, or even smoking cigarettes. Cigarettes will give you lung cancer ... but pot only makes you laugh and have fun."

Nancy had a lot of questions, and both Christopher and Fields went on and on and on ... about how cool it is to smoke pot. They told us it was even big in Europe, and England, and really everywhere.

"Anyway", Fields continued, "it's a lot cheaper over here, because there's no oceans separating Asia from Europe. Asia is where the best pot comes from. We got a hold of some hash smuggled in from Turkey. Hash is the best part of the marijuana plant compressed together, and would cost a minor fortune in the States ... but we got a righteous brick of it, the size of a mason brick, for only $100 in Paris. We'd like to smoke a couple bowls of it with you guys tonight, and party hardy. What do you say?"

Nancy replied, "I don't know ... you guys are crazy. Are you sure it doesn't hurt you?"

"I swear Nancy, it doesn't even give you a hang over the next day. You can take it or leave it, just like beer ... it's not addictive at all."

I jumped in, "So you have some with you ... right? Let's see it. I want to see what it looks like."

Christopher pulled out a bag from his fatigue jacket. Inside the paper bag was a square of tin foil about 3" by 3". He opened the tin foil, and revealed a dark brown, gummy looking substance ... which was hashish. It was late 1966 and the very first time I was ever exposed to any kind of drugs.

Nancy said, "How would you ever smoke that stuff?"

Fields pulled out a big pipe and said, "We cut up little pieces of hash with a knife, and mix it together with cigarette tobacco, put it in the pipe ... and fire up. Come on! Let's party a little here!"

"What do you think?" I asked Nancy.

"I don't know ... I guess I'll try it if you do. I hope we don't get caught or something!"

"Who would ever find us out in the boon-docks like this?" Christopher replied.

Immediately, Fields got a knife out, and started whittling, and chopping on the block, while Christopher busted up a bunch of cigarettes into a pile of tobacco on our kitchen counter. It was very interesting to watch them, and before I knew it … we were passing the peace pipe from person to person.

My preacher friends demonstrated inhaling a lung full of smoke, and holding it as long as they could. I gave the pipe a huge draw, and the hot smoke burned my throat, and was harsh. I could only hold it in my lungs a couple seconds before I started coughing. It was the same for Nancy. She coughed immediately. We kept filling the bowl of the pipe with the mixture of hash, and passing it around. After a couple times, I more or less got the hang of holding the smoke in for much longer. Might as well see what this stuff can do.

For a little while it didn't seem like anything was happening, but then I started feeling a little lighter. Something Fields said hit my funny bone … and then almost immediately everything seemed incredibly funny. Nancy was also laughing about nothing. Christopher looked like someone pasted a huge smile on his face. I started explaining something very, very important to everyone … but in mid-sentence completely forgot what in the world I was just talking about. Now that was really funny. We were in this one TOGETHER!

For some reason we were all sitting on the kitchen floor. Time seemed to take on a new dimension. "Like, haven't we been sitting here only about 10 minutes … but I can't even remember what life was like before this 10 minutes. This 10 minutes feels like one heck of a long 10 minutes. Did I tell them that … or did I think I told them that. I need a beer … Well … sunk-in-a-ditch … I didn't think it after all, cause … Thank you Nancy for the brew … You doing alright smiling one???"

I made a big mistake … I tried to stand up. Suddenly I weighed 800 pounds, and could hardly lift a leg up to take a step. The room literally started swirling and I had to lie down. This was no longer a good deal. What's a good deal about gaining 660 pounds in ten minutes … but anyway I made it to the bedroom, and stretched out on the bed. Everything was OK from there, and I could hear everything from the kitchen to downtown Orleans … in **super-stereo!** Let em laugh. Who gives a dang. It will do them good … "Hey Nancy … come here … listen … I can't move … but get me something out of the refrigerator!"

We became human piranha. We ate everything in the refrigerator …

and everything from the cupboard. I never got off the bed, but before I completely zoned out, I finished a bowl of cold peas ... one by one with my fingers (without even lifting my head off the pillow). It was amazing.

I didn't realize it then ... but that hash from Paris was probably one of the most potent doses of tetrahydrocannabinol that I would ever get my hands on in my entire life. The sticky resin said ... **"LET ME INTRODUCE MYSELF!"**

CHAPTER 11

"WESTWARD HO"

My plan for getting out of France worked like a charm. My marriage was another matter. Nancy was as perfect of a wife that any 19-year-old could ever possibly find. She loved me, and was faithful. She was a hard worker, and kind to everyone. She had my baby … a flawless 8 pound 6 ounce boy with blond hair and blue eyes. He was born on February 28th, 1968 … five months after I was discharged from the Army. About the only complaint I had … was that my wife was very, very jealous. While we were stationed in Texas, I came home to find a pile of ashes on the kitchen table. It was the remains of all the photographs of Linda, and any other girlfriend from my past. I didn't like it, and eventually her worst fears became reality. I'm not trying to make excuses … it's just the sad truth … I started messing around. I wasn't happy being married.

From France the Army transferred me to Fort Hood, Texas. I spent the last seven or eight months of my military career as a security analyst. I was finally promoted to Spec 4, and worked in an office with several civilian government employees, several officers, and several WACs … female soldiers. We processed Top Secret, Secret and Confidential security clearances, and were able to read many of the juicy FBI background investigations of prospective candidates. It was with one of the WACs that I began cheating on my wife. I felt horribly guilty afterwards, but it's just like they say … each time became easier.

In mid-September of 1967, the day that I thought would never-ever-ever arrive… finally came. As a matter of fact, the United States Army discharged me about 10 days early for some unknown reason. After serving three miserably long years, I was finally "honorably" discharged … and still a teenager. I turned 20 about a week after I was released. All I can say, is that I had a recurring nightmare for almost a decade … in which I was "somehow" back in the Army. I would invariably wake up in a cold sweat ... so relieved and happy that it was only a bad dream. It happened over and over.

Back in good old Fremont, I found a job working for Linders Dairy ... and I became a milkman. It beat the Army. Nancy and I rented a cozy little house on the west side of Fremont, and our little boy ... Troy M. Sachs arrived that next February. I really loved my tiny little son ... but Nancy and I were having a "tough row to hoe". In the spring I happened to go down to John Lewis' house one Saturday morning. There was a huge log in his back yard that had washed up from some long forgotten flood ... and it was the spot where all my black friends shoot craps. We were drinking, and in the midst of one such exciting dice game, when my wife came angrily walking up, roughly pushing our four month old baby in a stroller down Bidwell Avenue, and demanded in a loud, almost hysterical voice ... that I come home **immediately**! I was furious, and it was actually John Lewis who calmed me down enough, to load the stroller in the car, and take my family home. We had some terrible arguments. It got real sad. I completely left once, but after a few days felt so guilty that I went back. We had our good times, but the bad times were not good for any of us.

There came a time when I heard that Linda and her family were in town. I told Nancy that I was going to visit them, and if she gave me any crap about it at all ... I was gone. I meant it. Art greeted me with a big handshake at the door of the home they were visiting, and even though it was slightly strained ... it was so good to see them. No one objected that I take Linda out, and we went for a drive.

I found out that right after our last conversation, in which I had informed Linda that I was getting married ... right after that she met a young soldier, and accepted his marriage proposal. She got married only a couple months after I did. They already had a little boy, who I briefly saw that night at the house. Her husband had been transferred somewhere, and she was to join him later. As we drove around out in the country, I asked Linda if she was happy. She threw the question back at me. I told her ... "Not really."

She told me her husband was a neat guy, but that they had their share of ups and downs. However, she added, "Everything is too complicated now. I have a baby, and you have a little boy to raise, and we shouldn't even be talking like this."

I told her, "Look … let's make a date for ten years from now … and if nothing else changes, at least we can have one more time together that belongs only to us."

She laughed and said, "OK … it's a date. We better get back now, or my dad will get worried."

It was the last time I was ever with Linda.

One day Nancy was looking at The Fremont News Messenger, and said, "Wasn't your old girlfriend's last name McCloy? There is a picture of a 'former Fremont resident', who died in Colorado."

I grabbed the newspaper, and with an unbelievable shock … there was Art … Linda's dad … my close father-like friend. I couldn't believe my eyes! It couldn't be him! I only had time to see his name under the picture, and read … "dead at age 38" … when I was slammed with grief so hard, that I cried for hours. Nancy had never seen me cry. I went into the bedroom to be alone. "It can't be Art … it just can't be him!!!" I finally pulled myself together enough to find their phone number in Colorado. I dialed the phone. Barbara answered, and I started crying while I was talking to her. I don't even know what I said. What horrible empty feelings in my chest. "Why … Why … Why???? How come all the good people die??? What's the deal??? It's just not fair."

They brought his body back to Fremont. The funeral home was only a few blocks from my house. I went to say good-by, but the waxy looking man in the casket didn't look anything like my friend Art. Barbara came up and thanked me for coming, and calling on the phone. She told me … "Art thought the world of you Roger, and I'm so glad you came."

I didn't get over Art's death. It stayed with me, and I would talk to him at most every crisis point of my life. Many conversations. How cruel and unfair life is. Thirty-eight years is nothing. He died from sugar diabetes. Art went into a coma, and left this world, and all of us who loved him. "Son-of-a-_____!"

The pastor of my old Lutheran church came by and visited Nancy and I. Probably my mother had said something to him. She was very concerned, because I had totally rejected Christianity. My parents didn't go to church anymore, but at least they professed to believe. Pastor Glover spent a couple hours with us in our home … and in my opinion I made a fool out of him and his beliefs.

I said, "Do you mean to tell me, that every Jew, or Moslem, or Buddhist, or pygmy in Africa, who never even heard of Jesus or Christianity ... that they are all going to hell? It doesn't matter that they might have been loving, caring, honest people, who sacrificed for their kids, and did the very best they could? And just because they were raised in a culture that overwhelmingly believes in some other religion ... and just because they don't convert to Christianity ... that God is going to send them to hell for all eternity? Is that what you really believe?"

Pastor Glover picked up his Bible and held it up, "That's what it says in this book, and I have to believe it. If a person does not have Christ in their life, they are going to hell."

"Well Pastor, you're wasting your time with me, because I can't buy that. I'm not going to stop my kids from going to church or anything, because I don't want to mess with their eternity if I'm wrong. There's a lot of good things about religion, but I can't pretend to believe something that I don't believe. To me it's all a crock of crap, and I really don't want to talk about it any more. Thanks for stopping by."

I was still troubled about Art. As it always does though ... time marches forward, and sometimes things get back to normal. But, I didn't get back to normal. What is normal? Life just ... "keeps on keeping on". I got in a bad argument with Nancy in Port Clinton, which is seventeen miles from Fremont. I took off on foot from my parent's cottage, and left her the car. I hitchhiked back to Fremont, went to a drug store ... and called up an old girlfriend. She was my X-cheerleader girlfriend, who I had broke up with long, long ago, in order to go back with Linda, of course. I told her I wanted to see her ... and she said OK. After I hung up, I had to call her back and say, "I forgot, you have to come pick me up, because I'm on foot." I had corrupted her as a freshman in high school, and now I was about to do it again as an engaged young woman.

Not only was I full of guilt, disillusioned with marriage, and milk trucks in general... but I was also tired of Fremont. As much as I love cornfields and Old Betsey, I was bored and hungry for some change. Maybe I'm just wired that way. Things had settled down between Nancy and I. My secret cheerleader was pregnant, and went ahead and married her fiancé. I had wrecked my car with her and I in it one time, but that was all repaired now ... and ... "what the hey... I wonder what ever happened to Cliff Davidson."

I hadn't even thought much about Cliff for a couple years, but now I realized, "We were supposed to go to L.A. and start an art gallery. I wonder if he ever left Arizona, and actually went to L.A.?"

I told Nancy one day, "Do you remember that artist friend I told you about? We planned to start an art gallery in Los Angeles after I got discharged. I'm going to take a long shot, and call information in L.A. to see if they have a number for him."

Nancy reminded me, "Didn't you say his last name was Davidson? Even if he did move to L.A., just think of how many Davidsons there must be in a city like that."

Anyway, I dialed and eventually got the right operator who asked … "Can I have the city and listing please?"

"Clifford Davidson in Los Angeles."

After a short pause … she said … "That number is 213-681- * * * *."

I was shocked to get a number so quickly, but nevertheless thought, "what's the odds that it's the right Cliff Davidson on the first shot?" I dialed the number.

There was about two rings, and then … "Hello."

"Is this Cliff?"

"Yes."

"Were you in the Army in Germany and … "

The voice cut in … "Roger … dang … is that really you? I can't believe it! How the heck are you? How did you find me?"

"I called information, and took a big old long shot, because I didn't even know if you left Arizona, or went back to Hawaii, or where you are, but I remembered we talked about starting an art gallery in L.A.… . So, did you start one?"

"Heck yes … well, not a gallery, but I have a bitching studio, and I'm also attending Chanards Art Institute. It's a blast. Come on Rog … hurry up, and get your ___ out here!! What are you waiting for?"

We talked and talked just like old times … and then I hung up the phone.

"Nancy … Cliff wants us to move to L.A. and go in business. Let's get out of Fremont. What do you say?"

So, when Troy was 6 months old, we packed up all our belongings … and followed the trail of so many of our ancestors … "Go west young man!" … "Ride-em, ride-em, ride-em … get them doggies moving …

get them doggies moving ... **RAWHIDE!!"** (Help me out here Rowdy Yates!)

My dad gave me his "old" spare Frito-Lay truck. I bought a tow bar to haul my 1965 Pontiac behind us to California. The truck was the old style with a separate cab in front, and a fourteen-foot box on the back. The whole rig looked like a wreck, but it ran good, and had decent tires. My dad said that if I just take it easy, we should make it with no problems. We saved enough floor space in between a baby bed and some boxes to sleep at night ... so that we wouldn't have to pay for motels. We didn't have any money to speak of, but I figured we'd have enough for gas, food, and a month's rent. Nancy was a real pioneer, and more than game for the whole adventure. I stuck a loaded pistol under my pillow ... in case we got bushwhacked.

It took us about 10 days to reach California. I decided on the way, that I wanted to be a better husband and father. Troy was such a beautiful baby boy, and so little and helpless. Nancy was the best of mothers, and I had hurt her. She didn't deserve that. We did quite a bit of sightseeing, and side trips down good old Route 66. It's the reason why a 5-day trip turned into 10. I even went fishing. It was neat, and I had my little Brownie 8 mm movie camera catching the highlights. We finally made it safe and sound, just like my dad said. However, he had to wire us some money when we arrived, because the portable bank completely ran out. We were stone-broke ... but all excited and chomping at the bit ... to start a new life in California!

CHAPTER 12

"LA 1968"

We came up over the mountains into Southern California on Interstate 10. I had never seen highways like these with three, four, and five lanes of traffic going in one direction. It blew my mind for a while. I had to watch, and keep track of traffic on all sides of me. It was a new experience. Plus, I was driving a pretty big truck, and pulling a big old Pontiac Grand Prix behind that as well. Soon, I got my first taste of freeway congestion, and stop and go traffic jams. We followed Cliff's instructions, and got off the Hollywood Freeway on Alvarado Street. I drove straight over to his art studio, because it was late morning and Cliff was working.

Just like in Mannheim, Germany ... I found Cliff busy at work in his studio, paintbrush in hand. It was really great to see him again. He was working on a logo for a new fast food chain ... "Taco Bell", which was due to open shortly. I introduced him to Nancy and our baby. He hadn't changed much, except no more army fatigues. Thank God. His studio was upstairs in an office building, right down the street from Chanards

Fine Arts College where he was attending. After shooting the breeze awhile, he locked up the studio, and we followed him over to his place. He drove his nifty and original 1938 Ford coup.

Cliff had already made arrangements with his landlady for us to rent the 2-bedroom apartment right next door to his unit. The single story apartment building was on Virgil Avenue in Hollywood, about half a block from where Sunset Blvd and Hollywood Blvd merge. We initially had the small, but significant problem, of having run completely out of money on our trip west. However, my dad came through the next day. He wired us enough cash to get into the apartment. For the next three years this little apartment with it's narrow rectangular courtyard, and set of concrete steps going to each unit, became our home.

I had only met Cliff's wife briefly in Germany, but now we became next-door neighbors. Her name was Julie, and their three and a half year old daughter was named Tracy. Julie was very reserved but always friendly. As Troy started walking and talking, he spent lots of time with Tracy. Nevertheless, we never really got to know Cliff's wife. She kept pretty much to herself.

I immediately started looking for a job, and the first week was hired at Such Construction Company in Compton. Daily I fought my way, back and forth, through about 20 miles of freeway congestion. My starting pay was $3.15 per hour. Nancy got hired at California Federal Savings and Loan as a teller. She did great at her job. The bank was walking distance from our place. Cliff and I planned to start a combination art studio-gallery, but it was taking a little time, because we were both on a "low budget show."

I had made my mind up that I was going to be a good family man ... but something was going on in Los Angeles back in 1968. It was called the sexual revolution. There were radical longhaired hippies, and flower children everywhere. Beautiful girls with no bras and mini-skirts would be pumping gas into their little VW bugs at the corner station. The students were protesting about Vietnam, and the rock concerts were taking on mammoth proportions. I loved the whole rebellious feeling in the air.

Cliff was no help at all, because nothing had changed in his unhappy relationship with his wife. He shocked me one day by openly admitting

... "It's really bad. Sometimes I masturbate four or five times a day. It's the only way I can make my brain function so I can get some work done. I'm a Scorpio and I have to have sex, or I'll shrivel up and die."

We decided that the price of free love sounded pretty reasonable. But where can we find a couple of these liberated little hippy chicks? Cliff and I spent lots of time at his studio, but soon, much of the time that we were supposedly making art ... was spent looking for love in the wrong places. I had finally turned twenty-one, and we discovered a hep little L.A. nightclub called "The Garage". Seven days a week this converted grease pit had a live band. It was packed with bodies gyrating to the tunes of the times ... The Beatles ... The Rolling Stones ... Jimi Hendrix ... Janis Joplin ... Canned Heat, and on and on. The bands played all their songs, and sounded almost as good as the original artists. The music blasted so loud that I think it permanently blew my eardrums partially out. Both of us got involved with a series of "west-coast girls". One of my girlfriends from The Garage eventually became Cliff's second wife several years down the line.

After about eight months I got laid off from the construction company. I set up an art studio in one of our bedrooms, putting Troy's baby bed in our bedroom. It was hard getting started as an artist, because supplies and everything were expensive. Cliff helped me with some extra brushes and so on, but I needed immediate cash.

The term "starving artist" had quickly taken on a personal application, so out of necessity I applied for a job at Adhor Farms. They hired me, and I had to join The Teamsters Union, Local 441, and the whole nine yards. So now suddenly, I was delivering milk, and cheese, and butter, and orange juice to homes all over central Los Angeles. It paid real good money, especially if you were a crook, like many, if not most of the deliverymen at that time. Of all my faults, I never could get into being a thief. After about seven months on the job, I had a big fight with Nancy and went on an extended weekend drunk. I eventually went into the office, and told them that I quit ... but they said ... "No you don't, because you got fired yesterday."

I was relieved to be free from that job. It seemed to be jinxed. People were turning up dead left and right all around me. For example, one of my fellow workers came back to the dock one late morning, and told me ... "You wouldn't believe it, but up on my route this morning there was a bunch of murders. There were bodies in the front yard, and inside this house, and even in the back yard. There was a pregnant woman in the kitchen, and some (blankety-blank) tied her up, and apparently cut her baby right out of her. I was one of the first on the scene. It was incredible. I never seen so much blood in my entire life."

We found out later that it was Charles Manson and his zombies who committed the murders. The pregnant woman was Sharon Tate, who I had just seen in the movie, "Valley of the Dolls". I wished to God that I could get my hands on the person who did that to her. It made me crazy thinking of what I would do to them. I felt somehow connected, because I learned about the murders from an early eyewitness. I heard some of the gory details while the story was just breaking. But within hours, every TV station, every radio, every newspaper, around the world were continuing to shock us more and more with the emerging facts of the massacre. Charles Tex Watson was the monster who butchered Sharon Tate.

About half of my milk route was to convalescent homes. People were disappearing on a regular basis, and many of those left behind lay there in diapers with their mouths gapping open ... waiting their turn to vanish. Others just shuffled around. One old man would start screaming the minute I walked in ... "Help me! Young man, please help me! They're trying to kill me. Call the police! Call my daughter. Please get me out of here! Oh God please!"

A big fat nurse came over and yelled ... "Shut your mouth James! Your daughter came last week, and who knows when she'll come back again. The police don't care about you, and if you don't shut up, I'll make you lay in that bed all day long!"

That particular convalescent home smelled like urine so strong that it practically burned my nostrils. I would hold my breath, and get out as fast as I could. I lie not. Speaking of burning nostrils ... I also delivered all the dairy products to the Pico Grill, which was a small "Grandma type" coffee shop on Pico Ave. The owner was a wiry old lady named Faye, who would pour me a cup of coffee, and talk my ear off for about an hour. I always got along real well with old people. I love listening to their stories ... and they love telling them.

Faye was telling me, "Don't deliver anything for the next two weeks. I'm going to take my first vacation in forty years. I never close this place up, but I've finally decided to take a couple weeks off. I haven't got anything special planned. I just need a little time off. So, be sure to get here early, Roger, on June the 14th, because I'll be needing everything for the breakfast crowd that day."

Well, I'll never forget June the 14th, 1969. A heat wave hit L.A. for almost all of that June. On the morning that I was supposed to be early at the Pico Grill ... I overslept. My regular time to arrive was about 4:45 A.M. As the sky was getting light, around six or so, I pulled up to the back door of the restaurant well over an hour late. The door was locked, and I feared the wrath of Faye. I didn't know what to do, so I walked around to the front door. The coffee shop was dark inside, and the sign on the door said "CLOSED".

I almost left, but decided to try the door. It was unlocked. Something didn't feel right. I partially opened the door, and looked inside the dark store. As my eyes adjusted, I saw something on the floor about ten feet inside. It was a body. It was the body of a black woman who had been shot in the head. Her head was about twice the normal size, and had big streaks of blood coming out of it. She was lying on her side, and one arm was partially raised. Then the smell hit me. It almost knocked me over!

My reeling brain was thinking ... "There must have been a robbery, and she got shot in the head."

Just as I thought that, from out of the rear darkness of the store, a large man appeared. My heart about jumped out of my chest. I thought it was the killer. I should have slammed the door, and ran for my life ... but instead I yelled out ... "What the _____ is going on here!"

"What the _____ are you doing here, and who are you?" was my answer ... as the man continued to walk toward me.

"I'm the milkman, and I deliver to this place."

"Well, I'm a police detective. The pie man got here first and called us. Let's step outside."

"What happened? Was it a robbery?" I asked.

"No. It's really sad. There's still money in the cash register, and no sign of any kind of struggle. It looks like she was closing the place up, and sat down to drink a cup of coffee. She must have put the closed sign on the door, but didn't lock it yet. The coffee cup is still half full, and has mold on it. The rest of the place is clean as a whistle. She must have had a stroke or a heart attack, and fell on the floor and died. From the blood it looks like she hit her head. The door was open for the whole two weeks. Apparently no one even tried the door, because the place was all shut up. The pie man said she was a real nice lady."

"You mean that's Faye ... the owner? She's white ... not black!"

"She is now. She's been lying there for two whole weeks, during a heat wave in a closed up store. It looks like her head actually swelled up and burst. Rigor mortis set in a long time ago. It's bad, but the worst cases are when we find someone dead in a car trunk. One time we found a body that had been shot, and in a trunk for months. The smell was so powerful that when we opened the trunk, it got in our clothes. We had to burn them. You never forget that smell! This is not exactly the greatest way for us to start our day, is it?"

"That's for sure. I can't imagine anything smelling worse than this," I replied.

Death was such a monster. It took Art. It took a bunch of my schoolmates. Ruth Ann Ballman, Denny Wadella, Clayton Williams, Ted Namn, Chuck Pense, and many more were killed in car wrecks while still in their teens. Sweet little Cheryl Haar died in childbirth at age 19. Sharon Gracemeyer wrote a note and hung herself. Ken Sovano was a pilot, and shot down in Vietnam. Bobby Flores was killed on the day he arrived in Saigon. One of our own crippled planes crash-landed into the truck he was being transported in. The soldiers under the heavy green canvas in the back of that truck, probably never knew what hit them. What is life all about? Just like that ... it can be snatched away.

One minute Faye is making me laugh with her quick humor, homespun philosophies, and cranky personality ... the next moment I see her ... she is a decomposed pile of flesh laying on a floor. But then of course, for Faye, the dreaded moment struck on the eve of her first vacation in forty years. "It's time to get drunk!"

For multiple weeks I would smell that smell every time I'd get in my truck. It had to be in my head, because there was nothing in the truck. I searched. There were several other deaths on my milk route, which I won't share. This is getting too morbid ... but I did manage to fulfill my "drunk-wish" a few weeks later while on my route ... just a few blocks from the reeking Pico Grill. It was a strong contributing factor to my early retirement.

I had this one elderly black man, who would have me come inside his house, and put the milk in the refrigerator for him. He was an old bachelor, and the place was a huge mess, with piled up boxes, and old worn out furniture. But he was real funny. On this one particular day he asked me … "Do you have any orange juice on your truck today? I got some Vodka if you got some OJ. How about having a couple snorts with me, if you have time?"

Well, we finished the bottle together, and it was a big one. We discovered that Adhor's orange juice was especially made for Vodka. It went down like the best of German beers … but the Vodka kicked like the old famous mule. It was hours past the time I was due back in Glendale to gas up, and unload my empties. My gracious customer called my supervisor, after I drove off, to apologize for detaining me, and warned of an approaching storm. It was definitely on its way.

I **kicked** the death smell out of my cab, and decided to see how much a 20 year old, snub-nosed milk truck could make up for lost time. It did pretty good. I saw this hippy hitchhiking, and slammed on my brakes. He says, "Far out man … a milk truck! Isn't it kinda late to be delivering milk?"

"Just get your ___ in here, and hang on if you want a ride," was my suggestion.

It's a major miracle that we didn't run into a cop. I was making record-breaking time down Western Ave … the longest, straight as an arrow street in the United States. I was focused. We spotted two chicks thumbing for a ride, but I was going too fast to stop, so I went to the next block, and wheeled around to go back. They saw me and were waiting. I pulled up and said … "Are you ready for a joy-ride?"

As they jumped aboard one of them said … "We're in!"

I didn't disappoint. No hitting on them, no drugs, "no lie" … just plain old speed and straining sheet metal. Every bottle in that truck had a nervous breakdown. My hippy friend was frozen, and couldn't think of one cool thing to say. He didn't have time. The girls were just hanging on and laughing. It was one of the wildest rides of my life.

They all bailed around Griffith Park, still laughing, and wishing me good luck. When I finally made it to Glendale, I jumped out of my truck without parking it or anything, and marched in to see my supervisor. I told him … "You know, even though you guys are so _____ing cheap that your trucks are antiques … that one of mine does pretty good! You need to give the mechanic a raise. I'm a little late … but I sold all kinds of _____ing milk today. You know … you'd think people would get sick of drinking that crap day after day … What do you think???"

He was laughing, but trying not to … and said, "I think you need to get home, and sleep it off. Mr. Johnson called and told us that he held you up a little today, and your wife called and is worried … so you better get home."

I was positive that this was my last day on the force … and decided to continue to give my supervisor a real hard time. I wanted the most bang for my buck. I told him the sorry truth about the entire retail milk industry. But, everything I said just made him laugh more and more. I couldn't get him to fire me no matter what I said. However, a couple months later, Adhor Farms sent **both** of us out on the cold hard streets. "Sorry about that."

Cliff and I had finally established our own art gallery and studio. It was named Round Table Studios, and was located at 443 S. La Cienega Blvd, on the edge of Beverly Hills. Later he changed the name to The Golden Palette. It was a perfect location, because La Cienega was the art center of the entire west coast. The whole street was lined with well-known galleries, and studios, and high-class restaurants. We were on the tail end of the street where Restaurant Row began, but it was a great location.

The gallery was mostly Cliff's baby, because he had gone full time artist, while I struggled to get on my feet, and pay the bills with other jobs. Cliff already had a relationship with a big agent and wholesaler. He had clients and connections from his college also, but before long he worked me in as a partner. Cliff taught me how to paint with oils on LaCienega, and we specialized in seascapes. He was selling a few seascapes in the $800 range, and lots of them in the $200 to $400 range. We got an order from a dealer in New York to mass-produce this one particular seascape. Cliff and I set up a system, and produced a ton of them. I got to know lots of insiders in the art world, and lots of weird and eccentric artists also. I remember how excited I was when I sold my first painting in the gallery. It was a partial nude that I painted, and a doctor bought it for $75. An agent wanted me to mass-produce a little farm boy I painted, but it took me too long on each one for the money. The gallery was fun … but we still starved. There were always more bills than money.

After the time Nancy and I had smoked that hash in France, I never messed with pot again. I didn't like the way it knocked me off my feet. I liked good old fashion beer. However, one day I picked up another hitchhiker. He was a really mellow kid, and we got in a big old conversation, which led to the subject of marijuana. This guy was a couple years younger than me, and still lived with his divorced mother. I gave him a ride to his house, and he invited me in. His whole room was full of pot plants. He even had some on the patio out back. I asked him what his mother thinks about pot growing all over her house.

He said in his slow monotone voice ... "Oh, she's alright. She don't like it ... but is cool about it. That hash you smoked was probably a little heavy for just getting turned on. Let's try a joint of my stuff. I think you'll have a much better high. It's home grown and really nice."

He pulled out several joints already rolled up, and I had my second experience smoking pot. He was right, it was nothing compared to my previous encounter a couple years back in Orleans. We talked a lot and had a few laughs, and then I was even able to split, and successfully pilot my big bad 421 cubic inch Grand Prix. My new friend had also sent me off with an extra joint for the road.

The next day at the studio, when I told Cliff about my young pothead friend, he said ... "Do you have that joint with you? Let's smoke that puppy! I've been wanting to try pot for forever!"

I had left it back at the apartment, but Cliff insisted that we go get it **immediately**. We spent a good part of the day running back and forth across L.A. County after one little joint. Finally we had it, and after locking the front gallery door, in the confines of our back room studio, we fired up. Cliff loved it, and turned absolutely bright red from laughing so much. It was the beginning of a long love affair with cannabis for my artist friend. He enjoyed getting stoned much more than I did, but even so, we passed many a roach clip back and forth over the months and years ahead.

I decided to get some more college. I couldn't afford Chanard or Art Center, where I really wanted to go, but I enrolled at Los Angeles City College. It was free. Of course, I majored in Art. The campus was only a brisk walk away from our place. It was over on Vermont Ave. I would take Troy to the babysitter, and then rush off to classes. LACC was located on the former site of UCLA, before John Wooden's undefeated Bruins moved to the Westwood campus. I applied for my GI Bill college benefits, and started receiving checks in the mail. It was great ... to get paid for going to school. At least something good had come out of my military service. I had hated high school ... but at age 21 ... I loved college. I got all A's and B's, except for a couple incompletes.

Cliff's homemade board

Not only was I getting into the art scene, the college scene, the hippy scene, the L.A. adultery scene, and the anti-war student movement ... but Cliff had immediately introduced me to the Pacific Ocean. Every chance we had we drove down Pacific Coast Highway, and parked near the famous Malibu pier. We'd put on wet suits, and attack one of the most perfectly shaped waves in the world, right there within a few hundred feet of Alice's Restaurant. It was absolutely beautiful. It took me my first whole summer to learn how to stand up and turn right. My compulsive addictive behavior kicked right in. Sometimes Cliff and I would be in the water before sunrise, while the ocean was calm, shiny-smooth, and totally glassy ... and still be in the water by late afternoon. We would only appear on land long enough to slam down a couple deep-fried tacos, across the street at the local "Jack-in-the-Crack". I even watched Cliff shape, resin, and make his own board from a blank piece of foam. He is so talented. I absolutely got hooked on surfing.

Los Angeles in the late sixties was a radical humming place. But I was having a severe identity crisis. Was I a family man, or a hippy? My hair was getting long. Was I an artist, or a milkman? Did I want to go in business, or burn down the establishment? Maybe I should just surf every single day like some of the Malibu regulars ... and simply let life, and the whole sick world sort itself out. Here comes a set!   "OUTSIDE !!!"

CHAPTER 13

"KINGS AND SILVERS"

My Aunt Lula continued to send me letters. As always she would put in a clipping of a poem, or a little inspirational article about Jesus, or a special prayer. She would write about her latest bus journey to see the flowers in Pennsylvania, or a tour to Washington D.C. She was always going somewhere. I was happy that she was getting so much out of her retirement years. Lutheran Senior City in Columbus, Ohio might be expensive, but it seemed to be ideal for my Great Aunt. She was presently taking a bus tour to Oregon, and wrote asking if it would be all right to come down, and spend a week with Nancy and I in California. We wrote back and told her we would be looking forward to it.

A couple weeks after her visit, I received another letter from my Aunt. She wrote to tell me how disturbed and concerned she was about me. My mother had told her how adamantly anti-Christian I was … but she saw first hand the discord in my marriage, and the rebellious direction my life had taken. I had a beard and had bleached my hair. I marched in a war protest on Armed Forces Day with thousands of protesters led by Tom Hayden. Police helicopters flew overhead as we flipped them off. My Aunt saw the giant poster of a bank check hanging in our front room. The picture on the four-foot giant personalized check was of a Bank of America building completely engulfed in flames. Demonstrating students had burned it down, because BofA majorly helped finance the Vietnam War. I felt terrible after getting her latest letter. I sincerely loved my Aunt Lula … but what could I do? Pretend to be somebody that I'm not?

I met this girl named Shari, who was 29, and had recently broke up with a man that she lived with for ten years. I was shocked to find out she was eight years older than me. After about a month I told her that I was married. However, since I never took her to my place she had already guessed it. She was a former model, and had recently developed a rare eye condition. She had beautiful blue eyes, but one of them was going partially blind, and turned green. I really liked her, and for six months we had a very steamy relationship. She suggested that maybe we get an apartment together ... but I couldn't do it because of Troy.

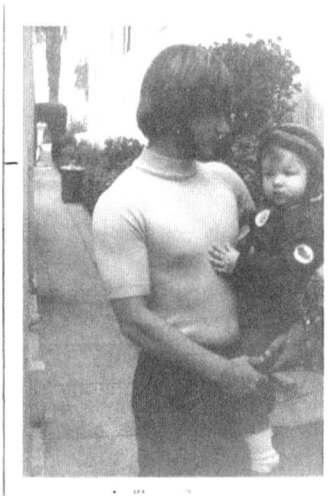

Nancy found out about her. In a big fight she badgered and badgered me to admit that I had been with someone else. In a fit of anger, I finally spilled the beans with my big mouth, and told her, "So what … our marriage is a joke anyway!!" She cried and cried and cried. She screamed and threw things. When I would want to leave the apartment she would hide my keys, and beg me not to leave, and things like that … but mostly she cried. I was absolutely miserable, and consumed with guilt, but didn't know what to do. Poor Troy had to listen to all of this. I felt like the most evil person on the face of the earth.

Cliff was having the same problems. Julie came down to the studio one night and went berserk. She threw paint all over the studio. She is of Mexican American decent, and her Latin temper manifested itself with **flying colors.** I wasn't there, but the "trail of paint" spoke for itself. Cliff and Julie's days were numbered. She finally left him and returned to Arizona. Later she filed for divorce.

At LACC I finished my second semester. I was doing great at school, but my life was a total mess. Nancy only knew about the one girl. I felt so sorry for her. I lied and swore that it was a brief encounter with this gal, and was now over. But in reality, there was a growing procession of different relationships. I was becoming more and more a part of the promiscuous L.A. landscape along with its drug culture and college scene. I was even sleeping with her best friend from work. It was like a growing seductive snowball, or rather fireball, and I couldn't help myself. I wanted to be single and free. The grass looked so perfectly green in every other direction.

Speaking of green grass, every noon hour on LACC's grassy common area, there would be a bunch of hippy Jesus Freaks. They'd have a couple guitars going, and would all be singing, and smiling with these big happy loving smiles. They had Bibles, and sometimes there would be 20 or 30 of them. I used to wonder how in the world they could honestly believe all those fairy tales. I envied the peace and love that seemed to shine from their faces ... but I stayed as far away from them as I could. In between classes one time, a petite young blond tried to tell me about Jesus at a concession area. I practically bit her head off ... "Don't try to peddle that ____ing crap off on me!" After I spit her head out, I couldn't believe how totally rude I was to the poor gal. Where did that come from?

In Geography class I made friends with Hubert Jackson. He was my first African American, L.A. born and bred soul mate. We became super tight. He told me he lived in the "Golden Ghetto", which was between Watts and Culver City. I was Acing Geography, because I love the outdoors, and nature, and the elements. It's one of my favorite subjects. Hubert, however, needed a little tutoring ... which we did between nightclubs, women and pot. He took me on many personal guided tours of night-time South Central L.A. I was totally accepted. Many times I was the only white at this party or that party. He also spent lots of time in my home, and I even fixed him up with Nancy's best friend from work. He reciprocated with a very eager beaver black beauty. We ran together for several years. He was married also, had a couple kids, but Hubert and his wife seemed to have a much smoother arrangement than Nancy and I. They simply didn't ask each other questions ... at all.

I even went to City College's summer session, and pulled a 4.0. I need to focus and get a degree! About that time Nancy and I moved into a house on Ardmore Street, on the other side of the Hollywood Freeway. By now Troy was three years old. Cliff and his wife had long since separated, and Cliff was now living with my old girlfriend, Toni, in a nice modern apartment near Santa Monica. After I took my finals, I hitchhiked up to the Columbia River, because I wanted to catch a real live salmon. The Columbia River separates Oregon and Washington. I had read a story in Field & Stream about the incredible salmon runs up that river. There was also a big rock concert, called the Satsop River Festival, which was scheduled right after Labor Day weekend. I wanted to catch some salmon, and catch the concert also. This was a wild adventure I was about to take, but unfortunately it finished off my marriage.

Besides surfing in the Pacific Ocean, I also did quite a bit of fishing. Being a mid-western boy, I was amazed by the bonita, and yellowtail, and the weird looking halibut with both of its eyes on one side of its body. I fished from the piers and jetties, and took the cattle boats out into deep waters. But I always wanted to catch some salmon, and they were not to be found in the Southern California waters. I borrowed an eight-foot long fishing pole, which wouldn't break down any smaller, and stuck my thumb out on the freeway entrance heading north.

It was about 95 degrees outside in L.A. and dry as a bone as I started the trip. From Sunset Blvd and the entrance to the Hollywood Freeway a VW bug picked me up. I had to let the fishing pole stick out of the window, but my longhaired friends, with tie dyed clothes and beads didn't think it was a problem. They took me about 75 miles, but I had about 1100 more to go. The next ride was in a big old Buick, and the driver was going all the way to Seattle. What great luck! He was a friendly red neck, and was driving like a bat out of hell. He wanted to get there in a hurry. We drove all afternoon, and all night at speeds up to 110 miles per hour. We were literally flying. We only stopped for gas.

Before dawn we were completely through California and Oregon. At my request, they left me off on the Washington side of the bridge that crossed the famous Columbia River. I had only cat napped as we flew down the Interstate, but now as the first light of a new day was barely breaking I was real tired, but excited. I started walking down the road. It was overcast and super quiet. Right away I got a ride, and asked the man how far it was to the mouth of the river. He told me it was something like 80 more miles paralleling the river on this little road. He could only take me a few miles to his turn off, and then dropped me off in the middle of nowhere ... in this endless forest. I stood by the road, and looked around in total wonder.

I flashed back just one day. Yesterday I had stood by the freeway on a normal August day in Los Angeles. It was super hot and dry as could be. The sky was smoggy, and the hills, and mountains, and sky were mostly brown. Now, suddenly like magic, practically every square inch of **everything** was beautiful shades of green. The forest was green, the floor of the forest itself was blanketed with millions of huge green ferns, and even the side of the road was covered with thick long green grass. The only thing that wasn't green was the overcast sky, and the tree trunks. It was still real early in the morning, and I wasn't in a big hurry to get my next ride. I was content to absorb this radically peaceful new environment for a while.

I got my wish, because for the next few hours, the only vehicles that went down the narrow green road were huge logging trucks ... and even they were few and far between. I like to travel prepared. I had a backpack, and sleeping bag, and all the essentials for hitting the road ... plus my eight-foot fiberglass-fishing pole. I sat on top of my pack and just waited. It was absolutely quiet with only a few birds singing and chirping away. I wondered if I would ever get a ride on this lonely road. I thought a lot about my life.

After about an hour I heard an unusual noise way off in the distance. It was really weird. Then the noise started getting closer, and closer, and louder, and louder. Soon I figured out what it was ... it was huge drops of rain hitting the millions of leaves in the forest. It was radical. I never heard rain like that before. There was no wind or thunder or anything, but the actual edge of the rain pattern marched right through the woods, and suddenly started pouring buckets on top of me. I mean I was **instantly** getting soaked.

I jumped up and started opening my pack, because luckily I had a cheap plastic tarp inside. It was about 6 feet square. I carry one to put over my sleeping bag at night. It keeps the dew off when you wake up in the morning. I fumbled around, and finally threw the tarp over my gear and me. I sat there under that plastic trying to get situated, and listening to the rain just absolutely pound away. I liked it, and felt like I was on another planet. It also reminded me of being a little kid back in the woods in Fremont in one of our forts or hideaways. Soon though, I was having a hard time staying dry, even with the plastic. It started coming down so hard that streams started flowing under my feet on the side of the road. I had to move, and find higher ground. It just kept coming. I was also trying to keep a little opening to see if any cars would come along, and rescue me.

Pretty soon I gave up trying to watch for cars, because rain just kept pouring in no matter how I made the opening. I just completely covered myself up under the plastic tarp on the side of the road. I had to stick my fishing pole out, because it was way too long. I figured I'd weather the storm in this humid living body bag, and worry about a ride later. It had to stop some day. I started worrying that a car might run me over, while I'm under here so close to the road. That would be lovely. The raindrop novelty had long since worn off, when I heard a vehicle go past. Then I thought I heard a faint horn. I pulled the plastic back, and saw that a pick-up truck had stopped about 50 yards down the road.

I jumped up, and started running with all my gear. The truck was now backing up, and when we met, a man jumped out of the passenger side, and helped me throw my stuff in the bed of the truck. I wrapped the plastic around my pack, and the guy yelled through the rain … "Open that cooler and grab three beers."

What a trip! I grabbed the beer and jumped in between my two benefactors. The driver looks over at me with a grin, and says … "Dang, we're driving along in the middle of nowhere, and here comes a pile of green plastic by the side of the road with a _____ing fishing pole sticking out of it. My brother in law says … 'What the hey, if there's a **fishing pole**, maybe there's a **fisherman** somewhere under there. So, how in the holy heck does anyone end up under a piece of plastic way out here anyhow?"

The other guy butted in, and said ... "By the way, did you catch anything under there?"

I liked these guys instantly. I opened my beer, and told them, "I hitchhiked up here from L.A. because I want to catch a salmon. I want to catch at least one. I heard that the Columbia River has the best salmon fishing in the United States. I didn't know I was going to get half drowned in a forest though."

They joked and kidded with me, and I couldn't believe my good luck. They were going all the way to Illwaco. The driver's name was Steve, and his brother-in-law was John. They lived across the river in Oregon. Every year they cross over to the Washington side of the Colombia River for a major salmon fishing trip. Their annual excursion was always scheduled over the Labor Day holiday. We drove along for maybe an hour or so, windshield wipers going all the way, stopping only to grab a few more beers out of the cooler.

My hair was shoulder length by then, and to my "rescuers from down under" ... I was a real live hippy. They were super interested in California, and L.A., and we had fun shooting the breeze. They were probably both in their mid to late thirties, married, with their flannel shirts, hiking boots ... and had gone all out for this trip. They told me they already had their boat, and a camping trailer parked by the mouth of the river. They were making another trip to bring 2 fifty-gallon drums of gas for their boat. They buy a commercial fishing license, just for their annual trip.

Steve said ... "We always catch enough salmon to pay for all our expenses, plus have enough canned and smoked for ourselves to last us a whole year. So what do you think, Hippy, do you want to go fishing with us?"

I said ... "Heck yes!!"

For the next two days, I had the most radical fishing experience of my life. It could be a short Field & Stream story in itself. I'll sum it up real quick. We launched out in a 18-foot boat way before dawn, and headed out through the mouth of the Colombia River into the dark open sea. By the time Steve cut back the throttle to start rigging up our gear, I looked back toward land, and saw the most glorious sunrise in my life coming from behind the mountains. It was worth being alive just to experience that one spectacular moment. I can't describe all the brilliant colors, and shapes of the clouds that were stretched out in the sky ... above the mountain-lined horizon. It was amazing.

We started trolling immediately. The sea was calm but had big rolling swells. John yanked his pole, and for five minutes fought a big old salmon. I hated to admit it, but I was feeling a little queasy. I felt a powerful hit, and yanked my pole straight up. In the middle of reeling in my first ever salmon ... I handed my pole to Steve, and started puking over the side of the boat. All day long I was **down** in the front of the boat with my eyes closed, periodically getting up to vomit some more of my wonderful cereal, until the dry heaves finally kicked in. They are the worst. Steve would say stuff like ... "Don't worry about it Hippy, we'll be heading back, in about ten hours."

Steve and John caught fish all day long. I stayed in my prone position. By late afternoon we headed back for the river. As soon as we got into the calm water, I felt better, and tried fishing again. I hooked and landed my first salmon. Then all of us caught several more, before we finally beached the boat on a big sandbar, to clean the fish. There were two kinds of salmon that we caught. One was Chinook, which get up to 70 or 80 pounds, and the other was Coho, which are much smaller ... in the five to twenty pound range. They called the Chinook ... Kings ... and the Coho ... Silvers. John caught one King that weighed 63 pounds. I felt pretty bad about whimping out all day, but as we headed back for the campground, Steve yells to me over the noise of the outboard motor... "Well, do you want to go out and puke some more tomorrow?"

I said ... "Absolutely!"

They both laughed.

That night, we cooked a big meal of crab (that we had illegally poached from some traps on our way in), drank a few brews, and really had fun. They even had vegetables from their gardens back in Oregon. Then, they really surprised me, and pulled out a lid of grass. What a trip. These guys were full of surprises. Steve was telling me all the advance news about the upcoming rock concert. It was making big headlines in the northwest. I was going to hitch up there after one more day of fishing. They were both saying they wished they were ten years younger, and able to just drop everything to hit the road exactly like I was doing.

I wished they could come with me. These guys were a blast.

The next morning we set sail again. This time when we reached the channel at the very mouth of the river, the ground swells were over 20 feet high, and breaking on the left side of the river. They decided they could get through on the right side, but warned me that we might not be able to get back in for a long time. Our 18-foot boat went up and down between the troughs, and those swells were much bigger than our boat. It was scary. We got over them, and out into a much rougher ocean than yesterday. Lo and behold, I felt completely fine … but John started heaving his guts out. He said he hadn't got seasick since he was a little kid. It made me feel great! I laughed as he gagged and choked.

John recovered faster than I did, and we nailed fish all day long. One time we had five big fish on at once. You talk about frantic gymnastics in a little boat. We each had a pole, and there was two "meat hooks" attached to the bow of the boat (another illegal maneuver). Every line was going wild with big fish on them. Lines were crossing, and we were trying to get the net on this one or that one. I think we got two of them in the boat. It was a blast, and a dream come true for me. I had two of my salmon canned at the cannery. They tag your fish, and can it overnight for one dollar a pound. I gave the rest of the Kings and Silvers that I landed to my well-deserved friends. The next morning I wished my fishing buddies farewell, and have never seen them again. I was off to the Satsop River Festival.

CHAPTER 14

"PAY TO PLAY"

After picking up my salmon from the cannery, I stuck my thumb out and headed north deeper into Washington state to find the Satsop River. My backpack was considerably heavier with all the one-pound cans of salmon. I ate some right away. It was **so** good. I felt totally alive and full of energy. I pushed aside all my worries about my marriage. It had been four days since I left, and I decided to call sometime later that day. Fisherman Steve had drawn me a map to get to the rock concert. Better than that, the sun was shining.

It took me most of the day to get to the concert. It was definitely in the boon docks. Finally, I was dropped off by this huge field filled with cars. There must have been a town nearby, but I never saw one. Every time I thought about calling home, there wasn't a phone anywhere to be seen. Now, I would have to wait. Someone told me they were not allowing any more cars past that particular field ... and the only way to get to the concert was a three-mile hike on foot. I started walking. With all my gear it took a long time. Along the way there were scattered farmhouses with huge fields on all sides. One fence had a big sign attached which read ... "NO TRESSPASSING ... SURVIVORS WILL BE PROSECUTED". That sign set the tone for the whole concert. In my life I attended quite a few big rock concerts, but The Satsop River Festival has stuck with me the most. When all the trouble started, most of the big name bands, like Ike and Tina Turner bailed out. They were smart.

I'll never forget walking through the concert gate. **Immediately** a row of vendors were calling out to the new arrivals advertising their merchandise ... only these longhaired, bell-bottomed peddlers, with rolled up bandanas around their foreheads, were yelling ... "Orange Sunshine" ... "take a trip to remember folks". Somebody else was yelling even louder,

"Windowpane here... only $5 a hit." I couldn't believe it. I passed the psychedelic section, and a guy motioned to me saying... "Hey man, I got three finger lids of Acapulco Gold for only $15. Need some smoke for the party? It's some bitching weed!"

A cop was standing back by the gate only 50 feet away, and I asked one of the peddlers... "What's the deal, do the cops around here just let you guys sell dope right in front of them?"

With a big smile he explained ... "When they organized this concert, they made a 'no-bust inside' deal with the pigs. It's legal inside here dude. Isn't that ____ing far out?"

What a trippy place. I was super tired from traveling and hiking all day, but kept moving. I walked down a muddy dirt road toward the main crowd. There were thousands and thousands of people in the distance. I missed the first day of the concert. It had rained hard on everyone the night before. All around were tents and makeshift shelters constructed of American flags, cardboard, crooked tree branches, and whatever. There were huge mud puddles all around. Everywhere else was just plain mud. Little half naked kids were playing in the cold puddles, splashing, and running, and sliding. They were covered with mud and had snot running out of their noses. A 15-foot long dumpster was absolutely running over with empty Boone's Farm Strawberry Wine bottles. There were piles of Boone's Farm wine bottles all over the whole concert, plus beer cans, soggy paper, and trash everywhere.

I could hear the music coming from the stage area. Finally I reached the half loaded crowd, which was fanned out in a huge open field. The stage had real tall towers on both sides with gigantic speakers and lights. The main field was mostly grass. I found a dry spot way back in the crowd, and decided to just lay down and rest. The sun was still high in the sky ... but I tied a small rope to my pack, and to my wrist in case I fell asleep. I didn't want to lose my camera, or my salmon. I closed my eyes, and almost dozed off; when I heard a CRACK ... CRACK ... CRACK. My eyes popped open at ground level, only to see boots and legs stampeding toward my head. I was about to get trampled big time. I jumped up with a shot of adrenalin, and joined the crowd not knowing what the heck was going on. A biker had pulled a gun out, and shot somebody about 30 feet from me.

This crowd didn't exactly feel like a summer of love type happening. It felt more like a huge Manson family look-alike reunion. I can't remember any of the groups, except Quicksilver, but anyway, that night the music was pretty good, and thank God it didn't rain. I smoked some pot with a few folks, but didn't really get to know anyone. About midnight I found a row of trees by the perimeter of the concert, and rolled out my sleeping bag. It had been a long day.

In the morning it was **really** cold and clammy. Instead of 23, I felt like I was about 103. Every muscle in my body felt stiff. I was on the edge of a big open field. On the other side was a small road with two residential mobile homes. I noticed a black hearse type station wagon, and a bunch of men in suits going in one of the trailers. A young guy came walking up to me, and motioned ... "Hey man, do you see those guys over there?

They are the coroners. I went over there a little while ago to borrow some water. I found out that the 13-year-old daughter came to the concert last night. She got a hold of some kind of drugs and overdosed. Hey man … they found her dead this morning in her bed. What a bummer!"

As I watched I saw the men in suits carry out a covered up body, and put it into the black station wagon. I could feel death in the cold air. "Art … I can't believe I'm watching this … she didn't even make it to sweet sixteen. How stinking cruel! There seems to be a pattern down here. Oh God, what her parents must be feeling right now. If I were that father, I'd probably want to drop an atomic bomb on this concert. Art, what should I do? How do I deal with the misery in this life? I feel so helpless."

I almost left the concert, but I didn't. As I walked back to the main area, I passed a guy who looked like John Lennon with braids. He was sitting lotus style next to a big Indian TP. He was totally nude, and had his eyes closed like he was meditating. On both sides of him were two females in exactly the same position, and just as nude. One was real skinny, and the other one was a Mamma Cass with big-time drooping breasts that probably weighed 20 pounds each. There were about six little kids running in and around them. "This place is too much."

The next major event that morning was the watermelon man. A local farmer got permission to bring a big dump truck full of watermelons into the concert to sell. There was a dirt road that circled the crowd and went right in front of the stage. Anyway, this young stout farmer stopped his truck, and started selling watermelons. While he was making some transactions, a wiry young hippy climbed up on the other side of the truck, and started pitching some watermelons into the crowd. The crowd went wild, and started cheering and going crazy.

The farmer climbed up on top of the truck, and kicked at the guy stealing the watermelons. The crowd booed. Then, about three more guys started climbing up on different sides, and did the same thing, quickly pitching watermelons into the frenzied crowd below. Everyone cheered some more. The farmer continued to punch at a couple of them, and then jumped down, hopped into his cab … and roared down the road by the front of the stage.

The M.C. grabbed the microphone, and said, "Hey look you guys. This is really not cool! It's not cool to rip off the dude's watermelons … but it's even more uncool for him to drive like a maniac around a crowd like this ... So, I'll tell you what ... just ____ his watermelons! Let him alone. OK?"

Well, the crowd wasn't into leaving him alone. Several more heroes started climbing up on the truck pitching watermelons. The driver got on top again, and started pushing people off and punching them. Then one guy managed to get on top, and punched out the farmer. The crowd went berserk, yelling and screaming and cheering. The farmer finally sat on the top of his cab, with a bloodied face, and just watched as about a dozen guys almost completely emptied his truck. They threw out hundreds of watermelons. Then, the farmer blew all of our minds, because he jumped back into his truck, and absolutely roared off again ... only this time he drove straight through the crowd over people, and tents, and campfires ... and I couldn't believe my eyes. People were running, and jumping out of the way, and it was total chaos. I never found out how many people were hurt or killed, but I saw several helicopters fly people out.

The whole Satsop River Festival was a total bummer. I was ashamed to be a hippy, if this is what it's all about. Much later they announced how many babies were born during the concert ... and everyone cheered again. I didn't. On that final night, I saw a guy fall from the top of one of the towers like a rag doll, and land with a thud. People said, "Wow man... did you see that???" ... and kept drinking their Boone's Farm. I was more than ready to hit the trail.

The next day I made my way back to Interstate 5. Several of us were hitching a ride on one of the on-ramps, when a real good-looking gal pulled up. We all hopped in her car. I was in the middle in the front seat. As we started heading south down the highway, I looked over, and saw that our pretty chauffeur was crying. She glanced back at me, and said ... "I'm sorry but I just broke up with my old man, and I'm probably not the best company right now."

We drove for about a half hour, and found out that she was going all the way to San Francisco to visit her best friend. After awhile she asked if one of us could drive, and I volunteered to take over at the helm. We talked and cheered her up, and found out that she was a real adventurer herself. She had hitchhiked cross country twice all alone, and things like that. She was foxy, and handled herself real well ... kind of like an Indiana Jones side kick ... tough as nails but beautiful. Nevertheless, she was all tore up about this guy she just left.

The other hitchers eventually reached their departure points, but since I was going all the way to L.A., I was left alone with my hurting companion. She invited me to crash at her girlfriends place in Pacifica, just outside of San Francisco. She said, "My friend lives at her parents house right on the ocean on top of some cliffs. It's so beautiful there. Her parents are just total sweethearts. I'm positive it would be cool for you to spend the night, unless you want to keep trucking through to L.A. tonight."

I was all for sticking as close as possible to Ms. Jones. She could tell, and I could tell that she could tell. We pulled up into the driveway of this gorgeous home, with a pretty blond and her parents running out to hug my sexy companion. I felt a little out of place, but soon everyone was going way out of their way to make me feel right at home. It was such a loving family. The middle-aged husband was some kind of dean at UC Berkeley, and they made this huge meal. It was really cool. We walked out on the back deck, and watched the breakers smash into the rocky shoreline about a hundred feet below.

My rebounding friend asked if I would take her on a drive. She wanted to show me a beach that she loved. We spent the evening walking down this incredible northern California beach under the starlight. It seemed perfect. We found a cave and went inside. This radical young gal really affected me. I knew I would never see her again. My life was too crazy, and her life was too crazy. Somehow I felt like we were soul mates … young hurting people trying to make sense of a senseless universe … fighting back as best as we could … but losing.

The next day I hitched down the coast route through some of the most beautiful country in the entire world. To cap the whole trip off, a small flatbed truck picked me up just before Big Sur. There were already about five hitchhikers on the back. I found a spot on the flatbed, and hung on. One chick even had a big German shepherd faithfully lying next to her. The truck was a **real** old model, but newly painted, and running super good. In the cab there were three longhaired dudes, who looked like they were from the backwoods of Tennessee, or maybe The Satsop River Festival. I couldn't hear the music through the wind and traffic, but all three of them were pounding on the dash, pounding on the inside of the roof, and rocking out to the silent tunes. They were laughing and warhooping, and had a half-gallon jug of wine, which they passed out the window a couple times to us. We could hear the music blasting through the wind when the window came down. They had a joint going in front, and we had a couple going in the back.

I became a little concerned as we started taking the curves in Big Sur real fast. But that was nothing ... because pretty soon, without touching the brakes at all, the driver swung off the road into a gravel view spot ... staying about six inches from the guardrail at full speed. A huge cloud of dust and rocks flew in the air behind us. The old flatbed swerved back onto the pavement ... and the three guys continued pounding on the roof. The driver stomped on the gas pedal, and we roared up to the next thrill. We left that pavement about ten times into gravel, and I thought we were dead ducks for sure ... on each upcoming curve. My companions on the flatbed in the rear were hanging on for dear life. Rin-Tin-Tin was doing the same. A few times I could see the ocean almost vertically below us, and I thought we were going over for sure. It looked like about five thousand feet to the bottom. I finally gave in to the experience, and figured ... "If this is it ... this is it! Why the heck fight it!" After that death-defying conclusion ... I felt all right, and somehow knew that we would survive.

I arrived home in L.A., fishing pole in hand, after about ten days on the road. It seemed like it had been ten years since I left. Nancy was real happy to see me. Troy was so perfect with his longish blond hair and blue eyes. I had finally called from a gas station, and let them know I'd be back sometime that particular day, according to my luck catching rides. I was glad to be home, but inside I was even more unsettled ... and consumed with guilt, anger and confusion. Unfortunately it showed.

Nancy said that night... "You don't love me at all do you?"

I did ... but not the way she needed, and wanted, and deserved. I couldn't put on an act any longer, and again I tore a piece of her heart out. A few days later Nancy came home from work, and said she had talked to her mother. She and Troy were returning to Ohio. They were taking a train at the end of the week.

On a Saturday, I believe, some friends from Nancy's work came, and picked her and Troy up from our house to go to the train station. I kissed my three and a half year old son good-by, and watched both of them walk down the sidewalk to a strange car. Something died inside of me.

My brother Randy was living with us at the time, and when they drove off … I had to get away from him to be alone. I went into our empty bedroom, and started crying, and crying, and crying … and then crying some more. I was starting to pay the heavy price for my fun in the sun. **You pay to play.**

CHAPTER 15

"THE WHITE HOUSE"

Nancy and Troy returned to our hometown in Ohio on a train. As they drove off to the station, I cried my stinking eyes out. "Well, here it is Einstein ... you got your wish ... on your own in California." I never realized how absolutely empty I would feel. Over there was our 8" X 10" picture of Troy in a glass frame. He was 2 years old then, and had his little baseball jacket on ... the one with all the different major league team patches. I numbly packed the picture away in a suitcase. It was years before I could even bear to look at it. The big old three-bedroom house on Ardmore Street seemed like a morgue. It was. My brother Randy went back to Ohio a short time later. I enrolled for the 1971 fall semester at LACC ... but dropped out after several weeks.

As she was leaving, Nancy had said through tears, "You can be free Roger ... that's what you really want ... isn't it?"

I was dead inside. Time slowly clicked by. I got a job working for a company that had a contract with HUD, The Department of Housing and Urban Development. My job title was "relocation specialist". A college friend got me the job, and I really enjoyed it. Before that job, I drove an ice cream truck all over East L.A. ... part time. That was an education. A bunch of Chicano gang guys robbed one of the other drivers, and pushed his truck over on its side. But worse than that ... it took months to get the stupid little tune out of my head, after driving up and down every street in the barrio all day long.

　　I also had a super-short career climbing 80-foot palm trees, with a rope and spikes. The tree trunks were about 3 feet in diameter at the bottom, but about eight inches in diameter up at the top. We're talking six, seven, and eight stories high. I thought I had a few guts until I tried trimming those palm trees for $3 apiece. Speaking of money, I had more or less completely stopped working at the art gallery, and besides, Cliff was in the process of moving the studio to a garage in Malibu … right across the street from the Pacific Ocean. So, all in all, working for HUD turned out to be my main gig immediately after Nancy left. By necessity, I was at the same time learning the fine art of blocking out painful memories.

　　Another good friend of mine from LACC was a neat guy named Pete Bauer. He was, in my mind, what a real hippy should be like … soft-spoken, totally non-violent, inquisitive about everybody and everything, and just a super-mellow nice guy. He was into nature, and music, and getting loaded with all of his friends. He was also a good mechanic, and had an old Ford van named "The Blue Max". Later on, he joined the Peace Corps, and went to Africa for a couple years.

Nancy didn't like Pete, because he seemed to be a main character leading me farther down the "tune-in and drop-out trail". He lived in a communal house with a bunch of other students, and hippies of both sexes. I spent a lot of time at his place. Pete had thousands of dollars of stereo equipment that he brought back from overseas. In another life, he had been a shorthaired swabby in Uncle Sam's Navy. The music at the house would be so loud, that the entire framework would literally vibrate to its foundation ... as the spell binding voice of Jim Morrison and The Doors took us into another mystical world. **"Riders on the storm."** I also loved to mellow out to the velvety songs of Roberta Flack. There were posters on most every wall, and beads hanging from the doorframes. A shiny giant poster of "The Hulk" was resined onto the fiberglass wall of the main shower. The house was almost always full of people with maybe one or two freeloading couch potatoes.

A couple weeks after Nancy left Pete swung by, and told me, "Hey Rog ... David is moving out of the front bedroom if you'd like to move in over at our pad. David is one crazy dude. He has been sleeping with Debbie for quite awhile, but about a week ago her sister Jackie came over to the house. Man ... you should see her! She's a total knock out, and David about crapped his pants. He gave her a ride home, and hasn't been back for a week. Debbie is totally freaking out. It's a trip Rog. I never saw a chick so totally freaked."

Pete continued his story ... "Now Jackie is telling her sister that she's sorry, but that she's **madly** in love with David. She is dropping out of City College, and they are going on a trip all the way around the States, and up into Canada in David's new van. You heard they're trying to repossess the van, right? That crazy ____er hasn't made one single payment since he bought it a year ago. Anyway, Jackie is paying for the whole trip with her savings. So, we have some empty space. If you want the room dude ... it's yours. Everyone at the house thinks it's cool for you to move in. How about it?"

I was more than game to exit my morgue, and thus began one of the most radical living situations I ever experienced. I loved every single minute of it. There was never a dull moment night or day. Not that there wasn't some yelling and screaming about dishes, or about this slob, or that slob. We ended up putting a pay phone in the hallway after a few explosive dramas related to the bill. But other than that, it was really neat. The gals kept us all in check as far as housekeeping, and would even share a home cooked meal every once in awhile. Lacy taught me how to bake a chicken with a couple cans of Cream of Celery soup, some carrots and peeled potatoes ... bake for about an hour at 350 degrees, smoke a joint, and devour it with greasy fingers like a bunch of cannibals.

Stump made a beautiful homemade "Aggravation" board, and we probably played 100,000 games of Aggravation over the next year or so. We smoked so much dope knocking opponents back to the starting line ... that it's a miracle we have any marbles left at all. Stump was also the biggest board game instigator, and always had a bag of pot stashed away when everyone else was out. We'd get high right on the front porch, play aggravation, and crack up about Stump's day at work. He was a drug counselor for the State of California.

The landlords were an elderly Jewish couple who lived right next door. They liked Pete a lot and were really nice. I got along real well with them also. One time, I helped Pete sandblast and paint a house up in Hollywood Hills, and pretty soon our landlords wanted us to paint the house we lived in. We really worked hard on it. It was a labor of love ... and rent. We scraped, sanded, and patched the whole house ... and then gave it two good coats of white paint. By the time we finished it looked great, and we named the house ... "The White House". Pete took an old electric Coke-A-Cola sign with a light inside, and made a new announcement. He hung and wired the rectangular sign above the front door, and it read in big letters ... 'The White House'. Next to that in smaller letters it said ... "The First Family ... Pete, Lacy, Roger, Debbie & Stump." On the roof we had a huge American Flag stapled down. It was about 18 feet long. On the front window we had a king-sized political sign that read "Lick Dick in 72". Next to the sign was a three-foot set of the Rolling Stones' famous tongue and red lips. It's a miracle the house never got raided ... but we never did.

" Bob, Stump & my brother Rob"

I planted a garden in the back yard. My ancestral green thumb kicked in, and pretty soon we had tomatoes, and corn, and zucchini, and all kinds of vegetables. Right in the middle of the garden I planted a nice sized patch of marijuana. One day the landlords' wife was complimenting me on such a healthy looking garden, and asked ...

"What's that in the middle that you're growing there? Is it some kind of vegetable?"

I answered ... "Oh no, it's just some ferns that I like." Then, I quickly changed the subject ... "Have you seen your friend Lilly around, because she wanted me to paint some of her rental houses. I guess she liked the job we did for you."

Pretty soon my ferns were above the corn, but thankfully the landlords never mentioned it again. However, even though my elderly Jewish neighbors were no longer interested in my garden centerpiece, it must have caught the eye of some fiendish, lowlife, traitorous friend or acquaintance. Soon everything else in the garden was dead and shriveled up … but my crop of cannabis was at least ten feet tall with buds, and seeds, and all the right equipment. We picked and sampled a few leaves by quick drying them in the oven on a cookie sheet, and it was dynamite.

I finally decided to harvest my illegal crop. However, that very weekend I went out of town with a girlfriend, only to come home to a bare back yard. There was one lonely male marijuana plant left. I knew instantly that this single stalk was my "thank you plant" left by the rip-off, for all the months of loving tender care. I realized that ten foot tall marijuana plants, right in the center of L.A., was a little crazy anyway. It was amazing they lasted as long as they did, with all the traffic we had. In fact, it was lucky they didn't cause even more trouble. Nevertheless, I was vigorously playing Dick Tracy, and absolutely sick about the whole thing. I think I know who did it Bob!

WITCH TRAINING

I had a very strange thing happen after living in The White House for a month or so. My good friend and housemate, Lacy, who suddenly fell in love with Pete, (and two bedrooms became one) … well anyway, she had a friend in Pasadena whose mother was a practicing witch. Lacy came home one day, and announced that she was in training to become a witch.

I asked, "Let's get this straight … **Who** is giving **who** lessons?"

After Lacy smacked me with a couch pillow, she said, "Come on. Stop goofing on me. I'm really serious. I'm learning all kinds of trippy stuff, and it's a rush. OK, check this out."

Lacy pulls out a deck of oversized cards, and coaxes me into participating. They were Tarot Cards … and she was giving me a "reading". Soon Lacy was saying, "Dang Roger, you have three fertility cards, and a death card … whatever that means. That's a drag. Let's do it again."

I said, "Forget it Lacy. I don't believe in any of that crap anyway. It gives me the creeps."

The very next week I found out from Ohio, that Nancy had left California pregnant with twins. Within days of that news, Debbie, our other female resident, announced … "Guess what Roger, I woke up this morning and found my IUD on the bed!"

I had temporarily followed crazy David's footsteps, and now Debbie was terrified that she was pregnant as a result. About a month later, a doctor confirmed that she was going to have a baby. Three fertility cards ... and now ... unexpectedly ... three babies. I started getting concerned about Lacy's budding witchcraft, but still figured it was a bunch of coincidence, and stupid hocus-pocus. Nevertheless, I decided to never again get predictions of the future. At the very least, it was definitely bad luck. I couldn't believe it. Three babies.

Speaking of bad luck ... for several years I had noticed that one of Grandpa Ira's superstitions seemed to be operating with uncanny consistency. If you find a penny heads-up, it was good luck. If it was tails ... look out, because bad luck is on the way. I didn't really consciously believe in it, but the pattern was working itself out in reality, just that way. I'd see a penny on the sidewalk, heads up, and that day a tax refund check would show up early. If I found one that was tails ... Troy would fall off his tricycle, and skin up his nose or something. I wrote it all off to coincidence. Still, I'd be real happy whenever I found a penny heads up.

My roommate Debbie was divorced, and had a 6-year-old son. She had joint custody with her X. However, their totally energized boy lived with his dad almost 99% of the time. Occasionally, he would be tearing in and out of The White House a weekend here, and a weekend there. Debbie informed me that she absolutely was not going to have another child. I told her, I'd take the baby, or to at least give him or her up for adoption.

Her response was, "No way am I going to go through that again, only to give the kid away ... forget it!"

So, she went out and killed our child. I was absolutely sick about it. She spent the night in a hospital, and was all bent out of shape that I didn't get her a card, or come see her, or get her flowers. I was a fire-breathing liberal, but could never comprehend how anyone could deceive themselves into thinking ... that a baby only becomes a baby after it takes a short little trip down a birth canal. On that one, I express **my right** to break away from the deluded pack. To me, life itself is a miracle, even though it can kick your butt from time to time. I might be the sorriest excuse for a father in the world ... but I'm sure Troy wouldn't appreciate having his brains sucked out, because I'm a lousy father... and neither did my other helpless child.

"Sorry Debbie … that I couldn't conjure up more sympathy for you. I realize it was an unwanted child, and also that society encourages, and justifies what you did to our baby."

Just before Christmas I decided to hitchhike back to Ohio. I would spend the holidays with my family, and right after that, Nancy was due to deliver the twins. I hit the road again, and had another series of real-life adventures, which I don't even feel like talking about. I love hitchhiking cross-country. It took me about five days to cover the 2400 miles.

Back in Fremont, Ohio I met with Nancy a couple times, and talked with her on the phone also. I was really considering giving our marriage another try … but was completely torn up with indecision. Troy spent loads of time with us at my parent's home. Nancy was really good about letting me spend time with him. It was so hard to know what to do. Then one day, Nancy and I got in an argument at my parents home. She went home crying. My father-in-law immediately called me up, and read me the riot act. He is about 6'4 and weighs about 270 pounds. He threatened to break a baseball bat on me if I stepped one foot on his property … and blow my head off with a shotgun. It sounded about right.

A few weeks later, while Nancy was in the very final stage of her pregnancy, my mom came home, and was red-eyed and crying. She said … "Roger I have some really bad news. I went with Nancy for her checkup, and the doctor told her they are only getting one heartbeat now … and to expect the worst for one of the twins. He said the other heartbeat is strong, and everything should be OK for one of the babies."

My mom continued to cry, but bravely went on, "I have some more bad news. It's about your mother. When it rains, it pours. My doctor ran some tests on me, and I found out today that I have cancer."

Some things I will never forget … and I'll always remember the numb feeling that hit me, when in a matter of moments, I found out that one of my children was presumed dead, and my mother had cancer. It was one of those brutal times when … "Life sucks".

A couple weeks later Nancy delivered two baby girls. The news got increasingly worse. One of the twins was stillborn, and the other one died shortly after birth. Both of them were around 8 pounds. Poor Nancy was beside herself with grief, but named one of them Michelle, and the other one Melissa.

My dad took me to the funeral home to make arrangements for two little plots at Oak Wood cemetery. I asked the funeral director if I could see the twins. He started talking about them like little monstrous pieces of meat ... "You don't want to see them. Believe me, there's nothing there. The biggest blessing is that they didn't live."

I said, "What do you mean there was nothing there. The two babies weighed over sixteen pounds, and I want to see them. Were they deformed or something?"

He responded in an indignant tone, "You can't see them. They're in formaldehyde inside plastic bags. They were completely deformed, and like I said, there's nothing there to see."

I started getting sick inside, and ticked off at this little cold-blooded weasel of a man. He continued trying to convince us the twins were hardly human, and was raising an eyebrow ... that I wanted a few graveside words spoken over them by someone. As my dad and I walked to the car, I decided to go back inside, and beat the "crap" out of the insensitive, presumptuous jerk.

My dad was saying ... "Come on, and get in the car! It's not worth it. We have enough problems on our hands without you landing up in jail. He's a total jerk, but so what? There's lots of jerks. Think about your mother."

We drove off, and splashed our way home through the half melted snow. A couple days later I met my father-in-law at the graveside. It was just he and I who said farewell to the two tiny lives. He didn't shoot me, and even shared a half pint of whiskey that he pulled out of his pocket in a flask. I always liked Norm. We used to go fishing and hunting, and played pinochle with our women folk. In the fall they would have regular sweet corn feasts at his house. He could eat at least a dozen ears of corn by himself. I felt terrible that my marriage to his daughter was upside down. Good-by Melissa and Michelle.

As much as I love Fremont ... it gave me a real connection to the movies. Fremont can be Peyton Place all the way. Soon, I was hearing rumors that the babies were stillborn and deformed, because I was a longhaired doper. The truth was, that up until that time, the only drugs I had ever used was alcohol and pot. I really don't think they are gene-altering substances. I was angry and sick inside.

DENNY'S PAD

One of my high-school friends lived in a nice modern house, way on the other edge of Fremont. His name is Denny Cramer, and he was attending Toledo University. He also worked as a caseworker for the Sandusky County Welfare Department. He was divorced, and lived with a long-time girlfriend. They had a 2-year-old boy, who was "Little Denny".

I spent a lot of time at his house, and after an argument with my father I moved in for a while. I was considering whether or not to stay in Fremont. I even applied to become a social worker, and took the state exam in Columbus, Ohio. Denny gave me the inside scoop. He told me to lie on my application, saying that I had a B.A. and two years of counseling experience. He said they never check, and if I could pass the 3-hour exam, I would start out as a GS-4, which paid much higher. I passed the test, and was put on a waiting list for a job opening.

In the meantime, my friend was into some other drugs besides pot. He introduced me to "black beauties", which were some potent amphetamines. They helped him stay up until the wee hours, cramming for a test. He was a straight A student in spite of working full time, and being a total party animal at every opportunity. The black beauties made me stay up all night writing and rewriting a letter to a girl I just met in Toledo. The next day when I read the letter … it didn't make any sense at all.

One day Denny and I were driving around in the country, which was a relaxing and safe way to smoke pot. As we were being amused by the endless cornfields, Denny says, "Hey my friend, it's time for the WFRO news. I think you'll get a charge out of it."

Denny snaps on the car radio, and we started listening to all the latest farm reports, and weather, and then … "now to announce the candidates running for the fifth congressional District, we have the Republican challenger Dennis Cramer trying to unseat the two term Democratic Congressman (so and so)."

I had just taken a big hit off the joint that Denny passed me … when I heard his name running for Congress. I about choked on the smoke, and we both roared with laughter. God help Ohio, and the United States, and even the world … if friends of mine can get elected to anything. We had a total blast. It was so weird. Denny was forced to withdraw from the race, because he was already a government employee. He didn't want to give up his job to run for office.

Then Denny talked me into trying some PCP. Here I was, the world traveler, and California hippy … and my own hick-town Ohio friends were into drugs way more than I had ever dared. What is the world coming to … but then … "The heck with it, I might as well live up to my reputation."

I decided to experiment with my first psychedelic drug. I'll never forget it. We were in Denny's living room, and we all ate a couple of these little aspirin sized pills. Just after we ate them, the doorbell rang, and this family came filing into the house. They were one of Denny's caseload families. Here was a young husky husband with his super talkative wife, who was about ten years older. They had a sixteen-year-old daughter, and a couple other smaller kids. Everything seemed strange, but I was thinking that those pills didn't seem to be doing anything. We were all drinking wine also.

No sooner had I thought that thought, when I had my mind absolutely blown. I was sitting in a chair, and the TV was to my right, and the kitchen was on the other side of the sofa to my left. The hallway to the bedrooms was behind my right shoulder. Denny's girlfriend and the welfare lady were in the kitchen making something, and talking real loud. Suddenly, the room reversed itself. I hadn't budged an inch … but now the TV was on my left, and the kitchen was way down on the right side … with Joann still banging pots and pans. The bedrooms were now behind my left shoulder … and I almost totally freaked out. I was never so disoriented in my life. I couldn't believe my eyes. Everything was in reverse!

I stood up, and tried to explain this phenomenon to Denny. However, he had just switched sides along with the room, and I became so dizzy that I had to find my bedroom. It was down this "other world hallway" to my left … but, thank God … there was my bed. I stretched out, and tried to stop my head from swirling. This was definitely more intense than the hash back in Orleans. I knew it would end, but who knows when. I was looking at a pair of shoes beside the bed when suddenly the bed started to lift off the ground, and slowly head for the ceiling. My eyes were wide open and I watched as the shoes got smaller and smaller, as the bed got higher and higher. It stopped about six inches from the top, and slowly went back down. I was freaking out.

A million other things happened, but eventually I passed out for a while. I felt something pressing on me, like in a dream, and I could smell something real sweet. As I was regaining consciousness, I realized that the pressure was from a girl lying on top of me, and she was kissing me. The smell was from the wine she had been drinking. It was the 16-year-old welfare daughter. She was saying ... "Please take me to California with you ... you're so cool ... I'll do anything to get the ____ out of Ohio."

Her mother's voice echoed into the bedroom, and the girl quickly jumped off the bed. I looked up at the doorway, and there was about six heads looking into the room stacked up around each side of the doorframe. They were literally stacked on both sides of the doorframe. The mother, the new husband, Denny, Joann, and a couple kids below that. They were lined up on top of each other. It was so weird. They wanted me to get up and eat some stew or something. I instantly was convinced that the mother was trying to poison me, and I told them to go away. They all went away except for the girl, who was standing next to a mirror. When I looked at her, she had a huge dagger in her hand. I jumped out of the bed, and grabbed her arm and said ... "Give me that ____ing knife!"

She said ... "Take it. It's not a knife. It's just my brush. You're tripping big time. I'll help talk you down. Everything will be OK. Just promise that you'll take me to California."

Finally her parents made her leave, and I heard them all say good-by, and leave the house. Outside it started to rain, and then there were flashes of lightening. A violent electrical storm was raging away. Thousands of bolts of lightning lit up the sky ... one after another. The whole house shook with occasional huge bangs. It seemed like a hundred years had passed since I was in the living room. I was looking at the ceiling, and I saw the shape of a head that looked like a picture of Jesus. I looked away to my right, and the whole wall started to turn into deformed baby flesh. I absolutely freaked out.

I ran out of my room, and out the front door into a driving rainstorm. I started crying and screaming ... and this was the first time I ever cussed God out. I lie not ... the bolts of lightening were coming down all around me. The light show was definitely intensified by the PCP, but it was real, and the lightning continued to streak across the black sky as the rain poured down. I literally called God every name in the book, and **dared** him to strike me dead. I thought that any second I would be fried to a crisp by a huge column of fire, but they all missed … hundreds of them … to my left, and above my head, and to the right. Lightening and blasting earthshaking thunder was everywhere. Denny was yelling at me through the pouring rain from his front door to come inside … but I stayed outside crying and cussing until I was almost frozen, and soaked to the bone.

About a week or so after my showdown with God, I gave Pete a call in Los Angeles. After I told him all the sad news, and all the hassles I was having in Fremont … Pete said … "Hey Rog, come on back to the White House. We are family too, and right now, you need to get the ____ out of that place! We saved your room because I knew you would be back. Life is kind of dull without you around … **so come on home.**"

CHAPTER 16

"BARBARIAN"

Troy spent the weekend with me at my parent's house. I was going to hitch back to California on the following Monday morning. A young guy named Richard came to pick me up. He was a friend of Dennys', who I had met on this visit. Richard was handsome and completely normal looking, except that he had been deaf since childhood. I learned to sign the alphabet, plus we used a notepad to speed communication up sometimes. He was giving me a ride to the Interstate, which was about 50 miles away. This parting was a thousand times harder than back in California. Troy was four years old, and begging me not to leave.

He started crying, and asked, "Why do you have to go to California? I don't want you to go. I never get to see you."

My mom went and held him, and was holding back her own tears. I told my son, "I have to go back and finish school, but I'll come back as much as I can. I love you Troy, and I know that your mom, and your Grandpas and Grandmas will take good care of you. I wish I could be with you every minute, but I can't. I'm sorry. Give me a big hug."

I picked Troy up, and hugged him for a long time. My mom said. "You probably should just leave now, because you have a long way to go. Troy, I want you to help me today, and I'll give you a big surprise. OK? Daddy will call you up real soon when he gets to California."

I forced myself not to cry, but felt totally hollow inside as I walked out of my parent's beautiful home on Oak Drive. While Richard backed out of the driveway, Troy was holding my mother's hand, and waving good-by from behind the window. Neither one of us in the car could talk now. I had a huge frog in my throat, and hurt so bad inside, that I can't find words to describe it. I almost told Richard to take me back, but something kept me paralyzed in the front seat. Tears finally streamed down my face, and the leafless trees flew past the window. I quickly whiped away the tears. I was determined not to break down in front of Richard.

My silent buddy dropped me off at a remote entrance to Interstate 70, and I experienced the second loneliest time of my life. This on-ramp was way out in the northern Ohio countryside. It had started to snow on the ride out there, but after shaking hands with Richard, and spelling out "Good-by my friend", it really started snowing hard. Richard's car vanished into the whiteness.

It was a cold, wind-blown snow. Not a gentle, floating type of snow-flake ... like the last loneliest time in Vienna. However, I was dressed for the weather this time, with long johns under my jeans, and a heavy jacket. I bundled up with my sleeping bag around me, and sat hunched up on my backpack with my thumb out. A recurring sensation of being this tiny little insignificant speck on a huge planet ... descended upon me ... a tiny speck on a planet, which is a tiny, tiny speck in the universe. It took a couple hours to get a ride, and pretty soon ... I was as cold as my cold-blooded heart. "How could I leave my family, and do this to Nancy and Troy???"

One way to escape certain aspects of reality is to simply get into the task at hand. When your out in the elements, and exposed to every level of society and humanity, it quickly becomes a matter of survival ... to get your head into a cross-country trek. Many times I would wonder what it must have been like for the pioneers, just a hundred years or so ago. They would take six months, or more, to travel as far as my thumb could take me in four or five days. I faced a few dangers, but nothing compared to the monumental challenge they faced. America is one big place, with a little bit of everything to throw at you.

Finally a sympathetic soul rescued me from the snow, and I was off and running. In Indiana a couple college students from Ball State picked me up, and invited me to spend a night at their pad. They were having a party that evening, so I got to eat good, meet a bunch of neat people, and even sleep on a heated waterbed. For some reason they treated me like a celebrity. California has this magic about it that can definitely get you some mileage. The trick is to keep your mouth shut as much as possible ... before you blow the mystique.

In the morning a couple longhaired students cooked a big bacon and eggs breakfast, and they drove me back to the Interstate. Around St. Louis, or somewhere, I got stuck for quite awhile, but finally this snazzy little sports car pulls up, and I hit the jackpot. The well-dressed shorthaired driver was heading all the way to Arizona. We took off like a bullet, and the first thing he said to me was ... "I hope you can drive, because I'm going straight through to Dallas, about 1100 miles, and I could use some help."

I told him, "Not a problem", and we zoomed through huge sections of Middle America. I drove about two thirds of the way. It turned out that my styling friend was actually on medical leave from Vietnam. He started telling me about how radical it was over there. He said that the unit he was in had seen all kinds of action, but the biggest trip for him was all the drugs.

He asked me, "Are you into drugs? Probably a stupid question with the long hair and all."

I answered, "Well, until recently I only smoked pot ... but I tried some PCP, and a few other drugs back in Ohio. In fact, I was first turned on to drugs myself while in the Army, in Europe. What's the drug scene like in Vietnam?"

"They have everything. I never did any drugs before I got drafted. I come from a relatively good family. They have a few bucks, and I had a pretty sheltered life. When I got to Nam, it was like another world. It was another world. Not only could you get blown away, but the officers, and everyone, are either using, or dealing, or turning their head the other way. I started smoking pot, and snorting coke, and dropping acid, like everybody else ... but the killer for me was the heroin. I just slipped right into it, and the next thing I know, I got hooked real bad. It took over my whole life, and now my parents, and everybody, are trying to help me. I'm all screwed up. I have to report to Fort Huachuca in a few days."

I said ... "Dang ... from looking at you, I would never guess you're into heroin. I saw a little bit of it in L.A., but decided that I'm staying totally away. In fact, I was going to stay clear of psychedelics too, but 'with a little help from my friends' ... in Ohio ... I about wigged out on some PCP. I'll never do that again. What's heroin like? No one has ever actually told me what it's like."

Keith, who looked more like Tab Hunter than a junkie, got very animated, and began explaining his experience with one of the most powerful and deadly drugs on earth. "Heroin, as bad as it is, has to be the best high there is. Nothing compares to it. When you get off, everything seems perfect. Not one thing in the whole world matters. If you can imagine, it's like sitting on a hill on a warm spring day, with the smell of freshly mowed grass, and the wind, and the sky, and everything is just perfect. It's almost impossible to describe the high, but that's about the only way I could relate it."

He continued, "You probably heard about the down side. If you get hooked, and it takes awhile to get a 'Jones'... then, you get sick as the dickens when you come down off the drug. You **have** to get another fix, and there's no, "ifs - ands - or - buts" about it. Junkies will always say, 'I got to get well ... I got to get well' ... meaning they need another fix. It turns into a living nightmare. I kicked when I came back to the States, and have been clean for a couple months now. I thought I was going to die withdrawing. I don't want to go back, but got to admit, it's incredibly hard to stay away even after your de-toxed."

I was amazed to hear his story, and we drove for about twelve hours at speeds up to 100 miles per hour ... all the way to Texas. Keith was going to visit some friends of his parents, in a suburb of Dallas for the night, and explained that he couldn't take me to their house. He was very apologetic, and tried to explain about the upper class Texan, redneck mentality. I told him I was stationed in Texas, and felt that I already knew a little about, the good, the bad, and the ugly, of the Lone Star State. Keith suggested I camp out, and he'd pick me up in the morning to continue our journey. We got off the main highway, and headed way into suburbia USA. He finally dropped me off by a large field, across from a small strip mall, and some nice homes. It was about a mile from his destination.

It was after sunset when Keith dropped me off, but I could still see. I was totally exhausted from staring at the highway for hours on end. I walked a couple hundred feet into the field to get away from the road. Since the Colombia River trip, I now carried two plastic tarps in my backpack ... one to put under my sleeping bag, and one to put over it. I stayed nice and dry that way. I rolled out my gear, and was asleep the second I closed my eyes.

I can't remember much of my dreams, but I know I was deep-deep-deep in dreamland. It must have been real late, but who knows how much time had passed. Anyway, in this one dream I hear loud crunching sounds … then I hear voices … and suddenly I realized I'm not dreaming. There is someone right above me. A rush of adrenalin propelled me out of my sleeping bag, only to see the barrel of a gun pointing at my head. The cop holding the gun jumped backwards with a loud gasp.

"Jesus you just scared the crap out of me! I almost blew your head off boy! Son-of-a-_____! Get up! What are you doing out here?"

Two cops took me to their squad car, and kept me for about 2 hours. They searched me, and took my ID, and radioed in for every kind of warrant check in the world. While we were waiting and waiting, to find out if they could haul me off to jail, the one cop kept telling me how lucky I was that he didn't blow my brains out when I jumped up.

He said … "Let me tell you, we were patrolling around here, and I shined my spotlight out into the field, because I thought I saw something suspicious out there. We saw this roll of plastic, and decided to investigate. As we walked up, I thought maybe it was a body that someone had dumped. We pulled our revolvers anyway. When you jumped up like that … I can't tell you how close you came to having a pretty little hole in your head. **Man** that shocked the _____ out of me!"

He added, "You know … people around here don't have much use for longhaired hippies. What the heck brought something like you clear out in this neighborhood?"

I "politely" gave them the rundown of my circumstances, and told them about Keith picking me up in the morning. (When faced with overwhelming force … be polite.) I sat in the darkness in the back of that police car forever, but finally they talked on their radio some more, and handed back my ID. They told me to keep moving in the morning … and let me go. What a rush that was!

I woke up in the morning, and it was already light and past 8:30. Keith was supposed to pick me up at 7:30 or 8. I hoped he was just running late, and didn't leave me. I had no idea where I was, or what direction it was back to the highway. I brushed my teeth with water from a plastic bottle, and packed up. I waited awhile, and then decided to walk over to the strip mall, and buy some milk and donuts or something. After buying some breakfast goodies, I walked back outside.

There was a man getting out of a car, just as I turned down the sidewalk. I didn't pay any attention to him … but he signaled to me, and told me to come over to his car. I asked what he wanted, and he flashed a badge at me. He told me … "Get in the car."

I got in the unmarked car, which had a police radio inside, and he made me hand over my ID again. I said … "What's going on? You guys kept me up half the night running checks on me, not to mention almost accidentally shooting me. What did I do now?"

The detective replied … "People around here get real uncomfortable when someone like you shows up. We already had several calls about you. One of the business owners is worried that you are going to rob them."

As he radioed in all my information from my California drivers license, just like the night before … I started getting a little less polite … "Do you really think, I'm going to get up, brush my teeth, roll up my sleeping bag … right in sight of all these stores … then walk across the street … rob them, and hitch-hike away, with all this gear?"

"Well, you got to realize that this isn't California. People around here are a little paranoid when it comes to hippies, dopers, and hitchhikers. Just relax, and if you were clean last night, the computers will show you clean again. Go ahead and eat your food. This might take awhile."

It seemed to go a little faster, and about an hour later I started walking down residential streets. The undercover cop, or whatever he was, gave me some complicated directions to get to a road that would then take me to the main highway. As I walked along, I had to put my coat in my pack. Lugging all my gear was a real chore. Before long it was pretty hot, and I was sweating like a pig. I thought I made a wrong turn, and asked a man in his yard where the main road was. He gave me more complicated directions. I figured Keith was long gone. He must have come by while I was still sleeping, but didn't see me. It was about 10:30 AM already.

Finally after walking forever, I saw a gas station on an upcoming corner. I was so happy. I went up and asked if I could have the bathroom key … and went in to freshen up. Actually, I locked the door, quickly stripped down, and took a wonderful sponge bath right out of the sink. It felt so good. I washed my hair, tied it back in a ponytail, and hurriedly pulled out some clean clothes from my backpack. I was almost ready for the world again, when there was a knock on the bathroom door.

A man yelled, "Hey, there's a guy out here looking for someone from California. Is that you?"

I thought … "Oh no, what's happening now?"

Then I yelled back, "Yea, that's probably for me, I'll be right out."

A couple minutes later I walked out, and discovered a little sports car along with my long lost buddy … Keith. I was totally shocked.

As we sped away, I asked him … "How did you find me?"

Keith said, "Are you kidding, that was the **easiest** thing I ever did! About every two blocks I would ask someone if they saw a longhaired guy with a backpack. This lady would say … 'He went down that way about 45 minutes ago' … the next lady would say … 'Oh my, he turned to the left way down there'. Hey man, your famous… you're the talk of the whole dang county. Every single person I asked knew all about you. Finally, I stopped here … and they pointed… 'He's in the bathroom'!"

I looked out of the passenger window, at all the nice homes with their manicured lawns, and said …"Hey Kieth … thanks a lot for finding me. I'm really happy that you had a nice visit with your family friends … **now get me the _____ out of here!"**

We drove all the way through Texas, and headed for New Mexico. Kieth told me he had stayed up real late with his friends, and didn't even wake up until about 9:30 AM. We got to Arizona, and then, finally to the turn off for Fort Huachuca. It was way after midnight. Kieth said adios, and left me off in the middle of a vast desert. I tried to sleep in the ditch, but my pillow turned out to be a giant anthill. It freaked me out, so I sat on the little shoulder of the highway, with semi-truck after semi roaring past me all night long. None of them would stop, but each one caused a mini windstorm … hour after hour. Right after the sun came up, a car finally picked me up, and took me all the way to LA.

I was so relieved to be back at The White House. It also didn't take long to get back into the swing of things. My attitude had changed a little. I had this …"Whatever … what's the use … you be you … and I'll be me", attitude. I stuffed the anger, and guilt, and confusion. I got back into surfing, and college, and all the things I had been into before. I went wild.

Our friend David, who took off with pretty Jackie, had returned from their epic journey. They pulled up in front of The White House with all kinds of antiques roped on top of the van. They had traveled all the way to the east coast, and all over America. They had purchased most of their antiques up in Quebec. About a week after they returned, David totally dumped Jackie. He had spent all of her savings. He had also gotten back into heroin, which none of us knew at the time. Jackie was freaking out in her sisterly fashion.

David was also Jewish. A Jewish junkie is a sight to behold. At least he was. He came up with all kinds of bizarre schemes, and rip-offs, and behavior. But he was such a likable little guy with a big smile on his face all the time. He was the kind of guy who would stab you in the back, but you still couldn't help liking him. He would go through lengthy theatrics saying ... "Gee Rog, I didn't know it was **you** I stabbed. Honest to God!"

The girls loved David. Once upon a time, he was even married to a Playboy bunny. They were on the Newly Wed Game when they first got married. I didn't see it, but Pete said David was the crack up of the show. One day he was driving down Sunset Blvd., and saw this beautiful girl in another car. When they both stopped at a stoplight, David jumped out of his van, and ran over to her car in the middle of the street. She rolled her window down, and he said with a big smile... "Oh God, your so gorgeous! I can't believe it! I **couldn't** just let you drive away out of my life ... **please, please, please,** can you give me your phone number!" She laughed while people honked their horns ... and then she pulled over and jotted down her number. Later David was waving the piece of paper around for all of us. He was crazy.

He told me one day how he got on permanent SSI disability. He said ... "What I did, was go downtown to the L.A. General Hospital, and I told them ... 'Please help me, I feel like I want to kill someone!' They locked me up in the nut house section of the hospital. You can't believe that place. They had a couple shrinks work on me. I just sat there **staring** at the floor most of the time. But after about two weeks the weirdoes, and real nuts in that place, were driving me up a wall. I figured, man this isn't worth it. I told the doctor ... 'Look, I just pretended to be nuts, so that I could collect SSI ... **let me out of this _____ing place!!!** But he didn't believe me ... the lousy _____ing shrink didn't believe me, and kept me in there another month! Dang Rog, I wish I could just take you down there for one day!"

• • •

While I was working for HUD helping people find new apartments, I got my hands on a little extra money. I was getting tired of paying ten or fifteen dollars for a little baggy of pot all the time. So, through a friend I bought a pound of pot for $110.00. I sold most of it, and still had plenty of private reserves. A lid is supposed to be a whole ounce, but with a little stretching, I think I got a couple extra lids. It was my first ever experience dealing. Not exactly big time money, but it paid for my pot, and gave me some extra cash to boot.

I hung out with Cliff from time to time. However, he was still living with Toni, and they were having their ups and downs. I would also go out on the town a lot with my black friend, Hubert Jackson. One night Jackie invited me to a party at her apartment. After David broke up with her, I saw her registering at LACC, and we took a class together. Soon we became lovers, which really ticked her sister off even more. For about a month or so it was pretty intense, but we eventually went our separate ways. However, we were still seeing each other once in awhile. On the night of the party, Hubert and I decided to go to this club in the San Fernando Valley, and if that was dead, then we'd check out Jackie's party.

Well, the hot club out by Valley State in Northridge wasn't so hot that Saturday night, so Hubert and I doubled back over the hill. Jackie's apartment was right in the heart of Hollywood. It was a classy apartment on the second floor. Hubert and I both had more than a little buzz going by the time we climbed the stairs to the party. The place was packed with people. The music was going, and every room was full. Jackie had lots of girlfriends, and they all seemed to be as beautiful as she is. I didn't see anyone I knew, but finally we found Pete sitting on a couch.

I sat down next to Pete, and before I even had a chance to acclimate myself to the new atmosphere ... he leans over next to my ear ... "Roger, I wish I was like you, because I've been sitting here for over an hour listening to this dude on the other couch. I never feel like this, but I'd like to just punch him right in the face. He makes me so sick. He's sitting over there, and those four girls are just eating up everything he says. He's putting on a show for them, and just listen to him for a while. You'll see what I mean. He is the most conceited, overbearing jerk I ever had to listen to!"

I laughed because it was the first time I ever saw Pete even hint at violence. I focused on the ongoing conversation next to us. I tuned into this guy for a while. Hubert went to the kitchen, and brought us both back a mixed drink. Jackie and her friends were obviously much higher up the social ladder, than The White House crowd. Everyone was dressed to kill, including the four girls laughing, and giggling at our charismatic friend.

I didn't really listen to this guy to form an opinion ... Pete's analysis was good enough for me. He said something ... and I butted in, and said ... "Oh that's a bunch of crap."

The guy looked up, gave me a dirty look, and continued his latest story. I waited a couple more sentences, and said ... "You're full of **it**."

"What did you say?"

"I said you're full of ____."

He said ... "Look fella, if you say one more thing, I'm going to get off this couch and ... "

"One more thing."

We both jumped up and I tried to punch him, but somehow he grabbed me, and we both fell back on his couch. As we fell, I was able to get in one good punch to his mouth. I heard and felt him wince, but then it turned into a wrestling match. He was quite a bit bigger than me, but I got him in a scissor lock around his waist, and with my left hand I grabbed his Adams-apple. I thought I was in big trouble. I was on the bottom, but every time he would rear back to try to punch me ... I would squeeze my legs together with every ounce of my strength, and dig my fingers into his neck, until he went limp. I did that about five times. He had blood covering his face, and finally a bunch of guys pulled us apart.

I'll never forget this next part ... because as they took him into the kitchen a crowd of people, mostly girls were completely around me in a big circle. A couple of the girls were saying ... "You animal!" ... "Look what you did to him!" ... **"BARBARIAN!!"**

As they were calling me names, I spun around in a 360 degree circle with my arm locked straight out into their pretty faces ... giving them all the finger. While I was doing that, with my clothes pulled apart, and my hair hanging way down ... I actually felt like a barbarian. "What would Aunt Lula think of me now?"

Anyway, I know Pete was proud of me.

They accused me of using brass knuckles, because he was cut so bad, but that wasn't true. It was just one lucky punch. Hubert goes … "Dang Roger, that's the first time I ever saw someone kick somebody's butt from the bottom! Let's sky brother. I don't think they like you here."

CHAPTER 17

"SIX KILOS &
A HEARTACHE"

I was sitting out in the Pacific Ocean watching the horizon for signs of a new set. The water was real cold, but my wet suit kept me nice and toasty. The Malibu Pier was off to the left, and about six other surfers were scattered around me. Nothing was coming in at all. The guy sitting on his board next to me struck up a conversation in the lull. I found out that he was from San Diego. I had never met anyone from our neighboring city to the south, and somehow we got onto the subject of cannabis.

"I hear that a lot of marijuana comes through San Diego from Mexico and South America," I said.

My new surfer buddy was named Dan, and he replied … "For-sure. Every once in awhile, my buddies and I cop a kilo or two, to keep the home fires burning."

"What can you get a kilo for down there?"

"We paid $125.00 for the last ones we scored."

"You gotta be kidding. Could you get me some for that price, if I came down?" I asked.

"Not a problem. If you get enough of them, then I can make a little coin myself, but anyway, you won't have to pay over a buck and a quarter. Heck yea, I'll help you out dude … come on down."

Finally a set of waves magically appeared, and we all started to paddle into position. The first swell formed, and was peaking right behind me. I was in perfect position. Dan and I dug in, as the power of the wave overtook, and captured us. I jumped up right in the pocket, and was instantly heading straight down the face of a six-foot wave. After a quick right turn, several of us were shooting across a **perfect** wall of water …

on one of the consistently beautiful Malibu waves. Dan was right ahead of me, and let out a war hoot. I love everything about surfing, including the danger, the smell of salt water, and the ever changing, peaceful-but violent, Pacific coast. I even love waiting on my board for the next thrill … which sometimes can be hours away. The rest of the world with all its problems seems to be a million miles away on another planet. I discovered why "many a good man", and a few beautiful surfer-babes … can get totally addicted to surfing.

Dan and I caught several waves, getting separated in the process. Later, I found him sitting on the beach. I told him I was definitely serious about our previous conversation, and I'd be in touch, as soon as I scraped up some money. He gave me his phone number in San Diego.

"Sounds like a plan my man. Just give me a call before you come down" … Surfer Dan replied.

One evening I was visiting a little tavern, right around the corner from The White House. It was a popular little place with a couple pool tables, and a very sexy barmaid. I met a guy named Frank, who was from New York City. He was handsome, had his accent, and a great natural build with iron pumping type arms, even though he didn't work out. He wasn't the typical rude, insensitive, loudmouthed, arrogant New Yorker that I seemed to run into, from time to time. Even though he looked like he could rip your head off, he was real easygoing, and almost shy. I could relate to that, because in certain settings, without chemical support … I can bomb real bad. I absolutely refused to take speech class at LACC.

Frank and I hit it off real good, and he bet me I couldn't get the barmaid to go out with me. She was one of these gals with a radical figure, and beautiful face. Her bust was not just big … it was Dolly Parton style. I'm not complaining Dolly! That evening I was just exactly drunk enough to get her laughing, and to Frank's amazement, she went over to the cash register, got a pen, and wrote down her phone number for me. What a trip she turned out to be.

The first time I went to her upstairs apartment, she showed me tons of her artwork. It was mostly pen and ink drawings of nude characters with exaggerated body parts, and things like that. The drawings were really well done, and looked very professional … but totally weird. She liked to draw about sex, but didn't want to partake. Outside, below her apartment, I heard someone let out a blood-curdling scream ... that went on and on and on. A few seconds later someone else let out another scream. It came from a garage below where several of her neighbors were practicing "primal scream therapy". I felt like I was in the Phallic Twilight Zone Apartment.

My busty friend wasn't into screaming ... she was into L. Ron Hubbard. Still on the hunt, I attended three or four Scientology meetings with her, and discovered how the engrams from my mother's constipation is the source of all my problems. I bought a copy of their Bible ... "Dianetics", and finally got my barmaid into The White House for a night. A couple days later she came back to the house, and taped up a big sign in the living room, which said ... "ROGER IS A CREEP". I was **clear** after that.

I made a great first impression on Frank. He thought I was his long lost big brother or something. I honestly will always love my, "sometimes", mixed up partner from the Big Apple. To add to my image I had just traded my Pontiac for an honest to goodness chopper. It was a customized 1947 Triumph, but almost looked like a Harley to me. The front end had been kicked way out, and the handlebars were in a zigzag shape. It had suspension in the rear hub, (which is unique), and had lots of chrome along with a tall sissy bar. The taillight was in the shape of a swastika. The whole frame was painted metallic green with just the right amount of detailed flames. My old leaker was a neat old ride. It almost killed me many a time.

Frank had a Jewish girlfriend back in New York, who was **madly** in love with him. Her parents had moved the family to California, from my understanding, primarily to get Dale away from him. Frank had had a string of bad luck back there. For example, one day he was simply walking down the street in the Bronx. Two of his friends and he, were going to cross a street, when a speeding taxicab cut around the corner almost running over them. One of Frank's buddies managed to kick the rear side panel of the cab as it shot past.

Several blocks or so down the road, a huge man jumped on Frank's back, and started thumping on him. However, the three musketeers managed to get the best of their attacker, to the degree that the man lost an eye from a kick to the head. The police came. Frank's two friends had run off, but Frank stayed, figuring ... this guy had just attacked him ... why should he run? Well, it was the taxicab driver, of course, and Frank did almost a year in jail before his trail even got started. Dale's nice, well-to-do family didn't want her to have anything to do with Frank.

Amazingly, Frank also wanted to break off the long-term relationship. He wasn't in California to follow Dale. He just wanted to get away from New York. Nevertheless, Dale pursued him in classic fashion, and they more or less got back together. She used money, she used tears, she used sex. Frank became one of our couch potatoes at The White House for a while, and on one of Dale's visits from not too distant Woodland Hills, she brought a friend of hers along, who was visiting from New York City.

This attractive young blond had a huge smile, bubbling personality, and great sense of humor. She wanted to go everywhere, and see everything that California had to offer, and I decided to take her, or at least tag along. She loved to drink wine, and would even smoke a little pot. Her name was Jill, and back in Flushing, New York, she was engaged to a law student. She was also the exercise instructor for an exclusive health club on Long Island. She had a terrific figure.

Over the course of her two-week vacation, she enjoyed my company enough to break off her engagement, and quit her job. Her boyfriend back in New York was totally freaking out. One day he called the pay phone inside the house, and was literally crying and begging over the phone. Jill signaled for me to come over, and she held the receiver so I could hear also. I felt sorry for him, and thought it was pretty cold-blooded of Jill, but obviously she was over him. Jill stayed with me an extra month before returning to New York to get more of her things. Before leaving, she helped me with my job working on the HUD project, and loved it. She wanted to live with me.

There was a little, tiny abandoned one-bedroom house behind The White House that was real run down, and I made a deal with the landlord to fix it up and rent it. While Jill was back east, I cleaned and fixed it up enough to move in. Pete and I had already painted the outside. I had several girlfriends just before I met Jill, and one in particular I was pretty serious about. However, they literally vanished from my thinking, although I was still human. A lot was going on at The White House about the time I was moving into the rear house.

Jill was going to stay a little longer in Flushing, which ticked me off. However, she changed her mind, when she detected a hint of all the female activity around The White House. Like, for example, I was sleeping in the little house one brightly lit morning when a cute, beautifully tanned girl, came in the front door, took all her clothes off, and got under the covers with me. I never saw her before in my life. Eventually, I found out she was visiting from South Carolina, and temporarily staying at crazy David's pad, along with her friend, who I also had a little fling with, and liked even more. David had a lot of overflow. Jill never found out any of this, but her female perceptions knew something was up. A little jealousy goes a long way.

Soon, I was going to LAX in "The Blue Max" to pick up my real heartthrob. For the next year or so, I would experience the thrill of victory, and the agony of defeat with this gal. We probably would have got married, except that my divorce wasn't final. We really loved each other, but somehow managed to put ourselves through the mill. We went from L.A., to Ohio, to New York, Florida, back to L.A., and finally ended up in San Diego. I got hooked on her worse than Vietnam Keith got hooked on heroin, and the withdrawals were almost deadly.

I was involved in the 236 Project, working for HUD, and what was happening was that the government was giving incentives to developers to renovate run down inner- city apartment buildings. The developers would get long-term loans at something like 3% interest. In turn, they would make about 20% of the refurbished units available to subsidized, low-income people, for practically nothing. When a building was sold to one of these developers, all the tenants would get a letter in the mail, informing them that their building had been sold … and a re-location specialist would be contacting them. That was me. Everyone was usually real happy to see me, because the letter also mentioned money. They would get paid to move, according to the size of the family, plus I had to help find them a new place. It was almost social work, and Jill and I both loved it. She said it was the only job besides working at the health club that she liked.

I saw all kinds of extreme cases of human misery, as well as unexpected love in these firetraps. Scores of individuals captured my heart. People are very special when you take the time to get past the thin veneer. I could have written a book, weaving about a dozen of these lives together. It would have been a story of desperate cries, and hidden heroes of love. As much as I go to war when I'm drunk, I really have a soft spot for just about everybody, although ... I have met a few people I didn't like ... Will.

In one dark and dingy building, I knocked on the door of an old widower. He was a large man in his seventies, with big hands and a weathered, intimidating brown face ... but he was so friendly and warm. One side of his face was slightly pulled down from a stroke. He was an Apache Indian named Henry Garcia. He had lived in that building for twenty years or something like that. He said ... "Well, my wife and I moved in here after we had to sell our home. She got cancer and I nursed her for many, many years. I watched her die right here in this apartment. That's her picture right over there. I never planned on moving again, and figured I'd probably die here too ... but I guess the good Lord has something else planned for me."

Henry fixed me a cup of coffee, and we talked for a long time. He wanted to know about me. He was such a gentle man. He said he had done construction and odd jobs all his life. For about a decade he said he worked for Humphrey Bogart, as his handyman. Henry gave me several personal glimpses of the movie star.

He said, "Sometimes Mr. Bogart would lay on his couch for two or three days in a row, and just drink and drink, and sleep, and drink some more ... but he was always very nice to me."

After a building has been renovated, the displaced tenants have top priority to move back in. Or they can move into any other available unit in the 236 Project. We found a great apartment for Henry in another completed building. It was in a better neighborhood on Berendo Street, and just perfect for him. The apartment was right in front on the ground floor, bright and well lit, and everything was brand new inside ... carpet, appliances, paint, and the whole nine yards. Henry was **so** thankful and appreciative.

I was still working on the little house, and asked Henry if he knew anything about fixing a ceiling. In our one-and-only bedroom, the ceiling was half caved in. Jill and I were sleeping in the front room until our own renovations were completed. Little by little it was getting fixed up. I came home one day, and Jill had painted all the windows on the inside of the house. It looked great, and she was all excited and proud of herself. Henry agreed to come over on the next Saturday to help me demo, and replace the ceiling.

When Henry arrived we were still asleep. Our bed was just a mattress on the floor like most hippies, but as I invited Henry in, I noticed that he was a little uncomfortable seeing my living arrangement with my girlfriend. Nevertheless, he was very polite. I also remembered that when I asked if he could come on Sunday, he kindly said that he couldn't, because he was a Christian and would be going to church. We worked most of that Saturday, and Henry did a great job. We completely replaced the ceiling. Although he was in his seventies, he was still strong as a bull. I really liked and respected Henry.

Eventually he told me incredible stories about being raised on the reservation in Arizona. He was sent out into the wilderness for two weeks when he was thirteen by the medicine man ... to be accepted as a warrior in the Apache tribe. He could only take a piece of string and a knife. He said he slept in trees at night to stay away from animals, and could remember looking up through the top of the trees at all the stars. He made a bow and arrow with the knife and string, and had to kill small game to survive. After two weeks he had to return, and present himself to the medicine man ... who examined his eyes and overall well-being. Henry passed the test, and was recognized as a young Apache warrior.

His father was the Indian Marshal on the reservation, and was judge, jury and executioner. He told me intriguing stories of his father's exploits, which I'll tell about later. He also told me how unjustly the government treated his family after his father was thrown from a horse and killed. Later in life, Henry was on an aircraft carrier in World War II, and shot by a German warplane off the coast of North Africa. He showed me scars from 30 caliber machine gun holes in his stomach, back and legs. He was airlifted to a hospital in Italy and almost died. Like I said, I could write a book just about Henry and his neighbors. What a sweet and interesting man. We finished our project.

Jill had some money in the bank, and I told her about my surfer friend in San Diego. I touched bases with Dan, and Jill got enough money out of the bank for me to buy six kilos. On the appointed day we drove south together to meet this kid. In San Diego we got there early, and had to wait hours for Dan to get off work. That evening he took our money and sent us to a Denny's restaurant in San Ysidro, near the Mexican border. **Again**, we waited, and waited, and waited ... and thought for sure that we were either going to get busted, or ripped off for all the money. Finally, Dan drove up with the "load". Feeling totally paranoid, we transferred everything into my borrowed car. I discovered that drug dealing can be very emotionally draining no matter how good looking your partner is.

We drove back to L.A., making it past the immigration checkpoint, and I began selling my merchandise. It was great. I recouped our initial investment, and still had lots of pounds and lids, and money set aside to go back east. We were planning to go home for Christmas. Jill was very uneasy about the dealing, and told me ... "If you get rich doing this, I'll help you spend it ... but if you get caught, I'm not waiting five or ten years for you to get out of prison." (What a loyal moll!)

We had a trail run of sorts one early morning. All the pot was in a closet, and somebody knocked on the front door. I looked out of the little window on the door, and saw a uniformed policewoman. I yelled, "just a minute", and frantically, but quietly threw all the pot out of the bathroom window into some bushes. I hoped the place wasn't surrounded. Then, I answered the door, with my heart beating a million miles per second. It was a marshal, and she was serving me with some kind of a warrant. I signed something, and was so relieved to see her walk away.

A few months before I met Jill, I had a brief affair with a married gal. She lived out of town, and I had trouble seeing her, especially after Bob ruined my chopper. She suggested that I take her extra car, and have it registered in my name. She was still the legal owner. It was about the only time I ever messed around with a married woman. I don't know how she explained away her car to her husband. Anyway, she wanted her car back, after it became apparent that our relationship had vanished along with her wheels. I felt bad about driving that car around for all those months, but it feels even worse to be on foot in Los Angeles. She finally resorted to the legal machine to get her car back ... thus the marshal.

This old girlfriend came to The White House about a week later and picked up her car, and then was supposed to drop the charges, which I guess she did. I never heard any more about it. Jill wanted to go out to see what she looked like, but I wouldn't let her. Anyway, it was a close call. Even if that marshal lady had served the papers back when my "ferns" were in their prime ... I would have been busted. They had been located about eight feet directly in front of my door ... ten feet tall. I had harvested the lonely male plant only about a week before that knock on the door. But more than anything, it bothered me that I got my "Dear John" notice from Jill ... even before I was off to the pokey.

I learned about a place that needs people to drive vehicles back east. It was advertised in the L.A. Times. All you pay for is the gas. They give you over a week to make the cross-country drive. I went down and got a brand new Dodge van with about 28 miles on the speedometer to deliver back east. The dealer mapped out our southern route, which we were not supposed to deviate from, and they allotted us about 2800 miles or so to get to this town in Pennsylvania. Pete showed me how to disconnect the speedometer cable when I got to the allotted miles, and how to reconnect it. Jill and I loaded up all our belongings, including my disabled chopper, and we hit the road.

It was a fantastic cross-country trip. We immediately disregarded the boring route, and went up through Vegas, Utah, and Colorado, which was an absolute winter wonderland, and then all over the place. We stopped in Ohio to see my family, and then I took Jill all the way to New York City. She was going to spend Christmas with her family, and me with mine. I doubled back through Pennsylvania, and on the last allotted day I reconnected the speedometer with about 30 miles under our limit registering. My cousin Steve met me, and drove me back to Ohio.

Jill called me up at my home about a week later, and said she couldn't stand being apart. My parents agreed if she came to Ohio, that we could stay in one of their 50-foot house trailers up on their property in Port Clinton. I also had a court date set for my divorce. This time, I drove my father's van, and went to pick up Jill, along with much of her furniture. We were back together in a frozen wonderland. Along with two house-trailers, and a nice classy cottage, my parents also owned an actual little beach right on Lake Erie. One of the trailers was about a stone throw from the sandy shoreline, and became our home for several months. A few weeks after moving in, we borrowed my brother's old car and drove to Miami, Florida to visit Jill's divorced mother and new husband. It was a great trip. Jill's step dad took me to the Orange Bowl to see a NFL playoff game between the Cleveland Browns and the Dolphins. I don't think he was too thrilled about my cheering for the Browns ... who won.

Back in Ohio, I sold most of the pot. I also went to work for my father again, driving one of his Frito-Lay trucks. He insisted I cut my hair, so Jill and I went to Toledo, and bought a longhaired wig. I put it on, and had it professionally styled and cut short. My dad thought I looked great, but about flipped out when I pulled off the wig revealing my pinned up pony tail. Nevertheless, he went along with it.

We stayed in Ohio until about May, but something happened to me. Jill said I changed, and I know I did. I was having another identity crisis I guess. I started to be clingier, and exactly like I hate. Nothing felt right, but I was powerless to reverse the drift. Jill started pulling away from me. We started having terrible arguments, and one time I threw her out in the snow half nude. Another time, I filled up a wastepaper basket full of water, and threw it on her in the bed. It was the wastepaper basket that her former boyfriends had filled up with change. The pennies, nickels, and dimes were all out in the snow also. I had become jealous just like I hate. She left me, and went back to New York.

My mother had surgery for her cancer. The verdict was … they think they got it all. Thank God. Let's keep our fingers crossed that it doesn't come back! I would see Troy pretty often, but I was a miserable excuse for a father. The divorce became final with a totally sad encounter at the courthouse with Nancy. She tried to talk to me in the hallway after the hearing, but I literally ran down the hall and out the door to get away from her. What a sad mess things are.

I hopped on a bus heading for New York to try to patch things up with Jill. I had to transfer buses in Toledo, but on the way up there I got in a long conversation with three girls sitting in front of me. They were Christians, and real nice. They said they were on their way to a Bible something or other in Lansing, Michigan. One of them invited me to come along to their event. I wasn't rude this time, but told them I had already been through the drill with other Christians.

I really didn't want to talk about religion. Instead, I unloaded all my heartaches on them about Jill. I talked and talked and talked. When I got to my transfer stop, I stood up to go, and one of the girls said … "I want you to take this with you. It's my personal New Testament, and **please** take it with you! I tried to push it back to her, but she kept insisting, and then I noticed that everyone on the bus was looking at me … so finally I just took the Bible, and got off the bus.

In New York, Jill and I almost made up again, but then didn't. We were at La Guardia Airport ready to fly back to California, but I sensed that she didn't want to go. At the ticket gate she decided to stay in New York. Instead we bought a ticket for myself. While we were waiting for my plane, I took a knife out, and was going to kill myself. Jill saw the knife and screamed. She took off and ran hysterically through the airport, and then into a women's bathroom ... with me right behind her. She locked herself in a stall, but I crawled over the top, and held her while she cried uncontrollably.

The other two loves of her life had threatened, and even attempted suicide over her. One of them by driving into a concrete wall with Jill in the car, breaking her ankle, and ruining her budding career as a prospective Radio City Hall Rockette. I was making it three for three. It was a pattern. As I ran through the crowded airport behind Jill, I remember the faces of the startled people, and especially the women in the bathroom. They were looking at me like a crazy man ... and I was.

I thought I had been to the bottom of the barrel a few times already ... but Jill took me to a basement that I didn't know existed. More like I took myself there over her. I hitched back to Ohio, and eventually to LA. I returned to The White House about fifteen pounds lighter, and feeling like a whipped puppy dog. What comes around goes around. She did to me, what I did to Nancy.

CHAPTER 18

"IT'S JUST A BOWL OF CHERRIES"

San Diego, California in 1973 had something like 300,000 people. It seemed to possess a small town personality ... on a big city playing field. The beach communities down there were very different from each other, and of course, the wild and woolly Ocean Beach was every hippie's favorite hang out. The climate is absolutely perfect all year long. Not too hot ... not too cold. The ocean cliffs and tide pools attract millions of tourists each year, along with the help of Sea World, Balboa Park, and the San Diego Zoo. The local people seemed radical to me, and more for-real than anyplace in California. In addition, San Diego is a border town, with a million Mexicans smashed up against a long ragged fence ... panting to get into America. A huge naval base lies just south of downtown. Thousands of military personnel are woven into the area's fabric. The international airport butts up against the north side of downtown, and jumbo jets practically touch down on the 5 Freeway. It's amazing to watch. San Diego has many faces. It is my favorite city in the whole world. I was on the way.

To revisit La Guardia International Airport for a moment ... from inside the toilet stall of the women's bathroom, I had calmed Jill down enough for us to leave and go back to her apartment. The following day I bought a bus ticket to Ohio, and said my farewell to Jill. She told me she just needed some space for a while. My original intentions of coming to New York, and patching things up, had gone from bad to **insane**. Nothing was going right. What a jerk I was. I agreed to split.

Several hours into my bus ride, I told the driver to stop the bus. I couldn't take it ... I had to go back. I didn't even know where I was, but somehow around nightfall I made it back to Flushing, and found Jill's darkened apartment building. No one was home. I waited outside ... and then I waited, and waited, and waited. Hours went by and it started to drizzle. Soon a cold, steady rain was falling. There were some huge bushes up close to the tall multi-story apartment building, and I got under them to try to stay dry. I was freezing. As the night wore on, my mind started working overtime, trying to figure where Jill was, and what she was doing. I actually prayed for the first time in years ... "Please God, let her come home alone!"

Some time in the wee hours of the night a car pulled up, and I heard voices. As I came out of the bushes half drenched, I saw Jill, and her sister, and a guy. Jill looked up and said ... "Roger! What are you doing here??? Oh God! Oh God! Oh God!"

I said, "Is that Tommy?"

Jill said, "Oh God ... this isn't happening!"

Tommy the law student said something to me. I told him to "Shut up" ... and then attacked him. In response to my valiant efforts he punched me real good right smack in my eye. Bang! My forward momentum pushed him down some stairs leading to a basement door, and I managed to pin him against the wall. I had my forearm on his throat like Art had me years before. I pushed like crazy cutting his air off.

He started pleading saying in a choked voice, "I can't breath!"

Jill and her sister Lynn were freaking out, and screaming at me to let him go ... which I finally did.

Winded but still feeling half crazed, they talked me into coming inside, and acting civilized. Lynn made some coffee, and I sat down in Jill's kitchen.

Tommy sat across from me, and made the brilliant remark ... "Now what did that prove?"

I shot back at him ... "Just shut up or I'll kill you!"

He responded in a real calm, matter-of-fact attorney like voice, "I'm going to forget you even said that."

"Well keep running that mouth, and let's see what happens. I think its time for you to get the _____ out of here."

I believed I had let my rival off a huge hook, when I had his air cut off. However, as Jill tended to my swollen eye with an ice pack ... I didn't look, or feel much like a victor.

Tommy left, and I spent one last night with Jill in the Rotten Apple.

After my sorry experience in Flushing, New York, I took my black eye and broken heart back to Ohio. I feel sorry for this one guy who picked me up hitching. He made the big mistake of asking about my eye. For half of Pennsylvania he had to listen to my lovesick story. He was a well-dressed man in his thirties or forties. I know he felt the utter emptiness in my voice, but couldn't do anything to help. He kind of tried. Normally I wouldn't disclose much to a stranger … but I hurt so bad that it didn't matter what people thought, or what they said, or anything. It's the worst kind of pain … to lose someone you really love … especially when it's fresh.

"Seems like I've been down this road before." … I told myself … "But this is a thousand times worse. Maybe I am growing in my ability to hurt. I never got suicidal over Linda."

From Ohio, I gathered my gear and returned to Los Angeles … "Bye mom and dad, and Troy, and my silent twins."

In California, Frank was living in my little house, but I was able to get my old bedroom back inside The White House. Pete, Stump, Lacy and Debbie were all still there. It was great to be back. They basically told me to suck it up, and forget Jill. Easier said than done. Nevertheless, they had lots of confidence that I'd be all right. A couple weeks later, Jill called. She was in Florida with her mother.

"What are you doing in Florida?"

"I had to get away from everything and everybody." She continued … "I'm so confused Roger. I called my mother, and she talked me into coming down here. So how are you, Rog?"

"I'm all right. It's good to be back in L.A. So what gives, I thought you were going back with Tommy."

"He wants to, but I don't know what to do. I had to just get away and think. I miss you Roger."

I didn't say anything for a while. My brain only works so fast. Finally I said, "So what do you want Jill?"

Her voice sounded soft and far away … "Do you think we could just start all over, and it could be like it was in the beginning? I thought maybe I could fly back out in a couple weeks, if you still want me. Do you want me to come back?"

"Jill, you know I never wanted to break up in the first place. The whole thing got way out of control. But man, I'm just beginning to feel alive and human ... and not that excited about letting you rip my heart out again. So tell me some more about Tommy. You mean you didn't get back with him?"

"He came around but like I told you, I was a mess, and couldn't handle any of this. I had to get away from him and you, and everybody, and just figure out what to do with my life. I'm still confused, but now I'm thinking maybe we should give it another try. I need to fly back to New York, and take care of some things, and then if you want, I'll fly to Los Angeles in a couple weeks."

I said, "Jill, if you want to be with me, you hop on a plane for California tomorrow or forget it. I'm not going to play a bunch of guessing games about who you're going to pick, and all that crap. I love you and miss you, but if you're not on a plane to LA tomorrow then don't bother."

She said, "Roger, I have to go back to New York. I only have a few things with me."

"Then forget it Jill. I'll see ya later." ... and hung up the phone.

I joined Pete in the front room who was drinking some beer, and listening to the stereo. I grabbed a beer out of the refrigerator myself, and tried to mellow out with good old Pete. What a neat guy and good friend. His love life also had had its dramatic twists. A few months back he fell head over heels for this girl in City College. The problem was, that when he broke it off with Lacy, our budding Samantha came totally unglued. Lacy cried, threatened suicide, and even went over to this new gals apartment while Pete was there, making a huge scene. It got extremely ugly on several occasions. However, the fireworks were pretty much over now, and Lacy was back in her own bedroom. She was making noises about moving out of The White House entirely, which was major. For some reason, I had a little more empathy for Lacy than I would of had in the distant past.

The pay phone sounded off, and someone yelled for me. I walked down the hall and answered the phone. It was Jill again. She said, "I booked a flight into LAX for tomorrow."

The next day we were in the Blue Max heading down the Santa Monica Freeway to the airport. Pete was driving. For the first time since Europe I was completely without wheels. It sucks. I had even traded my disabled chopper for a quantity of pot and cash in Ohio ... and then the kid never completely paid up. All of my drug money surpluses had long since evaporated. However, Jill and I were back together ... back in the sunny Golden State ... back at The White House. It was great, but it was different. For one thing we didn't have our little house anymore.

I said to Jill after a few days ... "Let's move down to San Diego. We both like it. I've thought about moving down there a lot of times. Anyway, there's nothing holding us in L.A. right now ... so let's sky. What do you think?"

She was game, in spite of the fact that we were almost totally broke. It never had taken much encouragement to get Jill up for an adventure. So the next thing you know, like a couple tourists, we were on a Greyhound bus heading for San Diego. We arrived at the downtown San Diego bus terminal in the absolute middle of the night. We had a few suitcases, and exactly $220 to our names. After lugging our things for several blocks, I discovered that downtown San Diego in the middle of the night in 1973 wasn't as romantic as my previous visits. In fact it was downright spooky, and dark like a Batman movie. The streets were deserted except for a few creeps. They looked at us like hyenas ... but with the help of a little adrenaline, we found a dingy hotel.

The next morning we bought a newspaper, and started looking for rentals and jobs. We needed to get out of the downtown area ASAP. We called from the hotel phone about a house for rent, and somehow by city bus, thumb, and foot we made it across town. The San Diego sun was shining away, and it was glorious. At one point we got completely lost, but so what. Finally, after wandering around a little, we cut across this big lush canyon on foot. I asked directions from a young guy, who magically appeared walking down our winding canyon path in the opposite direction. The house we were going to see was south of town on the other side of the 94 Freeway. He stopped and drew us out a map and everything.

Then he said ... "Hey ... house hunting is hard work. Why don't you two take a little break, and smoke a dubbie with me in this beautiful canyon. Welcome to San Diego!"

We floated out of the canyon even more happily disoriented, but eventually made it to our destination. We were able to rent the house, which like our place in L.A. was a house behind a house. Only this one was much bigger, with about half an acre of land to boot. A young earthy couple with several kids lived in the front house. They were real friendly, and helped talk the landlord into approving us, even though we didn't have any security deposit or last months rent, or references, or anything. We lied and said we were married. In our favor the house had been sitting empty. The landlord even arranged to have new carpeting put in.

Soon we were somewhat set up. The new carpet was in, we painted, and acquired a few furnishings along with several well-placed orange crates. I got hired driving a taxicab … even though I didn't know one street from another in the entire city. What an embarrassing challenge, when every single passenger had to give me directions. I mostly worked the taxi line at the airport. With her previous experience, Jill got a job at a Jack La Lanes Health Club teaching exercise classes. She loved it. They even wanted her to be in a TV commercial. A neighbor gave her a ride to work each morning. Everything went real smooth for a couple months. I planted a garden, (which gophers destroyed), and also planted some well-hidden pot plants. We got a little puppy … then a second one. We made some friends. I had everything I wanted, and should have been happy … but I wasn't.

I couldn't stop thinking about our break-up. I questioned Jill about a thousand times if she slept with Tommy. She swore she didn't … but I was positive she did. I badgered her. I used every kind of homespun psychology … and finally she confessed that he slept over a couple times. What a ding-dong I was to badger her. She cried and cried. I had never been the super-jealous type … but now I was totally overcome. I could dish things out … but couldn't take it. The male ego doing its ugly thing.

Nevertheless, my emotions were real and out of control. The downward spiral of my relationship with Jill was the straw that broke the camels back for me. Everything in my life was screwed. My twins were in plastic bags of formaldehyde. My mom was continuing to fight cancer. I was full of guilt over hurting Nancy, and poor little blue-eyed Troy. I had been faithful to Jill since we righteously moved in together … but now she was screwed too … by the guy crying and begging … as she quietly giggled … holding the phone so I could hear. "____ it all." … "This life sucks, and I'm not a very successful player."

An evening came when I went on auto-self-destruct. I freaked out. Before the night was over, I swallowed most of a bottle of prescription downers. I wanted to die ... but was also scared of the "big step out". I spit some of the pills into the toilet at the last minute. Enough medication made it's way into my system to intensify my delirium. Later I tried to stab myself with a kitchen knife, but the knife wouldn't go in. I really didn't want to die ... I just didn't want to live. While yelling at Jill, I picked up a water glass, and slammed it on a kitchen counter. Glass exploded and mangled my right hand, cutting the tendon in my little finger, and slicing deep into my palm. Blood shot all over. Jill was uncontrollably crying, and ran out of the house to the neighbors. Soon, I was all by myself in a fog world, only to be aroused by faceless cops who took me to a hospital. I woke up in a small room with padded walls. My right hand had a huge bandage on it. It was the Mental Health Section of Mercy Hospital ... a real live nuthouse ... and I was a real live ego-shattered suicidal basket case.

I don't remember much of the first few days at Mercy. They had me on some kind of medication, which made me sleep most of the time. I remember some counselor, or maybe he was an orderly or something, because he was young ... but anyway the whole time I talked to him, I cried like a baby. I didn't even care. All walls had come down. Then I slept some more. Occasionally, I came out of my padded cage to eat, and swallow more little pills. When I finally had enough of my senses to discern the surroundings ... I decided with a chuckle that the real San Diego Zoo was in the basement of Mercy Hospital. Prospective specimens to this place literally had to take an elevator way down to the bottom, like a shaft to hell, to reach the security doors of our loony bin. And then, only the real McCoys were allowed into these exclusive quarters.

At some point, I finally met the unseen master planner of my immediate life. He dictated the combination of drugs to feed me, and had very little to say except, "How are you doing?" He seemed very calm and collected ... wrote a couple things down on a note pad, and was gone for another three or four days. On the other hand, who knows how often he came, I lost track of time. They made sure I signed papers for Medi-Cal stickers. Eventually my body must have adjusted to the medication, because I didn't feel like sleeping all the time. I started to enter into the "general population" and life within the Co-Coos nest.

It was required that we go to group, so I sat on a chair in a circle with about ten of us in a little room. I decided I wasn't going to say anything ... and so did everyone else ... for about five minutes. Then this one girl jumps out of her seat, and sits on the floor facing the wall, and says ... "I'm not sitting on that chair any longer. I'm not even supposed to be here, and if Doris says one ____ing word, I'm going to kick her wimpy little tail!"

This other girl bursts into tears, who I assumed was Doris, and this other hard looking chick said ... "Shut up your ____ing face Sheryl ... if anyone belongs in this hole, it's you. How many times have you come back now? You scrawny little witch!"

Our ringleader in his white uniform finally spoke up, and said ... "How does it make you guys feel the way Sheryl and Connie are talking right now?"

With that question we were off to the races. If only I had smuggled a tape recorder into that room. We had every demonstration of anger, pain, withdrawal, denial, hopelessness, and despair that I could think of. It was the greatest therapy of my life, because as screwed up as I was ... without saying a word, I realized I was probably the sanest person in that room ... except for the counselor ... and he had to be crazy to do this every day for a living.

My shrink talked to me about Jill. He said she was real confused, and considering going back to New York. He warned me that if I wanted anything of our relationship to be salvaged, it couldn't take another blow. I was surprised that she was still in the state. She came to visit, and we talked on the phone. She was working with the doctor. But in my heart I knew it wasn't going to work out ... too many earthquakes.

I got to know a few people, and their circumstances ... like this one middle-aged woman, named Mary. I found out from Sheryl, who talked a mile a minute, 24 hours a day, that this was the second time the lady has been in here. The first time was about seven years prior. This slender attractive woman had come home to discover that her husband had killed three of their children, and then committed suicide himself. She totally snapped, and was in Mercy for months. She was finally discharged. However, now she was one of the silent ones in my regular group sessions. Her only surviving son had recently committed suicide. Mary came home and found him, just like she found the rest of her family years before. I felt the total blankness that emanated from her presence. My heart ached for her.

After about a week or so in the hospital, they let me have three hour passes to go outside. Mercy Hospital sits right next to the 163 Freeway, right at the top of a steep hill coming up out of a huge canyon. Jack Murphy Stadium, hotels, and the 8 Freeway lay down in the expanse below. Balbao Park was a short distance away in the opposite direction. I walked down by the Freeway overpass, and climbed off the side, down into the landscaping. It was like a jungle in there with huge bushes and trees. Like a little kid, I worked my way through the underbrush until I found an opening where I could see everything. There was a steep concrete wall directly below me. The freeway was about twenty or thirty feet down, cut into the side of the hill, and the cars couldn't see me. No one from above could see me either, because of the lush green canopy above me. I sat there for hours during the next two weeks, just thinking, and watching the traffic file past. I loved that spot.

The psychiatrist strolled in one day with his clipboard, and called me into a private room. He asked me a lot of questions, besides "How are you doing?" and he seemed like a nice enough man. The thought hit me, and I asked him … "Do you believe in God?" It was the first time I saw him get rattled. In all our other encounters he was the picture of Mr. Control … calm, soft-spoken, and very professional. Now for some reason, he got all stiff and defensive, and finally said … "What does that have to do with anything? Why do you ask?"

"I don't know. It's just that I'm in this place with my life a total mess, and you are trying to fix me, and seem to have it all together. I was just curious if you believed in God," I answered.

He was still very uncomfortable, but continued … "Well, it really has no bearing on anything, but no, I personally am an atheist. I don't believe there is a God per say."

A weekend was coming up, and I was given a weekend pass to go home. Jill came to the hospital, and the doctor gave us a ride to our place in his new Mercedes. It was the first one I ever rode in. I asked him how he liked it, and he gave us a humble speech on what a great turning radius it has for a large car. Pretty soon we were back at our little abode with Buku and Partner, our little puppies.

The place was all fixed up. Jill had prepared a candlelit dinner with a bottle of wine and all the trimmings. It was just like when we first met. We spent a perfect weekend together. On Sunday night, when it was getting close to the time for me to return, Jill said ... "What now my love?"

I told her ... "Jill, I love you, and will never forget you, but this is good-by. You need to go back to New York. I'm going back to my nut house, and eventually we'll both be all right. Please take care of yourself. I'm sorry for all the grief I caused you."

Jill was crying and held on to me, and I kissed her good-by, and said ... "I gotta go ... I love you."

I walked out of the house into the dark. I was numb. I looked back, and the last glimpse I saw of Jill was through the window. I walked like a zombie in the dark to a distant bus stop. A nice young black guy was waiting there also, and said ... "How's it going my good man. Life treating you OK?"

I looked into his friendly eyes, and said ... "It's just a bowl of cherries."

CHAPTER 19

"I GOT A PLAN"

In the State of California if you're over 21 years old, they can't keep you in a mental health hospital, without your consent after a few days. That is, unless you've broken the law, or pose some kind of threat to yourself or others. I had signed a consent form to stay past the initial 72 hours. Not that I enjoyed Mercy Hospital ... I just knew I needed a little help. Not only did my brain need some mending, but I was also having a real trial learning to be ambidextrous. The tendon I had cut left my little finger without movement of any kind, plus I had stitches, and a huge bandage to contend with. Eating and writing left-handed didn't come easy. So anyway, I had started my second or third week in Mercy. It seemed like another lifetime ago, when the cops had taken me to the emergency room.

The shrink brought me a letter from Jill. She wrote in part ...

"I'm going back to New York and hopefully we will both heal up. If you truly don't want anything to do with me ever again, I understand. I love you and love the way you genuinely care about people. I am so jealous. If I am carrying your child I want you to never worry about him or her. I will care and love this child with all my heart. Please let me know how you are doing. Love, Jill

What a radical relationship we had had. Jill is such a neat person. But, I knew it was history for us. I'm glad it ended on the note it did. A romantic candlelit weekend is probably not the normal way to end a relationship. The glimpse of her through the window, as I left in the dark, was the last time I ever saw her. I'll never forget that moment.

Although I had never cheated on Jill, (after we started living together) ... I had in the past never been completely faithful to any girlfriend, or especially to my X-wife. I figured it had finally caught up with me, and I got what I deserved. Like the street says, "What comes around - goes around". In her defense, I practically drove Jill away. Self-destructive tendencies? Probably.

Back in Mercy Hospital, I was having lunch, when Sheryl and a pretty girl named Carla, came and sat across from me. Carla was 18 years old, real petite and quiet. We were joking around and having a fun conversation ... making out like everyone in the place was nuts except for us. I think the meds made me a little more uninhibited, because I leaned forward, and boldly announced to Carla ... "I'd like to sleep with you sometime." She immediately shot me down, and said, "Thanks for the invitation, but the feeling is not mutual."

The rejection didn't bother me at all. The next day I spent a lot of time with Carla, and found out why she was in Mercy. When she was fourteen years old she had a baby. A baby having a baby. Her little girl was now four years old. Carla said she was always pretty shy and timid. After having her child she dropped out of school, and had a real hard time with life in general.

She tried to get a job, but said ... "Every time I would try to even fill out an application, I would get so nervous that I couldn't fill it out. My hand would start shaking, and I would just leave. I went to a counselor who talked me into coming in here. He wants me to take a break from everything, and concentrate on healing up."

Broken people talking to broken people. Pretty soon Carla changed her mind about my proposition, and we became nut-house lovers. She snuck into my room after lights out, and I took her to my jungle hideout by the freeway. I bought some wine at a nearby liquor store, and we threw our own ... "me Tarzan ... you Jane " party. I hate to admit it, but Carla was the best medicine for getting over Jill, that the doctor didn't order.

One night several of us got an evening pass to go to a concert at Balboa Park. It was a free concert, and the park is walking distance from the hospital. Sheryl, who had become my buddy, Carla, another guy, and myself all hiked over to the concert hall. We didn't have any drugs, but we pooled our money, and bought a pint of hard liquor to smuggle inside. I forget who was playing, but it was packed out. The music was super loud. The whole place smelled like pot. People were passing joints around from every direction. It was a wild concert. San Diego is radical.

A real friendly girl was sitting next to me, and her boyfriend passed me a pipe. The girl whispered in my ear … "Try this, its some bitching pot laced with morphine."

I never heard of that combination before. We all smoked a couple bowls and got really loaded. Pretty soon, the girl asked me … "Where are you guys from?"

I raised my eyebrows, and looked at Carla. She started laughing. I slowly looked back at our generous friends, and said … "You wouldn't believe me if I told you."

"Hey dude, you'd be surprised what I believe. Come on … where are you guys from?"

I looked back at my line of companions, and all four of us started cracking up. Pretty soon I had tears in my eyes from laughing so hard, but I cleared my throat, and told my new friends … "OK, the truth is, we're from the ____ing nut house."

It was hilarious. They didn't believe us at all, and figured we were just tripping on the drugs. For sure! We laughed, and laughed, and laughed. We bought some pop to mix with our liquor, and shared that with our friends. We had a crazy old time.

We had to be back by 11:30, and I'll never forget walking back to that hospital. When we got on the elevator, it reminded me of the spaceship in 2001. I was so loaded I thought it was never going to stop going down. Finally Hal opened the door, and we walked down this massive hall to another silent metallic door with a lone buzzer on the wall. Before I pressed the button, I told everyone … "This is it … we have to take these ____-eating grins off our faces … and be 'normal'!!" We all rose to the occasion, signed in, and faked them out real good.

One day the staff called everyone into a main room. We had a big group therapy session, instead of our individual small ones. As usual, I didn't say much of anything, but this one stout shorthaired guy, in his late twenties or early thirties, was offering his opinion all the time. At first I thought maybe he was a frustrated bully, or control freak, until I got to know him. His name was Charles Howell. He came and ate lunch at my table the next day.

During the meal, he told me … "What a picnic this place is! I voluntarily checked in, hoping "the powers that be", will have a little mercy on me. I was thrown in jail with my third DUI in a row, and they are trying to disbar me from my law practice. If they do that, I'm screwed. I'm taking anabuse again, but I might have cooked my goose this time. On the other hand, I don't know how long I can put up with this crap around here. How long have you been here?"

"About two and a half weeks."

Charles wanted to know my story, and I gave him the short version. We hung out quite a bit in our free time. He was real interested in my lifestyle of hitchhiking cross-country, and other adventures.

One day he said ... "That's my main problem. I feel like I missed out on life. I've never done any of the things you've done. I started going with my wife when we were only 15 and 16, and then we got married a couple years later. I went to college and law school. I worked my tail off there, and now I work even more, at the tune of about 60 or 70 hours a week. I mean I enjoy the financial benefits, but I'd give anything to just be free. There has to be more to life than this ridiculous little cubical bull-____ routine. Don't get me wrong, I love my wife, but she knows I'm not happy. The drinking is way out of hand. A couple weeks ago, I woke up beside my car on the side of the road, and didn't even know how I got there."

Charles asked me to get a pass, and go with him on some errands the next day. We took off in his sporty car, and the first place we went was to a grocery store, where he bought a couple bags of groceries. Then we took them to a family, who he informed me, were clients of his. I never did figure out the story behind all that, and didn't ask ... but the middle-aged woman was very happy that Charles brought the food.

Our second stop was along a middle class street, lined with storefronts. Charles parked and said ... "I'm going inside to get a massage, and a little tail. Here's forty dollars for you. You don't have to pay me back. We deserve a break."

I looked at the money in his hand, and said ... "You mean your going to pay $80 for us to get laid by a couple whores? Man Charles, I've been so broke lately, that I can't imagine forking out that much money. I'll just wait here for you ... its no problem."

He didn't say anything for a minute, so I continued ... "If that extra $40 is burning a hole in your pocket ... I could use a little loan right now, more than sex."

Charles just looked at me. It was obvious that he felt foolish. When I realized the struggle he was having, I insisted that he go on inside, but he changed his mind. He gave me the money, and asked me to help remodel the basement to his house, saying I could earn some cash when I leave the hospital.

We drove across town to Point Loma. As we headed toward the ocean, through an upscale residential area, the scenery got more and more beautiful. Most every yard had manicured tropical landscaping. I couldn't imagine how much the huge houses cost. We finally pulled up to a castle of a home. It was Charles'.

The house was three stories, with a separate garage, swimming pool, and the whole nine yards. Charles gave the grand tour, and then showed me the basement. He was fixing it up like an expensive bar-lounge combination. It looked about 90% finished. I loved it. He had a pool table with a cool leaded glass hanging light, expensive electrical beer signs all around, along with a long first class carved wooden bar and stools. Everything was top notch. He had bought the lumber off an old weathered barn, and paid to have all the paint scraped off. He wanted me to help veneer all the walls with the rustic looking planks. I was game.

I only stayed a few more days in Mercy Hospital. Long enough to finish a mug, which I made out of clay on a potters wheel, painted with glazes, and fired in a little kiln. (Actually, a staff member fired it for me after I left.) I would miss a few things around here ... like the ping-pong games, beating each other with flexible bats ... to release our pent up aggression ... and especially all the nut-house clowns, with their hilarious one-liners. What a trippy place down here in the basement of Mercy Hospital. Charles had baled out before I did. He couldn't take the place. Carla had gone home also.

One parting memory that has always stuck in my mind happened at the dinner table a few days before I left. It concerned this beautiful young blond, who never said a word. A lot of the patients were quiet and withdrawn, but this girl just stared into space, and never made a sound. I figured she must have been a LSD casualty or something. This particular evening she was picking at her food like normal, with a gal (staff person), who helped her eat. She probably only weighed about

100 pounds or less. It was relatively quiet, when suddenly, out of the blue, she threw her tray of food into the air ... and simultaneously let out a blood-curdling scream at the top of her lungs. Silverware, food, broken glass, and the tray were crashing everywhere while she clung to her chair with both arms locked at her sides in one continuous scream. It sounded like she was getting murdered.

Several other staff people ran to her as she continued to scream non-stop. The hair on my neck was standing absolutely straight up. It was the most radical gut wrenching screams I ever heard. They were trying to pry her loose from her chair ... but she wouldn't let go. Finally they got her loose and carried her, kicking and screaming, out one of the metal doors. I couldn't imagine such a tiny girl having so much volume. After the heavy door closed, we could still hear the muffled screams for a while, and then there was silence.

Everyone in the dining area just sat there for a stunned minute or two in total silence, and then this one clown loudly says ... **"Well ! ! ! Who in the ____ does she think she is!!?"**

Too much ... what an experience Mercy Hospital was. I'll definitely never forget it ... and I'll never forget my fellow hurting sojourners. I fear greatly for most of them.

They released me to a halfway house in Chula Vista, a few miles south of San Diego proper. The place had been a single story motel. It was nicknamed "Vista". The doctor suggested I stay there for a period, or at least until my hand healed up. He emphasized that until I got on my feet I wouldn't have to worry about "a hot and a cot". The food was edible, and I did get my own room. They continued feeding us little pills with each meal. A specialist back at Mercy Hospital was wanting to do a tendon graft on me. He suggested taking one of the two main tendons from my arm, and tie it into my hand, and up my little finger. After giving me a lesson on evolution, (why humans only need one tendon in their arm), I agreed to have the operation. Otherwise, my little finger would be hanging on my hand like a piece of rubber. Nevertheless, I had to wait until I was completely healed up before they could do the surgery. Being at the half way house was a good deal for me, but it was another trip in itself.

I settled in at Vista for a couple days, and then took a bus to Charles's house. I had already helped him a time or two on his project, met his wife, and had stored my belongings under his rear deck. This particular day he told me that no one would be home until later that day, but Charles left the rear kitchen door open for me. On the long bus ride, I noticed a pretty girl sitting by herself up ahead of me. The bus was almost empty, and I went up and sat by her. Her name was Shannon, and she had boarded the wrong bus. It was late morning and after talking awhile, I invited her to spend the day with me. She agreed.

I told her I was helping a friend fix up his basement. Shannon about freaked when we walked up to Charlie's massive house, and into the kitchen. The house was so beautiful. I gave her the now familiar grand tour that I had recently taken. She was really impressed. We spent the whole day together surrounded by luxury … getting to know each other. It felt like I owned the place. Just before Charles's wife was scheduled to come home from her job, I changed my mind about doing any remodeling, and Shannon and I split. Eventually we took separate busses. I got her phone number, and gave her my phone number in Chula Vista.

Although Shannon was a bright spot during those days, I was doing some real soul searching in my abundant free time. Here I was 25 years old, in a strange city, completely broke, with a crippled hand, and mending heart. For months, since arriving in San Diego, I had never let anyone in my family back east, or friends in LA, know where I was. Especially after ending up in Mercy Hospital, and now in a half way house. I was a stranger in a strange land. I figured this had to be the bottom for me, but discovered that life goes on … even at the bottom. I lost my fear of disasters.

One day I walked to the library in Chula Vista, and checked out some art books. I brought them back to my little dimly lit room. One book was on Leonardo da Vinci. I really got into his life history. I've always loved his art. He became my favorite artist after I read the book about him. There were lots of pictures of his paintings, and drawings and sculptures. One painting was a self-portrait when he was an old bearded man. It captured my imagination. I started drawing some of the characters in his paintings with pencil. While drawing, I had this very, very strange experience … I felt like I had drawn that person before. It was really weird, but the feeling didn't go away. I could practically visualize this one kid in 3 D full-life color. I didn't lose any sleep over it, but it really made me wonder.

The County or State had assigned a caseworker, and she came by to check on me. I gave her a sob story, which was all true ... but seasoned with generous amounts of gloom and doom, stitches and heartbreak ... far above what I was actually feeling at the time. I wanted to make sure I stayed eligible for a while longer. However, after she left, I really did feel super depressed. Although the bottom was not so much to be feared ... I was getting sick of grubbing around for a pack of cigarettes, or my next meal.

I sat around and thought and thought about my life. Suddenly, in that little room in Chula Vista, California, I developed a plan. I made the strongest commitment to myself that I had ever made. I felt like the old Wild West Doc Holliday ... "I have absolutely nothing to lose, and don't give a flying ____ anyway."

I decided that starting with nothing but my wits, and a little welfare money, I was going to get into mainstream drug trafficking ... if it killed me. I was going to focus all my time ... all my energy ... all of my life toward that goal. Total commitment. I was going to see how far I could take this thing ... and who knows ... I might even beat the system after all. I had tasted the fruit of small-time dealing, and realized the incredible financial opportunities, if you're willing enough, or crazy enough to risk your freedom and your life. I was in ... both feet ... down and dirty ... "Let's play jeopardy mother ____ers!"

From my little nut-house room in Chula Vista, I was about to embark on a radical adventure that should have done me in. The next two years of my life would explode. I didn't care, but for sure, I was squarely on ... **THE ROAD TO OBLIVION.**

PART II

"LA MESA"

Ernesto

CHAPTER 20

"ALONE IN T.J"

A shovel full of dirt came flying through the air, down the deep rectangular shaft, and hit the top of a casket with a muffled thud. The sound rising from his mother's wooden casket was the most shocking moment of the fourteen year olds' life. It became imprinted on his mind and aching heart. Young Ernesto Hernandez knew in that instant that he was totally alone ... totally alone in the world ... totally alone in the dirt streets of Tijuana, Mexico. Even though he had relatives surrounding the grave, he knew he was alone. The shovels continued to fill the hole and cover his mother forever. Numbness filled his being. It was 1956, and T.J. was just a small border town a little south of San Diego. Ernesto followed his relatives to a house. His wheeling and dealing Uncle Phillip proceeded to get them both drunk ... but the stinging hard liquor didn't take away the emptiness.

Elena Orosco was the first death in the Orosco family after they settled in Tijuana. Her funeral was about the only time the local relatives all gathered together in one place. The family patriarch, Uncle Henry was there. The elderly Carmen, Uncle Henry's sister and Ernesto's grandmother was also there. She had watched her daughter slowly waste away from cancer. Now a daughter was gone. Her surviving children, Consuelo, Ralph, John, and Phillip, Ernesto's tios and tias, said their goodbyes to their sister. Ernesto's young cousins were there, Angela, Henry, and Rudy, as well as Ernesto's grieving young sister, Dora, and his two-year-old baby brother, Ricardo. What would they do now?

Ernesto knew his relatives would help as much as they could, but his street-wise teenage senses also knew how out of control most of their worlds were. Flashy Uncle Phillip is a drug dealer among other things. Connie and his mother had both pulled tours of duty at local nightclubs. They did what they had to do to survive. It was a hard life in Tijuana. Ernesto would have to look out for his sister and baby brother. There was no real father.

It's an interesting story how the Orozco family ended up in Tijuana, Mexico. About the time that my grandfather, Ira McDonald was in West Virginia, Ernesto's Uncle Henry was in the merchant marines. For long periods of time he lived around the world. He lived in Hong Kong, Europe, Brazil, Alaska, New York, and all over during his seagoing career. He told me that as a young man he met some Confederate soldiers who had fled to Rio de Janeiro after the American Civil War. He said there were a lot of them in Rio at that time. Eventually he took a job in Fontana, California managing a ranch. He spoke excellent English. He brought his sister Carmen, and her young children from Mexico City to live on the ranch with him. It was somewhere around the year 1924.

Consuelo Orozco was just a baby when Uncle Henry moved the family to Fontana, California. She grew up with her brothers and sister on that ranch. Eventually she boarded a country school bus with the other local kids, and went to elementary school in San Bernardino. She never even learned to speak Spanish. America was her home. When she was fourteen years old, Uncle Henry decided to visit some relatives in Mexico City. They stayed down south visiting with their relatives for several months; like many Mexican families living in America do ... they visit for months not weeks.

The border had always been wide open, and Uncle Henry never had a problem going back and forth between the two countries ... but as the Orosco family attempted to return to their home in Fontana, they were refused entry into the United States. The immigration laws had changed, and it was no longer an open border. Connie was devastated. She was stuck in Nogales, Mexico with her relatives, and everyone was totally broke. She told me ... "I couldn't even speak Spanish, not even to my own mother."

At age fifteen Connie got married. Connie Orosco became Consuelo Brown. She met and married an older American man. She lived with Mr. Brown for only a short time, but then returned to her family in Mexico. She was pregnant but never lived with Mr. Brown again. She gave birth to her oldest son in Nogales, and named him Henry. He was born in 1940.

Shortly after that, the entire family moved to Tijuana, Mexico. Eventually Connie added two more children from different relationships to her family, Rudy and Angela. Her brother Ralph went down into southern Mexico and disappeared. John somehow became a college professor in Mexico City years later. But the youngest brother Phillip, stayed in T.J. and fell into a life of drugs and crime. He somewhat helped Connie and her sister Elena, as well as his mother. They all struggled to survive. Tijuana possesses a bagful of harsh realities that only third world survivors can fully relate to.

Connie's slightly older sister, Elena Orozco gave birth to Ernesto David Hernandez on April 22nd, 1943. (Little did young Ernesto or I know … but someday our future lives would be intricately entwined … to say the least.) Back in the forties in Mexico, it was another world. Ernesto's mother Elena never legally married. Nevertheless, she was a very protective mother to Ernesto and his sister Dora, who was four years younger, and to little Ricardo who came along a distant twelve years later. She managed to send them to school and keep food on the table. Still, her children never knew a close mother-son, or mother-daughter relationship. Ernesto was always in the streets in the neighborhood.

When Ernesto was around five years old, he had an encounter with his grandfather that put an indelible stamp upon his life. I asked him about it recently, and about his early years in Mexico. He told me in his interesting version of the English language ...

"When I was a little kid about five, I lived around some of my father's family in Tijuana. I met this other young kid the same age, and learned that he was my cousin. One day he invite me to meet my granddad. It sounded fine because I knew who he was. Nobody in my family ever told me anything about him, and I never asked anything. But I knew he was my granddad. I always saw him from a distance. People in the neighborhood told me.

So the first time that I came into my grandfather's house, he really put me down. He told me that in his house there was no room for a "bastard". So that was the first and last time that I talked to him. That was the first time I heard that word. I asked my friends what the meaning was. I knew it was something wrong or hard, because I didn't feel right when the guy use it. When they told me what it means ... I knew I did something wrong ... because this guy don't like me. That word haunted me for years and years.

As a little kid, when I heard the word "bastard" it made me angry. Later on I decided it was not worth fighting. If someone said that I was a bastard, I said ... "Yeah that's right!" It became part of my life ... being hard and mean. That's a bastard ... being hard and mean. So I grew up like that. I never saw my grandfather again. I never even walked on that side of the street again.

One of the biggest blows as a kid happened when I was about nine. My mother was sick and couldn't go to work that day. I knew what kind of work my mom did. That she worked in a bar. I could ignore people when they would talk about my mom working in a bar. I could ignore things that I heard the ladies do. My mother was really sick and needed money that day. She gave me a bunch of tokens, stamped pieces of paper, from the bar, and sent me to change them for her. She had never let me go there before. You can ignore things, but when you go to the bar and ask for the money ... you knew that she was living a life not even worth mentioning.

I never knew what a real family was, but then for a while my mother met a man named Manuel. He is my little brother's father, and for three years he was my step-dad. We all lived together. From the time I was about eleven until I was fourteen it was like a family. I had a mother and father, sister and little brother. It was the best time of my childhood. But then my mother got real sick and died. Manuel couldn't handle it. He really loved my mom, and when she died he fell apart. He hit the bottle and we ended up at my Aunt Connie's house with my Grandma, and a house full of relatives. My sister Dora finally went with her Godmother to live.

My aunt's house was real small and we were poor. There were seven of us living with Connie … my Grandma Carmen, my cousins … Henry, Rudy, Angela … my brother Ricardo, and me. Nothing was free … everybody has to work … everybody has to eat. We lived there for three years. At the end of the six months of my mother dying, I asked my uncle Phillip, because he was kind of in charge of the family … I said … 'I want to study'.

He told me … 'You want to go to school and study… but then your brother needs to eat … you need to make a decision.'

I understood what he means. I started to work on the streets of T.J. when I was fourteen. I quit any idea of going to school and I decided to work. I didn't have any more school after I was fourteen. I just keep on reading books. I had always read the magazines about wrestlers. Ever since I was a little kid I wanted to be a wrestler like the pictures I saw. Our house was only a block away from Revolution Blvd, and I liked the bright lights, and Jai Alai, and all the people … and the action. There was the bullring and Caliente, which is the big racetrack, and then the tourists. It was time to hustle. Everything seemed normal to me."

Ernesto continued his story about his life in Tijuana, Mexico.

"One thing I never liked was physical labor. I improved my English. I worked in Curio shops on Revolution Blvd. I worked like an errand boy. I do this and that for guys making money. Drug dealers. Pimps. Anybody that needed a favor … I was there for them. Even Phillip, my uncle. At first he taught me to go into stores and steal, and shoplift. He taught me the trade as a kid. I did small robberies … mostly from people I knew. Anything that was safe. Then Phillip began to use me for drug drops. Not big deals, but it was a beginning. He started with pills and pot. Later on he introduced me to powders. Heroin and coke. He taught me how to fold the papers ... how to use the spoon ... how to use the measuring scale. He was a good teacher.

I made money and I liked the money, but I never really saved any. As much as I got, I gave away. I was very careless with the dollars. I gave Connie money. Everybody had to pay at the house. Like I said, it never really felt like a family with my cousins. It was more like a boarding house. Everyone was going in and out. As a matter of fact, I never got along with my cousins. They never got along with me. It was that way even before my mother died. After she died it was worse, because I was like the guest that you don't want.

I didn't like it ... they didn't like it ... so we would fight. Every time I had a chance to have a problem with Henry or Rudy, I would take them on. Sometimes the two of them at once. It was one of the reasons I improve my wrestling skills ... is through my cousins. They were good guys to practice on. Henry was three years older, and I was a year older than Rudy."

I interrupted and asked Ernesto ... "Did they ever get the best of you?"

He said ... "They always got the best of me."

I was surprised and asked again ... "They always got the best of you, they always won?"

Ernesto said ... "No, I always won."

I explained to Ernesto . . . "In America, when someone gets the best of you ... it means they won."

Ernesto thought for a second and said ... "No, in Mexico it's different."

He continued ... "I usually practiced my wrestling holds on them. But then there were times when we had good times together. Times when there was peace in the camp. That didn't last too much, but sometimes there was good times. Henry and Rudy never got involved with drugs or anything. They always got good jobs. For me, I didn't like people giving orders, so that's why I didn't like that kind of job where you're suppose to submit to your bosses. I was too independent. I think I was very ambitious. I learned that if you keep yourself in one job, you never learn very much. I wanted to be my own boss. That's what I did.

When I was seventeen everybody wanted to move out. Connie was trying to do her own thing. She was thirty-five or thirty-seven and still young ... so she decide to move away from us. I ended up living with my grandma. Everybody was splitting. I was single. So I lived with my grandma and Phillip for a year. I wasn't working for my uncle anymore. I had graduated from his trade school. He was doing his own thing ... I was doing my own thing. He was always my hero, but now he kept his distance, and I kept mine. I was independent. It was not easy to handle me. I was a hot potato. I had my own dreams and one of them was to be a professional wrestler.

Through the years, I knew where the gym was. The gym was in Zona Norte. It's an area of Tijuana. It's like a red-light district. I remember when I was about ten the guy told me, 'when you have a body, come back and I'll teach you'. It took about seven years to develop a body. So I went up to the gym and tell the guy ... 'Big enough now?' By that time I was six feet, and almost two hundred pounds. The guy ... his name was Ichero wanted to help me. He began to teach me. He had been a professional wrestler and was now a trainer. I worked at his gym and other gyms, lifting weights, training. Then another guy came up from down south of Mexico. He began to train us.

I was surviving, and all the time taking care of my young brother

Ricardo. My sister Dora had a real hard time also, but she was five years older, and didn't need as much help as Ricardo. I turned a professional wrestler when I was 19. It was a little bit before I marry the first time. I was only twenty when I got married. I left my grandmothers at that time. Ricardo came with me. My brother was with me all the time. He was six years old now. He was ready to go to school.

I had met a young girl in my neighborhood. I was the guy who married the girl next door. We lived happily maybe a day. No … we spent four years of a good marriage. I was straight with her for those four years … no other ladies. We had two kids. The firstborn was when I was 20. We married and the first one came. It was my daughter Elena. A year or so later came Ernie. We were living with my wife's mom, who was working and kind of in charge. I was working at a couple gas stations besides my wrestling career. It was good money at the gas station. We would cheat the tourists with their change. I also worked as a bouncer in nightclubs, and enjoyed beating up American marines. They fight pretty good. I was also still dealing drugs a little besides.

It was a heavy load to carry … being a wrestler and having nice girls around. So finally I was no more honest with my wife. I started running around again, and everything began to crumble. So we got separated, and I ended up having a huge problem with the law. It was also the same time my X-wife started to become a cop. I became a criminal … and she became a cop.

EL PUEBLITO

My cousin Henry came into the picture again. He was going to steal something from his work and from his government job. It was a bunch of copper. Henry already had been stealing it before, and other guys from his work were doing the same thing. I didn't know anything about it. One day we were drinking at Henry's place and we ran out of beers. Henry said he was going to get some money from a friend, and he needed to stop at his work. My young cousin Rudy, Phillips son, not Connie's son, was also with us. He was only around 15 or 16. I went along with Henry only for the ride. I didn't know anything about a robbery. He went to his work to steal the copper. But it was a set-up, because the cops knew somebody was stealing things on the weekends. They were waiting. We got caught right there at his work, and we end up in La Ocho, the 8th street jail. We stay there 15 days.

Henry stayed around 7 days, and he point the finger to me and Rudy. We didn't have anything to do with it. But that's how things came out. I end up doing time in La Mesa that I'm not supposed to do, because I didn't do anything wrong. I was there 3 months, and I came out of the prison with a fianza (bail). I had to pay twenty-five hundred dollars. It was real hard to find that money. I was free for two years fighting the case. I got a lawyer. I fight it, and I was sure I would win the case. My lawyer told me all along we were going to beat the charges. But then I think Henry made some kind of deal. I don't know how it came out, but I was the only one who did the time. One day I was at my work, and the Federales came and took me to the prison. They told me, "you're done, you lost the case" … and they took me directly to La Mesa. I spent from 1970 till 1973 in La Mesa. Three years.

I already knew what La Mesa was like from the 3 months I did inside. Besides, I had friends there. Prison was not something I feared … I didn't like it, but I didn't fear it. I knew I had to do something in La Mesa to survive, so I became connected. I was not broke when I came into the prison. I had been dealing more heavily and wrestling. I had cash and friends. Plus I had Yoli with me. I was living with her right before I came inside the second time. She helped me and brought me things. She even lived with me inside from time to time. It was a common thing. We had two kids during my time in La Mesa. A boy and a girl. I named the boy Omar, and the girl Jasmine.

I bought a caraca in about a week after I arrived. I started working for the big guys inside La Mesa. I started with small stuff to prove I was the man they were looking for. That's how you start being connected. They give you small deals, and see if you can handle it from there. They want to see if you have connections outside. They want to see if you have good runners. So I had friends. You don't need too many to do business.

That's when Hector came into the picture. He was my main connection on the outside. I would get him drugs from my people on the inside. He would sell them and bring me the money, and I would pay my connections. It's like a chain. We have to trust each other because inside you're like security. If something comes wrong you're the one. There's nowhere to hide. That's why you need someone you can really trust to do business. I worked with different guys inside from Sinaloa.

They liked to front merchandise to me from their people on the outside. We did a lot of business.

I was inside about a year, and then one day I discover Johnny. He was by himself, and I just happened to like the guy. I don't know why. I found out he was an American. So I invite him to my caraca. We became friends. He even used to baby-sit my new kid. He wrote a song in San Quentin called … "Two Cheese Crackers and a Bottle of Beer". It is really funny. Maybe he sang it to my kid. We were roommates until he had enough money to get his own deal. Not too long.

Even when you're connected in prison there are times when you end up broke. I would sometimes pimp my girlfriend at those times. You don't want to be broke inside La Mesa. It seems like when all else fails there is a woman around. People ask how I know the kids are mine, but you know when it happens … even though at that time I didn't care. But I know they're mine.

After a long three years inside El Pueblito, which is what they call La Mesa, I was released in 1973. By now I knew lots of dealers and growers and smugglers. Prison is like a university of crime. I got my degree. I started working right away with some of my connections. I also continued to work with Hector and another guy. We smuggled lots of merchandise to America, and made a lot of money. But I made a big mistake after a few months, and with the money I decided to go out on my own. I took a load and got busted by the border patrol in the States.

"YOU WILL ALWAYS BE A CRIMINAL"

I did everything the right way, but I needed one more guy. I had mules help me cross the kilos. I had a driver in the States to pick up and deliver. We stashed the load in the night like before, and had the car come pick up the load in the morning. We always pick up when all the workers are going to work in the morning in America. We also know when the border patrol makes their run near our different spots. We time it.

When the car arrived, my mules helped me quickly load the kilos and they split. But because I didn't have anyone to pick up the money, I had to go myself with the driver of the American car. Everything was going smooth, and we were well on the way. Then a car came up from behind us with flashing lights. A border patrol had seen our car come into the area with one guy, and come out with two. It was a bust. If they didn't see two guys, there would be no reason to stop our car.

The border patrol pulled us out of the car and handcuffed us. They put us on the dirt. I had a gun under my arm, but they didn't know I had a gun. While I was lying on the ground I told the guy in Spanish that something was hurting me under my arm. The pistol really was hurting me, and I wanted them to take the gun. It was no good to me when you're handcuffed. They made a big fuss about the 38 revolver.

They took me to San Diego County Jail. I only spoke in Spanish. There was some reason why they didn't give me more time. One reason was that the guys from the Treasury Department interviewed me without my lawyer being present. That's why they only gave me a year and a day. The judge was upset because he had a cinch case. He was supposed to give me more time than that. The reason he wanted to give me five years or more … he told me in a real strong way … he said that I am a criminal, and I would never do better than that. The judge was very upset, and said that if he had the chance he would throw the book at me. He was even more upset about the gun. I found out it was from a load that someone stole in San Jose with another bunch of weapons. They made a big deal about the gun, and wanted to know where I got it. In court I had an interpreter, because from the beginning I never let them know I spoke English. At the end the judge looked straight at me, and told me he knew I could understand. I just stared at him.

ON THE RUN

They sent me to Lompoc. I escaped from that prison after about a month with two other guys. We ran full blast down this big hill in the middle of the night. At the bottom of the hill all three of us hit a wire fence for cows. It was so dark we couldn't see the fence until we were flying in the air. All three of us went up at the same time. I hit the dirt hard on the other side of the fence. It was a shock. We ran a long time and hid, and only walked at night. One of the guys split up and one stayed with me. His name was Flaco, which means "skinny". In the day we would sleep and rest.

We hid in some bushes in the morning, and there was a house up a big hill. A German shepherd dog barked at us all day long. My friend was hiding farther down a gully not too far. I heard the lady yell at her dog a bunch of times. I thought for sure that dog was going to get us busted. When night finally came we continued to walk. We walked from Lompoc to Buellton through the hills. We had on prison clothes like Army greens … but we didn't look suspicious because there was a bunch of guys who wore Army greens at that time. A bunch of hippies, and guys from Vietnam wore the same clothes. We made it hitchhiking to Santa Barbara. From Santa Barbara we hitched to Thousand Oaks to the house of a friend of the guy I escaped with. I spent the night in T.O. and a guy drove me to T.J. the next day.

When I got back to Tijuana, I went to look for Jesse, the girl I had been living with. She was a friend of Hector's girlfriend. When I came out of La Mesa I changed ladies. I always told Joli I was going to do it, but she didn't believe it until it happened. Now that I was free again, I got happy and started working. Jesse had what was left of my stash. She also was pregnant. She had a baby girl later.

I went looking for Hector at a club where he hung out. I almost had a huge problem there, because Hector had been cheating with this guy's old lady, and the guy killed him. Hector was dead. The killer and his people thought I was coming for revenge because he was my friend. I told them I didn't even know he was dead … and that it had nothing to do with my business. Hector had a history of messing with other people's women, and it got him killed. I was sad, but there was nothing I could do.

I would have to start all over again. How many times? I knew I could do it. I still had connections. Nothing comes easy. I decided to go visit my friend Johnny back in La Mesa."

CHAPTER 21

"THE STREETS OF SAN DIEGO"

In 1973 from my dim little room in Vista ... my half-way-house of choice ... I took stock of my present situation, and really my whole life ... and was ready for radical. I had enjoyed my limited experiences dealing pot, and decided to kick it up full throttle. Before I could fully implement my master plan, I realized I had to deal with the huge hole I was in. It would take a little time. I thought to myself, "Let's enjoy the ride up from the bottom as much as possible ... because who knows when, **or even if**, we'll ever meet the Wizard". I was willing to die trying. I was totally committed to my plan. I mean for the first time in my life I completely 100% dedicated myself to a course of action. Like Doc Holliday of old, I figured it was a deadly road to walk down ... but what did I have to lose? I figured that this planet is in reality a huge minefield. The casualties are everywhere. Look around. To beat the system ... was to not become a casualty. To beat the system was to be free. Free from a lying hypocritical society. Free from being a working class hero for forty years of meaningless sweat.

By now I had become part of an American subculture ... long hair, student protester, drugs, free-love, rock & roll, hang ten, and power to the people ... but still, I had never been completely on the pavement. That was about to change. At the half way house I was one step away from the street. However, after a couple months or so, I left Chula Vista permanently. I gravitated to Ocean Beach. It was a radical time to be cast into the wind. I was learning real quick how to survive and thrive on practically nothing ... save up a few coins for capital investment whenever possible ... and party hardy. It was a trip.

Before I left Chula Vista, another thing that I did with my free time was to start a journal. I've started many of them during my life since Jr. High school. I don't know why ... I just love to read them years later, although most have long since vanished. Maybe everyone should keep a journal. Time flies so fast. Jill and I started one together from the day we met. She was very faithful in keeping it up ... recording every intimate detail. It was now in a suitcase under Charles' back porch, and she was fast becoming just another memory. While sitting in my little halfway house one day I started to write. Like Leonardo, I've started a thousand projects, but completed very few. This latest journal was just before I left Chula Vista, and only covered five days ... before things became too crazy again.

• • •

TEN BUCKS

June 21, 1973 (Thursday)

Last night went to Ocean Beach with Shannon. We met at the Plaza, and took another bus. We were looking for Longbranch Street, where a big party was supposed to be. Shannon looked cute with a small summer top on. I bought 2 quarts of beer. I had $3 left to my name. We found the party at the end of the street. KGB was suppose to provide some live music, but everyone was just sitting around waiting ... plus drinking and smoking dope. We got a couple hits occasionally off someone's weed.

It was really warm out. It had been around 100 degrees during the day. More and more people kept coming. O.B. people really party. A rare sight is someone over 30. Finally, in front of an apartment building, they set up a band and started playing. Everyone was ready. We kept getting hits off everyone's dope. The cops were standing by, but not busting anyone.

Shannon and I ran out of beer and went back to the store. There was a big line of Ocean Beach hippies, students, and party freaks. We went back with 2 more quarts and a bag of peanuts, which we were definitely putting away. We both had the munchies bad. "Who gets the last peanut, Shannon?" Pretty soon the cops made the band quit ... because of complaints. We sat on the grass and smoked a lot more, and were really getting off. We had fun.

The hundreds of people were yelling, and upset because they shut down the music. Some bearded guy in a 2nd story apartment put his amp outside on a balcony ... and got on his guitar for the crowd. He really got down. Everyone shouted their approval and continued to boogey. Some hippy chicks can really dance. Shannon couldn't drink any more, and I kept finishing it up. Around midnight, the cops started kicking everyone out. Walking down the street with a crowd, I asked this dude if he had a light ... "or perhaps a joint".

He said ... "Wait a minute and I'll fire up."

He lit a J and went around giving super shotguns to everyone, (taking a joint inside his mouth ... fire first, and blowing a thick stream of smoke directly into our mouths). About 10 of us got ripped in someone's front yard. Only in OB would this be normal. In San Diego County, unlike LA, it's also legal to drink on the street. You can sit on a curb, or walk down the sidewalk, or beach or anywhere, and chug-a-lug all you want. It's cool. We caught the very last bus. Shannon had to change busses at the Plaza. I didn't. I passed out after Shannon split, and this dude woke me up, when I got to G Street. It was far out. How did he know? When I got back, Max was there and we rapped for a while. I like him. He was in Patton. (It's an asylum for the criminally insane and hard-core nuts.)

Max woke me up this morning at 7 for breakfast, but I said, "screw it", and went back to sleep. I thought it over, and decided to ditch the summer class at Southwestern. I got a letter from Jill. She's not pregnant. She sent pictures. She wrote around 3 pages. I thought about maybe writing back, but decided to forget it. Some of the pictures brought back hundreds of memories. This life can be dangerous.

I went to the library and went through some art books. I read about da Vinci. I'm going to go back and check them out when I get a library card. I keep wondering if I can do anything really good with my art someday. I have a feeling inside I can, but I wonder if I'm just dreaming.

I have about 90 cents left to my name. I called Shannon. We are going to do something tomorrow. Carla called after supper. She wants to go out Saturday when she gets her mother's car. I want to go to the Del Mar Fair.

Fire On the Mountain

June 22nd, 1973

Almost missed breakfast again this morning. Max and me and a couple other guys snuck into the motel next door, and went swimming last night real late. It felt good after another 100 plus degree-day. This is not normal San Diego weather. I bought a pack of cigarettes, and a Moby Jack to completely zero out my fortune. Twenty-five years old with not one cent to my name. You get a different perspective of this world when you hit the bottom … and it's not all negative.

Max and I are going to the plasma center next week. I did it once while Jill was still here. Our dippy-hippy pot-growing neighbor told me about it. It's a bummer. They take out a pint of blood, take the plasma out, put back the rest … then take out another pint of blood, and do the same. All the time you lay there with a **big** ____ing needle in your arm. About 1 1/2 hrs. Finally, they give you $5. You can do it twice a week.

When I told Max about it, he says … "Hey man, we can go score a lid". After all that hassle, I don't think I want to spend it for a lid, but I didn't say anything.

I called Charles, my lawyer friend, this morning to see if he needs any more help. He is super-busy as usual, and doesn't need any help right now. I was hoping he'd be able to keep me busy, the way he talked when I met him in the hospital. He's been good to me, and I hope he gets his thing together somehow. He's my living proof that money and "things" don't insure happiness, or anything else. It blows my mind to see someone with almost the opposite situation as myself … and find him more ____ed up and miserable.

Got my first welfare check later today and cashed it. Not broke anymore! I opened a savings account trying to stash enough to buy a kilo or two. Put all of the money in the bank except $10. Probably shouldn't have done it, but I couldn't see going through the weekend broke.

Called Shannon and we decided we'd do something down here in Chula Vista. I walked down to Mayfair, and bought a half pint of Seagrams 7 and a bottle of 7 up. Usually don't drink so much hard liquor, but lately it's been fun … mixing our own cocktails … street style. She called back while I was eating, and I returned the call. Her girlfriend answered, and said something came up with Shannon's X-old man, and she split.

That kinda changed the situation. I decided it would be a good night to check out Imperial Beach. They have a band at "The Clock". I hitched down there, and took the booze and $2. It was only 6 and the band didn't start till 8:30. I walked to the pier, sat on the beach, and broke out the Seagrams. I watched the surfers and some little kids playing. It's good for my head to be alone, an outsider to everyone except my own thoughts, and watch the world function on.

The 7-up was warm and didn't make the greatest chaser. The whiskey made me think about John Lewis, and the surfers made me think of Jill. She watched me surf many, many times. I drank half of the whiskey on the beach in an hour or so, and decided to ration it according to the buzz, and not reach my peak by 8 … before the night even got started.

I walked down the pier, and watched the water and surfers directly below. I love the ocean. I smelled a nice odor drift by, and three kids about 17 were firing up a J. I asked for a tote and they turned me on. Went to The Clock, and hid my bottle in the bushes outside. The dude I met the first time I went down there was there, and we talked. I bought a draft at 25 cents a glass until the band started. I bought 3 beers, and played a game of pool (lost), and had $1 left.

The place was still empty, and I was wondering if I'd make it through the evening. I rapped a long time to a waitress. Vicki. She's 23 and a little doll. I decided when the band started, and beer went to 50 cents, to find another way. Vicki got 3 hits of speed from one of the band, and gave me one hit.

I went outside to a 7/11 store and bought 2 more quarts of beer, and a 6 pack for this underage dude, who made up the difference for my beer. Everyone was happy. I went back to the bushes, poured out the 7 up, and filled the bottle with Bud. I put my jean jacket on, and put the bottle inside the arm, under my armpit. The half pint fit easily in the other sleeve.

It was about 8:45, and I could hear the place starting to turn on. I was completely broke … but had a good head start, with half a gal of beer and some whiskey left. I sat inside, got a glass, and checked out the music. The place was really filling up, and I "coolly" slid out the 7up bottle, and filled my glass with beer. The only person around me was some straight looking dude, who looked like a swabby … eating his heart out for one of the foxes on the dance floor. However, he comes over and busts me.

He took the 7-up bottle and apologized, saying … "I'm sorry but that's what I get paid for."

He didn't find the Seagrams. I sipped and sipped on the glass I had left, and finally couldn't take it, and went out back. I grabbed a quart of beer from my stash and walked around. A bunch of people were getting into an old pickup, and a dude yelled for a hit of my beer. I said sure and asked if he had any smoke.

He said … "No, but we just got ripped at a little party up the street. You should check it out."

"Where's it at?"

After chugging some more of my beer he said … "It's in the second apartment building, on the second floor, to the left, the middle door. Ask for Tim, and my name is Larry. Good luck and thanks for the brew compadre!"

The pickup took off like a bat out of hell, with the guys in back hooting and carrying on.

I wasn't sure if I had the right place, but I tapped and hesitantly opened this apartment door. A whole bunch of people were sitting around on the floor talking. Instantly, I forgot all the names I had been told, and stupidly said … " By a chance does anyone have any smoke?"

Everyone was looking at me standing in the door. There was this big pause. I was an inch from the flight mode, when finally this one guy says … "Sure … come in … we can't let a dude get away UNSTONED!!!"

I started laughing, and was in, in a second. He throws me a lid and some zigzag papers. Then they said they'd get out "The Whale". It was a long glass tube, but huge. About 3 1/2" diameter and over a foot long. It was the biggest one I ever saw. Had a little bowl attached for the weed, and of course one little hole on top. You had to hold your finger over the little hole for about 5 big draws to completely fill the glass tube with smoke. The smoke curled around inside the glass and looked cool, until it was a total cloud. The hole you draw from was gigantic, and covers your nose and mouth completely. On the last draw you let go of the little hole and the smoke **flies** into your lungs. You get super hits.

I rolled about 10 joints also. They were playing 2 guitars and having fun. We drank and smoked and rapped and laughed for hours. Another guy showed up also. "In Concert" came on TV, and was warmly welcomed. I couldn't believe how stoned I was, and kept going. The music was great.

The new guy turns out to be their boss, and everyone is selling Kirby vacuum cleaners! It freaked me out. He wants me to come Monday and give it a try. I split half way through "The Midnight Special", and went back to The Clock. I was really wasted. The place was getting ready to close. There were drinks left all over. I drank one.

I tried to get a ride to Chula Vista with no luck. I started walking down the road, looking for Palm Ave, and finally discovered I was on it. That was convenient. I started hitching. When I put my thumb out, my right side seemed to be weightless. It was freaky and I dug it.

I got a ride from a middle-aged guy. He was pretty drunk. Ran a red light. I broke out the remaining quart of beer and we drank. I didn't know if he turned on, but I fired up the J. I had taken one with me from my Kirby party. I told him to pull over, and gave him a shotgun, like the dude did to us in OB. I gave him about 3 giant hits. It was funny. He was so drunk he was game for anything. By the time we got to E Street, he was about as loaded as me and laughing his tail off. We had a riot. He thought I was his best friend or something. He took me all the way home. "See you in the next life dude."

I saved half the joint, and half the Seagrams for Max. He wasn't awake, and I landed up calling Shannon, and gave her a hard time. Adele was working the office, and started giving me a bunch of crap about my beer. I was really out of it, but having fun. Finally made it to my room and crashed

Sat June 23, 1973

I got up with a super hang over around 10:30 A.M. Fragments of last night began to piece together. I remembered Shannon said she would call, and I wondered if she would. I couldn't remember much of the 3AM conversation, but I know it's not the coolest time to call etc. Carla called this morning and wanted to see me. She got her father's car. She got here around 11 AM, and bought me lunch at Jack-in-the-Box, because she didn't want to wait for lunch at Vista. She brought Kisha along. We went to her house, and on the way smoked the half of a joint I saved, plus drank the beer. We really got high, and I wondered how in the heck I ever smoked so much last night. Dynamite weed. We sat around her house and talked to her parents.

Carla's mother fixed homemade tacos, and we all ate. I got so full, I felt terrible. We decided to go swimming at Dan's house (a brother) in N. Park. I asked if we could pick up some of my stuff at Charles' house first. We did. On the way I heard on the radio there was a concert at Balboa Bowl. I wanted to go, but not with Carla. I really like her, but I can tell it would never amount to anything. She has been letting me know she is getting serious, and from what I know of her, she could get hurt. I am no good for her, especially with my plans. She is so sweet, but so naive. I really fear for her, and wish I could be what she needs.

We went to Dan's, but left. I convinced Carla to drive to my place instead of her house. I decided this would be the last time I'd see her. I got a message Shannon called twice. I told Carla I'd be right back, and went to the liquor store and called Shannon. She had been waiting for me to call and I was glad. She said she'd come down about seven. I lied to Carla and said the guy with Kirby was coming to pick me up at seven. At suppertime she split. I felt sad.

Craig, the director, gave me a hard time about last night. Adelle had reported me bringing the beer and all. What chicken-____!

He said … "That's one, you have two."

I said … "What are you going to do … put me in chains and irons?"

____ the small stuff people come up with.

Shannon didn't get here until after 8. We stayed in and talked and drank some beer and had a good time. Around 11 we decided to hitch down to I.B. We got one ride to K Street, and decided it was too late to truck down there. We hitched back and a friend of hers gave us a ride. We bought some more beer and went back to my place. Shannon spent the night.

Sunday June 24, 1973

We woke up around 10:30. I'm really glad Shannon got on the wrong bus when I met her. So far it's been good between us. She has been through some heavy trips herself, but is a survivor. We couldn't get concert tickets for Balboa, but we decided to go sit outside and listen. We took the bus. I asked Shannon if she wanted to get blasted today … and she said "Sure"… so we bought beer, Seagrams, and 7-Up again.

The concert, "Summer Sunday", was packed with freaks. Everyone had a bottle of something and dope. The cops were everywhere, and the place outside of the concert was packed with people in our situation ... no tickets. We drank and got a few hits from a passing number. The cops made us move away, and we landed across the street by a big building. Dudes were trying to climb the fence in several places. A few made it inside the concert without getting caught. Then after awhile a whole mob went for one fence. The cops ran over to stop them, and bottles started flying. A small group of black dudes did the chucking in the beginning. When the cops started banging on a couple innocent people, the whole crowd closed in, and the cops really started swinging their clubs like crazy.

That enraged an even bigger crowd. Guys were letting out war hoops and continuing to barrage the cops with rocks and bottles and curses. They were calling them "____ing pigs" and every name under the sun. A few guys were throwing punches at them, one on one. Lots of heads got busted open, and more SDPD cops came storming in. It was a little riot. One cop was knocked off his motorcycle, as he came flying onto the scene. He and his bike went sliding in circles down the middle of the street, not far from where we were standing. The whole place went crazy. About 10 people got arrested that I could see. It was over in about five minutes. I thought it was pretty stupid over a $5 concert. It was definitely exciting though. Black is beautiful, but those brothers kick started that whole scene, and then disappeared.

Shannon and I walked around the stadium. A girl called at me and said she knew me. I had seen her at a party I went to with Carla. (I'm getting known in San Diego.) Shannon was really high from the booze. I don't think she's used to seven-sevens. On the other side of the stadium, we found a big baseball field, where hundreds of people were sitting. We lay down. A guy sat next to us and pulled out a lid. We got up and smoked and smoked. I saw another guy that I met hitching last week to another concert. He had beer and some weed also.

Shannon and I both fell asleep on the grass ... no blanket or anything. We woke up and the place was nearly empty, and the sun much lower. It was freaky. It turned out they had let everyone into the concert. We went in also. Shannon saw her X there. We stayed until it was almost over and split. I caught a ride with a chick, and Shannon took a bus home. Had a little hassle getting back, but made it. Watched TV until late and crashed. I have 10 cents left of the 10 dollars I started the weekend with. That $10 sure went a long way though.

Got up Monday at eleven. I had dreams of Jill last night. Hope the day comes when there is no feeling left in me for her. I loved Linda as much, years ago, and now it doesn't pull a single string to think of her. I hope the same pattern will hold true for Jill.

I ate lunch … (garbage). Went to the library and spent the afternoon reading more art books. A chick with a UCSD T-shirt and no bra, sat across from me about 4 PM. She was cute and I wanted to talk, but felt weird in the quiet, crowded library. I couldn't concentrate on reading, so I checked out 3 books, and walked back to my little "Nut Commune" on Broadway. Sat here and wrote down all these mini-adventures for the last couple days … until this very moment … while I await some more _____ for supper.

• • •

One person that I mentioned is … Maxwell Franklin Jones. I'll never forget Max. He had been at the half way house for about a year before I arrived. We became real good friends. He always makes me laugh. He looks cool but almost comical with his shoulder length blond hair, billy-goat go-tee, and black top hat. He is shorter than me, but Max is big boned and powerfully built. He told me he was constructed low to the ground for "cornering". He talks real loud. One day he told me how he got sent to Patton …

"I flipped out a couple times after returning from Namn. All the radical crap that happened there, plus all the drugs I was using, put me in a psych-ward. I was pretty messed up for sure. While I was there this black dude jumped me, and started thumping my head. He was a big sucker, and I couldn't do anything. I grabbed this pair of scissors and stabbed him four times in the back. I got a finger in his eye, and tried to spring it. He was messed up **real** bad, but he didn't die. They sent me to Patton. I was there nine months."

Max hadn't been allowed to bring his car to Chula Vista, but finally they allowed him to get it. It was a $50 car … a 1961 Chevy. ("Beats walking.") It ran good, but two of the windows wouldn't roll up. I told Mike about my plan to turn some kilos, and enlisted my first partner. Max's comment was, "Dang straight!" We would sit in our room and party, while doing our ever-compounding arithmetic. Now that I had access to wheels ... it was one step out of our hole.

Max didn't want to totally leave the half way house yet, but he took me to Ocean Beach several times. One day we were in a big line of cars at the McDonalds drive-thru. There were also huge lines of people inside. That's why we decided to drive through. When our turn finally came ... the speaker announced ... "Can I take your order please?"

We gave our order, and then the girl's voice says ... "Would you like a "super-scoop" to go with that order?"

In his booming voice, Max yells back ... "A Super-Scoop ... What the ____ is a Super Scoop???"

I could hear his voice boom throughout McDonalds. The whole place started laughing. I could clearly hear the laughter through the little speaker. The waitress was laughing too, but she politely replied ... "A super-scoop is our new super-sized large french-fries ... would you like to try one Sir?"

Max turns to me, and says with a big grin ... "Well ... do you want a Super-Scoop or not?"

I don't remember what I said ... I was laughing too hard, but also felt like crawling under the seat, on our long wait to the pick-up window. As we drove away I said ... "Jones, you are one crazy mother ____er!"

Immediately defending himself he shot back ... "How in the **heck** do I know what a Super-Scoop is!!"

I hit the streets in Ocean Beach. I could write a whole book about the people and crazy times in just the first few weeks. I slept on the beach, in Jones's car, and at different party houses. I was in an apartment where some guys came home after robbing two sailors at knifepoint, in a phony drug deal. I got to know the president of an outlaw biker club. He had known Jones since he was a little kid, and looked out for him. He was also worried I was going to get Max busted. I met two girls who moved to OB from NY, and lived with them for about a month, getting romantically involved with one of them. I eventually shared an apartment right on the beach with a new party friend, but not for long. I was constantly on the move.

Max had borrowed some money, and together we bought a kilo. We drove up to LA and to the White House, selling our merchandise. It was my return from obscurity. Frank was living with Dale in my old pad. We had a great reunion, playing a nostalgic game of aggravation with

Dale as my partner. Frank helped sell some weed. We also spent time in Malibu with Cliff. Life was almost as crazy for him. He had married Toni, but now they were split up. He was managing a big modern apartment building right on the beach, in addition to his art studio. He was doing real well financially, and bought up the remainder of our pot. He had a girlfriend who was the estranged wife of a Hollywood producer. She was beautiful, but would match anything inside Mercy Hospital. Believe me.

After a few more days, Max and I headed back to San Diego, with two giant air conditioning vents going full blast, and a little extra money. "Let's keep on … keeping on, wild man!"

"I love the streets of San Diego."

CHAPTER 22

"O.B. TO BOULDER"

Ocean Beach made me feel alive. At the end of the main drag was the pier. To the left of the pier you could follow the incredibly beautiful and interesting coast, which is lined with solid rock cliffs, and thousands of tide pools. Eventually, the cliffs get bigger and bigger, until you run into a distant secluded nude beach. To the right of the pier, were the main swimming beaches, lined with fire pits and parking lots. It continued down for a mile or so until you run into a big old jetty. The jetty protects the waterway leading into Mission Bay and Sea World. I walked every inch of the area many times. It was always refreshing.

You could also build fires on the beach, and almost every night there would be parties at one or more of the fire pits. It was a great place to meet people, stay warm, get loaded for free, or whatever, around those crackling fires. Dogs could run free on the beach anytime. Drinking was legal. People were super friendly, and in Ocean Beach there was always, sunshine, surfers, fishermen, and beautiful girls in bikinis. The main drag, Sunset Beach Boulevard, had a card parlor, several taverns, head shops, hangouts, and restaurants. All the beach houses and apartments were of the older variety, not like neighboring Mission Beach or La Joya. The rent was cheap in O.B. and it was hippy heaven.

Someone gave me a stubby little blond puppy with big fluffy ears. I named him Obie, after the town. I loved that little dog, and it adapted perfectly to my lifestyle. It never caused any trouble. I had it fairly trained in no time. Jones finally left Chula Vista, and was living with his elderly mother. He got a little mutt also, which he named Fubar. When I asked where he got a name like that, he said … "It means, ____ed Up Beyond All Recognition." (Poor dog).

I continued to see Shannon from time to time. She was 19 when I met her, and had just broke up with her boyfriend. She got in a car accident while I was still in Chula Vista, and broke her jaw. It was all wired shut … and was liquids through a straw time. She was in a vocational school, at that time, learning to be a dental hygienist. Months later, I found out that she lied to me about the accident. Actually, her X-boyfriend had broken her jaw after seeing us together at the concert. She was afraid to tell me the truth figuring there would be even more trouble. However, I never saw him then or later, or even found out his name. What a jerk.

Shannon told me another sad, sad story one day … "I grew up in Indiana originally," she said, "and when I was nine years old, I was playing in the house, and found my father's gun in a closet. My brother was with me, and while we were playing I accidentally shot and killed my eleven-year-old brother. It was horrible. My parents freaked out, and took me to my aunt's house to live. They said they never wanted to see me again. I haven't seen my parents for ten years now."

Shannon continued her story … "I hated living at my aunts, and ran away. They sent me to other relatives out here in California, but I kept running away. They put me in foster homes for a couple years, and after running from there, they put me in juvenile hall. I have been in continuation schools, and one institution after another, until I was eighteen.

When I was about 14-years old, a couple of the girls in my dorm started fondling me, and caressing me. I didn't know what was going on, but eventually believed it was normal. I was starved for affection. This is probably freaking you out, but I was only with girls until I was 18. My X- boyfriend was the first guy I was ever with, and you are the second."

Shannon had moved into a small house with some friends, a slightly older couple, who lived together. She dropped out of school, and got hired at a massage parlor. Initially, she swore that she only did legitimate massages, although admitted that some of the girls were also prostitutes. After a few months, Shannon was making a lot of money, and doing more than rubdowns. She would give me money, and lend me money. When she moved to her own place, she said I could move in if I wanted to. Her place was outside of OB in another section of central San Diego.

I stayed with Shannon for less than a week, until she started complaining about something. I liked her too much for things to end in some kind of a blow up. Although we had a long intimate relationship, it evolved from lovers to being just good friends … especially as my dealing career gained momentum, and took me out of San Diego more and more. Nevertheless, I always just shook my head, and didn't know what to do for Shannon.

What a rotten hand she has been dealt ... and now things seemed to be going from bad to worse. Her recent choices weren't helping the direction. She also was the second person in my life to offer me heroin. I was shocked to find out she had tried it. I really got on her case about that. She said ... "Calm down ... I only 'chip'. There's no danger of getting hooked if you only do it once in awhile ... come on ... you should do some with me." I didn't bite, but tried to keep tabs on my friend from time to time. We went to see the movie "Jesus Christ Superstar" several times. Altogether, Shannon saw it 14 times. She thought it proved Jesus was a phony. She hates religious people. I loved the music, but thought the movie showed that he had supernatural abilities.

The time came for me to get my hand operated on, and I hitchhiked from Ocean Beach back to Mercy Hospital. Two longhaired characters pulled up in an old car and gave me a ride. The taller guy really looked like a doper. He had super long black hair, a long black beard, and eyes that seemed to be permanently at half-mast. He was big, but looked like he needed to go shoot a cow and eat the whole thing. His face was sunk in, and to me he looked like a Viking who had just been released from Auschwitz. In spite of all that, when he talked he had this deep gentle voice that made me immediately like him.

I was having trouble finding connections for kilos of marijuana at the time. I asked these two guys ... "Do you know where I could score a few kilos of pot?"

The big guy, who was named Mike, said ... "I don't know man. I used to move a lot of weed, but it's been awhile. I got into other things, but could probably hustle you up some. Anyway, I got busted awhile back, and took a little vacation. Right now I have to turn myself in next Tuesday, on a parole violation, and go back for another 90 days. MAN, I hate being locked up!"

At the hospital they pulled the car over, and talked to me for quite awhile longer. Mike said, "Maybe I can help you out, after I'm back on the street again ... and after you heal up from your surgery. Sounds pretty narly there Rog. Looks like we're both going to be out of commission for a while. You take care of yourself, and I'll catch you later on."

With that, they took off. I walked into the hospital and went "under the knife". The next day I was one hurting puppy in a medicated daze ... but was pleasantly surprised when my Ocean Beach girlfriend from New York visited me in the hospital. I had drifted away from her, but she brought me a plant, and a neat card signed with love. It really meant a lot to me. We drifted back together when I got out of the hospital. She rescued me a second time. I was on some pretty powerful pain medication, and had little stitches all over my hand and arm. At the tip of my little finger they drilled a hole in my nail, and there was a wire sticking out of it. I also had a partial cast to keep everything in place. Anyway, my finger looks all crippled now, but at least I can move it. It looks just like Grandpa Ira's little finger.

In a few weeks I was somewhat functioning again, and managed to buy four kilos with money I had scraped up from here, there, and everywhere. I had previously paid Jones back the money he borrowed, plus his share of the profit from our trip to LA. But now his biker friend talked him out of doing any more dealing. It was for the best. Nevertheless, Jones took me to LA, and dropped me off at The White House. I had phoned Frank. He told me that Lacy was taking a vacation from her job, and was driving to Utah to visit friends by herself in her van. She wanted some company.

We talked Lacy into taking us to Boulder, Colorado. I had heard that Boulder was a wild university town, with lots of freaks, and a healthy demand for drugs. She was hesitant about detouring all the way to Colorado, but finally said ... "What the heck!"

We had a good time most of the way, but just before Boulder, Lacy got upset about something, and really coped an attitude. She started snapping at us, and complaining about going all the way to Boulder ... and what if she got busted with all that pot ... and you guys make all the plans without considering me ... "AND IT'S MY ____ING VACATION ... AND MY ____ING VAN !!!"

I finally told her ... "I have to get away from you Lacy. I'd have stayed married if I wanted to listen to this kind of crap! Just drop me off in Boulder. I'll give you some more gas money ... but ____ this!"

She didn't think I was really going to split, but when we got to Boulder I put all my gear in my pack and said ... "Apeterstrain Lacy ... Frank, I'll see you later too."

Frank says ... "Hey man, I'm going with you."

It took Lacy months to forgive me for abandoning her in Colorado, but we made up. However, that day she drove away madder than a wet hen. Frank and I were on foot with over 8 pounds of marijuana in my backpack. It was kind of spooky. About the first thing we did was to carefully stash our gear in some bushes, and take a bunch of one-ounce lids onto the college campus. We were almost broke again and needed some cash. Right there on the University of Colorado campus, we walked around on the sidewalk saying, "You want to buy a lid?" ... to everyone who looked half-way cool to us. Within an hour we sold all that we had on us.

With our pockets full of tens and twenties we celebrated at one of the college hangouts called ... "The Time Out". It was a wild place. Boulder was living up to its reputation. I saw this one spunky longhair that looked like he might be a small time dealer. I went over and asked him if he knew where I could buy a lid of some good pot.

He said ... "Come out in the parking lot to my car in a few minutes. I'm going to talk to my friends for a little while. After you see me leave, wait a few, and come on out. You'll see me."

In a bit, Frank and I were in his car. He started telling me about the lids he had access to, but I stopped him and said ... "Actually, we are in from California, and have some pounds to unload. Do you know anyone who might be interested?"

We drove around and smoked some of my pot. Eventually he took us to an alley entrance of an old two-story house, and had us wait in the car while he went inside. About 10 minutes later, our "contact man", came back and told us to come on inside. We filed through the back door, into a house filled with hippies. There were a couple girls fixing some food in the kitchen. They casually said "hi", and our friend said ... "Follow me".

We pushed our way through some hanging beads, and went down a long hall. A curly headed dude walked past giving us the peace sign, on his way to the kitchen. Pretty soon, we came to a closet door, which our guide opened. Inside the closet, he bent over, pulled back a rug, revealing a trap door, which he lifted up on its hinges. Cool. I was getting into this place more and more ... a Rocky Mountain High White House.

The three of us climbed down a vertical home made ladder into the most psychedelic basement I had ever seen. The whole ceiling was draped with tie-dyed sheets, and a huge parachute. Tons of bold colors and wild shapes hung overhead. Posters were everywhere, along with more beads, candles, and assorted drug paraphernalia. Several incense holders were fully loaded, and sending up their tiny curls of smoke into the confined atmosphere. It smelled like a full-fledged head shop. The floor had old colorful rugs and big pillows. At one end of the room were two guys and a girl sitting on the floor.

A lanky guy with a long black beard and hair to match had us pull up a pillow, as we went through the greeting ritual … in preparation of the official pow-wow. He said, "So you popped in from far off California, huh? Nice. So what kind of goodies did you wanderers bring us today? Is it some Mexican commercial, or something a little more exotic?"

I retraced my steps back to the car, and brought in my backpack. We showed them our kilos, and spent the next hour or so having a party. The San Diego street pot, which was probably just an A grade commercial, had fortunately passed the peace-pipe test. What luck, to find such a good connection so fast. It was uncanny. Within half a day of arriving in Boulder, we had sold everything … plus had a trippy place to crash, and mingle … and come back to. They wanted more on our next run. We were definitely adopted into the tribe with almost celebrity honors. A pretty squaw brought us all some homemade stew to cure our ever increasing munchies.

Our bearded friend was a mover and shaker in the Boulder scene. His name was Steve, and he informed us … "In the future, if I know your coming ahead of time, I can turn a lot of product for you. How do you like my little hide-away office? I kind of dig it down here, and do a bit of biz to boot … but I also manage a rock-n-roll band. Most of the freaks upstairs are either in the band, or shacking up with someone in the band. Pretty dang good local talent. You'll have to come to one of our gigs. Anyway, stay as long as you like. We always have room for another body or two."

Frank and I stayed in Colorado for a while longer, getting to know Steve and company much better, and then hitched back to L.A. Before leaving, I told my new friends in Boulder that I would return for-sure with more merchandise. I still couldn't believe how lucky we were, to immediately find such a perfect outlet. It sure beat selling lids on the university sidewalk. I was super encouraged and energized. My master plan was moving forward. The working capital had more than tripled, in spite of a few serious parties. I could have bought a car, but figured I should invest all of it in pot ... at least one more time, before spending a big hunk on transportation. "Let's shake those dice ... come on seven! Eleven, you'll do just fine ... but then of course ...Vegas will have to wait along with the wheels. You're much too dangerous with my pockets full of money."

In LA I stayed at The White House for a few days. Crazy David came by and invited me over to his place. He had rented a house similar to The White House situation. After staying there a week or so ... that's when I found out, (for the first time, from his girlfriend), that David was into heroin. She told me how she found him overdosed, and almost dead. They filled the bathtub with ice water and threw him in. David was completely blue. He came around a little, and then they walked him around for about an hour or two, and finally got some coffee down him.

David pulled through, and still had his charm intact. His new place was like grand central station. I was lying in bed with an old girlfriend, when another girl came into my room at about 2 AM. She sat on the bed and announced that she lived down the street, and had finally got up enough nerve to come over. She was about 23 and a little bit tipsy. I asked Lynn to go see what everyone else was up to. She shook her head and split. Our bold neighborhood greeter was very sexy, and extremely fit looking. She told me she just got off work, and then leaned over and kissed me. When I asked what she does until 2 A.M. she said ... "I'm a nightclub belly dancer." Things always seemed to be crazy around David.

The next day I got real upset, because a couple of David's friends came in with a van full of super expensive stereo equipment and other things. They had just robbed an exclusive house in Hollywood Hills. Then, to top it off, David came home after they left, and robbed the robbers. His girlfriend and he took everything of value in the whole house, and left the state in his elusive van ... the van that the VW dealer was still actively trying to repossess. I found out where he was heading, because he was having his SSI check sent to a friend of mine, and had contacted her to forward it to an address in Ohio. What a snake.

I had to get out of there, before I got busted or ripped off myself. Luckily, David didn't know about my cash, which was stashed under a mattress. One of David's junkie friends named Warren came by, and I told him I'd give him a hundred bucks to drive me to San Diego. He agreed, but said he had to make a quick stop to collect some money first. He guaranteed me that he wasn't going to score any drugs, and that he already had a fix earlier that day. The more I saw of heroin … the more I hated it. We split and Warren made his stop. He parked his little Toyota, and I waited and waited and waited, inside the little red car for almost two hours. The keys were in the ignition, so finally I took his car and drove off. I made a couple phone calls trying to find out what happened to Warren, and finally discovered that he was in jail. The apartment he visited got raided just as he arrived.

Warren had previously told me that he had just been released from jail, and that the car was his elderly mother's car … who was out of town for another ten days. The little Toyota had lots of miles and years on it. I figured that Warren might be up the river, for who knows how long. I had to get out of LA, and back to Ocean Beach. Nothing felt right in L.A. this time, except maybe the belly dancer. I cranked the Toyota up, and hopped on the 405 Freeway for San Diego. I planned on getting the car back before Warren's mother returned from her trip. However, that little car ended up in all kinds of predicaments over the next couple months.

I finally made it back to O.B. What a relief! I picked up my pup, little Obie, who was rapidly growing, and crashed at a friends' place by the beach. It felt so good to walk barefoot again down the seashore with my dog. The skies were perfectly blue, with the sun shining brightly away. The waves dipped and peaked, curled and crashed, and then finally slid up the sand around my barking and joyful pup. The girls would say …"Oh look how cute he is! What kind is he? He's darling!" I would walk to the long narrow jetty, and loved to see all the starfish hanging on the rocks. They totally fascinated me. For a while, that's exactly what I would do … hang out in Ocean Beach … until I could score another load of kilos.

CHAPTER 23

"MIKE"

The Ocean Beach scene had quickly become a part of me. A few pairs of jeans, lots of T-shirts, cut offs, and a couple nice shirts were the extent of my wardrobe. My hair was way past my shoulders usually back in a long ponytail. Barefoot most of the time ... it was me and my dog. Nevertheless, I felt pretty conservative compared to most of O.B. Like for example, the huge dude I saw hitchhiking down Longbranch Street one bright Southern California morning. His beard was about eight inches long. It hung straight down from a broad face ... and sort of blended together with this super long black hair. In fact, his hair more or less framed his whole upper body. I was thinking ... "Definitely another modern day Viking". As **my** little red Toyota approached the hitchhiker ... suddenly I realized ... it's Mike!!

I pulled over and absolutely could not believe my eyes. Mike looked like he definitely had eaten about half a dozen cows. He probably gained 40 or 50 pounds since he and his friend had dropped me off at the hospital about four months back. Obviously he had served the 90-day sentence. His eyes were no longer at a semi-permanent half- mast ... they were wide open and focused. His sunken face was all filled out. He looked great. I never saw anyone change so much in such a short time. In spite of all the weight gain, he wasn't fat at all ... just big.

He jumped in the car and said ... "Hey Rog ... long time no see! I've been wondering what the heck ever happened to you. I called the numbers you left me, but apparently you've been doing some serious trucking. Did you ever score the kilos you were looking for?"

I said ... "Gee Mike ... I hardly recognized you. Dang, you really look good. Is that what jail house chow does for a guy?"

"Well, I definitely had a bit of a Jones going the last time I saw you.

I kicked cold turkey in jail. It was one serious detox. But yeah, that's what happens when I get clean, I fill out right away. They have me on a program right now. In fact, I just got out of a half way house, but still have to test at the clinic. If I test dirty ... I'm back inside. But ____ that ... I'm not going back. I feel great. So how about you, did you get your arm sewed back together?"

As we drove away I said, "Yeah. See my little finger move? I couldn't do that before. It was a total drag though. My arm got all withered from the cast and all that. Hey man, I did find some kilos and sold them in Boulder, Colorado. It was a radical trip. I made some good contacts plus friends in Ohio want quantities. I've only been back in San Diego for about a week. As a matter of fact, I'm looking to score right now. So come on local boy ... show me where the action is."

Mike laughed and said ... "Pull into the Dairy Queen and let's feed these machines. If you have enough scratch to buy kilos, then I'll let you buy me lunch. I'm sure we can scare up some weed, Rog. It might take a little legwork. Like I told you before, I've been out of the pot scene for years ... but let's eat ... I'm hungry as a ____ing bear! Then we'll make the rounds. I'll show you a side of Diego that outsiders never break into."

Over the next few months, he did just that. Mike was really the first hard core "X-junkie" that I became friends with, (besides David). I had vowed to stay as far away from heroin addicts as possible, but in this case I couldn't help myself ... I really liked Mike. Even the legal establishment had given him break after break ... if for no other reason, than that he was so likable and easy-going. Mike told me that he had been busted three times for sales and possession of heroin, and only did six months in a minimum-security prison. According to him, that was totally unheard of. Nevertheless, short stay or not, he said prison and jail was the worst thing that ever happened to him ... and he was determined to stay away from smack completely.

Mike had grown up in a suburb of San Diego called Allied Gardens, and he did just as he said, introducing me to a whole new set of people. For about two weeks, we didn't have any success finding kilos. In the meantime, I was praying that Warren's mother didn't report her car stolen. I was getting paranoid every time I saw a cop. One day as we were driving around, Mike told me ... "Turn left here. I want to take you to meet one cool lady. Her name is Margaret. She is a widow. Her husband got killed years ago in a car wreck. She has three daughters, and their place is more or less the local hangout here in the Gardens. Check it out ... she is the only grown woman I know ... **that has never said or did one single uncool thing in her life**!!! Her son-in-law does quite a bit of dealing. Maybe Maggie can turn us on to him."

Mike's normally mellow deep voice had such conviction on it, in his description of Maggie that I was immediately curious. We pulled up in front of a little green house. At the door we were greeted by a young pretty girl about sixteen years old. She had long beautiful brown hair, and was a little on the plump side.

"Son-of-a-_____," she said and then yelled into the house ... "Mom, look who's here! Hey Mike, when did you get out of jail?"

"Hi Marta," Mike answered as we filed past.

We went into the family room, and there between the kitchen and a small dining area, was a lady sitting on the floor cleaning. She had a knife and a rag, and was scraping and poking at every little microscopic particle ... that was on or under the metal strip that separated the carpet from the linoleum. She looked up, and with this huge smile said ... Hi Mike. You're really looking good! When did you get out?"

"A few weeks ago Maggie. This is a friend of mine ... Roger."

"Hi Roger," Maggie said in her raspy voice, as she continued to scrape away under the metal strip.

Young Marta said with a friendly laugh, looking right in her mother's eyes, "Mom has cleaned the whole house about three times today, and now she's working on that metal band there for about an hour. Don't you think it's about time to give it a ____ing break?"

Maggie started laughing, "Mike, we scored some criss-crosses from Mexico, and I've been popping them all morning. I'm so into cleaning this place that it's driving me crazy! And Marta, instead of picking on me, why don't you go clean your room! **Believe me**, I didn't touch a thing in there! I wouldn't want you to have a ____-fit! So get the heck out of here if you're going to complain! I want to talk to Mike."

Marta calmly went down the hall smiling and shaking her head. Maggie sat there and chatted with us for about another hour, only stopping her relentless pursuit of perfection, when the conversation warranted it. She was a riot. Mike was asking her about her son-in-law, Steve. She told us that he was in jail himself, but was due to get out in a few weeks.

"I haven't heard any of the kids talking about kilos." she said, and then Maggie yelled into the other room to her youngest daughter... "Marta, get your ___ out here. Do you know anyone who has a load of pot?"

Marta came back in the family room and said ... "No, but try this", and she handed Mike a couple of neatly rolled up joints. Mike lit one up, and stuck the other one in his shirt pocket.

Maggie added, "I think David left some beer in the fridge, if you guys would like a beer."

So went my first encounter with Maggie. We sat there and drank up David's beer, and smoked Marta's pot. I wholeheartedly concurred with Mike's assessment of Margaret. One cool lady. I felt instantly at home in her house. Christie from next door popped in. The phone rang off the hook. Listening to the interactions of all the people running through that house was like watching one continuous sitcom. My face hurt from laughing by the time we split ... to continue our own relentless search ... for the ever eluding pot of Acapulco Gold.

For several more days Mike and I made the rounds with no luck. We stopped by to see Shannon one day. I introduced her to Mike. (It was prior to her renting her own place.) She also didn't know anyone with connections at the time, but we stuck around and had a little party. It was there that evening that Mike said to me ... "The heck with this crap Rog, let's go check things out down south."

Shannon said ... "Are you talking about Mexico, Mike?"

"I have a couple good connections down there." Mike responded, "They probably wonder where I've been for so long. Alberto is our best shot. He doesn't really deal with pot at all. But for old times sake, I'm sure he'll scare some up for me. I made him a lot of dinero in the past. What do you say dude? If we sky right now we can be at his door in Mexico in less than an hour."

"You're kidding me," I said, "How would we get it across?"

"One step at a time. Let's see what Alberto can do for us, before we worry about crossing anything. Where there's a will, there's a way. Anyway, it can't hurt to just check on things ... if you want."

I sat there listening to Mike to see if he was really serious. He was. I thought about it for around ten seconds, and said ... "___ it. Why not? Lead on Leon."

Shannon had been smoking a joint with us, and listening intently to our whole conversation. As we got up and headed for the door, she said ... "Are you guys really going to go to Mexico right now and try to score some dope? Are you both crazy!"

I got to admit, my blood pressure was up a notch or two as we headed south through San Diego and onto the 5 Freeway. Mike started telling me about different ways he had smuggled things across the border.

"I used to be hooked up with some people years ago who smuggled big quantities of pot under the floorboards of horse trailers. David whose beer we were drinking used to fabricate the false floors. It worked for a long time until finally they busted a load. One of the best bets is to put kilos inside each of our tires. I never did it that way myself, but I hear it works every time. You need to let about half the air out, and can't drive over 50 or 55 miles per hour. Faster than that the centrifugal force turns everything into kilos of powder. If Alberto can fix us up, I think that's what we should do ... the tire gig ... especially since we're not going to have that many units this trip anyway. It's taken so long to score your money is getting a little skinny. Here comes the border now. Say good-by to the good old USA!!!"

I had been to Mexico only once before in years past, on foot. As soon as we crossed the line ... it was totally another world. It felt like a demolition derby with old cars and taxicabs flying all around. Mike guided me through the maze, and past the churning downtown Tijuana. We headed out of town and drove to Playas De Tijuana, a small beach community where the new bullring is. It was about a ten-minute drive. Everything seemed so weird. It was a trip.

Soon, Mike had me drive down several streets lined with houses. Compared to some of the shacks around Tijuana, these houses looked like mansions. We pulled up in front of a two-story concrete blockhouse with a 6-foot wrought iron fence around it. In the front yard a huge spotted Great Dane was barking his head off at us. The porch light went on and a man called the dog into the house. Mike yelled out ... "It's Mike Martin, Alberto."

"Come up. I put the dog in the back, so wait a minute."

We went through the big iron gate and waited on the front porch. Alberto opened the door a few minutes later, and warmly welcomed us into his home. It seemed like a movie scene. Alberto was a thin Mexican

Fire On the Mountain

man wearing a fancy gold bathrobe. He had partially gray hair and looked around sixty years old. He was smoking a cigarette that was attached to a long shinny gold cigarette holder. The furniture was all gold leaf with black and red velvet. The coffee table looked like it belonged in an English castle. There were paintings of bullfighters and little statues here and there. A young attractive woman with bleached blond hair came down the staircase, and then hustled a two-year-old child up the stairs. She totally ignored us.

Alberto said … "How long has it been Mike?"

"It's been awhile Alberto."

"Are you ready to get going again? Business has been good Mike. A few months ago there was a lot of trouble. Several people I know got busted by Federales. I pay people to keep me with no problems. My people didn't move anything anyway, because we still don't trust any of these snakes. I pay but I don't trust. If I don't pay, I get busted for sure. Now things are quiet. I have moved a lot of merchandise these last days. I can front you a few pieces. Some good cheeva to get you on your feet."

Mike responded, "I'm staying away from smack Alberto. It almost did me in this last time. Roger and I are trying to hustle up a little weed. We have some cash customers who want kilos. I was hoping you could help us out."

Alberto looked at us for a while, and said, "I don't move mota. It's too much trouble for me. But for you Mike, I will get some. Come back tomorrow afternoon. But now I want you to try something."

Alberto had several rings on. One huge silver ring covered half of his finger, which he opened up like a locket. Inside it was packed with a white powder. Alberto produced a tiny spoon, and I snorted my first cocaine along with Mike and our host in this garish drug dealer's home in Baja Mexico. I talked and talked and talked … all the way back to the home of the brave and of the free … and then I talked some more.

The next day we were back in Mexico. Mike had brought an extra tire iron, and an air pump to break down the tires and pump them back up. I thought to myself that I must be absolutely crazy to be smuggling drugs in a car that is probably hot as a hot potato by now. "Anyway the ball is in motion … so here we go." We arrived at Alberto's place and gave him our cash. I only had enough to buy eleven kilos. He came back in a relatively short time. It was just getting dark outside. All my senses were high as a kite. I had to force myself to look calm and stay cool. Think and focus.

We thanked Alberto and went to the car. He had left the kilos on our back seat and then locked the car. We got in, I started the car, and turned the lights on ... but the lights didn't come on.

"Mike the lights won't come on! I can't believe it. We got a pile of dope sitting next to us, and we have to drive around with no lights! This can't be happening!"

"OK ... get out of here Rog. We can't sit in front of Albertos. Let's go up on the highway."

I drove through the streets toward the highway. A couple other cars didn't have their lights on yet, but it was getting darker and darker. We got on the main highway toward Ensenada and drove up to the tollbooths. I was totally paranoid with all the kilos sitting in plain view. We had originally planned to stash them in a remote canyon after leaving Albertos'. I still couldn't believe the bad luck. The lights on the red Toyota had **never** flickered even once before. What incredible timing! We were like sitting ducks on the highway.

Mike walked over to the tollbooth, and came back with a pair of pliers and a couple tools that he borrowed. We had a flashlight. I was positive a cop or something was going to pull up any second. We stuck out like a sore thumb ... the hood of our car up, two longhairs, with one hanging out from under the dash ... and a stack of kilos just sitting right there. It was a sure bust. I tried to somewhat conceal the marijuana by putting them on the floor. I could see the Mexicans in the tollbooth look over at us from time to time. Mike ended up cutting all the wires leading to the ignition, and started hot-wiring everything. He butchered the whole electrical system. After about a half hour of eternity, he got the lights to work ... and then with the touch of two wires we were into the Mexican darkness with our motor roaring, and lights blazing ahead. I couldn't believe we were on the road again and back in business ... but the lights were only the beginning of our trouble that night.

We went back to our original plan, paid our toll (after returning the tools), and proceeded on toward Ensenada. After a short distance, we got off the main highway and took a dirt road up some very steep sections, and way back into the hills. We turned the car off, unhooked the lights, and each of us expressed a huge sigh of relief in no uncertain

Fire On the Mountain

colorful language. We were high up in the Mexican boonies. Way off in the distance I could see the tiny lights from the Coronado Bridge in America.

"Well Rog … let's get these kilos into the tires, and get out of here. Do you know how to break a tire down?"

"Not really. I mean I've watched them plug a couple tires at tire shops. I thought you were the smuggling professional. Why Mike ? ? ? Don't you know how to break down a tire?" I asked.

"Heck no, but how hard can a tire be to get apart?"

We both started laughing our heads off, as we realized what a couple of sorry comedians we turned out to be. Mike said … "Give me that _____ing tire!" He grabbed the spare, and started wrestling with the little Toyota tire like a huge bear. We finally both got one side off the rim, and three kilos inside … but we couldn't get it back together … let alone, pumped back up. After at least two hours, I told Mike to forget it.

"Let's just stack the kilos in the recessed area by the rear window. If we cover it with the blanket that is already there, it will look like a normal rear seat without a window well. If we get busted … we get busted."

"OK with me Rog … let's do it!"

I looked back toward San Diego in the distance. The Coronado Bridge seemed like I could reach out and touch it. Oh how I wished we were over there already. What a fluke this escapade was turning out to be. Those tiny flickering lights might as well be a million miles away.

We carefully placed and concealed the kilos by the rear window, and headed for the border. As we drove along Mike was continuing my education …

"When we get to the border, look the guards in the eyes when you talk, and watch their lips when they talk. They even watch your neck to see if your jugular is pumping harder … so you need to stay calm. Can you handle it? Do you want me to drive?"

"I'll drive. I'll be all right."

No sooner did we reach the outskirts of Tijuana, when lo and behold, our third disaster struck! A cop car pulled behind us and turned on his flashing lights. I was in total disbelief and shock! Why are they pulling us over?

Mike cussed and yelled … "La Mesa here we come!" It was the first time I heard anything about "La Mesa", which is the infamous prison just outside of Tijuana.

Two uniformed Mexican cops walked up, and ordered us out of the car. I could smell pot real strong and was **sure** they smelled it. They interrogated us, and searched our glove box, trunk, under the seats, had us empty our pockets, but miraculously didn't look under the rear window well. They pulled us over because our taillights didn't work. Mike showed them how we had to wire everything because our lights went out. They hassled us for a long time, and then said, "OK … you can go."

As we pulled away, I realized that after the initial light crisis, the tire escapade, and being searched and interrogated by T.J. cops … that we haven't even reached the border yet. We still have to smuggle this whole load, in our hot-wired borrowed Toyota. What else could possibly go wrong? Nevertheless, when we got to the customs agent in our line … I looked him right in the eyes and answered … "American citizen."

"What are you bringing back from Mexico?"

"Nothing"

"What was the purpose and length of your visit?"

"We were just checking out the tourist shops in Tijuana."

He crouched down and looked at Mike … "What is your citizenship?"

Mike answered … "United States."

I saw the guards lips say … "Move on."

As we pulled out of the corridor leading to the 5 Freeway, Mike let out a huge war cry, and screamed … **"We're in the money!"**

CHAPTER 24

"WHAT A TRIP"

Mike and I were off and running. We grabbed our gear in San Diego and headed for LA. On our way out Mike had to pay his visit to the clinic. He tested clean. No heroin for about six months now. Right on. I don't know why the cocaine didn't show up. Anyway it didn't. Maybe the little bit we snorted didn't stay in his system very long. In L.A. I got a hold of Warren's mother's phone number. I dialed and Warren answered.

"Where in the heck have you been? Hey dude, you don't know what you put me through! My mother almost called the cops about a dozen times. I talked her out of it each time ... but it wasn't easy. You need to get that ____ing car over here right away!"

I interrupted ... "OK Warren hold on! What happened to you that night? I waited for hours and hours. I didn't know what to do. Eventually I called over to David's pad, and some chick said they hauled you off to jail. With all the priors you told me about, I figured you'd be gone for a long time. I **had** to get to San Diego. I'm sorry it took so long to get back. Things happen!"

Warren shot back, "Man, I got released from jail the **next** day! You don't know how close you came to having that car listed hot. Please get it back here today! I'm so glad you called!"

Mike and I met with Warren, and gave our somewhat unfaithful little red Toyota back. I hated to see it go. In spite of her untimely indiscretions in Mexico ... we had history. I get very attached to all of my vehicles. Anyway, Warren had his car back all in one piece ... except for a few taped up ignition wires dangling under the dash.

We spent about a week in LA and sold enough of our load to buy a car, and party with some old and new friends. I started seeing Dale's younger sister, who was now a high school senior. Roberta was blossoming into a beautiful young woman, and very streetwise too for an upper middle class Jewish girl. Mike hooked up with her sexy best friend, Pam. We had a great time. Roberta told me she could sell a lot of pot to her party friends in Woodland Hills. It blew my mind when in a few hours, she turned everything I gave her into cash ... piles and stacks of cash.

One day on our abbreviated stay in L.A. I picked her up after school. All the hep Valley kids were filing out of the school building with their books and teenage energy filling the atmosphere. Roberta had promised some pot to someone, and I was delivering it to her. I had heard on the TV news of fiendish people who supplied school kids with drugs. As I sat there waiting for Roberta to appear in the crowd of students, I suddenly realized that ... here I was ... **one of the fiends**! It really freaked me out. I quickly justified myself ... "it's only pot ... not psychedelics or hard drugs". Regardless, I never got near a high school campus again.

To find a car, I bought a LA Times and called some of the ads in the classified section. Pete took me to look at a 1954 Chevy that some kid had restored. It had a brand new fancy two-tone paint job, and the interior was completely done over in real black leather. It looked like showcase material. The father was quickly unloading the car, because his son had been irresponsible about something or other. I bought it for $300.00, which was nothing compared to what the kid had put into it. Unfortunately, he hadn't rebuilt the motor yet. It ran good, but used exactly a quart of oil every 300 miles. The plates were current for another six months, which was one of my operating necessities. I signed a phony name to the bill of sale, and off we went cross-country ... with a load of kilos and a case of SAE 30.

However, first, we drove back to San Diego where Mike tested again. I picked up my dog Obie, who had been staying with a friend. He was so happy to see me. We also stopped in to say hi to Maggie in Allied Gardens. Lo and behold, there was a stray dog at her house. It looked and was marked like a German shepherd ... only about half the size. It reminded me of Rex, my favorite childhood dog. Maggie said that if she couldn't find it a home soon, it was off to the pound. She couldn't afford to feed it anymore. So, I adopted the stray, and named him Partner. He piled into my hot 54 and instantly got along great with Obie. Once again we were off. This time our destination was Boulder, Colorado. We were becoming quite a troop ... two dogs, one X-con, and whatever I was, driving our Golden Oldie through the canyons of Utah ... leaving only a thin stream of black smoke.

I phoned ahead to Boulder that we were on our way. Steve was real happy and would be waiting. During part of the trek through the desert, I was sleeping in the back seat while the Viking took a turn driving. During that snooze I had one of the most radical dreams of my life. I mean it was totally radical and realistic. In it, I was back in Ohio running through a field. The thought hit me that if I jumped up ... I could fly. I wasn't sure if I was dreaming, (in the dream), and then was **positively** sure that I wasn't dreaming. I jumped up, and stayed suspended in the air about five feet off the ground. I came slowly down and tried it again ... several times. Each time going a little higher, and then doing different maneuvers. I taught myself how to fly with will power, and a kind of believing that I could do it. It was amazing ... I had every sensation of flying. The dream progressed into a whole adventure in another state, where I was rescuing some friends with people shooting at me ... and the whole nine yards. I was shocked and super disappointed when I woke up in the back seat ... on cold black leather, and realized it was just a dream. Since that dream I have had dozens of flying dreams. I absolutely love them.

We pulled in to Boulder after a day and a half of hard driving. Colorado Steve had bad news for us ... his best buyers had just purchased a bunch of pounds from someone else. Boulder was flooded with kilos right now. He was only able to sell about half of our load. He said if we could wait awhile there were several prospects for the remainder ... but they needed time to put some money together. We stayed at our Rocky Mountain hideout for about three days and had a great time. Mike scored a gorgeous University chick. The hippie pad never changed.

One evening we had an unusual experience along the lines of my dream. Only this time it came in the form of a supposedly true story ... that Steve told us. There were about a dozen of us present, both guys and gals. We were in the main living room of the big old two-story house. I'll never forget this tale. It definitely gave me food for thought.

We were passing around a joint that was clipped to the end of a long shiny pair of surgical scissors. Steve was sitting on the floor. He looked exactly like the manager of an early seventies tuned-in rock and roll band. Long curly black hair and beard ... lean, lanky, and mellow. He had a good rap. I liked listening to him. We were all having fun, as the conversation went here, there, and everywhere.

Steve looked at me and said … "I was wondering if maybe you got busted in California or something. I figured you'd be back **way** before this … a couple weeks max. As a matter of fact, I almost went to see Olga about you."

I said … "What do you mean? Who is Olga?"

"She's this lady who lives in a community back in the mountains … not that far from Boulder. Let me tell you about Olga. It's radical how I first met her. I have a friend who told me about a lady, who he said was 'in touch with the **teachers**' … and if I ever had any heavy questions about anything, to make an appointment with her. He said she was usually booked for about six months in advance, and that people from all over the world come to see her."

I thought Steve was pulling our leg, but as he continued the story I soon realized that he was dead serious … "So a few years back, I decided to go check this chick out. I called the phone number my sidekick gave me, and got her on the phone. This lady's voice told me she was booked solid with appointments, but that she would ask the teachers to see if there would be any cancellations coming up … ('yeah right'). Anyway the next day she had me call back. I did, and sure enough there was an opening in two weeks.

I was one super skeptical kid. When I got there and met with her … she asked what I wanted. I figured I'd give her something a bit challenging, so I told her I wanted to meet Jesus Christ. To my surprise, she didn't bat an eye, but told me to go into this other room. When I went into the room … immediately I saw this super bright light shining behind a man who appeared right in front of me. I couldn't see his face or features, but I could see that he had short hair and no beard. He was like a silhouette shaded by the incredibly bright light. It blew my mind."

(Now I was positive that Steve was feeding us a tall tale), and interrupted him … "You're kidding me right? I'm suppose to believe Jesus Christ was standing there in front of you???"

Steve said … "Hey … I kid you not! There was a man who appeared right in front of me in that room and he said he was Jesus Christ. It blew my mind … but I know what I saw."

I was into this story now because I could see how sincere he was. If he

Fire On the Mountain

was acting it was an award winning performance. Everyone in the room was on board. Mike was listening intently, but had no comments. I was the only one who kept interjecting questions. I was really puzzled ... "is this guy telling the truth? Steve doesn't seem like a flake ... maybe he is playing an elaborate hoax on us."

I said to Steve ... "So what did you say to him?"

Steve answered continuing his story ... "Well, he reached out and shook my hand. I couldn't really think of what to say ... so the first thing I said was ... 'Why don't you have long hair and a beard?'

Jesus said ... 'I never had long hair. It was just a myth.'

Then I asked him ... 'Why did you come 2000 years ago instead of now in modern times, when people could know for sure that you are real?'

Jesus answered ... 'I have come back. Hundreds of times. When I came the first time I showed people that we are all the children of God. We can all do the works of God by allowing love to rule. But when men saw the miracles working through me... they wanted to make me God. They didn't accept the responsibility of being Children of Light themselves. It was easier to deify me. When I refused to be their God ...they crucified me. They would have done the same today.'

I asked him ... 'Did it hurt when they crucified you?'

Jesus said ... 'No. I am in touch with every atom in the universe. I was able to release myself and my spirit into God's hands. The message is still the same, and I tell it again to you today ... We are all the Children of God. We have the ability within to be in touch with the divine. It is a matter of accepting and releasing the love of God to all mankind.'

After that, (Steve continued), he disappeared. When I left Olgas' I was **absolutely totally mind-boggled** and in a daze. I felt like a man with a mission. I started telling everyone that they are the Children of God. It was a trip. I'm originally from Mississippi, and went back home to tell everyone there also. But, it was the same for me, as it was for Jesus. No one would listen. I even went into the streets preaching to people that they are the Children of God. For a while I even wore a white robe. In one town they beat the ____ out of me, and the cops threw me in jail. I finally gave up, and came back to Boulder."

One of the gals said ... "Wow ... that is a trip if I ever heard one!"

The shiny scissors rotated back to me. I took a big hit but didn't know what to think. He was too sincere. I knew one thing ... I wanted Olga's address, and I was going to ask her exactly the same thing. I'd like to meet this shorthaired spirit man for myself. Steve gave me her phone number and address. I still have it.

It was taking too long to sell our goods in Boulder, so I made a couple calls to friends in Fremont. They assured me they could move the merchandise mucho pronto. So Mike and I piled into the Chevy and we were off to Ohio. Obie and Partner were doing great on the trip. I was looking forward to seeing everyone. It had been well over a year since I saw Troy last. I'd get this numb feeling every time I thought of him ... ("Oh God I hope he's OK"). It was October 1973.

Our time in my hometown stretched into a few weeks. It was a great visit, but the money came in slowly. We stayed at Denny's house out in the country. It was non-stop action. We attended several wild parties, went roller skating in Toledo on acid, got drunk at John Lewis', and went to painful extremes applying fake blood, for the annual American Legion Halloween party. We had a riot. I met a real cute girl at one of the parties named Heather. She had just graduated from Ross High School, and wanted to go to California with us. I told her she could if she did what ever I told her to do, whenever I told her to do it, with whoever I told her to do it with. I wanted to see what her reaction would be. She came from a strict Christian home. To my surprise she bought in. She told Mike and I ... "I want to run the border just one time with you guys ... I know I can do it!" The first thing I did was to share her with Mike.

Before we left Fremont, Mike and I had a meal with my parents. I spent several days visiting with Troy. I also spent a little time with my X-wife, even though she was engaged. She came to pick up Troy one day, and we sat in the car talking. She asked if I ever thought about getting back together. I told her I had, but that my life was way too crazy for a family. Somehow by the time she drove off ... we had left the door open that we might try again. She was going to write. I halfway thought about dropping everything, but my heart kinda sank ... because I knew it would never work ... I was too far into my master plan.

It was weird though, because on one of the visits at my parent's home the phone rang, and it was for me. It was the Sandusky County Welfare Department calling to interview me for a caseworkers position. After taking the State exam in Columbus, I had been put on a waiting list for over two years or so. How strange that they would call for an interview during the very few brief moments that I was at my parents ... like I'd been there all along in Fremont at that phone number. It made me think again about changing directions. A good paying job, that I knew I could definitely get into ... plus having my family back, was definitely food for thought. My wife wanting to try again, and that phone call was probably an open door to a sane life ... but instead we added Heather to our gang and headed for Mexico.

We decided to take the Northern route back to California ... so naturally that meant stopping at Boulder. We drove straight through to Colorado. Just outside of Denver it started snowing gangbusters. It became spooky. For one thing, our tires were not the greatest, especially as the driving snow started piling up on the highway. But, the biggest problem was the vacuum operated windshield-wipers on our old Chevy. They were having a hard time keeping the snow off the glass. About half way between Denver and Boulder, a big old fancy Cadillac went flying past in the fast lane. I was going real slow in the next lane trying to see. Apparently his wipers and tires had evolved into new spheres of efficiency. As the Cadillac shot past, a huge blanket of slush came flying on our windshield and just froze there ... completely stopping the wipers. We were totally blinded.

It was a horrible feeling. I pumped the brakes and finally stopped the car. Mike was cussing and rolled the passenger window down. He tried to knock some of the icy slush off. I looked in the mirror, and could see car lights coming behind us. I was positive we were about to get rear-ended. I yelled at Mike ... "Hey keep your head out the window and tell me when I'm on the shoulder of the road. We have to get off this highway!"

"OK ... come on."

I slowly inched forward and turned the wheel to the right.

In just a couple seconds Mike said ... "I don't know ... everything is solid white. You better stop!"

I put the brake on and the car **almost** came to a complete stop ... but then started sliding a little. In slow motion the front end kind of dipped down on the passenger side. Then we started to slide a little faster and pick up speed. We were going side ways. Heather started yelling ... "Oh no!!"

In a few seconds all hell broke loose. What a horrible feeling to be blindly shooting down some unknown incline. I could feel the car start to tip. I knew we were going over. Suddenly everything was upside down. Partner came flying into me. Heather was screaming. The car came crashing down on the hood. I was completely disoriented. We never wore seatbelts. The windshield busted out with glass flying everywhere. We continued to slide upside down for quite a ways, and then flipped over again onto the wheels ... and came to a stop.

Thank God the hill was just a big highway embankment, and not some major mountain or vertical something or other. The doors of our demolished car were both jammed shut, but we managed to crawl out through the windshield into the snow. Mike yelled out ... " Rog look at this crap!" He had hundreds of tiny pieces of glass and pennies in his hair and all through his long beard. My big jar of change broke on his head.

I immediately realized we needed to get our gear, and abandon ship before any cops show up. We still had a couple pounds of pot left in one of the suitcases and a lot of cash. As we got the dogs out, and all our gear ... a car stopped on the road above, and a man started yelling down to us ... "Is everyone OK??"

The Good Samaritan turned out to be a real friendly man who drove us all the way to Boulder. We made it to Steve's pad in the middle of the night. What a relief! The next day I grabbed a newspaper, and within a couple hours paid $650 cash for a 1969 blue station wagon. We decided to buy an airline ticket for Mike to fly back to San Diego. I drove him to the airport and he was off. He was in danger of getting violated for not testing on time. We simply abandoned the Chevy in the snow bank.

Colorado Steve was real surprised that we were just returning from Ohio. He had been expecting us with the next shipment by now.

He said ... "I had people who were hoping you'd be back through soon. They got their money together. I even went to see Olga, and asked her if you'd be coming back. She told me that you would return, and that you would be successful."

I was shocked that Steve had asked the lady who conjured up Jesus Christ anything about me. It gave me a totally eerie feeling ... that this lady had looked into the spirit world and predicted things concerning my life. Well, I had returned, but I don't know about the successful part.

I remembered Lacy's unhappy predictions from her Tarot cards. Something is going on out there. I wanted to meet this Olga, but it wasn't the time.

Heather and I spent another night at the house. In the morning I woke up pretty early and told Heather to take the car and go buy some breakfast groceries. I knew the refrigerator was basically empty from the previous nights' raid. She made a little list while getting dressed, took the car keys and was off into the snowy Boulder landscape. Less than an hour later, one of the guys in the house came into our room and hastily announced … "Hey, I think your girlfriend just got into a wreck!"

I thought he was kidding since everyone knew we just demolished my Chevy less than 48 hours ago. I sat up in my sleeping bag and said, "Come on Brian. It's too early to play with my brain."

Brian had obviously been outside. He had a sweater and heavy jacket on along with rosy cheeks. In a slightly winded voice he insisted … "I'm not kidding. Your car is in the middle of the intersection about two blocks down the street."

"Is Heather OK?"

"I think so. From here it looks like she's standing on the sidewalk."

I threw some clothes on and ran down the street. Heather was fine, but looked very exasperated and was closely watching my reactions. The right front end of our newly acquired station wagon was smashed in, and the tire was surrounded by mangled metal. A nice looking, well dressed elderly black lady was talking to the police. A tow truck had just pulled up.

Heather started telling me the details … "She slid right through the intersection and hit me!" It scared the heck out of me! She is a nice lady and feels terrible about it. She was on her way to Church. I didn't even know it was Sunday. I've lost track of time. She has insurance. It wasn't my fault!"

I calmed Heather down as they towed our car away. I felt sorry for the little old black lady as she gave us her insurance information. At least Heather had made it to the grocery store. We carried breakfast home in a couple plastic bags. Two wrecked cars in three days … pretty good.

The very next morning an insurance man called and came to the house. He told us he had inspected the car, and it would cost more to fix than it was worth. They considered it totaled. He wrote me a check on the spot for $975.00. He also drove us to the garage where our car had been towed. The garage man said the engine and everything appeared to be OK. The car just basically needed a new bumper and fender and whatnot. Also the tire wouldn't turn because of some metal pinned against it. I paid the man $25 to take a medal saw and cut away the fender until the tire was completely free. I drove it off the lot, and within two hours after cashing the check, we were on the interstate, dogs jumping around, driving down the fast lane in a slightly ugly Pontiac. It ran perfect, and literally cruised at 95 miles per hour. The snow zoomed by ... Vegas zoomed by ... and we made it to San Diego in record time! Plus, I felt pretty good about making $325 on a free car. So what if it had a couple battle scars.

"Hello California. Hello Mike. **What a trip!**"

CHAPTER 25

"RICH MAN'S SPEED"

San Diego! It was so good to be back. I found Mike at his parent's house in Allied Gardens. He was definitely glad to see us. Ohio Heather was enjoying the winter California sunshine and bumming around with us. We stayed in various places including a couple trips to Los Angeles, but usually ended up at Maggie's. Her little three-bedroom house was only a block away from Mike's mom's home in the Gardens. Maggie's house reminded me a little of one of my aunt's places back in Fremont … lots of action with people constantly in and out … lots of yelling and cussing, but nobody taking it very serious. Maggie was usually half broke, so I'd give her some cash, and chip in with groceries once in awhile. Eventually I moved into her spare room.

Mike had been to Mexico to his connection a couple times prior to our arrival from Colorado, and anxious to make another run. He said … "Alberto has some kilos lined up right now. He also has some good blow. Have you ever turned any coke, Rog?"

"Not really. It looks too much like heroin to me."

"Yeah, it looks like smack, but it's not in the same league at all. Heroin is heavy duty addictive. Cocaine is only seriously habit forming at the max. But most people can't afford to get their nose in it enough to be a problem. It's called "Rich man's speed." That's what it basically is … an "upper". Chris-crosses are for the masses. Cocaine is for the elite. It's really nice. There's some dang good coin in it if you don't party too much," Mike explained.

I had consciously stayed away from hard drugs, but coke was slowly creeping onto the stage. My master plan had been to get independently wealthy supplying the huge pool of tuned-in, and turned-on people … with some good old harmless weed. I didn't want to hurt anybody by selling anything harder than pot. But Mike made a convincing case about the pros and cons of smuggling and selling cocaine versus marijuana.

I asked Mike, "So what does Alberto have available down there? What's the PR and how much can we make?

"The coke he has right now is real good. It has lots of rocks. A piece is going for $600. We can probably triple our money here in San Diego."

"What is a 'piece'?" I asked as we drove down the freeway. Heather and Obie were sleeping in the back. Partner was at Maggie's. Mike had been rolling a few joints while riding shotgun during our dope education seminar. He fired one up, took a Viking sized hit, and passed it to the chauffeur …

"Mexicans are always trying to get over on you somehow." Mike finally answered. "'A piece is their version of an ounce. A real ounce is 28 grams. A piece is 25 grams. They screw us out of three grams. But like I said, the stuff Alberto has is pretty good. He might even front us on top of whatever we score. He has in the past, when I brought him a lot of business. We could step on this snow at least one full time, and make two ounces out of each piece. Besides it's a heck of a lot easier to smuggle little baggies of coke, than a huge stack of 2.2 pound kilos of mota!"

With a few more encouraging words and calculations, I added cocaine to the expanding product line. I figured it was **almost** as harmless as pot. Heather had been wanting to run the border with us. I was debating whether to take her on this next smuggling gig. However, first things first. We crossed the border, visited our Mexican connection to make plans and preparations … and then partied all night in the T.J. clubs. We got totally blasted. Revolution Boulevard … "hello".

A couple days later we were on our way South again. We left Heather in San Diego. I decided to invest all of the kitty in cocaine. I had this uneasy feeling, which I shrugged off. Every coin I found was tails lately. Mike had calmed most of my fears. In fact, our TJ connection had asked us on our last visit, if we would drive to Peru, and pick up a kilo of pure coke. He showed Mike the address of his source in Lima. He would front us the money, and split the profit with us if we would made the run. A kilo of pure cocaine for twelve thousand dollars. What a price. Nevertheless, I said absolutely "no way". I could just picture two longhaired hippies driving a smashed up station wagon through all those Central and South American countries with a kilo of cocaine. I had visions of armed soldiers tearing our car apart. I figured it was a sure bust. Driving around Mexico with drugs was crazy enough.

As we approached the border, Mike started telling about the different ways he used to smuggle heroin … "When I was strung out real bad, I would cross the border up ahead here all the time … sometimes daily. Usually I would 'kiester' the dope."

"What does kiester mean?" I asked.

"You divide a piece into several balloons, and then shove them up your rear. Sometimes we'd get a chick to put them up inside her. Other times we'd swallow a whole bunch of small balloons. When you get across the border you make a B-line to a gas station bathroom, and drink this crap, I forget the name of it … but it makes you upchuck like **right now**! The balloons fly out like ___ing bullets. A couple times we didn't get to a bathroom in time, and had to wait for them to pass all the way through."

I decided to ask a couple more stupid questions …"What kind of balloons do you shove up the ___? I think I'll **pass**. Anyway what happens if they break?

"Balloons are rubbers. When you make them up, you twist and fold, and they end up being double and triple wrapped. I never heard of one breaking." Mike added.

Years later I did on the news. A gal smuggling coke from South America had one burst in her stomach on a commercial jet. She died.

I opted for simply hiding the coke in the car. Luck was with us, and the customs officer just flagged us through the border … after asking the same magical questions… "What is your citizenship?" "How long were you in Mexico?" "What was the purpose of your visit?" We managed to keep our cool on the outside, even though every cell in my body was supercharged on the inside. "Back in the USA."

For the next month or two I got a hands-on education about cocaine. We bought a fancy triple beam scale, cutting additives like lactose, testing chemicals, etc. We made up one gram "papers", and sold full ounces as well. I learned to take a hot iron and seal up little plastic pouches of the expensive white powder, for transport out of California. Mike was a good teacher. He was also sliding back into his old ways.

Mike sold a lot of the coke, and also turned up with a new girlfriend named Kathy. He moved into her place, which was a house in San Diego that she shared with several other roommates. There were several parties in which much of our "product" freely disappeared up various noses. The money started to quickly dwindle. After one particular party that I missed, a gal was telling me ... "Hey Roger. You should have been here last night. Everyone was smoking dope, and horning coke, and drinking. We got **wasted**!" She continued ... "I couldn't believe Mike. He started shooting coke up with a needle on the back of his hand. It was gross. He was acting like a fiend, and had blood running off his hand and everything. It was too heavy for me."

I had become guilty of partying too much with the wares also, so I had a pow-wow with Mike, and told him that I wanted to switch back to Plan A, and cop some more kilos of marijuana. I told him ... "Hey we were making money before, but we are steadily losing right now. Besides that, I found out that you lied to me about that one ounce of coke with all the rocks in it."

I had never had any hard words with Mike before. He looked at me with a grin and said ... "Well Rog, You know what they say ... It's better to be the ____er, than the ____ee. And besides, it's also easier to forgive, than to forget."

It made me laugh, the way he said it. No denying anything. Just some smooth talking advise on how to deal with it. I couldn't help liking Mike even when I knew he had put the screws to me.

I told him. "OK ... it was only one ounce, and we still have a little coke left ... but I want to go down South, and see if Alberto can deliver us some more pot. No heroin or coke or anything but pot. Are you with me? We need to **make** money, not piss it away."

"Hey"... Mike said, "Let's go tomorrow and see what he's got."

The next day Mike, Heather and I drove to Mexico, passed through T.J., and met with our connection by the new bullring in Playas De Tijuana. Alberto told us to come down on the following Friday and he'd have some kilos. He tried to talk us into more coke, and also mentioned some heroin that he had. I told him we had a big market for pot, and that I wasn't very impressed with the cocaine trade. He said he'd get us the pot only as a favor to Mike. I could smell things closing up with Alberto.

On the way back Stateside we again stopped on Revolution Boulevard to party at our favorite nightclub. It was down a flight of steps in the basement of a big building, with a doorman, a band, and wall-to-wall people twenty-four hours a day. Heather wanted to dance all night, and when we wouldn't dance with her anymore, she danced by herself. She was good, and several times had told me about her dream of being a professional dancer. All three of us got real drunk. I felt good and loved kicking around with Mike and Heather. Heather had that 18-year-old mid-western spunk, and Mike was Mike.

Late that night we made our way out of the tourist area, past old run down buildings and shacks … and joined the multiple lines of cars at the border. There were probably 20 or 30 separate, long, bumper-to-bumper lines of cars leading to the actual border. All the booths reminded me of the starting gates at Hollywood Park … only this was more like a rat race. After making our way past the beggars and vendors, who walk back and forth amidst the vehicles day and night … eventually, the little green signal light went on for our car to pull up to one of the custom agents sitting in his booth. We had no drugs or anything to hide, but lo and behold the man put a slip on our car and told me to pull into secondary.

Mike was feeling a bit belligerent and announced … "I've been waiting for these mother ____ers to pull me in when I'm not holding! **Pull over there and let me out!"**

As I stopped the car, Mike threw open the passenger door. He got out and yelled in his deep voice at a uniformed agent who was walking by … "Hurry up and check this car out. I got better things to do than to____ around with you jerks!"

Mike walked straight toward the agent looking more like a drunk Hells Angel than anything else. Before he reached the agent he was addressing, out of nowhere, three other customs agents jumped him. Suddenly Mike was wrestling and cussing, and being drug toward some nearby offices. One of the bigger cops had a choke hold on him. Another one got his arm bent up behind his back. It took all of them to get him inside.

Heather and I got out of the car. Several other agents hustled us inside also … but didn't get physical. Inside they questioned us over and over, and looked through Heather's purse. They were writing down our names from our IDs on a report. Outside they were searching the car. Pretty soon one agent came over to us and said, "Pull up your sleeves and show me your arms." I showed him my arms.

After inspecting all sides of them, he said, "Do you know that your friend is a drug addict?"

I said, "Right now he is pretty drunk, but he doesn't use drugs anymore."

"Have you ever looked at his arms? He has tracks all over them."

"Yeah, I know he has old marks," I answered, "but, he went to jail, and has been off drugs ever since. He is just drunk right now."

The agent gave us a hard look, and then said ... "He has fresh needle marks. You need to wise up and watch who you associate with."

After another short wait they separated Heather and me. They took me into a room and searched me. I was totally clean and led back to a waiting room. Heather was still nowhere to be seen. About 20 minutes later a door swung open. A female cop and Heather emerged. As Heather walked over to join me, I **never** in my life saw such a shocked and horrified look on any gals face. Her eyes were huge ... her mouth was hanging open ... and she absolutely could not talk. I couldn't believe that she was totally unable to answer me.

"Come on ... What's the matter Heather?"

Finally she said ... {_ _ _ _!"

That's all she could say for about another 10 minutes. Finally she said ... "You would **not** believe what those jerks did! They stripped me, and did an internal search. I was on a table with stirrups and everything. I cannot believe it!"

Eventually they let Heather and myself go. They kept Mike. The next afternoon I found our troublemaker at his girlfriends. The border had released him in the morning, and he hitched back. I told him what they did to Heather. He said ... "Yeah, I guess I was feeling my oats a little too much. It was just that they've hassled me **so many times** at that place! I couldn't pass up the opportunity to give them a little crap back. As a matter of fact, I did ... they made me defacate in a bucket. Slimy creeps!"

The following Friday we still had a load of marijuana waiting to be picked up. Here we go again! I decided that Mike was too hot to come along. I told Heather ... "You stay at Maggies'. I can cross these kilos myself."

"No way! I want to come along. I'm all right. Really."

"Hey Heather ... this time we **will** be holding." I reminded her, "You were pretty freaked out the last time."

"Come on Rog ... I can do it. I know I can do it. It will even look better if I come along ... a couple college kids from Boulder with Colorado license plates. It would look strange if you were by yourself. At least I think so. Come on! Please! I want to get over on those jerks!"

What could I say? She had a couple good points, and convinced me that she was truly game. Besides, I figured they were slightly unlikely to find a load of kilos up inside Heather. If we got searched, our goose would be cooked long before she made it to the stirrups.

Mike borrowed a car, and we drove to Mexico separately. We picked up our merchandise, which was about 12 kilos, neatly wrapped in heavy paper and yellow cellophane. They actually looked pretty. However, my adrenaline was elevated way too high to appreciate much of anything, as we hid our stash in the station wagon. I could only afford about a dozen units, because our finances had dipped so low.

Here was the plan ... Heather and I would claim, if asked, to be traveling around from Colorado looking to move to the LA area. We had spent the day in San Diego, and were doing the tourist thing in Tijuana. The back of the station wagon had about five large suitcases, a couple small ones, sleeping bags, and about ten cardboard boxes full of my belongings. Most everything I owned was in the boxes ... clothes, books, shoes, art supplies, photos, pots and pans, and you name it. I had hauled my stuff around since returning from Colorado. In addition, we had all of Heather's gear.

The station wagon had a trunk of sorts, under the floor, way at the rear of the vehicle. It was a pretty big space. I had one huge cardboard box about 16 inches wide, and about 3 feet tall, that laid in there almost perfect. I was able to get a couple small boxes around the big box, as well as loose items, with several jackets draped on top. I could just barely get the door closed. Except for the little handle you would never even know there was a compartment under the floor.

After picking up our booty, I took the large box out, emptied it about two thirds ... packed the kilos in the middle, and then covered them with more clothes and household items that were previously in the box. Thus, the marijuana occupied the center section of that large box. Then we repacked everything back into the trunk, and into the station wagon. The remainder of the plan was to fake our way across the border ... and pray we didn't get any of the same border guards as we had a few days before!

This time we were completely sober. Mike was following several cars behind us. The lines were super long this time, but finally it was our turn to cross ... "What is your citizenship? How long have you been in Mexico?" (etc... etc.)

I thought we were doing pretty good. Then the guard looked in the back, asked a few more questions, and said ... "Pull straight ahead and park in a stall in secondary." He wrote something on a form, and put it on our windshield. I had the impression from his comments that the sheer quantity of stuff in our car, had worked against us.

I was in semi-shock. Heather was totally silent. "Oh no!" ... I decided not to give up the ghost until they actually had a kilo in their official little hands. They had dogs going through cars the last time we were there. In my mind I pleaded ... "God please give the dogs a day off today!"

As I drove the short distance to secondary, I gathered myself and calmly told Heather, "Just keep your cool, we're not busted yet. Are you OK?"

"I'm OK."

I parked the car in a stall and waited and waited. Nobody even came to our car. It seemed like forever. Finally, a heavyset customs agent came over, and looked at the paper on our windshield.

He told us, "Get out of the car. What are you bringing back from Mexico?"

"Nothing. We just looked around for awhile." I answered.

"What is in all those boxes?" he asked.

"We are moving to LA from Colorado. It is a bunch of our stuff."

He looked inside with a flashlight and then said ... "OK, take everything out and put it on these tables."

My heart sank a little more. Heather and I started unloading. I happened to see Mike drive past, and he was looking directly at us. I avoided looking at him. They must have sent him to secondary also. As we worked, the agent started going through our belongings. He looked at everything. He even opened up books and notebooks practically page by page. He made me unroll the sleeping bags and re-roll them. He took every item out of every box. He looked inside old letters that I had, and even read some parts. He asked questions about everything. He went through the glove box of the car. He knocked on side panels, pushed on seats, and went back to look through more suitcases and boxes. I took everything out except for the stuff in the floor compartment. The agent was busy searching, and didn't notice the floor compartment right away. He literally tore us apart for over an hour. It seemed like eternity.

As he worked, and time drug on, I watched all the hundreds of cars pass through the gates, and head out onto the freeway toward San Diego. I finally popped off at the agent, and said …"Look at all those cars being passed right through. How come you're hassling us so much? Is it because I have long hair or something? This isn't fair!"

I didn't want to press too hard, and tick him off, but figured a little offense was in order. The agent didn't respond at all to my remarks. He just kept searching.

Finally he finished everything on the tables. He walked to the back of the vehicle and saw the handle on the floor, and opened the compartment up. My heart skipped a beat. He looked through my jackets, and then took out one of the small boxes.

He said to me … "What's inside the big box?"

I said … "Just more of the same. Do you want me to take it out too?"

He looked at the box a minute and said … "That's all right, I'll look at it right here."

He opened one end of the huge box, and stuck his hand inside about a foot. I happened to look up and caught Heather's eye. We had a millisecond of non-verbal communication … of which we both said … "son - of - a - _____!"

The agent's arm came out of the box, with a shoe in his hand. Somebody is writing this script. He put his arm way inside again. I was positive I would see yellow cellophane. He came out with an iron. I was afraid to look at Heather lest he happened to read one of us. The agent opened the other end of the box, pushed aside some of the top clothes … and once again, forced his arm deep into the box from the opposite end. He pulled out a book.

To my utter disbelief, he said … "OK load it all back in." As he said that, he was writing something on a small form. "After you get loaded up give this slip to the exit booth … You can go."

"Keep your cool Roger. You're not out of here yet. Heather … you better be reading my mind. Don't be overanxious. OK? Let's take our time and pack things up right ... and then we'll **get the ____ out of here!**"

Fifteen minutes later, as we pulled past the exit booth onto the freeway, and into the night, we were both still in some kind of shock. Actually it was unbelief that we were free. I can't describe the feeling. It was totally weird. I guess my mind was having trouble catching up with events. Now I'm 99.9% busted ... now I'm 100% free driving down the 5 Freeway with a box of invisible kilos.

I finally said to Heather ... "What a trip that was. DANG! I can't believe they didn't have any dogs. UNBELIEVABLE! I can't believe he didn't pull out a kilo! You did good Heather. That's the last time I'll do it that way!" ... and it was.

CHAPTER 26

"A MONKEY NAMED ROSE"

I drove up to L.A. with Heather and Obie, and some of our hard-earned Mexican commercial. In my absence, my other dog, Partner, had bit two people at Maggie's house. One victim was the mailman. The San Diego animal control people had picked him up. What a drag! I was real upset, but sorry to say, slightly relieved. Two dogs were definitely becoming a hassle … especially when you live on the road most of the time. Mike stayed stoned in San Diego with his girlfriend. I was getting increasingly concerned about our slow talking Viking.

In LA I re-united with Roberta. She was becoming more and more a beautiful young woman … a long shot from the skinny fourteen year old that I once knew. She had a new job, and looked so proper all dressed up. She seemed curious about my hometown-traveling companion. On the other hand, Heather was accustomed to me being with different girls. She figured out real quick that I had special feelings for Roberta. Heather played her part perfect, and gave me total space.

We made the round of friends and acquaintances. In fact, Heather found out from home, that some people from Fremont were in LA. One of them was an old high school classmate of mine … a crazy but cool guy named Joe Connors. It's a small world. We looked them up at some apartments in the San Fernando Valley, and several wild parties ensued. We had a blast. Roberta's pretty friend Pam tagged along to one of our events, and at a certain dramatic moment, grabbed her blouse, pulled it over her head … and yelled out … "Let's orgy!" Soon, the other girls matched Pam's 19-year-old bare breasts with their own. I can well imagine some of the stories that filtered back to Peyton Place Fremont.

The main downer to that whole episode was that Obie got lost. He had wandered over to a nearby park one morning. We followed his trail through the middle of the San Fernando Valley, with no luck. I couldn't believe it. Partner was one thing, but Obie was a part of me. I stayed an extra day just looking for him. We put signs up and everything. I was sick. I was pissed. When I'd get in the station wagon, I'd picture my little sidekick. He never gave me any trouble from the instant that he was handed to me out of a cardboard box. When Obie was excited he would jump back and forth from the front seat to the rear seat ... fast as a ping-pong ball. He was one of the best dogs I ever owned.

Roberta sold a bunch of pot for me again. Because of her new work schedule, she wasn't present for any of the recent wild parties. That was good. I didn't even want to share her in an all out orgy. However, she did unexpectedly come one morning to the apartments, and caught me with her girlfriend Pam. It was a bummer. She was really hurt. I was surprised how hurt she was, and realized too late that she was serious about us. I did a lot of fast-talking, which seemed to work, but our relationship was never the same after that. Roberta continued to be my friend and occasional lover, but the special something was gone. I was definitely in a losing mode ... two dogs and one fox.

A trip to visit Cliff in Malibu seemed to be in order. As usual he bought some marijuana. I stayed a couple days camping out in his art studio, and absorbing the ocean. Heather stayed with her friends in the Valley. It was good to be with my old Army buddy again. He was doing real good, cranking out lots of paintings, and even giving high dollar art lessons to the rich locals. Cliff and another artist friend of ours, Paul Kelly, continued to manage a large apartment complex right on the beach. They had a neat modern apartment on the third floor with an ocean view. Both of them spent about half of their time chasing and catching women. Cliff was the ringleader. He never changed. A friend of mine's pretty wife told me ... "Cliff even **thinks** with his organ."

Whenever anyone would suggest that Cliff might be a little obsessed with sex, he would say ... "Man ... I can't help it! I'm a Scorpio. That's how we're wired!"

Cliff was a trip. He loved three things ... sex, painting, and surfing. He knew nothing about current events, or politics, or even TV. He never voted and told me ... "Who in the heck would I vote for? I don't have time to follow any of that crap. I just hope to God that somebody knows what their doing."

One morning on my visit Cliff said ... "Hey Rog, I just got a phone call from my girlfriend. She works for this movie star. He has been asking if she could get him some pot. I told her I probably could get some for them the next time you came through. This guy, I forget his name, but he is a pretty big star. Anyway he wants you to come over to his house, and he'll buy a couple lids. He lives right here in Malibu."

I told Cliff, "Forget it. I'm not going anywhere. Tell him to come here."

They talked on the phone again ... "He wants to know if you can meet him down Pacific Coast Hwy by the market in half an hour. Hey this guy is on the level. He really is a big movie star. Terri has worked for him for a long time. I don't think you can order him around."

I said, "I don't give a ____ how big of a star he is. I'd like to help, but I'm not going to run around Malibu for a couple lids, taking a chance on strangers. Tell him to get in his car, and come here ... or forget it."

Cliff once again called his girlfriend, who in turn relayed my updated message. I figured our Mystery Actor would forget it, but about 20 minutes later Father Karris from The Exorcist walked into the art studio. I was amazed. It was an actual rush when he walked through the door. I had seen the head-spinning movie about three times. Jason Miller played the young priest. I sold him a couple lids at top dollar, and did my first celebrity interview. He was really a cool guy.

We got talking about the movie while sampling the pot. I asked him ... "Did any weird things happen while you were making The Exorcist? That was a pretty spooky flick."

Jason said, "You wouldn't believe all the things that happened. The set burned up three times. I went through a divorce. Several people died. All kinds of co-incidental disasters happened to people directly and indirectly associated with the film. It was uncanny."

I said, "Do you really think there was a connection between the disasters and making a movie about demons and whatnot?"

"Well, it's pretty darn suspicious to say the least," he answered ... "The worst thing that happened was with my young son. We were at the beach on a beautiful day, and everything was normal. My little boy was a short distance away playing in the sand. I saw this dirt bike coming down the beach real fast. Something told me, it was going to hit my son. Before I could do a thing, the motorcycle veered right toward my boy. I jumped up and yelled, but was totally helpless. As I watched in disbelief, it ran right over him. My son was transported to the hospital and is seriously injured."

We talked for quite awhile. Jason liked the pot. He was an art lover and impressed with the studio. I was surprised that Cliff didn't enter into any of our conversation. He was completely quiet with this little smirk on his face. I think he was slightly blown away having a movie star in his nifty little domain. It definitely was flashy.

Back in San Diego, Mike was getting back into heroin. I continued finding out little by little. Heather decided to fly back home to Fremont. It was time. Mike and I made up several sealed packets of cocaine and pot for her to sell in Ohio. We taped them to her legs, inside her jeans. We would miss our game little Midwestern smuggler. I drove her to Lindberg Field in our smashed up, dope infested station wagon. Before long, a shinny jet disappeared into the California sky ... "We had some real adventures Heather!! Take care girl, and don't get busted! ... PS ... send back my money ... less your well-earned cut."

A LAME PHONE CALL

I moved into Maggie's place for a while. Her next-door neighbor was a sweet girl living with her parents. Christie was about eighteen and owned a horse, which she kept in Lakeside ... a rural community about 20 minutes outside of San Diego. I went riding several times with her, and with one of her horsy girlfriends named Cindy. I really liked Cindy except that she had a steady boyfriend named Jack Crawford. He was a tall lanky guy, who I also thought was a cool guy. Jack became concerned after I went riding a couple times with Cindy alone. I found out from Christie, that he had called asking a bunch of questions. He wanted to know what we talked about when I was with Cindy and so on. I had never made any advances, because of Jack, although Cindy had told me that she was thinking about breaking up.

I called up Jack one silly day and said … "Hey Jack, this is Roger Sachs. I wanted to let you know that I've gone horseback riding several times with Christie and Cindy. I used to do a little riding back in Ohio when I was a kid, and I love horses. I'm not scheming on Cindy, (which I wasn't). Anyway, I don't hit on friend's old ladies."

Jack basically said that it wasn't necessary to explain anything, and that everything between him and Cindy was their own gig. He obviously was uncomfortable with my call, and didn't want to talk to me about Cindy… (but he had definitely grilled Christie).

In Lakeside I soon got to know some of the locals through the two girls. I sold a little pot to several of them. I was back down to selling lids again. The local kids hung out at this bachelor's place in the boon docks. Chuck, the bachelor, let the kids smoke dope, drink, and party at his house all the time. Chuck himself looked like a 35-year-old short-haired lumberjack. He was a cool guy, but totally square when it came to turning on. Even though he let the kids go wild … he was afraid to try marijuana, or any other drug. The kids tried and tried to get him to smoke a joint to no avail. He stuck to his beer.

Chuck also had a South American monkey named Rose. The monkey was something else, with beautiful markings, and a perfect little mask on her face. I think she was a Spider Monkey. Rose wasn't one of these tiny little monkeys. She was pretty big. I spent quite a few afternoons at Chucks, and got to know him pretty good. I was a little older than most of the kids, and besides ... I liked beer better than pot myself. Chuck suggested that I get a tent, and camp out on his property, since I was so mobile. He had a big piece of property and told me ... "just pitch a tent anywhere out back. No one ever bothers me. I don't even lock my doors."

So Christie, Cindy, and I had a good old time shopping at a big sporting goods store in San Diego. I bought a tent, expensive sleeping bag, Coleman stove, lantern, and all the goodies. It was fun. On the day that I pulled in with my gear, I had an unusual greeting. Monkey Rose was sitting on the fence intently watching me. The next thing I know, she ran up and jumped on my leg. I could feel powerful little hands lock on super tight. I didn't know what to do. I was afraid to grab her, and try to pry her off my leg. Rose's dark round eyes were looking straight up into my eyes. It was like she was pausing to see what I'd do. I stood still just hoping she didn't bite. Then, in a real quick move, Rose grabbed my belt, reached a long arm up, and snatched my cigarettes out of my shirt pocket ... slick as a whistle. The second she had my pack of Marlboros in her furry little hand, she pushed off of me, ran up a fence, and onto the roof of Chuck's house.

I yelled ... "Hey you little dickens ... give me my cigarettes back!"

Rose looked down at me for a second, and then started pulling cigarettes out of the pack. She was completely ignoring me now, and one-by-one, she pulled the cigarettes out, shredded them into tiny little pieces, and cast them into the air. My cigarettes came floating down onto the driveway in hundreds of little shreds. I really got a charge out of the little thief. Later I told Chuck what his monkey did. He said. "Oh yeah ... Rose will get your cigarettes every time. It's one of her specialties. You have to guard them for dear life, if you want to keep your habit going." Rose was a trip.

Shortly after setting up camp on Chuck's property, a gang of the young and restless descended upon his remote pad. I joined the festivities. There was a houseful. We were drinking beer and smoking pot. Several of the girls were saying ... "Come on Chuck ... take a hit off this joint ... it won't kill you! Don't be a party pooper."

Pretty soon half of the place was on Chuck's case trying to get him to turn on. Chuck defended himself ... "Look ... how many times do I have to tell you wild Indians, that I'm not ready for any of that. For one thing, if you really want to know, the main reason I don't want to smoke pot is because I can't inhale smoke … and I don't want to learn. I tried smoking cigarettes a hundred years ago, and it hurt my throat, made me dizzy, and I felt like **total crap**! I decided there's no fun or satisfaction in that. If I can't inhale cigarette smoke … I dang sure can't inhale marijuana. This is especially after watching you guys, cough and choke … and turn bright red with your eyes half popped out every time you take a hit!"

Everybody laughed and hooted.

I had a great idea … "Hey Chuck, do you like brownies? I'll buy if you fly."

Soon, we all ganged up on poor Chuck with renewed vigor, telling him how great marijuana brownies were … and that they were absolutely cough-resistant to 100 meters or more. I donated a lid of pot. One of the gals ran to the grocery store for some brownie mix. To tell the truth, I had never personally made any kind of brownies, let alone marijuana brownies … and no one else knew how much pot to put in … so we put almost the whole lid in one batch. After about 3 more beers, we pulled out, and cooled off our labor of love.

Chuck was still hemming and hawing, but he finally ate a big old brownie, along with the rest of us. The party kept on, but pretty soon I started to get a major buzz, that eventually hit me like a sledgehammer. I looked over at poor Chuck. He was sitting in a chair not saying a word … but looking avocado green. I couldn't believe how stoned I was! The place and the people turned psychedelic on me. It was heavier than the first introductory hash I smoked in France.

Chuck was mumbling, and then got this wild, terrified look on his face. We all tried to calm him down … but everyone was pretty blasted. Here, I had simply wanted to give him a mild intro to cannabis, since he was so paranoid … with an innocent little brownie. But now Chuck was not only afraid, he was mortified … and spinning out of control. He looked like a caged animal … and all of a sudden, he ran to the bathroom and puked his guts out. As the guttural splashing sounds echoed throughout the house … for some reason everyone started laughing … and we couldn't stop for nothing. Poor Chuck.

During the next couple months, I managed to deplete most of my hard earned cash. My master plan was taking a major setback, but not a problem. I continued living in the tent somewhat ... and Rose continued to eyeball my cigarettes. However, pretty soon I couldn't handle the freezing cold nights. Inside the tent, inside my down sleeping bag, I would sweat ... and then if I left even a crack open in the bag, I would wake up with an icy draft creeping around here and there. After several sleepless nights, I went back to Maggie's. Heather mailed me about half of the money she was supposed to send, and I have never heard from her since. The last thing I even indirectly heard about her, was from my brother back in Fremont, who said he saw her at Chuds. She was being drug by her boyfriend out of the bar. He drug her by her hair, while she screamed threats and cussed him out at the top of her lungs.

"Gee Heather ... what happened to the sweet young Christian girl?"

"Mike ... did we play a part in this creation?"

Talking about hair pulling... I went to another party at Mike's girlfriend's place. As usual tons of people were there. At the end of the night, a huge 250 something pound volunteer started ordering everyone to leave ... "The party is over folks ... time to book!" Everyone was leaving, but I had planned to sleep over on the couch, as I had many times. Mike was upstairs crashed with Kathy. This particular bouncer didn't know me, and didn't believe me, etc. He ordered me out. When I refused, he pushed me in my chest backwards. I tried to punch him, but several people jumped on both of us trying to break up the fight. As they pulled us apart, my foe managed to grab a fistful of long hair, and **wouldn't** let go. It felt like my hair was going to be yanked completely out, and made me mad as a hornet. Finally, I was pulled free of Chris Jackson, and several guys shoved me out the side door. They slammed the door and locked it.

I started screaming obscenities back at the overweight bouncer that might have shocked Grandpa Ira. I called him every name I could think of, and dared him to come outside. "Come on you fat, sorry, coward, blankety blank ... your twice my size ... let's finish what you started." I went on and on, and banged on the door. I could see him and a bunch of people inside. They were laughing. Finally Chris came up to the window on the door, and started making faces at me. When he put his face right up to the window with a huge mocking smile, I punched through the screen, and through the glass. He went backward on the kitchen floor holding his face. When he still didn't come outside, I finally got in my car and went over to Maggie's. The next day, with a huge hangover, I found out that they had taken Chris to the hospital. He had glass in one of his eyes. I felt sick to my stomach about the whole thing. To compound things for the poor guy, the following day he got his hand caught in a machine at his work. When I saw him at Christi's about four days later, he had a patch on one eye and a sling on one arm.

He told me … "When they take this patch off, if my eye is OK, we'll forget the whole thing. But if my eye is screwed up … then you and me are going to go about 10 more rounds in the ring."

I said, "Let me know. Sorry about the glass. I really hope your eye is OK. But if you want me, I'm here at Maggie's most of the time."

My homespun philosophy of, "what comes around - goes around", came true in a couple short weeks after my window-smashing fight. I stopped over at Maggie's house, and found out that Cindy's boyfriend had been looking for me that day. I had recently played an old drinking game that I learned in the Army, called "Here's to the Cardinal" with Christie and Cindy. We got real drunk. It never fails. When we ran out of beer, Cindy and I went to the 7-Eleven for some backup. Cindy had been kinda flirty. Half way back to Maggie's house, I parked the car, and did exactly what I told Jack that I would never do … hit on his girlfriend. Cindy was 95% unreceptive, but the 5% kept me trying for quite awhile.

Jack continued to be suspicious, and soon found out from Christie, on one of his interrogations, that **one** time it took us over an hour to get beer from the store. He then badgered Cindy for days to find out if anything had happened. Finally she admitted that I made a pass at her. The war was on.

If I know I'm going to get into a fight, I hate waiting around. I called Jack … but he was at his own birthday party at Kathy's place. I called there. He was at the store. I left a message that I was at Maggie's. I waited and waited, but no return call … so I drove to the party. Like a fool, I walked straight into the enemy camp. What was I thinking???

The place was packed out. I went into the house, and when I got to the kitchen, I saw Jack. The moment he saw me, he started screaming … "Let's take it outside mother ____er!"

Just outside the same door that I had recently paid to fix … I punched Jack as hard as I could … aiming for his mouth. He ducked, and I broke my hand on his upper forehead. It felt like I hit concrete. Everything went downhill from there. I was able to get him in a headlock, but he grabbed my crotch, and practically twisted my testicles off. It hurt like heck. I kept yanking on his head and neck, trying to get free of his below the belt tactic. That went on for an eternity until both of us were pretty winded.

Finally we separated. By now the entire party was outside in a huge circle around us. They were all Jack's friends. (Home court advantage fight fans). It was his party. The only ally that I had was Mike... and he was upstairs completely passed out. I looked over at Jack. He was breathing real heavy, and not looking so sure of himself. However, I felt completely drained. Right about then, one of the guys said ... "OK dudes ... Let's go round two!"

I hate braggers, but once in awhile I might have mentioned to someone, after a few beers, that I was definitely maintaining Grandpa Ira's record ... undefeated in every fair fight. That was true until Round Two with Jack Crawford. He completely knocked me out with a big old lanky-armed punch. I saw it coming an instant before the blackout. Twinkle-twinkle little stars. You really do see them.

While I was unconscious, (I was later informed), my vindictive friend got real macho, and kicked me about thirty times. My face looked like a piece of butchered meat. I lay there in a pool of blood for a long time. No one did a thing. Talkative Christie was there, and she screamed for someone to help. I woke up in the back seat of a car ... on Christi's blood soaked lap. I only remember bits and pieces of the jerky car ride, and of the hospital itself.

One of the kicks to my head had split my bottom lip completely in two ... just like Walker's in the 102nd Signal Battalion. "What comes around goes around Roger." Both of my eyes were completely shut. The doctors tried to X-ray my head. I totally fought them because every touch hurt so bad. It took about 3 people to hold me. I guess they eventually got their ghostly pictures, and I was mercifully knocked out with some kind of painkiller.

In the morning I called Maggie, and through painful crusty lips, asked her to send Marta to pick me up. The hospital tried to keep me, but I walked. When Marta finally showed up, she said ... "Holy molly! You're all ____ed up Roger! Are you sure you should be leaving the hospital?"

I went to Maggie's and lay in bed for a solid week. My grotesquely swollen face turned into a rainbow of colors … not just black and blue. There was yellow, and orange, and brown, mixed in with different shades of black and blue, and purple. When I finally emerged from the bedroom, I went to the Sports Arena to see Muhammad Ali fight Joe Frazier on closed circuit TV. It was the "Thriller in Manila". They literally beat the living crap out of each other … but I still looked worse than both of them put together, and I didn't even have multiple millions of dollars to show for it. As a matter of fact, I was almost broke. Anyway, I was truly glad Ali won. Once an Ali fanatic … always an Ali fanatic.

I felt that I pretty much deserved my fate, because of the stupid, lame phone call, that I had made to Jack, declaring my honorable intentions with his girl. Nevertheless, I don't kick a guy in the head, numerous times, after he is already down and whipped. While lying in bed for a week or so, wondering if I'd ever look normal again … I decided to let it all slide, and call it even-Steven … unless Jack pressed the issue again. If that happened, I would do my push-ups, and try Round 3. If he beat me again, I seriously decided to shoot him in a kneecap. I was determined to keep guns out of my business … but enough is enough, when people start rearranging your face. I clearly visualized Jack slowly dragging one leg behind the other one … and with each and every crippled step he'd be reminded … "It's not cool to kick a guy when he's down … (step) (drag) … it's not **even** cool to kick a guy when he's down … (step) (drag) … I don't think I'll do that again …"

However, when I saw Jack come out of Christi's house a couple weeks later, he didn't make a move toward me. That was the last time I ever saw him. My hand stayed real swollen for weeks on end, and eventually I went back to the doctor. They X-rayed my right hand, and that's when I found out that it was broke. An effort was made to set the bone, but it was too late. The sharpest pain I ever felt, was when two large doctors tried to press the bone back in place. It didn't work. My knuckle has permanently dropped down below the other ones. It's the one over my little finger … the one that now matches Grandpa Ira's crippled little finger. I exited the hospital wearing still another sling and cast for six more weeks.

Christie later told me that she had to help Jack put his jacket on, when he left her house. It had been a couple weeks, but he couldn't put a jacket on by himself, because his neck and shoulder was all screwed up from the fight. She said she laughed at him, and told him ... "Good! I'm glad Roger did some damage after all!"

That made me feel a little better. I also heard that Cindy and Jack broke up a short time later. What a merry-go-round this life can be.

While I was getting detoured from my master plan playing ... "Here's to the Cardinal for the first time tonight" ... Mike was cooking up more sinister things.

That whole chapter of my life was a bum trip ... just ask Chuck. It was all about dark and dreary. Maybe the only bright spot ... was a monkey named Rose ... and she was a thief.

CHAPTER 27

"THE BLACK JEW"

When things get tough … go to the beach. That's exactly what I did. I can never stay down at the mouth for long when I'm at the ocean. Too much power … too much beauty … too much life. I moved back to Ocean Beach. I looked around, and found a little house behind a house to rent on Longbranch Street. "De ja vu." It came with a nice unattached garage, and a little courtyard. With the little bit of money I had left, along with my dwindling stash of drugs to sell, I set up a small bachelor's pad … in the midst of hippie heaven.

Not only did I miss the smell of sand and salt water … but I missed my dogs. It was like one of my charismatic relatives said after a couple decades of marriage and divorce. He said … "Just think. A year ago I had a wife, and a house, and a dog. **Dang**, I sure miss that dog!"

Just before moving back to Ocean Beach, a good friend of Martas' had a beautiful Golden Retriever that had a litter of these perfect little velvety puppies. I went to look at them when they were only a couple weeks old … and for a discounted price of $65, I got to make second pick out of the whole litter. It was a tough decision, because they were all so radical. I finally picked one of the stout looking males that caught my eye. I named him Leo, and a month later was able to pick him up. He had papers and everything. I never owned a full-bred dog, and this one was the coolest canine that God ever thought up.

Leo was a gentle sweetheart, but one hundred percent male, all at the same time. We had a few bumps in the road. For one thing, it was slightly difficult to potty train him on the move. I had him about a month before I landed back in OB. The garage was perfect for Leo and for business. It was roomy, shady, and cool inside. Along with the courtyard, it was one big playroom for my new partner in crime. Leo's webbed paws started to radically expand. He got bigger, and bigger, and bigger. He would consume huge bags of Purina Puppy Chow (mixed with a little canned Alpo) … and what a joy to watch him grow and develop. He was with me always, wherever I went, with very few exceptions … and then if necessary I had a list of people that I could leave him with. He was an instant hit with everyone. Obie was far out. Leo was royalty.

I enrolled in a Junior College just to get the money from my GI Bill. I went to classes about two times, and then collected $250 a month for a whole semester. I had to do something to generate some revenue fast, before I went completely broke. At the same time I bought a couple more kilos in San Diego, and broke them completely down into lids to sell in OB … mostly to the sailors and locals. I liked the role of a wholesaler, rather than street level sales … but necessity calls from time to time.

THE NORMAL JUNKIE ROUTINE

I had pulled completely away from Mike. He was back into heroin big time. I subsequently heard through the grape vine that he got Kathy strung out real bad, as well as a whole set of kids in Allied Gardens.

What a bummer! I really like Mike, but heroin sure has messed up and controlled his life. From time to time, over the next few months, I would hear reports of his miss-adventures. Then I heard the news that he and Kathy got busted trying to rob the May Company. He had taken a hostage and the whole nine yards. Years later after he was released from prison, I finally learned the details directly from Mike himself.

It's another wild story, but here are the highlights. Mike and his girlfriend got really hooked again on heroin. They were doing robberies, and dealing, and the normal junkie routine. Apparently Kathy had worked at the May Company or something, and knew the inside scoop. However, when they actually did the robbery everything went wrong. Mike ended up taking a female employee hostage trying to get away. He forced her in an elevator at gunpoint. When the door to the elevator opened on the ground floor, there was a crowd of people, security guards, and police already waiting.

Mike told me ... "I yelled at everyone to back off, or I would shoot the girl. I put her head under my arm, and held the gun to her head. Everyone backed off, and I drug her over to the door, but the ____ers had locked all the doors. I started kicking the heck out of the glass trying to get out, but it was some kind of super thick glass. Even with my big old motorcycle boots, I couldn't break through. While I was kicking the glass, the girl managed to get free, and about ten Joe-citizens jumped me immediately, and started thumping the crap out of me. I thought they were going to kill me. They got the gun away. It wasn't even loaded. I didn't want to shoot anyone ... I just wanted drugs."

While Mike was out on bail on that charge, he and Kathy drove up to Oceanside, which is about fifty miles north of San Diego, and robbed a Jolly Roger Restaurant. This time they made their escape OK, but a couple miles down the road they saw a cop car pass them at high speed, going in the opposite direction. Mike looked in his mirror, and saw them spin around, and turn on their flashing lights. The chase was on.

Mike said he drove through a couple beach communities at around ninety miles per hour, sometimes on the wrong side of the street, and through red lights and stop signs. He wanted to get away. Pretty soon there was about five cop cars chasing him. He cut sharply across some lanes, and got on a freeway entrance with a cop car almost beside him. He heard a huge boom behind him. A shotgun or something blew out the entire rear window of his car. He pushed Kathy down on the seat, and when they got on the freeway he floored it.

Mike told me about the continuing chase ... "I was going over a hundred miles per hour down Interstate 5. When I looked in my mirror, it looked like a regular circus was following me. I'm not kidding. There must have been a dozen or more highway patrol and cop cars by now, with all their lights flashing like crazy, and a couple helicopters flying above us shining their lights down ... it was a trip. When we came up to the place where the 805 Freeway and the 5 Freeway fork off, I pretended like I was going to go down the 805. At the last second I swerved over onto the 5 Freeway. I figured if we could get more into town, I could lose them on side streets that I know real well. We could dump the car if necessary.

But, a couple more miles down the freeway they had a roadblock set up. There must have been six or seven cop cars parked all the way across the freeway. I saw a spot where two of the cars were apart a little, and I rammed them trying to bust through. It didn't work. My car got all mangled up in between two cop cars, and we went sliding down the freeway and finally stopped. A bunch of cops ran over with their guns, and screamed at me to roll the window down. I rolled the window down, and they pulled me right out the window. They started beating me, and then this big old police dog grabbed me in the leg. One of the cops yelled ... 'Don't let your dog put that **thing** in his mouth!!' Another huge cop was screaming ... 'Let me take him in ... I'll make sure he never gets there!' I was thinking ... 'O God ... don't let that big gorilla take me in!'"

• • •

But, I didn't know any of this back in OB, except that Mike got busted again, and was looking at some very serious time. All I knew for sure about anything ... was that I had to work my capital back up to a point where I could make some progress. I drove to Maggie's to see if Marta would help me sell lids on the Cliffs. She jumped at the chance to make some fast money, and asked if her friend Bobbi could help also. I figured it would be much safer for a girl to carry a bunch of lids around, walking down the beach, talking to guys, etc ... than for me. Early in the morning, while it was still dark, I stashed several bunches of lids along the cliffs in various places. When we would run out of a batch, a new supply was readily available. Later in the day, with the hundreds and hundreds of people, it would be crazy to carry that much pot around. After a short while in OB, I learned that several narcs and snitches, were watching the crowds for dealers, through binoculars from the pier ... but I planted all my booty well out of view of the pier. We only did it this way a couple times, but each time sold out by early afternoon. It was risky but very lucrative.

On the last day that we did the beach thing, this big black dude came walking past us by the tide pools. Marta had one lid left, and as he walked up she said ... "Hey dude, I got one lid of some fine smoke left. It's a healthy three-finger lid. Would you like it, so I can get the ____ out of here?"

He said ... "No thanks."

Marta turned back to me and said ... "Well, Bobbi and I are going to head back to the car, and we'll get rid of this last lid on the way. I'll see you at my moms'. Let us know when you want us to do it again. Did we do good ... or what? We sold those lids like hot cakes! Dang! Later Rog."

The black dude had walked toward the breakers, but after the girls left, he walked back toward me. He came up, as I was getting ready to split, and said ... "So what's happening my man? What's the give ... you got those young babes out here hustling lids for you on a Saturday morning? What kind of crap is that? Do you actually make a living like this?"

He talked a mile a minute, and was looking me straight in the eye with this huge smile as he talked. I said ... "Why all the questions? Are you a narc or something?"

"____ no!" he started loudly laughing ... "Do I look like a narc? What's the matter with you ... hippie dude ... I ain't no narc, and I don't fool around with a couple lids either. When I do something ... hey mister ... **when I do something**, I make some **serious** coin! You should be selling those broads hot little tails, if anything! Man, you don't know nothing!" He continued to laugh at me.

I liked him right away. It's hard for me to not like someone who is smiling and joking all the time. He wasn't being serious, but was definitely trying to figure me out. My black friends in Fremont used to "talk ____" all the time. They were geniuses at creating a whole new language … as they talked. In fact, I think my small town Ohio friends were even better at chucking and jiving than their west coast brothers. I loved it. However, this guy had a PHD in talking pure unoriginal "crap". It flowed and he was good. I was wondering, what the real bottom line angle was. I didn't really think he was a narc … but maybe.

"What's your name white man?" he asked.

I had recently adopted a new alias and told him … "Just call me Jake. What's your name?"

"Harry Specter … the black Jew … in the flesh mother ____er!" He busted out laughing, and put his palm out so I could "give him some skin".

I slapped his hand. He flipped it over in one motion and "gave me change". Harry was the most hand slapping, amplified brother I ever met. I would soon learn that every five minutes was five, high five, behind the back five, casual five, triumphant five … etc., etc., etc. Even when it was getting real old, and tiresome … it was all Harry … all the time … so much so … that I'd finally just laugh, and sting that big black palm. Handshakes were another whole trip.

Harry was something else. He was a big, big man, well over six feet tall, and built a little like Rosie Greer, or maybe even Reggie White. He probably weighed around 225 pounds or more, and carried himself real well. He dressed in expensive clothes, but not overly flashy. He did have a big old diamond encrusted ring, and a shiny gold watch, but that was about it. The most flashy thing about Harry Specter, the black Jew, was his huge smile, and jolly, joking nature.

In fact, on the walk back toward the pier he said … "Are you driving my man? You know what they say … **Money t a l k s but bull ____ w a l k s !** Are you walking?"

Before I could answer a word, Harry continued … "How about we grab my wheels, and I'll spring for a big fat steak somewhere. I was born hungry, and I want to talk possibilities with you at the same time. How about it Jake?"

I was game for a good steak, and thus was the beginning of a memorable partnership to say the least. Harry took me to his ride, which was a late model VW bus, and as we drove off, he started telling me that he had customers for hundreds of kilos of pot. He said … "Why screw around with a few lids, taking all that heat and exposure, when there is a righteous fortune to be made being the 'middle man'. The middleman has the best of all worlds. I hook up money if you have the merchandise, or I deliver the goods, if you have the finances. My job is to keep things flowing. It's other people's money and other people's dope … clean and quick. **Middleman is the name of the game!"**

I told him, "I've sold a lot of kilos. Right now I'm trying to get my money back up to start moving quantities again. I had a couple setbacks."

Harry started laughing again … "What kind of connections does barefooted Jake have?"

"Well, among other things, I have some Mexican connections, and I've done a little smuggling. I have some money people in LA, and Colorado, and here and there. But, before I say anything else, let me see your wallet Harry."

"What the ____ you want to see my wallet for?"

"If you're a cop or a narc, you probably have some kind of ID on you. So if your not, then its no big deal … just let me check out your wallet."

Harry cussed and bitched and tried to laugh it off, but when I insisted … for us to talk any kind of business, he finally threw me his wallet. I looked through it, and didn't find any badges or anything, but did discover why he was so reluctant. His name on his California driver's license was Marvin Alan Walker. I quickly memorized his real name and address, and said … "So Harry Specter is your alias. Well, that's no big deal. At least you're probably not a narc. My real name is not Jake James."

Harry tried to convince me that his real name actually was Harry, and that the ID was phony. That could have been, but for some reason, I never believed it. He asked if we could meet with my Mexican connection some time. I said … "How about right now?"

So we changed our steak plans to Carne Asada burritos. Within just a couple hours of meeting "Harry the black Jew" on a San Diego beach, I took him to Mexico to meet Alberto. Harry had been doing a lot of talking. I wanted to flip over a couple real life cards. I could tell he was impressed. It was actually a pretty uneventful visit, since it was only an introduction. Alberto was warm as toast, and told me that he had heard about Mike. I lied and told him that Harry was an old associate of mine, and that we had a customer who wanted a hundred kilos. Harry was asking what kind of price we could get. Alberto said he could get us a load for $90 a unit. We would have to cross them ourselves. We smoked a joint with Alberto and split.

Over the next couple weeks, Harry came around a lot. He always had a big wad of bills in a money clip. He loved to shoot pool and chase women. We partied a lot. He would take me to fancy restaurants. I enjoyed Harry, and was trying to team up with him, and tap into some of his customers and action. He was looking for new sources of drugs and deals. He said his customers wouldn't front any money for a smuggling gig. It was too risky for their blood. I finally got my first check from the V.A. for my college benefits. It was for two months and totaled $500. I got five one hundred dollar bills from the bank, and flashed them on Harry. I told him I had turned a load of pot for some people.

The next day Harry shows up, and brings me a gunnysack full of kilos of marijuana. He said ... "Here is some leftovers from a deal I just turned. Break them down, into pounds or whatever. Turn them quick. I'll keep bringing you more. Use your local connections or run up to LA. I want to help you get your stake up, so we can fry some bigger fish."

I started breaking ahead fast, and it also felt good to a have a real soul brother again. I hadn't had a close black friend since kicking around with Hubert Jackson. He had transferred to the University of Washington, after attending LACC, and was long gone. I was getting real tight with San Diego Harry, and had his phone number, but he never let anyone come to his house. I could understand the precautions, and didn't take it personal. I used aliases, and was on the move all the time. In Harry's case, he was either married or living with someone with kids, because I could often hear family type commotions in the background, and the same woman often answered the phone. I had memorized his address from his driver's license, but then forgot it. He would always come to my little pad in OB, and continued bringing me merchandise to sell. We partied together all the time. Our favorite hangout was a tavern near the beach called The Sunshine Company.

One evening Harry and I stopped in at the Sunshine Company, where everyone knew me as "Jake". We were drinking, and shooting pool, and having a good old time. Harry was practically a pro with a pool cue. He bragged about hustling people out of big bucks playing nine-ball, and setting chumps up in honky-tonk bars. I could only beat him about once every three or four games ... but he kept me laughing win or lose. Harry pointed out two girls, who just walked in and sat down. He leaned over next to my ear, after slamming a stripped ball into the corner pocket, and said, "Now that shorter one is one fine looking fox ... um. ... um... ummmm!"

Harry drinks Tanqueray Sevens almost exclusively, and when he went up to the bar to order another round, he turned on the fast-talking charm, and invited the pretty gals to join us ... which they did. We all played pool and had fun. Harry kept the conversation lively. The girls were continuously laughing. It turned out that they were on vacation from New York City ... of all places. The shorter one, the one that Harry had been drooling over, somehow gravitated toward me, and instantly Leo and I had a new roommate. Debbie moved in with me for the last couple weeks of her visit to California, and decided she wanted to be my "old lady".

Debbie was nineteen years old, very quiet and soft spoken, but definitely a gal of action. She came from a broken home, and had a wealthy domineering Jewish mother, whom she had totally rebelled against. She told me her mother shipped her off to a fancy boarding school, but eventually she ran off, and had been on her own since age 15. She was presently living with a guy, back in Manhattan, named Ken, who was about 30 years old. She was smart as a whip, had an IQ of about 160, in addition to being pretty as a picture. I thought she looked like a combination of Natalie Wood, Sophia Loren, and Pocahontas. We hit it off real good, and my fast paced, wheeling and dealing life style at the beach was A-OK with her.

After a couple weeks, Debbie flew back to New York City. I had invited her to come live with me if she wanted. She said she had to break things off with Ken, and get all her furniture and things out of his apartment. After that, she would fly back to San Diego. We talked on the phone a couple times a week, and then she told me it was going to take longer than she thought to return to California. From our conversations, I got the picture that she was still staying with this Ken guy, and I was in no mood for games. I enjoyed playing house with her, but didn't need another Jill in my life. I told her ... "Forget it Debbie. Don't bother coming back."

After hanging up on her, she immediately called back, and said she would fly to California the next day ... which sounded strangely familiar ... only this time I truly didn't care one way or the other. It was cool with her, and it was cool without her. At that point we only had about a two-week fling going. Nevertheless, the next day I drove to the airport and picked up my wandering New Yorker. She moved back in, and Leo was happily jumping all over her. Debbie made Leo a scarf out of a huge red handkerchief. He looked very hep. The next couple months were a good time for us living at the beach. We made several trips to Mexico, and partied with Harry and Debbie's friend Carolyn from back east.

Debbie also had friends in Ocean Beach, who she had originally been visiting. The house she had been staying in, was a little like The White House, with a much different personality. The alpha male of the house, was a guy named Chuck, who signed the lease, was a "somewhat" professional gambler at the local card rooms, and full time postal employee. His favorite past time was cocaine dealing, and filling his fenced in yard with nude sunbathers … especially of the opposite sex. One wall in the house was covered with pictures of his back yard garden of Eden. Debbie had soaked up some rays a few times while staying there. A couple of the girls coaxed Debbie and I to join in the nude festivities, but I wasn't that "free to be" and didn't like Chuck. When I wouldn't go to the party, they brought the party to me. Pretty soon my little courtyard had a line of totally nude gals stretched out on beach towels. Leo would playfully bounce around between the bodies, and I felt totally obligated to join the crowd. Someone grabbed a camera, and eventually that nude picture of me found its way into the hands of Debbie's mother. Nice introduction to a rich New York City businesswoman, with her office on the 54th floor of the Empire State Building.

One day Debbie was telling me about her mother, and some of her childhood experiences. She said that her parents were divorced, and that she really clashed with her mom for most of her life. Her mom sent her to a girl's boarding school. At the school there was a rumor that the place was haunted. Apparently the building was a mansion, previously owned by a young married couple. The young husband was killed, if I'm getting this right, and then the young widow never remarried, and grew real old grieving over her husband until she died. A ghost in the form of the young bride would appear to the students, and sometimes she would appear as the old scary widow.

Debbie said … "I walked into this room one time, and a rocking chair was rocking by itself, and then things started flying back and forth across the room by themselves."

I didn't believe her, but just like my friend's story in Boulder, Debbie swore it was true.

She said … "Another time I was sleeping, and when I woke up the young bride was standing next to my bed … and then she disappeared."

Debbie then told me how she and some of the girls got into the I Ching, which is ancient Chinese fortune telling. She said … "I've studied it for years. I'll show you how it works."

She got out a big book, which is their I Ching bible of sorts, and then told me to think of a question. As I concentrated on my question I was to throw these five coins. The coins form hexagrams, which can be interpreted by looking them up in the book.

Debbie said ... "You can use regular coins, but I have some original Chinese coins that I use. Do you want to try it?"

After my experience with Lacy's Taro cards, I didn't want any more Twilight Zone episodes in my life. At the same time, Debbie's stories reminded me of Steve's encounter with the mystic lady in Colorado asking to meet with Jesus Christ. It sparked my curiosity about what is really going on ... out there in the invisible realms. There are definitely some strange, and unexplainable stuff to put in your pipe. What about the mysteries surrounding the Great Pyramids and things like that? Plus, I kept hearing news reports on the radio of people who said they picked up a longhaired hitchhiker, who would talk to them about God. This hitchhiker would at some point ask if they believed in Jesus, and then would totally disappear from the moving vehicle. For several months there were multiple reports, which started on the east coast, and then headed west. Joking broadcasters would say things like ... "It looks like Jesus is heading for California folks!"

I told Debbie ... "OK, give me the coins. My question is ... is Jesus Christ actually who he claimed to be?"

Debbie said ... "I don't know if it will answer a question like that."

"Well, let's see what it says."

I threw the coins, and she started looking up the answers. It was all a bunch of mumbo jumbo, which didn't make any sense at all, except that the answers talked about heavenly things, and mystical this and that, and the other. It didn't have anything that you could grab a hold of. It sounded like a greasy politician's answer in a way.

My analysis was ... "the I Ching is a crock of crap."

Debbie defended it by saying ... "I never got answers like that one. Each hexagram talked about the same heavenly things ... and it didn't say he wasn't who he said he was."

I wasn't convinced. However, I was having an increase in the coincidental superstitions that I inherited from Grandpa Ira. Especially the one ... where if you find a penny heads up ... that is good luck. If you find one that is tails ... that is bad luck. Somehow I managed to expand the principle, and now I noticed that when I would reach in my pocket to get a dime for the pay phone ... if the coin came out in my hand heads up, it was a good omen ... if it was tails ... look out! I kept telling myself that it was ridiculous. Nevertheless, it kept coming true over and over. I did most of our dealing from different payphones, and it got to the point that sometimes I wouldn't make the call if the coin came out tails.

I thought ..."If I told anyone about this ... they would definitely think I blew a cork!"

Back to reality... Harry came by as usual, and wanted me to go with him up north to Oakland. He had some business to take care of. It was a crazy trip in Harry's VW bus. Debbie's friend Carolyn came along, and was suppose to be, more or less, with Harry. We drove straight through to San Francisco. It was a fun time for Debbie and me. Outside of the van there was a warm rain coming down as we entered a section of San Francisco. Debbie said ... "Let's go streaking."

I told Harry, "Stop the van ... my woman has this nude thing on the brain ... and we're going to do a little streaking."

Harry said, "Come on now!"

So we put on our birthday suits, and streaked through a residential section of "The City". We all got a charge out of it.

As we approached Oakland, we rented a motel. I stayed in one room with Debbie, and Harry stayed in a room with Carolyn. In the morning Carolyn came over, and was complaining about Harry ... how he couldn't take no for an answer ... and that he had a gun in his suitcase ... and that she wanted Debbie to hitch with her back to San Diego. In the meantime, Harry came out of his room, and was mad as heck.

He walked over and told us ... "I told her ... 'I don't care if you use me ... **but don't abuse me!'** ____ the bitch. Get your stuff out of the van ... I'm not taking you anywhere!"

Carolyn was crying, and asking Debbie to go with her, but Deb didn't want to be stranded in Oakland, California either. I tried to smooth things over, but Harry was adamant ... "the broad is gone!"

Finally we gave Carolyn some money, and took off, leaving her behind. She held that episode against Debbie for years. Thankfully, she made it back to Ocean Beach all in one piece. It was a rough neighborhood where Harry and her blew up.

Later that day Harry took us to a small house in Oakland. We were in a totally black section of town, and the house we went to turned out to be command central for a baseball and football numbers racket. Different guys kept coming and going. Harry introduced me to the main guy, who was all slicked out with fancy clothes and spit shined shoes. He was real friendly, and after Harry explained that I moved a lot of merchandise out of San Diego, he decided to explain the operation they had going in Oakland.

He said ... "Well my man, we move a little snow for sure, but mostly we are organized in other areas. We send runners out mainly to large factories and businesses. People buy the cards we print up, and check off who will win the game that day, and what the score will be. We pay off thousands of dollars to the cards that pick the right numbers. It's a going thing ... and we be doing this for a loooong time."

After talking to Harry for a while, he continued ... "you and your pretty lady should relax, and hang out the rest of the day. Later this evening we are having a little get-together right here. So there's food in the kitchen, beer in the box, and just about anything you want, if you look hard enough. Don't be shy. I have a little biz to take care of, so I'll be checking you out later on."

That night the house filled up with people. Debbie and I were the only whites in the jam packed little house. I've been the only "honky" many a time, and it's always been cool. Since getting served as a young teenager in Simmies Restaurant, (which is a wild little black tavern on Dickerson Street in Fremont), to all the super loud parties with my college partner Hubert Jackson, in the Golden Ghetto of South Central L.A, I have developed a deep appreciation for my black friends. They know how to throw a wild party and have fun. Tonight was no exception. Besides all the loud music, beer, wine, and mixed drinks, it was the first-and-only party I've ever been to, where the host kept a small mountain of cocaine piled up on a coffee table the **entire** night. People freely kept dropping by taking healthy dents out of the white mountain with one of the straws. I got absolutely totally buzzed, and was literally " the last man standing". I never talked so much in my entire life. I can't remember one thing I said, but I had my syndicate brothers cracking up until the wee hours. Harry had them convinced that I was a major mover and shaker in San Diego. This was in spite of my bare feet and Budweiser T shirt. Sexy Debbie by my side was a definite asset, and object of great interest and respect. One of the dudes **slyly** slipped me his phone number, when Harry wasn't looking. **"What a total con this life can be."**

CHAPTER 28

"TEN SECONDS"

Over the next few months life became a total blur. I continued dealing with my soul brother friend, "The Black Jew". He loved to eat expensive meals at expensive restaurants. I thought it was a waste of money … but had to admit that steak, and lobster, and swordfish went down real nice with a barrage of mixed drinks. We became real close. At least I thought so. We had a lot of fun and laughs. Harry continued to supply me with fronted kilos, and trusted me to turn them into cash, which I did. Nevertheless, he was very secretive about his personal life and connections, which was understandable.

Harry said his people had a huge shipment of kilos and needed buyers … did I know of anyone who could turn a big load in San Diego? I did have one connection that needed a hundred kilos, but it would be a couple weeks before they would have their money. In the meantime I talked some new friends into putting up $5000.00. Harry set everything up. I was instructed to meet this black dude right near Belmont Park in Mission Beach.

I took the money and followed directions. As I pulled into the appointed parking lot, a tall, youngish looking black man walked up and asked if I was Roger. We then walked to a private place across the street. He was acting real nervous. He said … "Man this is crazy." He repeated the same thing about three times as we talked. I started wondering what was so crazy.

I asked him … "Look, Harry said it would take you about 20 minutes to turn this thing around. Is there a problem?"

"No man … everything's cool. Hold tight right here and I'll be back. It won't take long. Do you have the money?"

I asked if he wanted to count it, but he said it wasn't necessary …

and split. The minute he walked away I was sorry I handed him the money. But then, I told myself ... "Harry has come through time after time. It's probably all right. Just do your part!"

Well, twenty minutes turned into forty-five minutes. I started to get a very sick feeling in my stomach. Forty-five minutes turned into an hour ... and I knew inside that I just got ripped off ... that is ... "unless there is some other explanation"... "Son-of-a-____." Just in case, I waited a full two hours, and then shot back to Ocean Beach to my place.

As I walked in the door, the phone was ringing. Debbie and Leo were standing by waiting for me. I answered the phone. It was Harry.

"How does the load look?"

I said ... "Harry , what gives? Your man never came back! I got a bunch of people to answer to!"

Harry said ... **"What!** Are you kidding me??? You don't have the units? No way! Hold tight and I'll call you back."

An hour later Harry calls back ... "Jake, the punk middle man ripped off the money. He is one dead nigger. By tomorrow that mother is dead! Nobody messes me around like this. Believe me, he is dead. I'll handle it!"

"Harry ... listen ... **and I'm not jiving you** ... don't kill anyone! Try to get the money back ... but forget this punk. He's a low-life, but it's not worth killing someone. I mean it!"

"Yeah ... well ... we'll see about that. We're tracking him, and he's going to wish his sorry black behind never landed on this planet. I gotta go!"

Over the next few days, Harry came by several times giving me updates on the search. He informed me ... "The dude is out of San Diego on the run".

Harry would make it up to me ... "no matter what".

I took him at his word. But the bottom line was ... the money was gone ... and I had to do some fast-talking to the losers. What a drag!

Shortly after that fiasco I finally met Maggie's son-in-law. His name is Steve Peterson, and he came in from Colorado with his wife Paula and their two kids. They were staying at Maggie's place. Even though I had just suffered the losses from the rip-off, I had some other customers who had cash for a big load. I definitely wanted to get in with Steve, because I knew he had Mexican connections. He had dealt with Alberto in the past, but he had even better connections. However, Steve had a dealing partner who didn't like me. I could tell. His name is Joe Monroe. Joe had a real big dog, which was part German Shepard and part coyote. The dog was a lean, mean, vicious machine, who would bare his fangs like a wolf, and **lunge** at anyone who came near Joe's car. Scary animal! He bit several people.

One day I went to Maggie's house and walked in ... in the midst of an emergency. Joe's dog had just went through the sliding glass door, and was bleeding half to death. I felt sorry for the dog as he limply bled like a stuck pig. Joe didn't have any money and neither did Maggie. I paid for the dog to get sewed back together ... and Joe and I ended up being super tight partners. We went to hell and back a couple times, didn't we Joe? But back then, that canine episode was probably the beginning of our little consortium. Steve, Joe and I began planning a major smuggling gig.

Both Steve and Joe had been strung out on heroin in the past. They had also both kicked cold turkey of their own free will. Joe told me how he stayed at a friend's house in Lemon Grove for about six weeks during his detox. He said ... "I thought I was going to die."

I was amazed ... how did all these X-junkies come into my life? After hearing some of their stories I wholeheartedly agreed with heroin's street label ... "the devil drug". It takes over! Every time I drive down the 94 Freeway south of San Diego past Lemon Grove, I think about Joe.

Steve was even more likable than Mike, my junkie Viking friend, who was now sadly locked up again. Steve had super curly blond hair and bright blue eyes. He was cool. His little three-year-old son, Cody, looked just like a miniature clone ... with exactly the same curly blond Afro and blue-blue eyes. Joe was pretty quiet and calculating, but Steve was a free-flowing talker. He could tell stories that would keep people spell bound. He is very unique, gifted, and intelligent ... with no education ... except the streets, and the drug world. I was excited about hooking up with these guys. It was obvious that they really meant business. I did too. Hopefully they would stay away from the "devil drug".

Debbie and I were still living on Longbranch Street in Ocean Beach. My brother Rick came out from Ohio and was staying with us. Rick is about four and a half years younger than me. We were always pretty close, like with all my brothers, but on this visit to California we took it to a new level. I really love, and trust, and appreciate my younger brother. He wanted to participate. I tried to put on the protective big brother cap ... but not very successfully.

Steve went to Mexico and met with one of his favorite connections, who lived in Rosarita Beach, to line up some kilos. He came back all excited, because **three tons** of dynamite weed had just arrived. We could move it all. I was able to get the money for a hundred kilos fronted to us from one of my customers. We would start putting a dent into that tonnage with a hundred or so kilos, and if everything went smooth, we could take it from there. The clock started ticking. Life took on a strange new dimension as we planned and prepared for D-Day.

Steve was the master planner. We were going to go through the hills, mule style, down some trails that Steve had used before. It was desolate country between the beach and Tijuana, a stretch of about ten or fifteen miles of uninhabited hills and ravines. Steve and Joe picked a drop-off point in Mexico, and a pick-up spot on the American side. Thousands of "pollos", (chickens in English), AKA illegal aliens, had worn trails everywhere through the landscape over the decades. Steve also spent a couple weeks carefully scouting out the two locations at the exact time we would be doing the real McCoy. He wanted to see how much traffic and activity were at those two critical locations. The remote locations had hardly any traffic, etc. Everything looked good. We would drop off at 6 AM in Mexico, and pick up at 7:30 AM in America.

The week before our run we got our equipment together. We bought a pair of good walkie-talkies. The nicest ones I have ever seen. They had a real long range, but we only needed less than a mile for our purpose. We bought high quality nylon duffle bags to carry the kilos in. I was borrowing my brother Rick's Vega hatchback for the transport vehicle. We rigged the rear door to open at a touch. We made sure that everyone had a good watch and we synchronized them. We wouldn't talk on the walkie-talkies, but instead they each came equipped with a built in beeper. We made up a simple code. One beep meant... don't turn into the drop-off location ... keep driving and come back in 10 minutes. Two beeps meant ... suspicious activity in the area ... drive into T.J. and come back in an hour. No beeps meant ... everything is cool ... make the drop. It wasn't the most sophisticated plan and arsenal, like some of the big boys with airplanes and multi-million dollar budgets ... but it was better than ninety percent of the gigs we knew of ... or had tried before.

The day before our event we all went south to Mexico. We did a partial dry run making sure that no one was observing us. My role was the drop off man. Debbie wanted to go along, and convinced me that she could handle it. We would spend the night at the somewhat famous Rosarita Hotel, and bright and early in the morning ... it was game time. But first, for the dry run, I drove from the hotel to the drop off point, timing exactly how long it took, so I would be on schedule tomorrow. The drop point was at a little road that crossed the highway. There is a small off-ramp, which I would get off on ... turn left across the bridge, back over the highway ... and then get on the onramp heading back the way we just came from toward Rosarita.

The onramp heading back south was sunk down in a gully, and not very visible from most of the highway. It was here on the onramp in the gully, that I would stop, and Steve and Joe would make the pickup. Steve would be at the top of a steep hill, which overlooked everything in the immediate area, and he could also see way up the highway as I approached. If anyone was in the area, or if anyone suspicious was following our car, as I approached, Steve would beep me off ... either for ten minutes, one beep, or an hour ... two beeps. Our only vulnerability and exposed time would be the few seconds it took Steve and Joe to run down the hill to our vehicle. It took them seconds to run down the steep incline to my car. Everything was looking perfect.

We all went back to Rosarita and went to a neat restaurant for some real Mexican carne asada and Coronas. The adrenalin was flowing pretty good by now. We could all feel it. After dinner Steve took my car to his connection and picked up the load. He brought the "fully loaded" car back, and we went to the hotel and to our room. We had carefully covered the duffel bags of marijuana and parked the car in the hotel parking lot.

Steve had hired a friend of his, Mike Hardey, to be the pick-up man at the end of the trail. He would leave in the morning ahead of Debbie and me, drop off Steve and Joe, and then head to his destination in the U.S. Mike slept in the extra bed in our room with Debbie and myself. I didn't know Mike, but had overheard at Maggie's house that he had been strung out real bad. He didn't seem to be loaded now, and was wide-eyed and fully alert. We had a good time talking. He had a gentle way about himself that made him very likable. (Seems like all my junkie friends are nice guys.) The Rosarita Hotel reminded me of Europe with the high ceilings and all. It was definitely hard to get to sleep.

In the morning we were off. Everything was on schedule. I felt like I was in a movie as our Chevy Vega zoomed down the highway, with our merchandise nicely packaged in the rear. Adrenalin definitely wakes you up in the morning and makes you feel alive. Debbie was keeping the walkie-talkie handy in case we got signaled. As we turned down the final stretch to our destination … no beep. No cars were even in my rear-view mirror. There's the off-ramp. We kept listening for a beep even as we turned up the ramp and took a left over the bridge. It's definitely a go now. I turned left again as we reached the on ramp … and then stopped as I entered the gully.

No sooner did the car stop, when I heard the rear door fly open and then swish -swish-swish … the sound of nylon duffle bags flying across the car carpet. Almost simultaneously the rear door slammed shut and I hit the gas. It took seconds. As I drove down the on-ramp and reached the highway again, I saw a black and white Tijuana city cop car go whizzing past on the opposite side of the highway. I couldn't believe my eyes. What is he doing out here??? He must have been driving about 70 to 80 miles per hour like most of the sporadic traffic on this stretch of highway. Did he see Steve and Joe? I looked in my rear view mirror, and to my disbelief, I saw the cop car way down the road putting on the brakes. As I watched, I could see him pull over and start to back up on the side of the highway. Unbelievable!

I drove like a bat out of hell back toward Rosarita. I was in shock! He had to have seen the guys … for him to be backing up like that. What in the heck is a city cop car doing out here in the countryside? It couldn't have been a set up. Not in a black and white marked vehicle. In all the years of going to Mexico I have never even seen a city cop car out on the open road. Unbelievable! Why didn't he come a few seconds earlier … Steve would have seen him and beeped me off. Or a few seconds later … we would have been long gone. Maybe Steve and Joe had time to get down the trail in the bush before the cop backed way down the road. He had a long way to back up! Oh God I sure hope so!

I screamed at Debbie … "This is totally unbelievable!"

As my mind raced away along with our speeding car… I continued thinking … "What are the stinking odds that this could happen anyway? There are multiple thousands of seconds in a day … what is going on? We were only exposed for probably ten seconds out of all that time… and what … a city cop car happens to drive by … at top speed … at exactly the moment we don't have radio cover. He couldn't have been following me! Even if he was, I would have seen him, and Steve would have seen him for sure. He must have come around the bend in the road after I crossed the bridge at positively and exactly the second Steve put down the walkie-talkie, and raced down to my car. You gotta be kidding! What should I do now … keep going south … or what???

I asked Debbie … "Do you think they had time to get away?"

We talked about it as we continued driving south. She didn't know. I was pretty sure they had time to get away. After about 20 or 30 miles I decided to turn around and head back to the States. There was quite a bit of traffic by now, and I was pretty sure the cop didn't get a very good look at our car. We turned around. Bad decision!

When we went past our drop off spot, a good thirty to forty minutes later, there wasn't any cop cars, but there was a van parked along the side of the road. We shot past our spot along with the rest of the traffic, looking straight ahead. Ten minutes later, as we came up to the cemetery outside of Tijuana a cop car was waiting. He immediately pulled out behind us with his lights blazing away. From the frying pan … into the fire. "Why didn't I keep going south … stupid jerk!"

The cop pulled us out of the car and walked us back to his patrol car. Totally busted. As we got closer I saw Steve sitting in the back seat. What a bummer! I wonder what happened to Joe? Hopefully he got away!

Now three of us were in the back seat. We rode in silence to who knows what fate. Debbie was holding up good … Steve made eye contact a couple times … but that was it … we continued in silence, as the cop car snaked it's way into Tijuana. We finally stopped on 8th Street, and the short overweight cop escorted us out of the patrol car,

Fire On the Mountain

and led us up to a large door. He seemed almost apologetic. Later, Steve told me that the cop asked for $200, and he would have let him go with the load. Again like fools ... Steve only had a few bucks on him. I had a couple hundred dollars on me ... but I was the wrong guy. We should have made sure each of us had some cash! We knew better. Steve had bribed his way out of a bust once before. We walked into Tijuana's 8th Street city jail ... commonly known as "Ocho". What a hellhole welcomed us!

Debra Fifi, Steven L. Peterson y Roger Carl Sachs, detenidos por la Policía Municipal en posesión de 120 kilos de mariguana.

However, first they took us up a bunch of stairs to the commandant's office. Maybe he was the police chief or whatever. The first thing I saw was all our kilos stacked up on the floor in a long pile. He and another officer who spoke English began negotiating with us for six thousand dollars to release us. I told them that I didn't even know Steve, but could get them $1500 from some friends. I wasn't even sure if I could get that. We went back and forth for about 20 minutes. Some plain-clothes officers came in, and the whole tone seemed to change. They took pictures of all our dope.

At one point I finally had a chance to ask what happened to Joe. Steve whispered to me ... "As soon as he saw the cop car he dropped his kilos and ran like crazy. He got away down the trail."

The police talked and gibbered away in Spanish forever, and finally one of the cops took us downstairs. We tried to continue to negotiate, but someone came back and told us that the Federalles had just made another bust of some Americans. Too many people now knew about our bust. All deals were off ... we were going to stay in jail. A major bust in the middle of our "possible release" was just a sick continuation of bad ... bad ... **bad luck** ... and ... bad ... bad ... **bad timing**.

But nothing compared to the ten **miniscule** seconds that changed our lives forever.

186 Paquetes de Mariguana se Decomisaron en dos Acciones

TIJUANA.- Un total de nueve individuos fueron puestos a disposición de la Agencia del Ministerio Público Federal después de que fueran detenidos en dos diferentes acciones emprendidas por elementos de la Policía Municipal, al encontrárseles en posesión de 186 paquetes de mariguana, de los llamados "prensados de a kilo"

Primeramente a las 1.30 horas del día primero de este mes, sobre la carretera a Playas de Tijuana y a la altura de la entrada de la colonia Lázaro Cárdenas fueron interceptados seis individuos cuando trataban de llevar a Estados Unidos un total de 76 paquetes de mariguana, en dos costales de lona.

Los detenidos son Ronald W Williams, Everett L. Emers, Paul E. Malens, Henry E. Huddlents Jr, Howard Charles Bradford y Rodrigo Rentería Jr., de 18, 23, 20, 19, 21 y 18 años de edad, respectivamente. Todos ellos son residentes del vecino Estado de California.

Las autoridades dijeron haberles incautado a los traficantes el auto Dodge 71 tipo panel, placas 24522 N. de California.

Casi 20 horas más tarde, elementos de dicha corporación municipal detuvieron a otros norteamericanos, a la altura de la entrada del fraccionamiento El Mirador, sobre la carretera a Playas de Tijuana, en posesión de cuatro costales de lona, que contenían en su interior un total de 110 paquetes de la nefasta yerba.

Los detenidos, que dijeron ser residentes de San Diego, California, son Steven L. Paterson, Roger Carl Sachs y Debra Eve Pitz, de 25, 27 y 22 años de edad, respectivamente.

Ambos casos quedaron en manos de la Fiscalía Federal, para que se ejercite la acción legal correspondiente, según se informó.

CHAPTER 29

"LA OCHO"

There were three stories of cells at "Ocho" …the T.J. city jail. We were escorted to the very bottom floor. They opened the iron bars and signaled for Steve and I to go in. Debbie was put in the cell next to us. Inside our cell was a crowd of prisoners … I couldn't believe it. There were nineteen men packed into a six-man cell, and we made it twenty-one in that little hole of reeking humanity. There were two metal framed bunk beds, with three bunks each against the two sidewalls. The mattresses were actually concrete slabs about an inch and a half thick. Between the two bunks there was about a five-foot space. Against the back wall was a totally grimy sink with no drainpipe. Instead of a drain, there was a five gallon plastic bucket under it to catch the water. Next to that was a toilet with no seat, and an old worn piece of plywood covering it. We walked in and found a tiny spot on the floor to sit down.

It was good that there were two of us. Some of the characters in that cell looked pretty rugged to say the least. They smelled even worse. Another thing in our favor was that the word had gotten out about our bust. When you have over a hundred kilos of any drug, you are probably connected with somebody. The other prisoners were watching us real close but gave us some space. Instinctively we played the role, showing no fear, pretending to be as relaxed as possible. I had Steve's back and I knew he had mine. We didn't have any problem. In fact, one of the guys gave us a blanket. Some of the men didn't even have one. There were two men on each of the concrete slabs which made twelve men on the bunks … the other nine of us had floor space. As night came on that first night, Steve and I shared the single blanket. It got real cold. What a nightmare this is! The overhead lights stayed on 24 hours a day, and you could hear the echoes of prisoners yelling and talking non-stop. To cap off our first night, a Mexican woman in the next cell with Debbie, was withdrawing from her heroin addiction. She moaned and moaned, screamed and cried, and moaned some more … all night long.

On the second day, two guys were released, and Steve and I commandeered the top bunk that they had occupied. It was great to be off the floor. Debbie was sending me notes, which I would answer and send back. Sometimes a trustee would bring them. Sometimes we would push them out on the floor where we could fish them into the next cell. She became more and more desperate as the days wore on. I still have most of the notes, which were written on the back of torn apart Mexican cigarette packs and other scraps of paper. A Tijuana lawyer came to visit us one day. My brother Rick was communicating with him. I sent a note to Rick through the lawyer to contact Craig, the investor whose pot was now sitting in police custody. The lawyer wanted $2000 to take our case. Rick was able to get a thousand dollars from Craig and friends, with the promise of the remainder when he got us some results. Rick was also trying diligently to get his car back, which had been impounded somewhere in T.J. About the third day they took Steve, Debbie, and myself out of our cells and a newspaper reporter took our pictures.

Several of the inmates spoke English. One of the guys was a real funny, skinny Mexican who told us about his career of stealing cars in San Diego, and Mexico, and everywhere. This was about his tenth time he had been busted for the same thing. Steve and I started calling him "GTA" which means grand-theft-auto. It made him kind of mad, but he finally went along with it. Then there were the times when nature called, and the guys would take the plywood off the toilet. The stench that filled that cell was absolutely unbelievable. I would push my face and nose between the bars of the cell, (even though the bars themselves were sticky and totally filthy), just to be able to breathe. The toilet didn't have a working flusher. What they did was take the water from the five gallon plastic bucket under the sink, and pour it into the toilet. It would slowly kind of gurgle down. I was determined to never sit on that thing.

After a few days, as I lay on my concrete mattress, with Steve at one end, and with the old plastered ceiling about thirty inches above my head, I started doing a re-run of the day we got caught. I went over everything in detail. Was there any indication that we were under surveillance or anything? Was it just a fluke? Or is it some strange sick coincidence?

I was positive that cop car was not following me. I was watching. Steve was watching from his vantage point. They don't have airplane, Mission Impossible, high-tech task forces following every small-time hippy suspect. Like I said, even if we were followed … it was impossible odds that he would have been able to time everything perfectly to catch us the way he did. Something is going on here! This could not be coincidence! Maybe somebody is trying to send me a message. Maybe God isn't exactly thrilled about my master plan. This is crazy, but that tiny microscopic window of time, when the cop saw Steve and Joe … out in the boon docks … is beyond belief … beyond coincidence!

Other strange things had happened before that. On my first smuggling adventure with Mike, what are the odds that the lights on the car would die exactly the minute we picked up the kilos? For over a month that car and the lights worked perfectly … day and night. Then, an hour later … we get pulled over by Mexican police. It was a miracle the cops didn't find the pot then! That entire night was probably a warning that I was on the wrong path. I didn't pay attention. Now look how everything has intensified!

"God if you are doing these things, then I'll change!"

I told Steve … "Hey man, I think God is trying to tell me something. This is too weird the way we got caught, and the way everything came down. I think I'm supposed to quit dealing."

Steve started laughing his head off … He laughed and laughed and laughed … "Listen Rog … We can't quit now! I know that this is really a bad scene, but we've got three tons sitting in Rosarita! We can rebound from this. What we need to do is to put our heads together, and work our way out of this mess. I'll take the fall, and you just do whatever it takes to get me out. They caught me with the load … so I'm screwed. But, they don't have much of a case on you. We just need to stick to our stories. Hey, I don't know you or your girlfriend. You never saw me before in your life. You guys are tourists and just went for the day to Rosarita. It's corrupt as heck down here, but they still have to have a case on an American. Listen, when something like this happens, and then you get out, it was such a nightmare that you just want to forget everything … but hey dude … please don't forget me! Get my butt out of here. Please! OK? This was just one sorry fluke. Don't fold now!"

Steve's 'ra-ra-ra' speech made me laugh, and I told him … "OK Steve.

I'll get you out, and I won't forget you."

It didn't make sense. Here we are in one of the sorriest places and circumstances on earth ... not knowing what the heck was going to happen ... but something told me to "keep on keeping on."

Later that night as I stared at the filthy, crumbling plaster ceiling a short arm's length overhead, I silently said ... "Sorry God, but I can't quit right now."

One of the amazing things that I witnessed inside of 8th Street jail was a cell almost directly across from our cell. We could see about a dozen or so cells on the other side of the building packed with prisoners. We could also look up, and see parts of the cells on the floors above. But this one particular cell right across from Debbie's cell had a huge curtain all the way across the front. It had a door with a window that opened on the top half of the door. When the window was opened I could see a TV set, and that it was like an apartment inside. Every day there would be well-dressed people coming up to talk to the man in that cell. We had up to twenty-one people in our cell. Debbie said there were six women in her cell. But there was only one man in the luxury cell. I asked some of my roommates what the deal was. I was told that the guy was one of the main criminals in Mexico, and that they had brought him here from La Mesa for protection. Apparently, there was some power struggle or something going on in the prison, and so they set him up here at Ocho. I only got a glimpse of him a couple times. What a contrast between the rich and powerful ... and the rest of us ... even in here.

On about the fourth day of our incarceration, they took us out of our cells, out of the jail, and across town to another place. It was the D.A.'s offices where we were to give depositions. Behind a big building was a little building with a lock-up holding room. The room was about 20 feet by 20 feet. Inside there was already about seven or eight people. Five of them were Americans. They were young Marines stationed at Camp Pendleton ... and they were also the ones busted the same day as we were. It was a bare room with no chairs or benches or anything. As we sat on the floor, we listened to the on-going conversation.

One of the Marines was saying "Why didn't you shoot that dude when you had the chance?"

The other young soldier responds ... "Yeah I know. I should have. I could have blown them both away easy. What's the matter with me?

Dang!"

They went on and on talking about their bust, and what they were going to say in their depositions. Steve and I asked them how they got caught. The leader of the pack was a guy named Chuck. He told us they did this same gig a bunch of times before with no problems. They simply walk the kilos down the beach. He said this time they picked up their load of pot, and then drove by the beach, stopping to change into some dark clothes and night gear. He said they were sitting there quite awhile changing, when some federal police pulled up to see what they were doing. They had all kinds of guns and firepower. The cops caught them by surprise, but one of the soldiers was in the bushes taking a leak, and could have got the drop on the feds. But, he choked and now was saying again ... "I'm sorry, I should have blown them ____ers away! It would have been so easy!"

I didn't know how serious they were about blowing people away, but they were almost comical to listen to. They started arguing about what to say to the D.A. Again I flashed on how unlucky we were, compared to these guys. Instead of having a lookout with radio cover, in an isolated place that takes seconds to transition, they drive up with a van full of drugs, park beside the road, and then sit there for fifteen minutes changing clothes! It's a wonder they didn't get busted sooner.

They argued quite a bit, but they also joked around too. One of the stouter guys was named Hank. He was nineteen years old, and I immediately liked the kid. At one point he said ... "This is way too serious around here ... What we need is a little music". There was a broom in the room, which he grabbed and pretended was a guitar. He started wailing on the broom, and singing some homespun rock-n-roll. He was a blast, and had the whole crowd laughing, including a couple Mexicans prisoners who never said a word.

Finally I told the platoon ... "What you guys need to do, is the same thing we are doing. Somebody needs to plead guilty ... and the rest of you work your butts off to get your partner out. You need to all get your stories worked out, and make sure they match up. It boils down to all of you going to prison ... or just one of you. They caught Steve with the goods, and I need to get him out. The choice was made for us. It's tougher for you, because you need to decide, and decide quick, what you're going to do before they start calling you in for depositions. At least you guys have five people to help the one who goes down. It's a whole lot better than all of you in La Mesa with no one on the outside to help."

Chuck says ... "That sounds right. We need to decide who is the one."

For about twenty minutes they went back and forth about why each of them shouldn't be the one. Chuck was saying, "I would, but I'm married and have a kid. I think it should be one of you single guys."

Hank didn't say much ... but finally he said ... "OK ____ it!" He started to half cry and was all choked up as he talked ... "I'll do it. It's always me! Why is it always me? Chuck is married, Ronnie is a seventeen-year-old punk kid" ... and he went down the line ... as to why he was the obvious choice. It was very dramatic.

By the time they took us in for our depositions, we all had our stories straight including the Marines and Debbie. Steve and Hank confessed to everything ... we all denied everything. They took us back to our hellhole cells in Tijuana. We didn't know if our strategy would even prevail, but after eight miserable days in a filthy, overcrowded Mexican dungeon ... it worked! Our lawyer came to the jail, and Debbie and I were released. All the Marines were released except Hank. The lawyer took us to his office in T.J., and had me sign a promissory note for the unpaid balance, which totaled $1000.00 for his services. It's still drawing interest and late charges.

Miraculously, my brother Rick got his car back. The only thing missing from the car ... was probably the only thing that could have linked me to Steve Peterson ... the walkie-talkie. I'm sure someone ripped it off ... just like all the weapons that the Marines had in their possession ... never became an issue. What do you think happened to them? The biggest miracle of all ... is that I didn't sit on that filthy, seatless, disgusting toilet for the entire eight days. How did I do that? I've never gone eight days without "sitting on the throne" in my life.

Poor Steve and Hank were off to La Mesa Penitentiary. Man!!!

CHAPTER 30

"LA MESA"

I had heard so much about La Mesa Penitentiary over the last year or so, that I had developed a vague picture of the place in my mind. When I finally wandered all around T.J. and found the place ... to see Steve ... it was nothing like I imagined. The prison was a couple large city blocks long and wide, with twenty-foot high concrete walls surrounding it. Multiple guard towers rose above the walls in strategic locations. On the outside it looked like most other correctional facilities we might drive past, even in America. On the inside ... it was another ball game. It is known as "El Pueblito" in Mexico. It means "The Little Town".

When I drove up, there was a large open dirt parking lot on the side next to the main entrance. An old man charged me an American quarter to park there. The entrance to the prison was a large section of iron bars about thirty feet wide, and as tall as the concrete walls. Within this section of iron fencing was a large gate, which opened wide enough for cars and trucks, and a smaller gate for people to enter. Two lines of visitors were waiting outside. One long line stretched way down the side of the prison, and was all women and kids ... and a shorter line was just men.

Behind the iron bars you could see across a short open area of about thirty feet to another large gate of iron bars between two buildings. Packed up against that second set of gates was a total mob of prisoners jammed against the bars yelling and shouting through the open area to the visitors waiting outside. It was loud, loud, loud. Behind this mass of humanity I could see a little of the inside of the prison. Above the constant yelling and clamor, would come the occasional voice of a guard yelling something in Spanish on a bullhorn. The whole scene reminded me of something out of a Mad Max movie. It was unreal.

Several of the inmates were yelling at me in English. "Hey wheto ... Hey you, who you want? Hey over here ... me!"

There were so many voices mixed together with the dozens of other yelling and screaming people, that I couldn't see which one of the inmates was addressing me. I finally made eye contact with a voice and yelled back ... "Steve Peterson".

About four guys took off running away from the mob somewhere inside the prison . . pushing people out of their way. More inmates just pressed in taking the place of the four runners. The whole crowd was a pathetic but scary looking bunch. About half of them looked like they could slit your throat without a blink of conscience. The other half looked like death warmed over. All of them had rags for clothes. Later I would learn that these were some of the "oudies", which means vultures. They are all addicted to heroin, and survive by begging from the visitors, working for other inmates, stealing, cleaning, dealing, and maybe even killing for the next fix.

After the entire women's line entered La Mesa, the guards started processing us men. I was barefooted as usual, and one of the guards pointed at my feet, and said something in Spanish to another guard. They looked at me with a smirk and a little disgust. Only the poorest of the poor go barefooted in Mexico. I didn't realize it was a cultural thing. Eventually, I figured it was a good strategy to continue playing the barefooted-broke-small-time-American-longhaired-hippy-want-a-be-whatever ... nobody. For the most part, it was true anyway. I definitely didn't want them to think that Steve and I were well connected, big time dealers, with lots of money ... just because we got caught with a good sized load. I went barefooted almost every time I entered La Mesa, and just smiled to any comments. I was quickly learning how things work down here, and the overall mentality.

Just getting processed as a visitor into the prison for the first time can be a real unforgettable experience. It was even harder for me that day, because for one thing I was by myself, none of the guards spoke English, and I don't speak Spanish. I had to play charades and play stupid. The guards walked around all dressed in black fatigue-like uniforms, with semi-automatic rifles and pistols. They all looked hard and impatient. A couple of them were somewhat nice. You go through this line, then that line. They stamp you after each line with different ink stamps on your arm. You look like a gang-banger by the time you get in the prison. They take your ID and put it in a little wooden box ... they type in the name of the prisoner your visiting on an ancient looking typewriter ... you sign your signature on a huge list ... they stamp you again ... they search you in a tiny room after another long line, and give you a little tag to take to two armed guards sitting by the second metal gate. At this second gate the guard takes your little tag, gives you a red chip, which looks just like a poker chip from Vegas ... and then finally after one more stamp, they open the gate and let you into the prison right in the middle of the mob of slithering, screaming oudies.

What a trip! The second I was inside there must have been a dozen hands on me begging for money ... "Please do you have a quarter or any pesos for me? Who you see ... me take you!! Please ... please Senior por favor uno dinero!!" All of them were saying the same things. I started pressing my way through the crowd not saying anything. Nobody was trying to stop me or assault me ... it was just a clinging ... begging ... relentlessly begging and pleading. They couldn't really rob you there with armed guards on the walls above. As I pressed through the crowd I recognized one of the four runners in the distance, who I assumed had previously went to find Steve. He was running back toward the gate from inside the prison. He was waving at me, and pushing people aside to get to me. Behind him I saw Steve walking toward us. I made my way toward the runner, and he finally grabbed my arm like he was my lead dog or something and pulled me the rest of the way through the crowd. By this time Steve was there, and we shook hands by grabbing each other's thumbs like all good hippies. Our victorious runner was standing by waiting for his reward. All the other inmates except for two or three were back up front waiting for other prey. Steve asked me if I had a dollar for the runner ... which I gave him. He wanted more ... but smiled as we walked away. I've often wished I could have taken about a hundred dollars in quarters and threw them up in the middle of that crowd. That would be a sight!

Steve said ... "Come on. Let me show you around this place. It is unbelievable!"

We started walking across a big open area. La Mesa actually did look like a little town inside ... dilapidated Wild West cutthroat town. In the distance I could see all kinds of little shops and restaurants like at a swap meet. Some of them were a little nicer than others. Some were the size of a closet. There were little tiny alleys, and walkways in and around buildings … some barely wide enough for people to pass in opposite directions. People were constantly moving around. There were women and kids everywhere. One of the restaurants was in a building by itself, had chairs and tables inside, and even had a big jukebox. There were run-down motel-like cement block buildings all over, crammed with little tiny homemade apartments. Some of the buildings were two stories. The little apartments inside were actually the cells, and are called "caracas". You have to buy your caraca or you sleep on the floor of one of four tanks or outside with the oudas. You have to buy your food … you have to buy everything … even a nickel for a few folded pieces of toilet paper to take a crap.

We passed one section of shacks and buildings made of scrap lumber, garage doors and about anything else. Nothing was wasted. Electrical wires hung overhead like spaghetti going in every which direction. It's a miracle the place didn't burn down daily. Steve pointed to a door where there was a line of people waiting to get in. The door opened, and a guy walked out and the next guy went inside.

Steve said, "That's one of the shooting galleries. You can buy a paper of smack in here for two dollars or less. It's like an assembly line. You sit down. They cook up the heroin in a spoon while they tie off your arm … load up an outfit and shoot you up. Then it's next in line.

There was a guard tower within plain view of the line of men waiting for a fix. This was like the Satsop River Festival times a million. I said … "The guards don't care about people shooting up right in front of them?"

Steve replied, "Obviously not … right? Listen, you can get anything you want in here. There's a "cavo" who's in charge of everything. If somebody tries something on their own, they end up sorry or dead. He's like the prisoner Godfather. Every ounce of heroin, every pound of pot, and everything else … he gets his cut. The guards get their cut, the warden gets his money. Like I said you can get anything you want in here, except alcohol. They don't want everyone rowdy, and drunk, and tearing each other up. They want everyone nodded out."

Steve continued … "You see all these kids running around? They live in here. If one of the parents is locked up, they just let the kids in to live with them here also. There's hundreds of them. Your old lady can shack up with you. Everything's possible for a few pesos. There are prostitutes, and fags, and everything in between. There's also stabbings all the time. Last night a dude tried to stab a guy because his hot plate was making smoke, and blowing in his window. This is a total zoo!"

It had been a few weeks since I was released from the T.J. jail. Steve was pretty settled in. We had sent him money with his wife Paula. He bought a caraca for $600. It was a one-time purchase. It was his as long as he was in El Pueblito. Like buying a condo. You have to work inside, unless you pay to be exempt. I think Steve paid a couple hundred dollars, and he didn't have to do any work his entire stay. His caraca was in D-tank, one of four large cement building about mid-way inside the prison. On the outside it looked like any old concrete building, except it had a single double sized iron door in the middle. On the inside it was Mad-Max material again. Almost all the Americans were in one of the tanks. However, one of the Americans had been inside La Mesa for twelve years and lived with the vultures.

Inside D tank was two floors of homemade caracas. From the first floor it was open all the way to the top of the building in the middle section. The second story caracas on both sides had a walkway about thirty inches wide with a rail to keep you from falling down to the first floor. The open area in the middle between the two sides of caracas was about twelve feet wide. To get to the second floor you had to climb up a rickety steep metal ladder like a fire-escape ladder. Steve took me to his pad. We climbed the metal ladder, went to the left and down the tiny walkway, squeezing past a few people standing by their doors, to his old worn homemade door. He unlocked a padlock to his home sweet home in the midst of hell.

Steve's caraca was about six feet wide and maybe ten feet long. In that small space he had a bed, and a few makeshift furnishings. He broke out some pot and we smoked a joint or two. I gave him an update on things back in San Diego. I was scrambling hard trying to get things going again. I wanted to get him out ASAP like I promised I would. He said he was meeting all kinds of connections inside, and that he would probably be able to help me out soon. Later he took me to see Hank, who was in another tank, and also to the caraca of a couple more Americans. I met most of them. They were all real glad to see another

American from the outside. I heard so many war stories about how they got busted, and about La Mesa ... and about the struggle to survive in this jungle. It was amazing. We smoked some more dope, and when visitor hours were over I was almost ready to stay ... but not quite! Everything about La Mesa attacked each of your senses ... the incredible rank smell ... the noise ... the danger ... the poverty ... the little kids running around like it was normal ... it was unreal. Thank God I didn't lose my little red poker chip!

Thirty years after my first visit to La Mesa this article appeared in the Riverside Enterprise Newspaper:

CHAPTER 31

"LIKE A YO-YO"

Out of Mexico and back in the sunny sanctuary of Ocean Beach. Back with Leo my faithful Golden Retriever! God bless America! God Bless California! Debbie was happy. The Mexican jail experience started to fade. It's so good to be free. I was determined to rescue Steve.

Harry came by. He said … "By the time I found out about your bust, you were already out. I would have been there for you dude!"

He told me about a big load of pot his people had in San Ysidro. It was perfect timing, because I had just met someone looking for a hundred kilos. My new acquaintance was named Rich, and he said … "My customers are flying in from back east next week. They have cash for at least eight hundred kilos plus, but want to start with a hundred. Can they get a sample of this load you told me about?"

I called Harry and he set it up. I met with this Caucasian guy in central San Diego and he gave me a sample kilo. In turn I gave it to Rich. Everything was a green light. Rich's people flew in.

On the night of the transaction, Harry and I were to meet Rich at a specified apartment. I drove there separately and Harry showed up shortly. There were several people there, including the gal who lived in the apartment. When she saw Harry she said … "I know you!"

It turned out that they had some brief acquaintance, and proceeded to get into this big old conversation. At one point the gal said … "Yeah, I've been living here just waiting for my old man to get out of a Mexican prison."

I cut in and said, "What prison?"

She said, "La Mesa."

"What's your husband's name? I was just there visiting a friend in La Mesa."

"His name is Joe," she told me.

After a short inquiry ... it turned out to be the same Joe that I had met a week or so earlier. Steve had taken me to a couple of the American's caracas, and Joe and his partner were on the circuit. They were locked up in D tank along with Steve. I had spent about an hour in their caraca, and heard everything about their bust. What a coincidence that I would meet his wife in the midst of a drug deal. What a small world that my black partner also knew her ... out of the hundreds of thousands of people in San Diego.

Rich, who was listening to all this said ... "Hey, it makes me feel good that you guys have some history. When I start working with new people, I get a little nervous. Now let's get down to biz."

Rich brought out stacks of cash, and lined them up on a coffee table for us to count. We were charging $160 a kilo. Harry counted out $16,000. I had also scraped up $3000 to purchase twenty-five kilos for myself. Harry told us the kilos were in a car in San Ysidro, and we would have to pick up the car and transfer the units. Rich sent his partner, a medium sized guy named Jeff with shoulder length blond hair, to go with my partner ... Harry Specter the Black Jew. Jeff had the money and strict instructions. They went in Harry's car, and we estimated that it would take about sixty to ninety minutes to consummate everything. They were off about 6 PM.

About 7:30 Rich started pacing the floor ... "Why is it taking so long?"

I tried to calm his nerves ... "Harry said it would take sixty to ninety minutes to turn this around. It's only been about that now. They'll probably pull up any minute."

We sat there in the apartment, and the clock crept forward slowly and forever. Every ten minutes seemed like an eternity. Rich became like a caged tiger.

"Something had to have gone wrong! ____!!! I have plenty of resources ... why did I mess around with new people. Man if I lose that money ... I'm in for some serious crap!"

As time dragged on I didn't say much more. I only assured Rich that Harry had consistently come through in the past. I didn't mention the time I got ripped off by the "middle-man". Harry had totally convinced me that he was a victim along with me. But now ... I too was beginning to wonder ... "Did that jerk set me up, along with everyone else, and then leave me here stranded with the people he's ripping off??? No way! If that's what's happening it means he did it to you twice ... you stupid idiot Roger!"

Nine o'clock ... ten o'clock ... and then at 11:30 PM a taxicab pulled up. Jeff came into the apartment breathing all heavy and dazed looking ... "I think I just got ripped off ... but I'm not sure!!!"

Rich was all over him ... "What do you mean, you **might** have been ripped off??? Where is the dope???"

Jeff gave Rich a complete run down ... "He took me to a little tavern, and said he had to call his people to deliver the car. He said they had parked the car with the load in the trunk near their location and a few minutes from the tavern. He came back to our table from the pay phone, and said the people wanted him to wait, because there was possibly someone watching the car. They saw someone suspicious driving in the area. They wanted to wait and make sure it was cool. They said to call back in half an hour.

We drank a beer, and Harry called back in half an hour. His people said it was probably cool, but they wanted to wait a little longer to see if that same vehicle came back again. We waited about 20 more minutes, and then Harry called a third time. This time Harry said his connection figured it was cool, but wanted Harry to come get the car himself. They didn't want to deliver it, didn't want a crowd, and wanted to play it safe. Harry asked me to give him the money, and said he would be right back with the load.

I told him no way. He called them back and told them what I said. They said OK, but they didn't want to move the car, and they were paranoid about dealing with a stranger. They didn't like the scare they had about possibly being under surveillance.

I told Harry that if there was a problem we would just wait or do it some other time. He said let's just give them some time, and they would probably deliver the car. We waited over another hour. He called back, but they said they would only do the deal if Harry dropped off the money and picked up the car. He kept telling me that it's all set up. That his people are serious movers and shakers, but are real cautious ... that he has used them on a regular basis. He said 'I can be back in a matter of minutes ... just give me the bag ... and let's get this thing over with.

Trust me. I know your friend at the apartment. I've been taking care of business a long time. Don't be so paranoid.'

He talked me into giving him the money. I finally gave it to him. The dude didn't come back. It's probably a rip-off ... but maybe it was a bust ... I don't know ... I'm sorry!!"

Rich was freaking out. He yelled at Jeff ... "The last thing I told you was, **do not let go of the money until you have the load!!!**"

Rich turned to me, and pulled out a 38-caliber revolver, and demanded ... "Where is your partner?"

It was the first time in my life anyone pulled a gun on me, besides the cops in Texas, and I started talking my hind-end off ... "Hey Rich ... we don't know for sure if it's a bust or a rip-off or what. I don't think it's a rip-off. I can't imagine Harry would rip you off, and leave me sitting here on the hot seat ... but if that creep did, then he got me too, because I had all the money I have in this deal. I'll help you get him, if it turns out wrong! I know a lot about Harry. I have pictures of him. I think I know his real birth name. I have phone numbers. Let's hope he calls and has some good news or explanation."

Rich turned to Jeff and said ... "where's your gun?"

Jeff pulled up his shirt. He had it taped to his chest, with the tape going all the way around his body to hold it in place. He started to un-tape the gun, but was having a hard time.

Rich halfway laughed while slowly shaking his head, and then said ... "What kind of total ____ is this? What would have happened Jeff ... if you needed the ____ing thing? What a sorry night! Listen Roger ... I'm going to take all the heat on this from my people. I'm too embarrassed to tell them the truth how all this came down. Help me try to nail this nigger if he's not in jail. At this point I hope it's a bust for his sake. These people he ripped off will go after him. Big time. They'll spend the money just for principle. Get me that picture, and everything you have. We better not find out you're in on this!"

I drove back to Ocean Beach to my place. My head was spinning. On the way I started thinking about how many people had to be working with Harry on this apparent rip-off. During negotiations I had talked to at least three different people, plus met with a fourth. It was pretty organized, and I could see how he was definitely setting me up from the beginning. I was conning him by making him believe I had more connections than I really did ... and he was conning me by trying to set up big deals, where he could rip off either the money or the dope. He probably didn't know it would take the better part of a year to get a big score out of me. All the kilos that he fronted to me were probably from their ring of rip-offs. I still believe that he enjoyed kicking around with me, but now I was worried that he might realize that I knew too much about him. He might come after me to clean up his tracks. I thought it was stupid to even go back to my pad in Ocean Beach. People get blown away in drug related deals all the time. He knows where I live ... but I don't have a clue where he is. He likes his ivory handled pistol. I thought ... "But I have to go back to get Debbie and Leo!"

When I blasted open the door to my little house behind a house ... I yelled at Debbie, "Grab everything of ours in this place right now, and throw it in the station wagon.! Did Harry call? **We have to get out of here as fast as we can!**"

I started grabbing clothes, and bedding, and everything we had. In about five minutes the car was about half loaded when I heard the sound of a Volkswagen engine come up the alley next to my place. My heart about jumped out of my chest. It sounded exactly like Harry's VW bus. I grabbed Debbie and we ran between two of the neighbors houses. I can't remember ever having a rush of adrenalin like I did at that moment. I snuck around the corner looking through bushes to see if it was Harry ... but it wasn't. It was someone else.

We went back to my place and within another five minutes we had everything including Leo packed up ... **and we were gone**. It was the fastest move I ever made.

Man ... from getting busted in Mexico ... to a partner in La Mesa ... and now a lousy major rip-off! "I'm getting totally ticked off! What's the deal!"

I met with Rich, and gave him the photos and everything I had on Harry. Rich told me ... "We already found out a lot about your partner. He's the ringleader of a regular band of professional rip-offs. He used to own a gas station, which he burned down for the insurance. He ripped off a bunch of people, and he did his homework. He backed down some really bad people here in San Diego, by putting contracts out on their wives and kids if anything happened to him. He knew their names, and where they went to school ... and he's a real snake. He also works with

Fire On the Mountain

the narcs, and plays both sides of the fence. They say he gets immunity for giving people up.

But he screwed up with you and me, because he don't know anything about my people. They're dug in … and have already put a contract out on him."

A couple days later I finally got Harry on the phone. I said … "Harry, you probably think you're pretty cleaver, but I think you screwed up this time. These people are determined to blow you away whatever it takes. It's a miracle they let me slide. Hey, I didn't see it coming. I thought we were tight. I thought you were for real. These people aren't going to quit on you for sure … so you better get ready!"

Harry went ape on the phone … "First, I didn't rip anything off, and ____ that wise-mouthed junkie Rich! I know everything about him, and his little Margo, and where he lives. If those punks come near me … we'll see who gets blown away!"

I said … "Rich isn't a junkie."

Harry said, "**Ha ha ha** … that's about how much you know! He's a stone cold junkie, and so is his old lady. He can run off with the mouth all he wants, but let him know from me that it's already paid for. He has a kid too."

"Yeah Harry, I heard how you work things, but it's not Rich who's coming after you. It's people from out of state. The people who's money you ripped off. Rich was just the middleman. Remember middleman? I don't even know who they are, but they have a lot of money, and they are really bent out of shape. I told you that these customers wanted to start with a hundred kilos and then do some serious business. Well, they're serious about finding you right now! And thanks a lot for ripping my money off, and leaving me sitting on the hot seat!"

Harry really flipped out … screaming obscenities and threats, and then he hung up. About a week later I met with Rich again and he gave me an update … "Your friend Harry is on the run. They scared him out of San Diego. They believe he is in Fresno. If he shows up in San Diego he is as good as dead. They know all about him now. Several contracts are out on him. My customers have cut me a lot of slack. You can thank me that I took all the heat on this! Your name didn't even come up."

I thanked Rich for real. After a few weeks I felt confident enough to temporarily move back into my place in Ocean Beach. The landlord didn't even know I had ever left. That was good. Craig my customer from Syracuse, New York, whose money purchased most of the 120 kilos that we lost in Mexico, came by to see me. He had also given my brother the money to give my lawyer. He was back in San Diego, and wanted to know if I could help him and his buyers recoup some of their losses. I didn't tell him that my illustrious career had just produced another major loss. Instead, after truly thanking him for his help ... I called Rich to see if he could score **me** some kilos. Craig had cash for another hundred units. Rich said ... OK Rog ... I'll drive my car into your garage tomorrow. Are you sure your customer has the dinero?"

"We have the money Rich."

The next day all went like clockwork. I opened the garage door at an appointed time. Rich pulled in ... we shut the door, and there was a trunk full of **real** kilos. I handed him the real cash, and we drank a beer.

Rich says to me, "You know Roger, the thought hit me ... could he have possibly been in on that rip off ... no way could you be that slippery ... are you ??? If you are, that would be one gutsy play ... but no way ... right?"

It made me laugh. I said ... "Hey man, I'm not a rip-off. If I could act that good I'd head for Hollywood. I like what we just did ... produce. This really helps me. The people who bought this load, are the same people who fronted me the money on the smuggling gig, when I got busted in Mexico. I'm giving them a real good price to make up for some of their losses, and I'm still making a profit. Did I show you a copy of the Tijuana newspaper when we got popped?"

rson y Roger Carl Sachs
sión de 120 kilos de mar

I went in the house and found the newspaper. When Rich looked at it he started to laugh … "Dang, the look on your face is like saying … 'Oh ____!!'

That reminds me, what did you think when I pulled my gun on you that night?"

"I thought … it's time to get chucking and jiving, cause this don't exactly look good!"

Rich laughed, finished his beer and took off. I covered the kilos up with a tarp, and contacted Craig. He came over with a partner of his. They checked out the load and were real happy. My brother Rick had re-surfaced that same day. Craig and partner wanted to celebrate by throwing a little party on the Ruben E. Lee, which is a Mississippi riverboat turned into a fancy restaurant docked in San Diego Bay. We paid my brother a hundred dollars, and locked him in the garage to guard the kilos. My business partners took a couple girlfriends to the floating celebration, and I took Debbie. We toasted with Margaritas, and ate probably the best prime rib steak I ever ate in my life.

One minute your down, totally in the hole, an inch from getting blown away … and a few days later you're a hero … toasting your clientele … with a pocket full of hundred dollar bills … and your fast-talking, scheming enemy on the run for his life.

It's just like a yo-yo … "YO YO" !!!

CHAPTER 32

"PARTNERS"

Three long years Ernesto had survived in La Mesa. His blood boiled whenever he thought about his cousin Henry. It was Henry's lying finger that had put him inside. Ernesto was guilty of a lot of things … but he was innocent of the charges that sent him to prison. Now that he was out, he would actually have to protect Henry … instead of breaking his neck for getting him busted. If anything happened to Henry everyone would assume Ernesto got his revenge. Nevertheless, Ernesto emotionally and skillfully tortured his cousin constantly … with threats, and insults, and mental gymnastics. You never knew for sure what he would do next. Ernesto could be very cruel if you wanted to play that game.

Now, over a year after being released from La Mesa, and after escaping from Lompoc Prison in central California, Ernesto was back in Tijuana. He would have to start all over again from scratch. What's new with that? Since fourteen years old he had been making something happen with nothing. Maybe he could revive his wrestling career. It would take time. He started checking around. He met some small time local drug runners who had a brother living in National City. It was a whole family of brothers, and other relatives, who were the mules for some big dealers in Baja. This family had scraped together fifty-five kilos of marijuana of their own, and had already smuggled them to the U.S. The kilos were stashed at the brother's residence in National City, a suburb of San Diego. They were hoping that Ernesto could line up some buyers in America. He made a deal with them.

Ernesto didn't have any buyers on hand, but decided to go visit his friend Johnny in La Mesa. If anyone could make things happen … even from inside a lockup … it was his sidekick Johnny. John Ellis is a Mexican American from Lake Elsinore, California. He had been in and out of different prisons for most of his life. Altogether over twenty years inside. He was presently doing a six-year stretch in La Mesa. Ernesto and Johnny had worked, hustled, and survived together inside "El Pueblito".

They call him Johnny Bigotis ... which is Johnny Mustache in Spanish. He is a little guy with a big mustache, and a ton of personality. In San Quinton they called him "German" ... because he is half Mexican and half German. Everyone likes John unless there is a problem. Then you might have a problem. (Steve found out that it was John who actually took a knife after the neighbor of his caraca, because of the hot plate smoke.) John knew people everywhere ... up north in the States, way down south into Mexico, inside and outside ... and he could literally sell ice to an Eskimo. Ernesto was hoping John could point him in the right direction to unload these kilos.

About the third time I went to La Mesa to visit Steve, he introduced me to Johnny. Steve had given me a great personal tour of the prison, but Johnny topped it all. He knew just about everybody and everything in the place.

The first thing he said to me when we met was ... "Hey Roger, its **r e a l l y** good to meet you! Steve has been telling me all about you. Man ... that was too bad you guys lost that big load!! That was terrible! But listen, I want you to come back next week, and meet one of my partners. He did time with me in here. We go way back. He has over fifty kilos on the other side right now. Do you think you could move them real quick?"

I said ... "Definitely."

Johnny smiled and said ... "This is what I want. I want to hook you up with Ernesto, and then you guys start working together. You get Steve out of here, and Ernesto will help me. You'll like Ernesto. He's real good to work with. Hey, let's go over there and get something to eat ... I want to introduce you to the owner of that restaurant over there. They make some **real** good machaca! Are you hungry?"

I liked Johnny Bigotes immediately. He was so full of energy and so animated. He never stopped talking and joking around. On the other hand, he knew when, and what not to talk about. Steve and Johnny had teamed up inside. It was a good combination. My partner was now paired up with Ernesto's old partner. We made the rounds of La Mesa again. The place never ceased to amaze me.

I gave Steve some money, (about sixty bucks), and told him about all the latest ups and downs of my recent adventures. The good, the bad, and the ugly. The good part was that Craig and his New York customers were "hot to trot for more pot". I had other customers too. Another good part was that I went looking for Joe, and found him at Maggie's one day. We started working together. Joe had good connections also. My master plan was steam rolling forward … however, I was beginning to see first hand how I could definitely die trying. Oh well … no pain … no gain!

While we were still in the Eighth Street jail together, Steve had emphatically instructed me … "When I get to La Mesa don't give me more than fifty or sixty bucks at a time. I can survive on that. If I start pressing you for more … don't cave in. No matter what I say … OK? It means I'm using again. I don't want to get strung out in a Mexican prison … it could be real bad news."

The next week I was back in Mexico, and back making my way through the mob of oudies. Soon I joined Steve and Johnny who were waiting for me by the park. There were two infamous prisoners in La Mesa who were known as "The Brothers". They were written about in a book named "The Smugglers". (I also saw a huge article in the LA Times all about them years later.) Anyway, they had built a little tiny park inside La Mesa. It was pretty nice. My friends were waiting for me there. Standing next to Johnny was a tall, muscular, mean looking character. He kind of had that Poncho Villa hard-core outlaw look.

Johnny says. . "Hey… Que paso Roger ? … this is my friend Ernesto. Ernesto … this is Steve's partner Roger!"

Ernesto's first impression … was … "how could this barefooted little hippy have any money?"

We shook hands, and that was the beginning of an amazing and unpredictable partnership. Neither one of us had a clue what was coming down!

We went to a restaurant and had some authentic jailhouse cuisine, and then went up to Steve's caraca. Ernesto took off with John, but we had made a plan to meet outside the prison a few blocks away after visiting hours. Ernesto was on foot … not barefoot. As we planned, he left the prison before me and would be waiting.

Pretty soon I too was being processed out of La Mesa. They searched me ... took my red poker chip ... checked all my stamps ... made me match my signature ... and gave me back my drivers license. Now to find Ernesto. I drove back toward TJ, turned the corner on the main drag, and there he was. He hopped into my car, and we took off. I enjoy driving in Mexico. It's a little like demolition derby ... or "let's play chicken". If you hesitate, the traffic eats you alive. The first thing Ernesto said, after riding with me for a few miles in heavy traffic was ... "You drive like a Mexican cab driver." I took it as a compliment.

By now it was pushing 6 PM, and we hadn't eaten since early afternoon with Steve and Johnny. Ernesto said ... "Do you like Chinese food?"

"Sure"

"I'm taking you to my sister's pad, but we can pick up some Chinese first. I think you'll like it." Ernesto spoke almost perfect English.

We picked up about 3 boxes of take-out Chinese, and he directed me the remainder of the way to his sister's upstairs apartment. No one was home. Ernesto broke out a bottle of El Presidente Brandy, and we proceeded to consume every piece of sweet and sour chicken in sight. By the time we finished the bottle we had all our business nailed down, as well as "life in the big city" pretty much figured out. Ernesto had me cracking up. He has a great sense of humor ... and is a fun drunk ... when he's not ticked off. I asked him how he learned to speak such good English. He said ... "Sesame Street ... and Big Bird". We connected real good, and even though he looked like a hit man, I knew we could do some serious damage by teaming up. We bought another bottle, and by the time I finally headed back for the border ... I had in essence ... actually become an aggressive-suicidal-drunk Mexican cab driver. Look out ... and get out of the way! It was great.

Within a few days Ernesto had me in contact with his people. He talked them into fronting the whole load to me for a couple days. I could have got a lot more money for the fifty-five kilos if I had more time, but we did all right. I turned them quick just like I claimed I could. Everybody was happy. During the transaction in National City, the Mexican brother living in the States took me aside and let me know they didn't want to work with Ernesto anymore. They wanted to deal directly with me. I played along.

I had to make a decision. I took Joe down to T.J. to meet Ernesto. We had planned to celebrate a little and do some new business. Ernesto said … "Come with me. I'm going to take you to meet someone. I want you to go up to the door and say you're a friend of Ernesto's. The lady is my Aunt. She used to live in the States, and speaks good English. Let's see what she says. I'm going to hide and wait around the corner of the house."

When I knocked on the door, a middle-aged lady with long black hair answered. I said … "Sorry to bother you, but I'm a friend of Ernesto's". I didn't know what else to say to her.

She immediately said … "Come in. Tell your friend to come in. My name is Connie …"

Joe and I walked in, and of course before much more was said, Ernesto came barging in laughing his head off. We already had been drinking. Connie smacked Ernesto in the head, and it was a fun time. There were several kids running around, and everyone was real excited that Uncle Ernesto was there with his friends. I knew that Ernesto didn't take many people to meet his mother's sister. Connie saw the big bottle of Brandy, and brought out four shot glasses from a cupboard. We partied, and ate, and laughed all night. They had a poloraid camera and we took a whole pack of pictures.

At one point during the night I told Ernesto. "You know, your partners want to cut you out. They told me they want to go directly to me from now on. What do you want me to do?"

Ernesto thought for a minute … "Do it. Go along with them, and later when everything is up with us … then ____ them, we'll decide what to do."

I thought it was a good answer. I knew somehow that I could trust Ernesto, even though in the future we would both fudge a little on prices. But I wanted to shoot square with him from the beginning, and build some trust both ways. I didn't like these other guys … but I really liked Ernesto. We made a pact … I'll handle things in the States … and he'll take care of business in Mexico. Together we would buy our comprades out of La Mesa, and carve out a nice little retirement plan for all of us.

Connie poured us a refill, and said … "Salute!"

She stayed right up with us … not a problem. I had more than another partner or another Mexican connection … I had me a friend. Don't laugh … How many do you have?

CHAPTER 33

"CHOCOLATE MESCALIN"

We were off and running. Soon, I discovered that Ernesto had lots of connections in Mexico ... some old and some new. We crossed several loads and I sold them in San Diego. Craig, my customer from New York was flying hundreds of kilos back east. He was fearless about boarding an American Airlines jet with expensive luggage jam packed with pot. Joe and I stayed real busy. We were making tons of money in the short run. When I'd go to Tijuana, we would use Connie's little house as our rendezvous. Her coffee table would be **completely** covered with piles of hundreds, fifties, and twenty-dollar bills as we counted out our booty. I loved our celebrations.

We would always give Connie a generous tip ... and would always throw a drunken party. On top of that she made the best homemade tortillas in the world ... the best refried beans and tacos ... and sometimes her hot sauce would make you sweat like a pig ... but it was good. I got real close with Connie. She had raised her own kids, Henry, Rudy, and Angela ... but now she was raising two of her grandkids ... Phillip and Dollia. I always considered her little house, "Connie's place", but actually her son Rudy paid the rent and lived there most of the time. He worked for the power company. He was divorced a couple times, and Connie was raising two of his kids. I became good friends with Rudy too. He didn't speak any English, which made it a little tough.

When we started working together Ernesto and I were both basically broke, and starting over. We worked with fronted merchandise, and other people's money. Pretty soon I had enough cash to buy a load with our own profits. We could take it back east and five times our money. Finally we could start to really break ahead. Everything had been going so smooth ... but then of course disaster strikes again. Our personal load didn't make it across the border. What happened??? What lousy karma I must have! Ernesto had been using a family of mules, who were real pros, without any problems. The next morning he drove up to their place in the hills to find out what had happened to our merchandise. They told him that some guys with guns had jumped them on the trail, and had ripped off the load.

Ernesto didn't believe them. He got the entire family out of the house, and he threatened to kill them one by one. He stuck a knife up to the throat of the oldest guy, and surprise, surprise ... most of the kilos were next door stashed in a car. We lost part of the load, but not the lion's share. What a bunch of snakes in this business.

I continued to take Steve money inside La Mesa, and he did start pressing me for more. He said ... "Listen, I didn't want to get hooked in this place ... and I know what I told you ... but it's too late. If I have to hustle and connive for a fix, I'm probably going to get blown away in this place. Everything is cheap, but I need more than fifty or sixty bucks every two or three weeks to survive. Cut me some slack!"

I did. Steve was starting to look pretty bad. He had lost weight. I didn't want him to have to steal and deal with the lower echelon of La Mesa. I gave him more dinero. On several of our more successful events, I started giving Maggie money to put away for Steve's "fianza". A fianza was bail. In Mexico it's just the opposite as it is up here in the States. Here in America we are innocent until proven guilty. We can post bail and get out of jail until we are proven guilty and sentenced. In Mexico, they throw you in prison first, and then when you're proven guilty ... they set a fianza or bail for an appeal. It's real confusing. We were keeping track of his legal case the best we could. Paula and Maggie had hired Steve a Mexican lawyer. We put away a couple thousand dollars for Steve's bail so far. Maggie kept it stashed in her bedroom closet.

I had finally moved out of Ocean Beach. I rented a house in central San Diego. Good things were happening business wise, but a lot of bad also. I tried to break up with Debbie a couple times after arguments. She would freak out. She would beg, and promise, and write me poems and letters. I loved and admired Debbie's spunk, but we were fighting way too much.

One early morning I woke up, because I thought I heard something outside. I glanced toward a window and saw a guy run past. Almost immediately my bedroom door busted open, and several guys with guns filed in. Our house was being raided by a large group of drug dealers. They were looking for a guy that had ripped them off for $10,000 worth of coke. It was a shocking way to wake up. They roughly pulled us out of bed. Debbie was completely naked, and folding her arms across her bare breasts. I could tell it distracted the intruders, and hopefully softened their "attack attitude" a little. One of the guys told her she could put her clothes on as they interrogated us.

They demanded ... "Where is Tom? Has he been here?"

I had sold this particular guy, and his partner a couple loads of pot a few months earlier. The people that "Tom" had ripped off, had succeeded in catching his partner in Ocean Beach, and they were literally torturing him. The posse of dealers brought him along and he looked like "death warmed over". I kid not. The captured partner had guided them to my place, because Tom was back in San Diego trying to buy a load of weed. In fact, I **was** the guy he was buying the pot from. Tom was at my house the afternoon before the raid! I had nothing to do with any rip-off, but he was scheduled to get a shipment of our kilos that very same day. I had even offered him our spare bedroom, but he opted to stay in a hotel room. If he had accepted my invitation he would have been upstairs when Debbie and I got pulled out of bed at gunpoint. There must have been five or six gun toting characters all over the house. They were not the usual longhaired hippy drug-dealing sort. They all looked like young clean-cut businessmen. One of the shorthaired invaders coldly told us ... "You can thank your lucky stars, and God that we didn't find Tom here! It would have been over for all of you!"

I moved again, and told Debbie to return to Manhattan. Enough was enough. I had succeeded in getting her locked up in a Mexican dungeon ... and almost killed two times since. This was too crazy to play puppy love. She was convinced that I was all she ever wanted ... but I was convinced that it was really her pretty little ego that couldn't handle rejection. I had seen the pattern at work a lot. She was supposed to fly back to New York in a week, but she ended up staying with friends in Ocean Beach. In the next few months, I lived in four different apartments and houses. Three of them I shared with Joe, and of course Leo, my dog. I also bought two different used cars during that same time period. We were moving fast, and not leaving much of a trail to follow.

Ernesto sent us a load of kilos one time that looked real unusual to me. The kilos were packaged much nicer than most, and the marijuana was a real dark color. When I sampled a joint it was like dynamite cannabis. I told Joe ... "Hey this is like some kind of exotic weed. We could break all these kilos down into pounds, and give it some kind of label, and triple our money right here in Diego."

Joe didn't agree. We had only paid for it as good Mexican commercial. We had promised this load to one of Joe's old partners and a good friend. (I wish I could tell this particular guy's whole story, but he promised to shoot me if I even mentioned his name in a book.) Anyway, Joe said to me ... "No way, I told __BLANK__ that we would deliver the weed tomorrow, and I don't want to try to pawn this off as something that it's not."

I said ... "Joe, listen, I've smoked some so-called Acapulco Gold that didn't get me as stoned as that stuff. We could easily get $250 a pound for this, and BLANK could still double his money! I'm not kidding."

He didn't buy my pitch ... and since it was already promised to his friend I conceded. By the way, our unnamed associate is also a friend of mine, and even though over thirty years have passed ... he still might shoot me. Even if I changed his name, the uniqueness of his radical story would quickly reveal his identity. Maybe some day... OK blank?

Anyway, about a week later we received a call to come see our friend. When we arrived at his place he said, "You know that last weed you sold us was absolute dynamite! Dang, where did you get that? Can you get us any more? Listen, it was so good that we broke it down into pounds and quarter pounds. We sold it as exotic Colombian something or other, and made a fortune! Are you sure you can't get any more. We'll pay top dollar."

I told him I knew it was real good, but that it had come from our Mexican connections ... and that so far every load has been different. I doubted if we'd get any more.

Then our friend kind of embarrassed me by putting both of his hands on my shoulders, and looked me right in the eyes. He said ... "You know Roger, I don't know too many people who would go to bat for a friend like you're doing for Steve. I don't even know if I would, but I want you to know that I really respect what you're doing. I talked it over with my partner, and we made such a kill on this last load, that we want to chip in $5000 toward getting Steve out of La Mesa."

He handed me an envelope with five thousand dollars in hundred dollar bills. On the drive back to our pad Joe said ... "I'm going to keep my ____ing mouth shut from now on!"

We drove straight to Maggie's house, and she added the cash to our kitty in her closet.

Craig had become such a good customer that we more or less took him in as a partner on all his deals. He was a doctor's son, who had attended Vanderbilt University in Tennessee. He got caught with some pot and sent to jail for like six months or something years before. I asked him ... "Didn't jail make you want to quit dealing?"

He said, "Heck no, that's where I found out what's happening?"

We sent him back to Tennessee several times, and he was majorly supplying the student body at Vanderbilt with our wares. He even got a group of his old schoolmates to invest money in our enterprise. He offered them fifteen percent on their money on each load that we crossed into America from Mexico. We had all kinds of cash. I sent Joe back with him on one trip to help out. Everything was going real good.

Pretty soon we all re-united in San Diego, and then made a victory trip to Tijuana to celebrate with Ernesto. We went to our favorite subterranean club on Revolution Blvd. and got absolutely totally blasted. At least I did. A photographer came by to try to sell us a picture. I was trying to give the entire universe the finger, but my new girlfriend kept holding my hand down. Ernesto is in the top corner with his hands crossed.

I moved in with my new girlfriend. She shared a four-bedroom house with several other people. Joe got his own room, and I bunked in with Sue. There was another gal, and another guy who lived there. It was a neat house right above Jack Murphy Stadium on some bluffs. I could look over the backyard fence, and see the stadium and most of the parking lot. We had a pool, which was totally green, and I had my first experience trying to get the water swimable. I cleaned the filter, added a bunch of chlorine, and pretty soon we were diving and swimming ...

until it turned totally green again. I finally gave up on the pool, but we had a lot of wild parties at our house.

One day I noticed that a car was broke down on the street by our side yard. Two longhairs were trying to get the vehicle going. One of the gals came in the house and said the guys outside wanted to know if we wanted to buy some "chocolate mescaline". She didn't think they were narcs or anything after talking with them. So, I went out to check them out. Even though I had decided to stay away from any form of psychedelics, I ended up buying a thousand hits from these guys for eight hundred dollars.

Everyone loved this stuff so much over the next couple months, that they were absolutely begging me for it. I sold a couple hundred hits to my old friend Rich, the one who didn't shoot me. I eventually found out he was using pretty heavy, just like Harry had told me. He also begged me for more chocolate. I sent several hundred hits to Nashville with Craig, and half of the student bodies' grade point average at Vanderbilt took a sudden dip. They had a no-bust policy at the university to bring your drugs in to the lab, and get them tested for content and purity. They took some of our chocolate in and the verdict was that it was a very pure low grade LSD, and not chocolate anything.

I also took Steve a hundred hits inside La Mesa. Paula smuggled them in like only a gal could. Steve sold most of them to the Cavo, the godfather of prisoners, who was one of the most notorious criminals in Mexico. His name was Alijo Fitch. He absolutely loved the chocolate mescaline, and also wanted more. I got invited to his caraca, which was like a huge, nice, second-story apartment. It was a mansion compared to Steve's caraca. Alijo showed me his huge collection of hand carved pipes that were made by inmates inside La Mesa. Steve said to the ruggedly handsome 'prisoner godfather' … "Hey Alijo … It was on the news that the Federalies shot and killed a smuggler over by the Texas border. Did you know about that?"

Alijo said … "It was one of our people. Anyway we killed three of the pigs yesterday, but they didn't say nothing on the news! … nada!"

I thought to myself … "I'm sitting here trying to act normal while a Mexican drug kingpin casually discusses blowing away three federal police over a cup of instant coffee. Crazy!"

Steve wanted me to do some business with Alijo, but I knew better.

Debbie was still in San Diego. I thought she had returned to NY. My favorite hangout in San Diego was a nightclub on University Avenue called "Neutral Ground". It was packed every night. One night somebody came in, and said that my old girlfriend was by the door, and wanted me to come outside. She couldn't get in because she was only twenty years old. I went out and we talked. Several times Debbie would find me there at my hangout, and beg me to come outside. Sometimes we would take off together, but I wouldn't let her know where I lived. I told her about the popular LSD that I had, and she wanted to drop some with me.

I told her ... "Everyone absolutely loves it, but it really doesn't do much to me."

Debbie asked ... "Didn't you see any trails, or colors?"

I said, "No, I just got real paranoid a couple times."

She said, "Well, probably you didn't take enough if it's a low grade or whatever. I've dropped acid ... I don't know how many times back in New York."

"I didn't know that. About how many times? Ten or twenty or what?

Debbie laughed and said, "We used to trip all the time. Probably more than a hundred times ... maybe more. Let's do some, and I'll help you see trails."

We went for a drive, and ate three hits of my aspirin-sized drug. I still had a good-sized personal stash. Debbie lit matches and waved them around, and eventually claimed she was tripping and seeing things ... but I still didn't see anything. I just felt real loaded and paranoid again. Maybe my brain doesn't react normal. Anyway, after a couple of our encounters, I insisted that Debbie give up on us as an item. I again told her I thought it would be better for her back at her home in New York. She had two close brothers that she often talked about, and lots of family. Now, she was telling me that she and her friend Carolyn were going to hitch back. Whatever.

To complete my chocolate story, one night at our pad by the stadium, we had a spontaneous totally unplanned party. Joe and I had invested in a couple ounces of cocaine from Mexico. I was beginning to enjoy snorting coke more and more. There was a bunch of us there, including this real handsome black dude, who I had never met before. We decided to snort some of our coke, and drop some of the very popular psychedelic. Pretty soon I was feeling very loaded. Since three hits didn't have much effect on me in the past, I decided to double up. The black dude and me ate six hits each. We snorted some more coke, and I felt great, but still no light show. We drank beer and laughed, and snorted some more coke. Joe was there, and Sue, and several other people including Craig. We were all in our large bedroom, with several of us on Sue's huge waterbed. For some reason I was zeroed in on the black dude. It was like we were reading each other's minds … and suddenly we decided to drop some more acid, and snort some more coke. Our ounce of coke was shrinking fast with all the people, but who cares. We ate a few more little chocolate pills. At last count we stopped at 21 hits each.

Someone went out to their car, and brought in a little gadget that looked almost like a flashlight. Only this was a little emergency beacon light that you put out on the road to alert traffic. A voice out of star wars said … "Watch this!"

Darth Vader turned it on, and instantly a beam of light shot out of the gadget straight over to my black friend. He was sitting across from me, and was smiling with a huge gleaming-white perfect smile. In total amazement I saw the large beam of pure white light hit one of his teeth … and then explode into millions of tiny beams of light that shot like lightning all over the room. It totally freaked me out.

I tried to ask him if he saw what I just saw … but I couldn't talk. I wasn't paranoid at all … just totally in awe. What kind of dimension is this? I scooted way back on the waterbed up next to Sue, who seemed to be acting completely normal. I looked around the room. The beacon light continued to send pulsating lightning trails around the room. It was beautiful. Then I noticed a hanging plant way in the corner of the room. The thought hit me … I can make that plant take off. Instantly, my mind made that plant grow, and sweep across the ceiling of the bedroom. In Ohio when I had tried PCP at my friend Denny's house, the hallucinations were quick, dream-like, and very mental … this was totally visual and continuous. Not only did the plant branches, and leaves appear, and move in crystal clear wide-eyed **apparent** reality … but they were also changing colors from beautiful shades of green, to deep purples, and all kinds of colors. The ceiling was completely covered, and I decided to make the plant sweep down the wall next to my dog Leo. It obeyed just like I had a huge invisible magic paintbrush. It was unbelievable! The room was a complete psychedelic jungle. But that was just the beginning.

Suddenly time itself took on another dimension. It seemed like I had already been wherever I was for a million years. I panicked, and now the trip became a living nightmare. It was just like a couple of the bad trips I had before ... only a billion times worse. I felt like I had lived a thousand lifetimes, and I was trapped forever. It was horrible. Twenty-five-billion, mind-boggling years later, I could hear Sue trying to talk me down.

As daybreak was visibly approaching the bedroom window, I took back control of my mind. I could begin to function. In fact, I was suddenly in TOTAL control. I decided to go fishing. I love to fish. Craig said he would go with me. I went into the front room, and there was my black friend staring at the wall.

I said ... "Hey, do you want to go fishing with us?"

He never said a word. He was sitting in a chair, and then he slowly looked at me with his mouth hanging wide open. His eyes had this confused blank look. His mouth stayed open in a fixed position. I tried to get him to talk ... but he was completely gone ... **completely**! I never saw him again in my life.

Somehow we made it to the docks. I'm sure Craig drove. Sue's father owned a sports fishing boat, and I think she gave us free tickets for a half-day boat. Pretty soon the San Diego coastline was way off in the distance. The sun had just cracked above the distant mountains, and I was continuing to see an incredible light show. It was so beautiful dancing across the bubbling ocean water like magic. You think the trip is over, but it has a life of its own. I then took control of the boat ... I caught fish, and made the deck hands do everything ... take the fish off ... re-bait my hook each time ... and I even went up on the bridge with the captain for a couple thousand years of roaming the ocean! "How could little pills ... do that ??? Even twenty-one of them?"

"That's enough of that!!!"

CHAPTER 34

"THEATER OF THE MACABRE"

Even though I was enjoying many parts of this season of my dealing career ... there seemed to be some sinister forces at work on many levels. Every time we would break ahead, right around the corner would be a disaster or two. It was a pattern that I couldn't break. I was beginning to get a little more superstitious than ever. As mentioned, I took my Grandpa Ira's belief that it was good luck to find a penny heads up ... I took that superstition about twenty steps forward. I continued to notice that when I reached into my pocket, and pulled out some change for the pay phone, which I did daily ... if the dime would come out in my **hand** heads up ... then that phone call would almost always be good news. I needed good news. It was beyond coincidence how consistently it held true. However, if the dime was tails, then it was invariably a negative response waiting on the other end of the line. What is this?

We didn't have cell phones on every living soul in 1974 so I used a series of indiscrete pay phones around town to conduct business. Some phone calls were so super important to our immediate future, finances, and freedom, that if the dime came out tails ... I simply wouldn't even make the call. I'd wait, or change direction, or whatever. It was crazy and I knew it ... but this thing was actually starting to have a measure of control over me. I never told a single soul.

Craig took a load back east with no problems, but while there in Nashville he called and told me he was buying a quantity of hash to bring back on the return trip to California. The transaction was going to take a few more days. I told him to absolutely forget it! I had things lined up with Ernesto, and we needed the money now! Well, he didn't listen. He lost all our money on a bogus hash deal. He was tied up in a hotel room, injected with a big dose of heroin ... and ripped off. At least that was his story a week later. I was so angry that I refused to do business with Craig or his partner back in Tennessee. I scrambled hard and got things going again without them. I had other customers. For over a month Craig literally begged me to work with him again. I finally did. After all, he got me out of a Mexican jail.

Then, our former associate Mike Hardey was found floating down the Colorado River with another guy. He had been our pick-up man when Steve and I got busted in Mexico. The two deaths were ruled accidental drowning, but Mike's death was pretty suspicious. It was common knowledge that he had been repeatedly busted for possession of heroin, but never did a day of jail or prison time. It was rumored that he gave people up and was a snitch. Not only did Mike turn up dead, but after I agreed to work with Craig again, we found out that the DEA, or FBI back east wanted him and his partner to come in for questioning. It was a murder investigation. Craig was told that they were only wanted for questioning, and were not suspects in this particular investigation. The authorities knew drugs were involved, but promised immunity from any kind of drug bust. They just wanted some answers. The murders happened at a customer's house in a neighboring state to Tennessee.

Apparently, this particular customer was involved in a drug deal that went bad. Someone came in and murdered every person in the house. The saddest part was that the young guy doing the dealing had a brand new girlfriend who was also killed. She was nineteen years old, and was at the house in question for the very first time ... and never left. How could all this death get so close? Even though this was in no way connected to me personally ... it was still way too close. I had pushed diligently to keep guns out of our dealing ... even though Ernesto seriously wanted to include them ... at least in Mexico. I was committed to "what comes around ... goes around". I was also constantly trying to make sure that everyone around me stayed away from heroin. My friends started calling me "Mother Roger". I simply wanted to enjoy life, and make a lot of money ... not kill people ... or see them OD on the devil drug.

I think the lowest I ever got in my life, besides Mercy Hospital, or our Ocho-jail experience, happened about this time ... one weekend in Tijuana. I had gone down by myself to find Ernesto. I had a lot of money on me. For some reason I couldn't find Ernesto anywhere. I can't remember all the details, or even why I was on foot, but I was. I went to a couple sleazy bars in frustration, and ended up getting really, really drunk. I remember worrying that I might lose the money, or get robbed, because of all the cutthroat looking people around me. It was a real rough section of TJ ... off the beaten path. I left a bar, and stumbled around looking for a place to stash the money. There was a building with a wide entryway, and some plants on both sides. It looked like some kind of offices were inside. It was late at night, and no one was around. I stashed the money under some rocks by the entry plants. Then I went to another bar and drank some more.

I finally decided to walk to Ernesto's sister's place to see if he was there. I figured it would be a mile or so, and then up this hill to her apartment. I took off, and walked and walked and walked. Everything looks different on foot in the dark ... especially when you can't even walk straight. It must have been around two in the morning, and I was lost big time. I was so drunk ... and the taste of Tequila was starting to make me sick. There were no streetlights, and I was in some real poverty stricken, filthy area of T.J. I slipped, and fell into a huge ditch next to an old concrete road going up a hill. I thought it might be the hill by Dora's place. I wasn't sure, and didn't care any more. I tried to pick myself up from the bottom of that ditch ... but instead I got totally sick. The tequila and tacos make horrible tasting barf. Believe me. I passed out.

The next thing I remember was waking up in that stinking, filthy, trashy ditch. I was covered with dew, and felt stiff like a corpse. It was now light outside, and as I looked up from my prone condition in the dirt and trash, I saw an old, very-very poor looking, hunched over Mexican lady looking down at me from the road above. She was about four feet tall, had her shawl on, and a very wrinkled up brown face. It was a weird feeling as she intently stared down at me in startled curiosity. She probably thought I was dead. I managed to move a little, and she turned away her gaze, and continued on a slow pace up the hill ... glancing back at me a couple more times.

"This has to be the bottom. What is your life coming to?"

I spent most of the day sobering up, looking for Ernesto, and searching for the money I had buried. About thirty buildings all had the same looking entry. However, instead of dark deserted office spaces … now the sun is beating down like crazy, and people are running around like Mexican jumping beans. When I was absolutely ready to give up, I finally stumbled onto the right place. The money was there. Thank God! Ernesto laughed his head off.

The problems I was having was nothing compared to the hell on earth that Steve was waking up to daily. I got in to see him as often as possible, but he was still on his own in probably the most notorious prison in Mexico. A local news station in San Diego did a story on La Mesa. They were able to come inside with a film crew. Roberto Salenas from Channel 8 News interviewed Steve. I never saw the broadcast, but lots of people told me about it. Steve's segment was the big hit. They repeated the story several times. It was one of the few highlights of Steve's nightmare.

I asked him what he told the reporter. He said … "He wanted to know all about La Mesa, and what it was like for an American to be locked up in a Mexican prison. He asked about my case and I lied my tail off!"

(Someday I'm going to try to dig up that broadcast.)

On one visit Steve was all excited, and told me about a huge incident that he eye- witnessed. He said … "I saw Alijo walking across the yard with one of his bodyguards. I always thought that this one particular bodyguard was more or less a punk. Alijo usually has about three bodyguards with him, but only the one dude was with him. I was up at someone's caraca on the second floor. I noticed a whole bunch of oudies waiting nearby. They were acting kinda nervous. I thought something was coming down.

When Alijo was pretty close to his pad they all ran over and attacked him. There were at least eight of them. One guy stabbed Fitch right away, and his bodyguard fought them back with his knife. Then he picked up a piece of rebar, and started really fighting them off. The bodyguard was incredible! It was like a pack of wolves lunging in at them from all directions. Every one of them had a big old knife. Usually the bodyguards have a gun, but for some reason he didn't have one. It happened right below me. I saw the whole thing.

The bodyguard bashed a couple guys real good with the rebar, and drove the rest of them back over and over. He looked like Errol Flynn in the movies. The pack did manage to get in and stab Alijo several more times though. A few other guys came in, and helped the bodyguard.

When that happened Fitch got free, and kinda held his arm up against his side, and went up the steps to his caraca. They took him out of La Mesa a little while later in an ambulance to a hospital.

That bodyguard blew my mind! You should have seen him! He was fighting like a madman for dear life. He saved Alijo! I was definitely wrong about him."

Fitch almost died in the hospital. Eventually he pulled through, but was in the hospital recovering for a month or so. In the meantime there was a power struggle inside La Mesa to take over Fitch's position as Cavo. Three different factions, led by three different men, took control, and divided up "The Little Town".

Fitch is notorious in Mexico, and greatly feared in La Mesa. When he was originally busted in years past, he allegedly had an eleven-hour shoot out with the police. He fought until he ran out of bullets. Now, everyone was warning him (even on the local radio) … not to return to La Mesa. He was given the option to go to other prisons, because of the death threats against him, but he chose to return to La Mesa.

Steve told me … "Alijo could have quietly returned with a little army around him, but instead he walked in by himself, no bodyguards or anything, with the whole prison watching. He definitely has balls of steel, and was sending everyone a message!"

Within about two months all three of his rivals were dead. He was back in total control of the prison. "La Mesa is too much!"

Later, Steve told me about all the homemade knives in La Mesa. He said some of them were really a trip. I told him to get me one for a jailhouse souvenir. The next time I came inside he arranged for me to meet with one of the lowlife "possible" killers … (who knows?) … who also needed money. I met with him behind one of the tanks. He wanted fifteen dollars, but I told him I only had five. He reluctantly handed me the knife for five bucks.

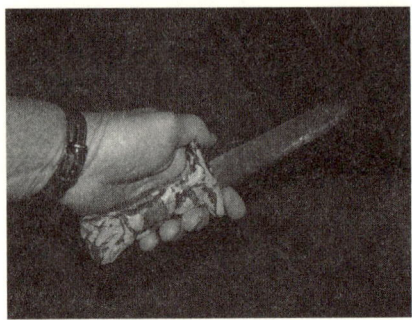

The knife was made out of a thick steel ruler, and honed to a dagger point on one end. It is slightly over ten inches long. The other end was fashioned into a handle by melting plastic bottles, or some kind of plastic, and shaping it around the steel. It must have taken a long time to make. Like a fool I smuggled that knife out of La Mesa. They patted me down and everything, but didn't touch my private parts where the knife was carefully hiding. The handle went from the crotch of my jeans to the point under my belly button. Ernesto said I would have received a minimum of four years if they had discovered that knife on me. At least it hasn't killed anyone for the last thirty-one years.

One day I was sitting in Steve's caracca, when Hank knocked on the door, and came in. He said … "Hey Rog, can you do me a favor? When you cross over to San Diego can you drop this letter to my girlfriend in the mail?"

I said, "Sure Hank."

Steve said … "Hank … have a sit, and help us smoke a couple joints."

Hank was still standing in the doorway, but he said … "No thanks. I'm going back to my place. I feel like total crap! I heard that Roger was here, and I just wanted to get this letter to him. Thanks Rog … I'll catch you guys later."

I took the letter with me, and put it in my glove box after I left the prison. When I got back to the States I was consumed with business. We crossed another load or two, and I even went back to Nashville with Craig. I forgot all about Hank's letter. I didn't get back down to see Steve for about a month. When I got back to La Mesa, I found Steve and

Johnny by the little park.

Johnny says to me … "Hey, one of the Americans died a couple weeks ago."

I said … "Which one?"

"The young Marine … Hank. It's really too bad because he was good kid! Everybody liked Hank. What a shame!"

I was shocked. I almost felt responsible. I had personally talked his little bunch of smugglers into picking one of themselves to take the fall. Hank had let all his friends off the hook, and reluctantly volunteered for "hell on earth". I remember him choking up with tears when he made that decision … like it was yesterday. What a total bummer!

He died from hepatitis contracted from a dirty needle. Hank was not a veteran junkie. He started using inside La Mesa. It cost him his life. To top it off Steve told me he had shared a needle with Hank a week before he died. He was positive he would get the same thing, and asked me to get him some medicine. I had no idea of what kind of medicine, so I called the Marine base at Camp Pendleton, and asked for a doctor. I finally got through to one, and told him about Hank, which he already knew about. I told him I had an American friend in the same prison, who had unfortunately used drugs, and the same needle with Hank. After a little hesitation he told me I could buy gammaglobin, (or something like that), over the counter in Mexico. He told me how much to give him and so on. We smuggled the medicine in to Steve.

I got the letter out of my glove box, and thought about what to do. It was addressed to Hank's girlfriend in Palo Alto, California. I figured I had to mail it … so I did. I often wondered what it must have been like for his girlfriend to get his letter several weeks after he was dead. Life is a trip. Death is a worse trip.

Lots and lots of other things happened over the course of the eleven months that Steve resided in "El Publito". He didn't die from hepatitis, but his health got worse and worse toward the end of his time. (Months after his release he almost died of TB.) We paid his fianza, and I actually picked him up when he was released. My girlfriend Sue went with me. We stopped and had a drink in T.J. on the way back to America.

Steve wrote a little story about his experience in La Mesa … and sent it to me years down the road (from an American prison). It goes like this …

THEATER OF THE MACABRE

By Steve Peterson

On Mexico's Independence Day, Cinco De Mayo 1974, I was arrested by the Mexican Police, and charged with smuggling marijuana.

I did not realize it at the time, but I was about to embark on a dreadful adventure. It was filled with misery, loneliness, horror, corruption, and human desperation ... a journey that would eat away at my soul for years to come, and leave scars that would last forever.

After spending eleven days of hell in an over-crowded jail cell, I was taken to La Mesa prison. La Mesa went by several names, but after being there for a short time, and watching this bizarre prison life unfold, I came to think of it as a theater.

The commandante, who was always behind the scene, and who had his pockets lined was the producer. The poorly paid guards with their wide brim caps and antique Pistolas, who were easily bought ... were the ushers. The upper class prisoners who flaunted their cocaine, heroin, and whores ... were the macho showmen of the stage.

The vultures were inmates who would sell their sisters and rob, steal, and murder for heroin. They looked like a bunch of derelict commancheros from the set of a John Wayne movie.

The Visitors were our audience - spectators in our theater of the macabre.

Sometimes the melodrama was uneventful. Other times it was ovation. I was just a bit player. I had a very small part in all of these theatrics. My reluctant audition was full of terror and stage-fright, but I got the part anyway. I learned to play it with my life.

In my caraca (my "dressing-room"), I would cook my heroin, and inject it into my soul. I used this drug to steady my nerves for all my curtain calls. Back on the yard (the stage) it was wheel and deal for the next fix. Sometimes hunger would dictate where my priorities were. Sex was only a feeling to suppress. I would masturbate for the same reason I shot heroin, whether I had a woman or not. My nerves were shot, and I was trying to bury all feelings.

My nights were spent in ritual listening to "Dark Side of the Moon" by Pink Floyd, while watching the silhouettes of the guards in their gun towers, and the shadows of prisoners scurrying across the yard. An occasional flash from the muzzle of a gun was all to be seen from my box seat at the window of my caraca. I sat alone in the dark, burning one, and licking the run in the zig zag paper, dreading my next performance, and wishing this long running play was over. I prayed that sleep would come easy, and dreams would forever take me away.

Morning came with the sun peaking over the east wall, and the guards storming through the tank banging their billy clubs against the caracas, and yelling "la cuenta." I jumped down off my bunk, pulled on my Levis, and stepped into my sandals. I headed out my door, and down the rickety stairs to the floor of the tank. I fell in behind some of the more unfortunates who slept huddled together on the crowded floor, and were dragging their bug-infested bedrolls behind them. I walked outside into the cool morning air, bleary eyed, with a chill in my bones, and in need of a fix. It was show time!

I was standing in front of the tanks contemplating on what the day had in store for me. All around me were men sick with tuberculosis and chest colds. They would spit their vile phlegm everywhere. Some of the prisoners were standing around open fires, burning plastic, tires, wood, or anything they could get their hands on to keep warm.

One of the more bizarre, but strangely fascinating sights was the transvestites. There were a dozen or so standing in line for the morning count. Dressed in their nightgowns with their obviously bleached hair, eye makeup running, limp wrists, and some in need of a shave … these pathetic looking creatures never looked worse than in the mornings. They were our God-awful chorus-line.

The morning chill is gone now. The sun is overhead and beating down. I can see heat waves drifting, changing, and dancing all over the yard. There's not a cloud in the sky with most of the population looking for shade, no doubt. I've lost so much weight, I've been able to sit back on my haunches for hours. The same stance I've learned to use to defecate, standing on the rim of our decrepit toilet. I feel a little better now, because after the morning count I scored a dollar paper of heroin, and it took the edge off.

Looking out over the prison I could see a few of the dealers standing in their usual spots. They were trying not to look obvious. The chorus-line is out in full drag. They're doing laundry across the way. They've got their hair pinned up, short-shorts on, and their blouses tied above the waist. They're talking that talk, walking that walk, and flirting with the men who pass by. Heck, after all it's summer!

There's an old man, a pot farmer from Sinaloa sitting down the way from me. He's eating watermelon with chilly powder sprinkled on it, fanning himself with his hat, and watching some of the inmates children play hopscotch.

In front of me, and up about ten meters was a fruit stand. The owner, with his big hat and machete always ready, was squeezing orange juice for two customers.

A young vulture who had been shot in the leg a few days earlier was limping across the yard toward the fruit stand. He was barefooted, and had a crutch under one arm. His leg was still bleeding. As the boy passed, I could see the handle of a gun sticking out from the back of his pants. I looked to the old man eating the watermelon. He nodded to me that he had seen it too.

Suddenly, I realized what was about to happen. Everything seemed to slow down as in a silent movie, frame by frame.

The young vulture drew his pistola as he approached the customers at the fruit stand. One of the customers saw the boy draw the gun. He stepped away casually. He was obviously in on this surrealistic murder scene. The owner with the big hat saw the boy too. He dropped what he was doing, and ran out of his stand. The man playing the victim turned around to meet his death. With a look of terror in his eyes, and his mouth wide open, the young murderer put a bullet through his heart.

The victim started to run, again in slow motion. As he ran past me, he was clutching his chest. The boy was taking aim for another shot. He fired again, striking the man in the back. He fell to his knees from the second shot. He was trying desperately to crawl away from his death.

He had a look of desperation that I'll never forget. I could see blood running down his arms as he collapsed in the dirt. I thought about how hard and uncaring I had become in this place. I looked over to the children playing hopscotch. They were also watching this drama unfold. Looking at their faces, I could see they too, were very hard, but still children.

Thus bathed in the horror of sudden death, in a sea of poppy induced apathy, I passed on through another day in this theater of the macabre.

CHAPTER 35

"ABSTRACT CROSSES"

Things had really been intense over the last year, but as I analyzed everything on a beautiful San Diego mountainside … I felt that I was making progress … in spite of all the setbacks. I was still "a clean machine" … meaning no felony convictions. In fact, I never even saw the inside of an American jail cell for any charge. I had great connections both in Mexico, and scattered across America. I was truly enjoying the fast paced, adrenalin producing, lifestyle of a smuggler. Every once in awhile I would give myself a pep-talk when bad things happened. However, basically I am an optimist, and don't give up easy. One of my favorite spots for soul searching and pep talks was under a certain tree. The tree was way up overlooking the ocean and the cliffs south of Ocean Beach. You can see for miles and miles of sparkling ocean, and tiny distant waves along an endless coastline. I took a deep breath, and said to the universe … "OK … **next** … bring it on!"

In early 1975 we put all our eggs into one basket, and bought two hundred kilos in Mexico. Ernesto had assembled our own team to run the border including his cousin Rudy. Again, not Connie's son Rudy, but his late uncle Phillip's son who was now nineteen years old. I really like Rudy. We partied hardy many a time along with kingpin Tio Ernesto. Rudy was good looking, and real easy going with a lot of guts. In the picture he is sitting between Ernesto and myself. However, all good parties must come to an end, and the border patrol busted our latest shipment. Our money was gone again, and several of Ernesto's workers were in the San Diego County jail … including his young cousin Rudy. What a bummer! Very disheartening! (Rudy ended up doing something like ten years in prison in the United States, and he came out very bitter against Ernesto and myself.)

Joe, Ernesto, Rudy & Roger

From that bust we scraped the bottom of the barrel, and survived another month or so. Then Ernesto talked one of his big-time connections in Tijuana to front us two hundred kilos on credit. Believe it or not … that load was busted. His connection figured it was just bad luck to lose a load, so he fronted Ernesto another 200 kilos. That load bit the dust with the other two. We lost around six hundred kilos in a couple months. All credit was cut off. Eleven of Ernesto's workers joined Rudy in the San Diego County Hotel.

Ernesto was in serious trouble. He thought they would probably try to kill him, but decided not to run. Instead for several days he walked around his block to say … "here I am." The drug lord sent a car by with a bunch of thugs to intimidate him, but didn't do anything. Later they would use his debt as a huge obligation and leverage. Ernesto was hitting the bottle so heavy during this time … that when I saw him, I hardly recognized my friend. His liver went upside down, and he turned yellowish. In addition, all his eyebrows and eyelashes **totally** fell off. A person really looks strange with no eyelashes. He went on the wagon, and started drinking turtle blood, and protein powder, and whatever to regain his health. He also began working out to start wrestling again. It was survival time.

Steve, Sue & Roger

By now Steve had just been released. In fact, as I mentioned, my girlfriend Sue and myself picked him up from La Mesa on that final day of his incarceration. He looked a mess, and was a shadow of the Steve that got busted with me eleven months earlier. It was scary. He was skin and bones, pale and ashen, along with a dazed, disoriented demeanor. We drove straight to downtown TJ, and celebrated his release with a stiff shot and a taco. A roving photographer captured the moment. Thank God he was alive and free. Mission accomplished!

However, in my mind, Steve soon became another major problem, and was way out of control, dealing and using heroin. I had done my part, helping to get him out of La Mesa. We talked all the time, but he knew I was down on dealing smack … so he basically did his own thing. He made a deal with two guys who had been on a rampage robbing gun stores all across the west coast. They had made the news several times, and had escaped after a shoot-out in L.A. They wanted to trade the guns for drugs.

The Mexican guys, who had the original fifty-five kilos in National City when I first met Ernesto, called and had another load. It was the same family of brothers who cut Ernesto out. I had continued to sell an occasional load for them. They would always front me the kilos, but insist that I sell them in San Diego quickly. I always did, but this time I decided to put them off, and take the pot back to my Vanderbilt customers. We were so broke that I figured they could just wait a week or so extra this time. Joe and I put a hundred kilos in our own rental unit, and made reservations to fly into Nashville with Craig like we usually did.

In the meantime I slowly became convinced that we were under surveillance. I heard a bunch of strange clicks on my phone when I talked to Steve. Maybe he was being watched or his phone tapped. I wasn't sure. I had two kilos of this new load in my car that Joe and I were going to take a look at. The rest we left in the storage unit. We drove up to our newly rented single story apartment.

I saw a car parked across the street, and a man was fumbling around in his glove box like he was looking for something. I put Leo's leash on, and walked my dog down the street. I casually watched awhile to see what the guy was doing. Joe went inside. The man in the car had on work clothes like he worked for the gas company or something. Pretty soon he got out of the vehicle, and went into the center of a bunch of apartments across the street. I couldn't see him anymore. I couldn't see if he went inside or what. I took Leo into the apartment, and told Joe what I thought might be happening.

Then I went out my back door, and in back of our apartment building. I ran a couple buildings down to a place where I knew I could see into the apartment complex across the street where the guy had walked into. Lo and behold he was standing behind a palm tree talking into a radio.

I ran back to our apartment and told Joe ... "We need to get out of here! The guy is across the street hiding behind a tree watching our place, and talking into a radio. I don't think they know we're holding anything, or they'd have broke the door down already. Let's act normal and you take the white car and split. If anyone follows you just lose him, or ditch the car if you have to. It's not in any of our names anyway. If everything is cool take the kilos to the storage. I'm going to go get Craig, and we're going to change our flight plans. I think our phone might even be tapped. We need to scramble before we get popped!"

Joe took off in one direction, and a little later I walked out with Leo, and drove off in another direction. We always drove in circles making sure that no one was following us. I left Leo with Sue, and the next day, instead of flying out of San Diego, Craig and I drove up to LAX, and spent the night in an airport hotel. In the morning we flew with several large suitcases of kilos into Memphis instead of Nashville. From Memphis we took a Greyhound bus to Nashville. I figured we were making it pretty hard to bust us on this run … in case they had learned anything about our regular routine. I rented a hotel room in Nashville.

Then another disaster strikes. We discovered that the pot was a bunch of bogus kilos. We never had a chance to check them out in San Diego. In the center of each kilo was about a pound of seeds. They were rip-off kilos. Some pot farmer in southern Mexico probably took a scoop shovel full of seeds, and filled the center section of each kilo. What a bunch of snakes! In addition to that … you'd have to smoke about ten joints to get a buzz. After all the hassles we had getting back east this time, along with almost a thousand emotional gyrations … and now this! "What is going on!"

We finally scrambled, and were able to buy a bunch of pounds locally of some really good weed. Then we tore everything apart, and mixed it all together with our huge stack of kilos. Craig and I had a frantic production going at top speed … with a gigantic mound of reeking cannabis on top of the queen-sized bed in my hotel room. If they only knew what goes on in some of these rooms! We threw out most of the seeds in a nearby dumpster, and were able to start selling some of our revitalized pot.

I called Sue, and told her that it was taking a lot longer than planned. She was so glad I called. She told me that the Mexican connection in Chula Vista had her phone number, and was threatening our lives. They were freaking out, and screaming that they were going to kill us! Sue was freaking out as well … and real scared. I told her to calm down, and assured her that they had no idea of where we lived. Thankfully, that was true. Nevertheless, I had her move out to our new apartment that I had just rented with Joe.

One of our regular customers in Nashville was a young college kid, who had several outlets for pounds and kilos. Like usual we fronted him some of our merchandise. He always brought us back the proceeds a few hours later. We gave him about fifty pounds of our remaining load in a combination locked suitcase. On his way to his delivery, a drunk driver ran a red light, and center punched our friend's car. His car was completely totaled. He woke up in a hospital. The cops came in, and informed him that he was busted for possession of marijuana. He ended up beating the case for illegal search and seizure … but I lost another 50 pounds. Can you believe it? The parade of disasters keep coming!

The next day this kid's father sent me a message through another college student, and was begging me not to harm his son. They gave me an envelope with $1500 in it, and the father promised to make payments for the rest. I was told that this kid got involved with a gang one time before, and was shot in a fight. It freaked his upper-middle class family completely out. The kid relaying the message, and the money ... said that the father was really **begging** and promising to pay the entire amount. I felt horrible. No way was I going to go after the kid, but I kept the money his father sent. (At least I never tried to get any more out of him.) We did manage to sell some pounds, but the money was coming very slowly.

Craig and I got in an argument. I had just about had enough of everything. We still had about half of the remaining load left to sell. I made a radical decision to break rank. I got up real early, and with a rush of adrenaline took off for California. I took the cash we had which was around seven thousand dollars, and left Craig a note saying that he could sell the rest. I'm sure he was shocked when he saw that I split. I was planning to go to L.A. ... catch a plane to Hawaii ... and start a new life. That's what I was thinking. I felt real guilty ... but was so fed up and tired of one disaster after another.

Instead of going to Hawaii, I went back to San Diego. Foolish move, but I couldn't abandon everyone. I felt bad about Ernesto. I knew he was on the hot seat, but what could I do ... except get things going again on my side. I also felt bad about Joe. He had been staying with a girlfriend, and was totally broke. I met with Steve and bought an ounce of coke and a bus ticket for my friend Joe to take back to his hometown in Illinois. He had told me that in a pinch he could break down an ounce of coke into grams, and at least five times the money back in Illinois. I felt this was the time for extreme measures. I found out later that he cashed in the bus ticket and never left.

I got together with Steve again, because he knew a guy that could get us a load of pot. All my other sources were dry right now. This man was a Mexican American man about sixty years old. He knew that we had moved a lot of merchandise in the past, and he wanted to help us over this rough spot. I talked to him on the phone. He told me he also knew about this family of brothers who I had a problem with. He told me one of the guys in T.J. had offered him $5000.00 to bring me to Mexico. They put a contract on me.

Fire On the Mountain

He told me on the phone ... "But ____ them! They are a bunch of small time people. We need to get you going again. Why don't we meet?"

I was a little reluctant to meet with this guy ... especially after he told me he was offered a contract on my head. What are the odds that a stranger would even know these same people? It was bizarre. But then, if he really wanted to do me in ... he wouldn't be broadcasting it ... he'd just do it.

I still wanted to be careful, so I told him ... "Look, I'll meet you at the main bus station in downtown San Diego."

So we met and worked out a deal for $6000 worth of kilos. He was a sophisticated looking man with his gray hair and all. Six thousand was all the investment money I had left except for around $600 and change. I met with him again a few days later, and fronted him the money. I was then to meet him the next day around noon to pick up the kilos in Chula Vista. I found a motel right near the 5 Freeway to camp out for the night.

It was a nice big motel room, and I decided to watch TV. The NCAA playoffs were on. I think it was the UCLA Bruins and Kentucky playing. It was an exciting game ... "but why didn't I hop on that plane, and go to Hawaii like I planned? Why am I trying to get this gig going again for the thousandth time? No matter how hard I try ... it's not happening!"

I turned off the TV and took a shower. When I stepped out to dry off, I noticed a design on the small bathroom window. At first I thought it was some kind of fancy stained glass or something, because the colors were so vibrant. It was a design that had three colored crosses. One real big one, and two that were more or less transposed beside and behind the big one. It was like a beautiful abstract design. Three illuminated radical crosses. Being half an artist I was amazed!

The window was high on the wall, and around 20 by 30 inches. The crosses were perfectly distinct and beautiful, but I couldn't figure out if it was man-made, or what. I got closer to inspect the window. Then I could tell that it was reflections from some neon lights behind the hotel from neighboring businesses. But how could they randomly happen to produce such a radical piece of art. The bathroom window had a texture to it for privacy, so I couldn't tell what kind of signs were able to combine, and produce those three crosses. I looked at the window for a long time. It was a strange coincidence to see three radiant crosses at this upside down point of my life. So many coincidences were happening. "What's going on out there?" I went to bed.

The next morning I got up and made another major life decision ... "Screw the kilos and the six thousand dollars, and beating my head up against one concrete wall after the other! I have a car and six hundred dollars left ... not enough for Hawaii ... but I bet I can make it to Alaska! ... This is it ... **I'm out of here!!!"**

• • •

I thought nothing could be more radical than all this wheeling and dealing ... Coming so close to losing my freedom ... so close to losing my life ... so close to achieving my goals ... and then to see everything vaporize over and over. I thought nothing except fiction could be more radical ... but I was wrong ...

What was waiting for me up north was far beyond anything I could ever imagine!!!

PART III

"CUSTOM PLATES"

KARA JANE

CHAPTER 36

"THE MEADOW"

Ernesto David Hernandez was boiling inside. "Where is my 'gabacho' friend and partner?"

A ruthless Tijuana drug lord had brought Ernesto in to see him. In Spanish he said … "You owe us mucho dinero Ernesto. You lost four hundred kilos of mine! We're thinking maybe you're just a drunk who can't take care of business. Que Paso? Is that what's happening with you?

Anyway, I have a job I need you to take care of. I want you to kill these two men. We'll forget about this other deal between you and me for now. How about it?"

Ernesto accepted. In fact if he was going to be killing people … "let's start with Gordo … I heard he is back in Tijuana … and then I need to find Senior Roger Sachs."

Gordo had worked with Ernesto for over a year, but had ripped off several thousand dollars that Ernesto gave him to pay for some merchandise. He had completely left Tijuana for fear of his life. The word was that he was somewhere in Mexicali. It had been almost six months, but now Ernesto heard he was back.

Not long after he was hearing these reports of his missing partner … Ernesto went to his Aunt Consuelo's house, and there was Gordo sitting on the couch. He was there trying to borrow a gun from Uncle Henry. Ernesto flew into a rage and started cussing out his obese former partner. He pulled out his gun but somehow the clip with all the bullets ejected onto the floor. It freaked Ernesto out because that had never happened. "How did that happen???" He started to load the clip full of cartridges back into the 45 automatic while he screamed at Gordo … "Get your sorry fat ____ outside!!! I don't want to kill you in my aunt's house!"

For the first time in her life Connie fainted and hit the floor. Gordo was paralyzed and wouldn't move off the couch. He softly said ... "You're going to have to kill me in here."

Ernesto put the gun to his head. He almost pulled the trigger. Uncle Henry was trying to get Connie up off the floor. The little kids, Phillip and Dolia were both crying. Gordo was completely white with terror in his eyes.

As Connie was getting off the floor with Uncle Henry's help she began begging Ernesto ... "Ernesto don't do this!!! Not in my house ... and the kids ... please!!! It's not worth it Ernesto. Let him go!!!"

Something stopped him from squeezing the trigger. Maybe it was the crying kids, or the old man, or the bullets ejecting ... or Connie's pleas. Ernesto told Gordo ... "Don't ever come here again. I should kill you right now! If I ever see you again I probably will."

Ernesto split.

• • •

When I left Chula Vista and San Diego heading for Alaska, my head was spinning. Spinning and numb at the same time. I felt like a fool that I had simply handed my last six thousand dollars in cash away. It was about the same feeling you get in Vegas ... after losing big time on the crap tables ... a sick, empty feeling. But it wasn't just the money. Six thousand dollars was nothing compared to what had gone through our hands. I had that "running away" guilty feeling. I was letting Joe down, and Ernesto, and Craig, and Steve, and Sue, and Maggie, and everybody. At the same time, I knew in my heart that I had given it my best shot. It's not happening ... at least for now. Whether it's bad karma on my life, or divine intervention, or colored crosses ... I don't know what it is. I just know it's time for "exit stage right".

I stopped and picked up my dog Leo, and hit the 5 Freeway heading north ... all by my lonesome. By the time I got to L.A. it was mid-afternoon, and I decided to call Roberta and say good-by to her. I stopped at a phone booth and called. I gave her a little run down on what I was up to.

She said, "Where are you now? Shouldn't you at least spend the night before you take off for Alaska? Are you sure about all this? I'm going to come meet you."

We met and had dinner, and she talked me into staying in L.A. for a while. Roberta and I had a lot of history together. She is one of my favorite people in the whole world. It was really good to get some objective input. I couldn't afford to rent an apartment or stay in motels on my tiny nest egg. Roberta still lived at her parents home in Woodland Hills, so I drove down to Malibu, and dropped in on my good old Army buddy Cliff. On my trip to Alaska … I never got past Los Angeles. Oh well … so much for plans. As a matter of fact … so much for Master Plans!

Cliff was real glad to see me. You know, you have a best friend … and then you move or something, and years go by … and then you might have another best friend. That's happened to me a bunch of times. Cliff is, and always will be, one of my best friends … no matter what! I crashed at his art studio, right on Pacific Coast Highway, a stone throw from the famous Malibu beaches. It was great. I started painting again and helping Cliff with different projects. It was just like old times … like Germany and like Round Table Studios. It was natural … and La Mesa, and people trying to kill me, and treacherous scheming drug deals … seemed a million miles away.

Cliff continued to live in the three-story apartment building right across the street on the beach. He shared an apartment, and managed the building with another artist named Paul, who was separated from his wife. Cliff was giving art lessons to a bunch of rich Malibu locals, as well as to one spunky middle-aged X-con named Gene. Gene had done a stretch in prison, and the state offered a career-training program for parolees. He wanted to be an artist, and Cliff was his "Great Master" … paid for by the State of California. It was far out. I enjoyed working beside Gene. We became good friends. I had the studio to myself at night.

Now, Cliff was being paid with taxpayer's dollars to help rehabilitate one of our wayward fellow citizens, but I don't know if Governor Ronald Reagan would approve of all his methods and tactics. We would smoke dope, drink wine, listen to the Moody Blues, and "Nights in White Satin" … and "Stairway to Heaven" … and then try to make the paint magically do something! It was funny.

But man … so much cannabis! I was a dealer, but had never smoked so much in my life. I remembered the time years back when Cliff made me drive clear across L.A. to get a little joint that a hitchhiker had given me. Since that very first marijuana cigarette he had really become a certifiable pothead. A very unique and talented pothead ... but probably not what Gene really needed. On the other hand, I seriously became absorbed into abstract painting. Normally I paint pretty tight and realistic ... but not with the Moody Blues and THC.

I spent a couple months living at the beach in the studio. It was a good time. I would see Roberta once in awhile, but we drifted apart again. Her job was in the city, and I think she had another boyfriend as well. Cliff was experimenting again with a new technique for making abstract paintings. Like I mentioned I jumped into the act. We took big sheets of smooth masonite ... four feet by four feet. We would gesso them with a couple good coats, and then let them dry real good. Then we poured generous sized puddles of bright colored poster paint on the masonite. Lots of colors with some overlapping and running around here and there, but with a minimum of control ... just good color placement. Then the fun part ... we took a big air compressor, and would blow the paint around mixing the colors together. You tried to control the shapes and the wild things the paint would do, but beautiful things would disappear, and new effects and colors would take their place. When they would dry it was completely different again. I loved it. Cliff would varnish them and frame them with a simple frame, and he sold lots of them.

One night, while I was alone in the studio I was staring at one of the abstracts that I had made. I was really loaded from smoking pot all day with Cliff ... and I was trying to decide if I really wanted to varnish this particular one. Parts of the four-foot square painting I liked, but other parts didn't seem to work. Of course the Moody Blues were blasting away because they are one of my all-time favorites. Then, I noticed the shape of a large whale-type looking fish about six inches long. In front of the creature was the backside of a man who looked like he was throwing something. I grabbed my brushes and painted into the things I began to see. It was incredible.

As I looked at the sea creature, suddenly I couldn't see it anymore because it became part of a man's face clear as a bell. I put a little more detail to that and then the painting did both things. It was truly dimensional. In just a section of about ten inches by twelve inches, there was a perfectly composed piece of art that would have made Salvador Dali amazed. It had a huge wave, and several other creatures, and a futuristic looking warrior who popped out at you. It was complete. It had a hundred things happening.

I know I was loaded, but this was not like the plant that I turned into a psychedelic jungle. By the way, a couple days after that LSD trip, I noticed the plant again. It was in reality a scrawny half dead vine with only a couple leaves still alive. But this painting was there, loaded or not … day or night. It blew my mind. On another part of the large abstract painting I saw another smaller picture … then two more. I had to do minimal accentuation … it was already there. I got the one ten by twelve, and about three miniatures out of that first four-foot abstract.

The next day I showed Cliff and it totally amazed him also. He said … "nobody could paint that again in a million years … no matter how hard they tried! Dang Rog!" He helped me carefully cut the little miniature masterpieces out of the large abstract. He had all the tools in his studio. We cut them out perfectly with a small jigsaw. Two of the smallest paintings were only about four inches by five inches … but perfect. I honestly believed they were priceless. I was going to continue to make a whole series of them exactly the same way.

While living at the beach I started connecting with a lot of new people. A pilot hired me to re-hang his collection of paintings in his Malibu beachfront home. Cliff didn't have time so I was handed the job. The middle-aged pilot had literally a couple dozen original oil paintings, mostly of different kinds of aircraft. I know nothing about interior decorating … but he was happy when I finished. Easy money.

Cliff had several girlfriends, and he never changed in his obsession about sex. I walked into the studio one day, and his whole art class was wildly dancing around totally nude. This one old rich guy who was freely jumping around with his little potbelly looked so comical, I had to force myself to not bust out laughing. The music was blasting, and one of the girls tried to get me to join in. It was wild. Cliff orchestrated a couple orgies in his apartment also … never a dull moment.

"KARA JANE"

While living at the beach in Malibu I remembered Topanga Canyon. I was thinking that I needed to look up an old girlfriend who I had met at a party in San Diego. She had told me a wild story about living on Clint Eastwood's land in a Gipsy trailer in Topanga Canyon, and raising a baby African lion. Her name was Sandra, and she had drawn me a little map to her remote hideaway. I still had the little map in my wallet six months later.

I dug out the map and drove along the beach to Topanga Canyon Blvd, which winds all the way through the mountains from the Pacific Ocean to the San Fernando Valley. It's about ten or fifteen miles of winding, mountain and canyon road. I followed directions to the Corral, which was a large nightclub out on a remote stretch of the curvy highway. Next to the Corral was a tiny dirt road, which took you way up in the hills. It was a well-beaten little dirt road because it led to about three different very remote destinations, but it was a trip in itself. There were huge dips and chuck holes and places you needed to drive uphill on the shoulder to avoid dropping straight down into steep gullies. About a half mile back into the wilderness you took a left on another dirt road, which was much nicer because it curved around in a big flat plateau filled with yellow mustard, and then it curved into a beautiful grouping of huge California Oak trees and Sandra's campsite. It was named "The Meadow".

I drove up there in my most recent brown station wagon. It was a 68 Pontiac, and the only meager asset left over from all the months and years of pursuing my Master Plan. Leo and I got out of our car and were immediately besieged by a huge dog. It looked like a German Shepard but much taller and ferocious. I grabbed Leo, whose fur was standing all across his back. The other dog was showing his teeth and acting like he was ready to attack. I heard Sandy screaming at her dog and running toward us. Up behind the dog was a wooden porch like platform about twenty feet long under one of the huge oak trees. Lying on a large bench was a beautiful African lion, intently watching the two dogs square off.

Sandra grabbed her dog and asked me to put Leo back in the car for a few minutes. She said … "It takes Jack a little while to warm up to new people, and especially new dogs. You can let him out after Jack settles down. They'll be all right. So you finally made it up here. What do you think? Isn't it cool? Did you see Kara Jane over there?"

I said … "Yeah, she's a little bigger than the pictures you showed me in San Diego. She's beautiful. Does she just run loose up here?"

"Definitely. Free as a bird. She's a lot bigger because she was only a couple months old in the pictures you saw. It took you awhile to make it up here. As a matter of fact today is Kara Jane's birthday. She is 8 months old today! Let me show you around. What have you been up to all these months?"

Sandra's place at the meadow was one of a kind. Luckily I was born with a camera attached to me ... so I shot a roll of film that day on Kara Jane's birthday. Sandy lived in a trailer that probably was a genuine gypsy trailer. There was another small trailer over by the next large oak tree. The whole camp was under a huge canopy of branches. There were also two tents.

In the center area of the camp was the large raised wooden patio deck, and a couple empty three-foot electrical spools used for tables. There were hanging plants and birdhouses and hummingbird feeders. Sandy had a rope swing, and one of the trees had a platform way up in the branches. There was no running water, no power, but across the little dirt road encircling the camp was the neatest little outhouse I ever sat in. A local carpenter built it for Sandy. It had a shingled roof, paneled wood sides inside and out, a nice framed-in window, and real comfortable custom-made toilet seats. Inside, Sandy had made curtains and hung pictures. Above the door was a sign that said, "Jesus loves you!"

In one of the tents lived a gal from the mid-west named Marcy. She had two wild boys about eleven and twelve years old. They had been living there quite awhile. In the other tent lived an unusual guy named Gustavo. He was good looking with a beard and long dark curly hair and dark complexion. I found out later he was from Argentina. A gal who was in the process of leaving her husband lived with him about half of the time. It was quite a little compound. I loved it. Sandy said Clint Eastwood either owned or leased the land, but she had squatter's rights and had been living there several years.

I spotted a big oak tree about a hundred yards across a side meadow from Sandy's trailer and said to Sandra ... "How about if I build a tree house over in that tree down by the ravine over there? I'm living in an art studio right now ... and I could dig living here."

Sandy said, "No. It's already getting pretty crowded the way it is. I had several other people want to move up here, but I had to tell them no also."

I said ... "How about if I give you $25 bucks a month to build a tree house in that tree over there? It's a little ways away and I can help haul water in my station wagon. You could probably use a few bucks."

"Really, you'll pay me twenty five dollars a month?"

So for the outrageous sum of twenty-five bucks I rented a tree and moved into the meadow. It was far out!

" Let's see all the people who want to kill me … find me now! Yeah if they do … I'll sic Leo and Jack on them! And if that don't work I'll sic Kara Jane … **the one and only totally free African lion in America** … on them!"

CHAPTER 37

"TOPANGA DAYS"

I moved up to "The Meadow" … but continued to paint with Cliff and stay at the studio quite a bit. At Topanga's local lumberyard I started buying plywood, and two-by- sixes, and two-by-fours, and nails, and whatnot. I got to know one of the young workers and without asking, after I paid the bill and was loading up, he would throw a bunch of extra wood into my station wagon. I'm not a thief, but didn't stop him either. I didn't have any money to speak of … and needed a whole lot of wood to make a tree house, and a sturdy ladder, and other supports.

I drew up a real neat plan. It was to be a two-story tree house way up into the big oak tree. My bed was going to be way at the top with a huge plate glass window directly above me, so I could look up through the branches and watch the stars. Over the next few weeks I finished the bottom floor, and a ladder, and had some of the walls framed. Pretty soon it was enough to move in … even though the place didn't have a roof yet. I was temporarily out of money and lumber. I did have a couple sleeping bags, a Coleman stove and an ice cooler. What else does Tarzan or a hippy need? Thank God that it didn't rain one time in six months of tree life.

One evening I was working with Cliff in the studio when Cliff says to me … "Look at this painting I'm working on. This is the one where I discovered the 'Golden Light Theory'." He went on to start explaining a whole bunch of things about this theory he discovered in the painting. It was total nonsense. I thought he was joking with me.

I said, "Cliff … what are you talking about. Are you tripping or something? You're not making sense."

Cliff left his painting and walked over to where I was working and looked right into my eyes … and said real seriously … "Listen Rog,

Fire On the Mountain

Michael and Peter and I were up on a mountain here in Malibu about a month ago and an 'angel of light' appeared to us. I'm not kidding you! It's happening! It's happening right now! It was revealed to us that Peter is an Apostle, and Michael is the Archangel, and I am the Son of David. It's even in my name … Davidson … Son of David … it's all part of the Golden Light Theory."

"Cliff … what in the world are you talking about? Did you and Peter and Mike eat some acid or something? This sounds way out there!"

Cliff responded, "I know it sounds crazy … but it's right here!" He started laughing and laughing, and walked back over to his painting. He continued … "it's the ultimate trip Rog! It's not just a trip … it's the ultimate trip! Listen Rog … you need to get on board … it's what's happening … just ask whatever you want … I lie not, ask whatever you want, and you can have it!!!"

He was laughing and throwing his arms around. It started to make me laugh the way he went on and on … it was absolutely crazy! I said … "OK Cliff … I can have whatever I ask for right? I want an Appaloosa horse. My friend Joe had one and he says they are the best."

I dropped the whole thing and really thought that Cliff must have finally tried some psychedelic drugs. I knew this Michael and Peter for over a year now. They were both pretty different. Cliff told me some pretty kinky things about Michael, which made me think he was probably bi-sexual. I had sold them some pot on previous visits. Michael worked for Wally Findley Galleries who supposedly had galleries in Hawaii, Vegas, Paris and London, as well as L.A. Both of these guys acted real uppity, and I was never sure if I liked them or not. They put together a real neat art show in Malibu at this mansion about a year previous that I helped with. Peter is a gourmet cook and served up some incredible meatballs. Supposedly lots of expensive art was sold that night. It was pretty impressive … but now I suspected that one of them probably fed Cliff some acid. I always knew that Cliff's brain and emotions should never do anything stronger than pot. But it was so crazy … I wasn't sure what was really going on.

Most of the time, in the short run, Cliff seemed pretty normal. But I was concerned. He would from time to time mention "The Golden Light Theory". On the positive side, he was still cranking out paintings, which was good. He did one of a cheetah, which I bought off him … for next to nothing. He still had his art students, and also continued to be romantically involved with the gal who worked for Jason Miller the movie star. His routine was for the most part ... normal Cliff Davidson stuff, if there was such a thing. He denied dropping any psychedelic drugs.

Our occasional artist friend Gary came around the night after Cliff told me to ... "ask for anything I want". Gary says to me ... "Hey Rog, why don't you take some of your paintings and join me at an arts and craft festival. I paid for a booth and this weekend it's happening up in Topanga Canyon. You don't have to pay anything, just help me set up and run the booth. They have it every year and it's really cool."

I agreed and the next day I was following Gary to the art festival, which was named "Topanga Days". I didn't want to sell any of my radical little paintings, because I was positively sure they were worth thousands of dollars. Nevertheless, I brought the larger one along to see what kind of reaction I would get. I figured I needed to do about twenty more before I could really try to market them. I helped Gary set up his easels and racks. He brought about thirty of his paintings. The day was absolutely beautiful and Topanga Canyon had a magical feeling to it. We were way back off the main road and the people came streaming in to the festival. There was some real good energy happening. It was a weekend that I'll never forget.

Everything was full of color ... the sky, the trees, the mountains and cliffs, the booths, the crowds of longhaired bearded dudes, and pretty hippy chicks with their beads and ankle bracelets. There was grandpa and grandma casually walking along, and here comes two cute little girls around ten years old riding through the crowd on their well-mannered spotted ponies. Off to my left was a little valley, and down about a hundred yards was a muscled young guy on a large front-loading tractor. He had about thirty screaming little kids running all around his tractor. He would slowly drop the bucket to the ground, and about half of the kids would pile in. Then he would raise the bucket about eight feet, and dump the kids into a shallow pond that he was parked next to. You could hear the screams of joy echo through the canyon, and the kids were absolutely covered with mud. What a breathe of fresh air this place was.

Something was happening. It felt like the air itself was tingling. The sounds and colors, and the smell of sage seemed to penetrate me. It was not a momentary thing ... it was all day. It felt natural and supernatural at the same time. I didn't understand and I didn't care. I felt totally alive. I drove back to the studio to pick something up and the moment Cliff saw me he said ... "What happened to you???"

"What do you mean?"

He said ... "You're face is shining! Something happened! What's going on?"

I didn't have an answer. I told him it was just a really cool festival, and that I had to pick up a couple things. We were going to camp out all night and I needed to get back.

We had a great time the first day, but Gary didn't sell any of his paintings. The next morning it was getting real hot by 10 AM. Gary said to me ... "Well, my painting aren't exactly selling like hotcakes ... so screw these people ... if they don't like my art, we'll just have to sell them some **watermelon**! It's going to get hot as blazes today. We can probably make a kill selling slices of cold watermelon! 'MAN THE FORT'! I'm going to go find us some melon."

Gary took off and came back in less than an hour with a pile of watermelon in his car. He was laughing and said ... "I drove down to the fruit stand by the ocean, and told the owner that we were raising money for a Catholic charity by selling watermelon. He dropped his price to a nickel a pound! What a chump!"

We sold watermelon all day. Gary was charging like seventy-five cents for a slice. I thought it was too much money, but it was fun having a hot item. I was sitting there at our booth in the bright hot sun, when Grandpa Walton from the hit TV series, came walking up. I found out later that he lives in Topanga, and has a cool outdoor theater for aspiring actors at his place. He said after a couple bites ... "The watermelon sure isn't very cold." (The local stores had completely sold out of ice.) " Sorry Mr. Greer." Our "hot" item was definitely not cold enough.

A few booths down they were actually selling something cold ... real nice cold beer. I absolutely love cold beer on a hot day. I spent some of our overflowing watermelon profits on Anhieser Bush, and by mid-afternoon was feeling my oats. People were going through our isles looking at Gary's paintings. I had my one and only painting displayed on an easel, and I saw a man and his daughter looking at it. The girl looked about twelve years old and she was pointing at something in my painting. Then the father looked real close and started pointing at something to show his daughter. They were looking at it for about five or ten minutes. That's a long time. I knew the painting hooked them in.

About that same time I heard someone making a ruckus behind me. It was a man who was staggering around and looking at Gary's paintings. He was a medium sized guy, and had a real tall, rough looking man with him. The drunker was snarling at a painting and said … "aaahhh … this is total crap!!!"

Gary was sitting right nearby listening to his cruel public.

Then the two guys walked past a couple more paintings and our "smart ___ art critic" says … "This guy needs to take up **carpentry**!!!"

I turned around and yelled at them … "Hey, it's time for you to get out of here. Keep your opinion to yourself and get going!"

The loudmouth came walking right up to me and said … "Well ____ you too!"

I told him, "Listen … I think you're a total jerk for badmouthing my friend's paintings … and if you don't get moving out of here right now, I'm going to bust your ____ing jaw. Your big friend here might help you … but not before I knock the living ____ out of you!"

The man squinted his eyes, snarled, looked up at his friend, and then back at me. I stayed totally focused on the art critic. My adrenalin was doing a great job. I didn't even look at the tall guy to see how he was reacting. I was going to deliver my promise any second. Then the drunk looked up at his friend again, and back at me, and said, "____ it!" He turned around and they both joined the crowd walking through the festival.

Gary came running up to me. He said … "Roger, that was the coolest thing I ever saw! Thanks for sticking up for me. Man, you got a righteous ton of guts. You backed that ____er right down! Did you see me behind those two guys? I was stabbing the butcher knife into the table the whole time you was in his face!"

I said … "No I didn't see that. I think it's definitely time for another beer! What a loser!"

In a little while Gary took off again to see if he could find some ice somewhere. Our watermelon was getting way-way too warm. While he was gone a man with a foreign accent came running up and started yelling at me … "I'm taking all these watermelons! Where is the guy who bought them?"

I said … "Who are you?"

He said real fast with his accent … "I own the fruit stand on Pacific Coast Highway, and this man comes yesterday to me, and says to me … real nice … that he is selling watermelon for a Catholic charity. I give him my price, and then people come and tell me he is selling **my** watermelon for a lot of money at the festival, and no ____ing church charity!"

He started loading up the remaining watermelons, and I didn't stop him. He drove off in a huff. Gary came back a little while later. "Where's all the watermelon?" (He was having a tough day.) I didn't tell him he got what he deserved, but that's what I was thinking. We finished the day off drinking beer. What a trip!

The whole thing really amused me. The magical feeling in the air persisted in spite of the recent hassles. I felt strangely relaxed and totally peaceful. I felt joy. It wasn't the brews. It was in the air!

"What is going on?"

CHAPTER 38

"KIMO JO"

It had been a great festival. I helped Gary pack up all his stuff and we took off in different directions. I had previously discovered the OPO. It was the local Topanga tavern. In cowboy days of yesteryear, it had been a real post office ... but was now converted into a rustic and rowdy tavern called the Old Post Office ... or OPO for short. I walked through the door, and was immediately loudly hailed ... "Roger!! What are you doing here??? Son-of-a-_____!!"

My old New York friend, Frank, came running up through the crowded bar, and gave me a bear hug. I was shocked to see him way out here in the boon docks. Many moons had long gone since I last saw Frank, and then that was in the middle of several million people in central Los Angeles. I said ... "I can't believe that I would run into you up here! Hey Frank ... this is really cool! Dang, what have you been up to?" I was really happy to see him!

A big old lumberjack looking hippy came over to us, and complimented ... "Hey dudes ... that reunion was down-home right-on cool. It's nice to have friends!"

Frank and I got a pitcher of beer and sat at a table. We caught each other up on all the latest, while the jukebox blasted away. I told him that I quit dealing. Frank had always told me that I was totally crazy for smuggling and cross-country trafficking. He had followed most of my career from afar. Now, he was saying ... "Things have changed for me Rog, and I've picked up where you left off!"

I said ... "Oh no ... I hope not!"

He didn't give any details, but we had a great visit. As we're sitting there at the small round wooden table, I was telling Frank and the friend that he was with, about my concerns about Cliff and his "Golden Light

Theory". I told him ... "It's really a trip. Cliff told me the other night, 'Ask for anything you want, and you can have it.' I told him I wanted an Appaloosa horse."

Exactly when I told Frank about asking for a horse, I felt this strange sensation like little bells were going off in the atmosphere or something. It was another deja vu type feeling. Like this all happened before, but it was different than that. I told Frank ... "Did you feel that?"

He laughed at me, and didn't know what I was talking about. I didn't exactly know what I was talking about. It was just something weird. But at the same time, it was totally real and tangible. Like another dimension had momentarily surrounded us. I lie not.

We stayed in the OPO all evening having a blast. As it approached closing time, the drunken art critic from the festival came over to us. He was about ten times more blasted than earlier in the day, when we had had our exchange of opinions. The bar was crowded all night, and I didn't even see him until he showed up at our table. He was so drunk that it was absolutely pathetic. Now, he was trying to be my friend.

He put his arm on my shoulder and said ... "You're all right! Are you for real? Maybe! Maybe not! Those mother ____ers took my license away. How about you give me a ride to my place? I'll let you ride my horse. I got this stallion ... a beautiful stallion. He's the best dang horse in California. You think I'm kidding? Come on give me a ride to my place."

I told him to forget it. "You acted like a total idiot this afternoon, and now you want to be my friend? You need to lighten up!"

I tried to get rid of him. As they were closing up the place, he was still hanging on to us, and bragging about his horse. I didn't even believe he had a horse, or anything else he said. Somebody in the bar overheard me, and told me ... "Yeah, Alfonso has some acreage here in the Canyon, and he does have a nice horse. Somebody needs to give the dumb ____ a ride before he kills himself."

I said to Alfonso the drunk ... "So you really have a horse?"

He staggered around again like a classic stumbling drunkard ... grabbed my shoulder with his hand, steadied himself, and got real close to my face. He squinted his eyes like he did a lot, and was being all dramatic. It was pretty funny. He said ... "I told you a thousand times that I got the best horse in California ... and I bet you fifty bucks that you can't sit on him for ten seconds!"

I told him, "OK ... it's almost two o'clock in the morning, and I'll give you a ride to your place before you stumble around in front of a car. Do you even remember where you live?"

"____ you!"

We piled into my car and took off. A couple miles up Topanga Canyon Blvd we turned up a side street to the right, and followed the windy uphill road a short way to his place. It was real black outside with no streetlights or anything. We parked and I followed Alfonso around his two-story house to a pasture in the back. There was a large wooden gate, and the rest of the fence was chain link. Standing behind the gate was the silhouette of a horse.

I told Alfonso, "Look, I don't have fifty bucks to bet you, but if I can sit on your horse for ten seconds ... I want to get a foal out of him ... OK? I was pretty inebriated myself, and was positive I could hang on for ten seconds.

He said, "Get on. But, first I want to tell you ... that he bucked off a dozen people in seconds, and he broke a rodeo riders leg ... but most of all he hates drunks!"

We didn't have a saddle, or a bridle, or anything but a short rope. I climbed over the fence next to the horse, looped the short rope around his neck ... and then jumped up on his bare back. The horse just sat there as relaxed as I felt. I started kidding Alfonso after about two minutes ... "Hey, this is pretty dang comfortable. What's the deal? When is ten seconds up? I don't think your horse wants to break my leg. Maybe he's too tired. You owe me a horse Alfonso."

I stayed up on the horse, and Alfonso was acting mind-boggled. He said ... "That's unbelievable. He's never been like this! I don't believe it! Listen, Kimo Jo is an Indian horse. They are one-man horses, and son-of-a-____, you got yourself a horse. I believe in stuff like this. That's your horse now!"

I told him I was living up in the meadow by Sandy's place, and didn't have any place to keep a horse ... and besides we had a lion. Alfonso said I could keep him where he was for free. He said he would get me his papers, because Kimo Jo was a registered Appaloosa, sired by Double Tree Jo, a champion horse in Arizona, owned by Alfonso's father-in-law. He only wanted $500 for bringing the foal to California, and raising him for five years. I could pay the money off in small payments whenever.

He sounded sober now, and said ... "Do you want Kimo Jo? It looks like he wants you!"

I said ... "Absolutely!"

I got to bed in my tree house real late, and was out like a light. In the morning, I woke up to the sounds of birds and honeybees. A beekeeper had a whole bunch of beehives pretty close to my tree. I never got stung, but you could hear them whiz past all the time. I lay there in my sleeping bag, and started thinking ... "That's a pretty big coincidence. A few days ago Cliff Davidson, (aka the Son of David), is acting totally bizarre ... but tells me to ask for anything I want, and I can have it. I tell him ... 'OK', I want an Appaloosa horse. When I told Frank, who shows up out of nowhere, about that conversation, I have a strange little experience like I entered "The Twilight Zone" ... and that happened the very second I mentioned an Appaloosa horse. Then, before **the very same** night is over ... I own an Appaloosa horse. But, not just an ordinary horse ... a young purebred stallion with a great bloodline, with no money down, and a place to keep him for free. This is crazy! What's going on here? Can this all be coincidence? What are the odds?"

Plus, the coincidence is even a little more intense, because the reason I wanted an Appaloosa in the first place, was because of my friend Joe in San Diego. He had an Appaloosa in Ramona, CA, and told me all about the breed. Now, this morning I wake up owning a horse named Kimo Jo, who is nicknamed **Joe**.

Something is definitely going on in my life ... and I don't have a clue to what it all means! But ... "Oh well ... it sure is a neat horse! Hey Chief George ... I hope you are thoroughly enjoying the happy hunting grounds on your faithful spotted warhorse!"

CHAPTER 39

"TREE RENT"

It was so cool living at the meadow. Sandy would buy Kara Jane chicken necks from a butcher. He gave them to her real cheap. She would get hundreds of pounds. At night Kara took off and slept in the hills somewhere. We didn't even know where. She would come back to camp every morning. She was literally a totally free female African lion. I was positive that she was the only one … on either American continent.

Sandy told me the story of how she ended up with Kara. She said, "I would baby-sit for this couple in the San Fernando Valley who owned exotic animals. They used them in TV commercials and whatnot. They had this one baby cougar, which you might have seen on the Lincoln Mercury commercials. It's the one that shows the cat on top of the dealership sign … and then it goes 'Meow'. That was their baby cougar.

Well, this couple went out of town for a while. While they were gone, some neighbors called the animal control people. They filed a complaint that my friends had illegal exotic animals, and that the animals were being neglected. The county came in and confiscated all of them and took them to the animal shelter. While the cats were in the dog pound, the baby cougar died of distemper.

After only two weeks, my friends came back and they sued the animal control people. They proved that they did have all the proper permits, and also had people coming every day to feed and care for the animals. The County settled out of court for ten thousand dollars, and gave them two or three other large animals. One of them was a baby lion only a couple weeks old. It was Kara Jane.

I continued to baby-sit for them, and also helped feed the baby lion. It was supposed to get fed every two hours around the clock. About the second time I came over, I saw that Kara Jane wasn't being fed regularly enough. I really got on my friends case about it. Then, the third time I came over the baby lion was barely hanging on ... and I told my friends ... 'I'm taking Kara Jane home before she dies!' I brought her up here to the meadow, and she's been here ever since."

My dog Leo never paid any attention to Kara Jane. Kara was already much bigger than my Golden Retriever when I moved up to the meadow. The only thing Leo paid attention to was the tennis ball that I would throw for him. He would chase it down twenty-four hours a day if you let him. One day he was intently watching my hand to see when I would release the ball. Kara Jane was intently watching Leo. She crept up slowly behind him, and playfully swiped Leo in the hindquarter. Leo spun around and tore into Kara Jane like he was the "King of the Jungle".

I never saw an animal move so fast in my life. Kara literally jumped backwards about fifteen feet, and climbed up on some tall benches. Someone took a picture right as all this was happening. I hope I can find it. Leo immediately turned around, and continued to focus on the ball ... like nothing happened. I was proud of him ... but Kara Jane could have eaten him for lunch instead of chicken necks if she wanted to. Bob Pino got 21 stitches from playing a little too rough with Kara Jane.

I was getting a little tired of being broke so often. After all, I had to feed a horse, and a dog, and pay tree rent every month. I had met a guy in Malibu through Cliff who would buy pounds of pot from me in the past. He owned a swimming pool maintenance company. He and his wife had a real neat house in Malibu Canyon, and to my surprise they smoked twice as much pot as Cliff. My pool man friend would fire up a joint before breakfast, and it was all day long. I don't know how he functioned, but he did. He wore shades. I ran into Ed one day, and he wanted me to score him some more pot. I told him that I was semi-retired, but that I would make a couple phone calls down in San Diego.

I called my old friend Rich, who had pulled the 38 on me ... (I'll always remember that). It had been over a year, but he assured me that I could pick up four kilos the next day. I had Ed front me the money and off I went. Hello San Diego. It was good to see Rich again. We hadn't done much business together after I started working with Ernesto. He said ... "Hey it's weird that you called after all this time ... because this morning your partner Joe called and wanted to know if I've ever heard from you. I told him, as a matter of fact, you are coming this afternoon to pick up something. What's happening, did you have a fall out with your partner?"

I gave him the short version, paid him, and took the four kilos out to my station wagon. Just as I was ready to get into the car, which was parked in the rear alley, Craig and Joe came running around the side of the house. They yelled at me to stop, and just then a black and white cop car pulled into the alley about four houses down. I sat the kilos down on the front seat. There were two cops in the car, and they stopped their patrol car, and sat there down the alley watching us. The kilos were just sitting there in plain sight in two brown bags.

I walked over to where Craig and Joe were ... "Hey we better be cool, or we're about ready to get busted. Don't you see that cop car there watching us? I have some kilos sitting on the front seat."

They both started yelling at me ... "How come you took off with all the money?" How come this and how come that!

If that cop wouldn't have been there, I know that Joe would have fired on me. No way could I have taken both of them, even though Craig isn't a fighter. Besides, I didn't want to fight either of them. I told them ... "I left you with an ounce of coke Joe, and a bus ticket. At the time it was all the extra cash we had. I left Craig with half of the last load in Tennessee. That load never got paid for, and I'm the one on the hook for it. They are looking for me on that load ... not either one of you guys. You should have made out real good on that Craig! Didn't you give Joe any of the money?"

I saw Joe look surprised, and glance over at Craig. I added ... "I just had enough of everything going sour. I wanted everything to work for us, but it wasn't. I tried to get it going again here in San Diego, but something wasn't right, and I ended up walking away from a deal losing everything. I've been scraping around in survival mode up by L.A."

I casually glanced down the alley ... "We better keep our voices down and act normal, cause for some reason the cops are still sitting there watching us."

"Joe said ... "How many kilos do you have in the car?"
"Four"
He said ... "We're taking half of them."
I said ... "Let's just keep talking normal until the cop drives past, and then I'll give you one of the bags. This thing could still turn into a

bust."

We talked about four or five more minutes, and pretty soon the cop car slowly drove past us. We acted like old friends, which I wish we still were ... until the black and white made a right turn out of the other end of the alley.

I walked over to the car, and handed one of the bags to Joe. I jumped into the drivers seat and took off. As I was driving away I heard Joe yell ... "Why should you get to keep the car?"

"Man ... what a mess. Now, two of my old partners are completely down on me, and they basically just ripped me off. There goes most of the pool man profit. It's a miracle I didn't get busted. It's a miracle the cop drove up at the **exact** second he did. What a coincidence that is! It could have been real ugly otherwise. They probably saved me from a whipping. Joe is no lightweight. What a coincidence that they would call Rich on the very day I was going there! It's been way over a year since I even talked to Rich. Craig and Joe hardly knew him at all. This is too weird!"

This must be another sign that I'm not supposed to be dealing. It must be! Look at the ten seconds in Mexico when Steve and I got busted. There is something totally fishy about that. It was impossible. Then Ernesto loses three loads in a row. Not likely. On the heels of all that ... I get a load of bogus rip off kilos. A kid gets hammered by a drunk driver, and loses a car full of our kilos. People putting a contract out on me! Now, I try to buy a couple stinking little kilos for a friend ... and I almost get busted and pounded on! How much clearer does it have to get? There is more going on here than cops and robbers! "I need to completely quit dealing this time!"

I drove back to Malibu and delivered half of my pot. Ed paid me and I still made several hundred dollars on the two remaining kilos. Most of the money he gave me was in twenties in a big wad with tape around it. I had a lid in my shirt pocket, and decided to stop and see Cliff. I had been drinking quite a bit, and we decided to go somewhere. I can't even remember where ... but as I'm driving along PCH I hear a cop car blast his siren at me for a couple seconds. I looked in my mirror, and there were the famous flashing red lights.

I pulled over, and the cop made me get out of the car. He said he was stopping me because I was weaving. I had forgot about the lid in my shirt pocket. The officer was just about ready to give me a sobriety test, when he noticed the big bulge in my shirt.

"What do you have in your shirt pocket?"

Boom! ... I'm busted by the Malibu police for possession, and possession for sales. They added the sales charge because of the taped up wad of money I was carrying. I didn't have any ID on me, because I had long ago lost my wallet with my driver's license in it. Cliff was all scared, but I told him not to tell them my name. I wouldn't tell them anything. They booked me, and photographed me as "John Doe". Cliff's girlfriend bailed him out a few hours later, but I spent the night in the Malibu City jail.

In the morning, with a big hangover, I cooled off, and finally told them my real name. Then, I could make a phone call ... so I called Debbie back in New York. I told her I was in jail, and asked if she could send me some money to bail out. They put me in chains along with several other prisoners to transport us in a little bus to the LA County Jail. It was really weird to look out the bus window, and see all the surfers, and girls in bikinis, and people going about life as usual down that familiar stretch of Pacific Coast Highway. Everything looks so different when you're in handcuffs, **and a chain on your leg.** What has my life come to?

LA County jail was really something. It was intense. I was finally busted in America. As we got processed in, a guy ahead of me in the long line of prisoners was having a real hard time. As the cops would read his charges, they would say ... "Oh ... we have an assault and battery on a police officer here!" ... and then they would knock him around. They stripped us, and showered us, and made us "spread them". Then they gave us some jailhouse clothes, a bedroll, and took me to a cellblock. The place seemed huge. As we passed this one oriental cop, who looked absolutely super clean-cut and healthy, he said ... "Now don't forget to go to church this Sunday." He smiled at me, and there seemed to actually be a sparkle in his eyes. I remembered that. Finally, I was put in a cell with two other guys. I was about to spend my second night locked up in America. I had avoided this completely until now.

I was just getting settled into my bunk, when someone yelled at me to roll up. I was getting bailed out. So, after another round of protracted processing ... I finally saw my pool man friend Ed. He said it took him over six hours to get me out. It was almost midnight. We went to a downtown restaurant, and ate steak and eggs. It tasted so good! It really means a **lot** when somebody rescues you from jail … I'm sure many people can relate.

The next day I went to the Malibu jail, and sprung Leo out of his dog jail. "What kind of humans do you hang with anyway?" He had been locked up in a kennel just outside of the jail building. I also was able to get my wad of money back, which helped. They had dropped the sales charge. I called Debbie in New York, and told her that I got out … and thanked her for sending me the money, which was waiting for me at Western Union.

Debbie wanted to come to California and get back together. I told her it wouldn't work, because if nothing else, I was living in a tree house. That didn't bother her at all. I told her "no". I went back to Topanga, and worked some more on my pad. I also spent a lot of time working with my horse. The only tack I had was a rope, and I would run him around the field and sit on him bareback. He was a headstrong son of a gun … but we got along. I finally got a bridle, and would ride him up in the hills. I loved it. I got two cats, and named one of them "Budweiser", and the other one "K & B". They disappeared after awhile. Maybe Kara Jane had something to do with that.

I went to court as time clicked on, and was offered a "diversion" … which meant that I could go through a drug program, and the arrest would not show on my record. It was a program for first-time offenders. I took it and was assigned a probation officer. I had to report to him for six months. I went to AA meetings weekly. They were interesting. Somehow, after a couple months I was totally broke again. I called Debbie, and she sent me some more of her savings.

Cliff shocked me about this time, and moved his art studio to Marina Del Rey. It was upstairs above a popular tavern called "The Glenn Bar". The place was right on the border of Venice Beach. The studio was much larger than the converted Malibu garage. As usual Cliff fixed it up really neat. Most of his art students continued with him even after the move. Cliff's ex-con student Gene was there all the time. I spent a lot of time in the new studio also, but didn't do any more painting. Cliff was still acting real strange, still talking about the "Golden Light Theory" … and other weird stuff. I was worried.

One of the Malibu crowd was at the studio one evening. It was a gal named Alita. She was a beautiful former model, probably in her mid to late twenties like I was. I had met her a couple times before in Malibu, but this time we connected, and I spent some time with her in her nice Hollywood apartment. She told me a couple stories ... one very sad ... and the other one very disturbing.

She said that she had lived with a man who was in the movie industry. I think he was a director or something. They had a son together, but things were not working out between them. When Alita broke it off, her boyfriend committed suicide right in front of her. He shot himself in the stomach, and slowly bled to death in their bathroom, while Alita frantically tried to get help. She said it was horrible. That had happened when her son was two years old, and he was now six. She said it had taken years for her to get over it.

More recently she said that Cliff, and Michael, and Peter had spent the weekend at her place after a party. When they left, she said her six-year-old son Mark, came to her and said ... "Mommy, Michael put his hand in my pants and stuck his finger up my butt!"

That blew my mind. Now I was positive that I didn't like the arch-angel, or his apostle friend. It made me furious. They were coming around Cliff's new studio all the time. At least Michael was. These guys are bad news ... sick news. What a slime ball Michael is!

On a brighter note, I was loving Topanga Canyon. My oak tree was right on the edge of a steep ravine. Long before I ever took up residence, someone had tied a big rope way up high into the tree. There were two or three places that you could take off from, and then swing out over the ravine. It was fun. There was one branch, higher up that was the most radical take-off spot. One of my favorite new friends in the Canyon was Little Rick, and he told me that several people were hurt trying the swing from there. One guy flew off the rope and broke his hip. They put a pin in the bone. Naturally I had to try it, but alas ... no problem. I swung out over the ravine like a pro. I did it a number of times.

One day someone told me about going berserk on "Maddog", which is Mogen David 20-20. It is cheap wine that is twenty percent alcohol. I had never tried it before. Besides, I'm really not much of a wine drinker, but I was in the mood to go berserk. By the time a couple of us drank a bottle or two, we ended up at my tree house. One of my friends pulled the rope over and swung out into the wild blue yonder yelling Tarzan or something. I told him to try the higher take off spot, but he said, "Lead on Leon!"

I decided to show them some of my skills ... and Mogen David and me grabbed the rope, and climbed up to our platform. The rope has about three big knots in it to help with the grip. Like before I took off and went sailing. Only this time there must have been a little slack in the rope. I started to slide down the rope in an instant to the next knot. I was holding so tight that it tore some skin off my hands, and when the rope was fully extended it gave a final snap. It shot me right out into the air. I flew over the top of a little tree below, and seconds later hit the rocky hard dirt.

As soon as I hit I knew I was in trouble. I had landed on my right arm and hand. I rolled over, and knew instantly that something was broke. My wrist and hand was at a strange looking angle. Both my wrist and thumb were broke. I actually moved the bone back in place with my other hand, so that my hand was again pointing in the right direction. It hurt like the dickens. I just held it and climbed up out of the ravine.

Lucky for me, my pool man friend Ed came walking up out of nowhere seconds after the fall. He had his nice shiny pickup truck, and drove me to a hospital in Santa Monica. It was the last time I ever bought any MD 20. However, on the ride to the hospital, I finished off the bottle. It helped kill the pain a little. It was a long miserable drive, but thank God

... **Ed comes to the rescue again!**

I called Debbie in New York, and told her if she wanted to check out Topanga Canyon with me ... we would see what happens. I was feeling super guilty for spending her money. So a few days later she joined me in the half built tree house. From a fancy apartment in Manhattan to an oak tree. She did real good ... right? Actually, I was very surprised and impressed with how well, and how quickly Debbie adapted to life in Topanga Canyon. She became good friends with Marcy living in the tent with her two kids. She got along with everyone including Kara Jane, and didn't complain about roughing it at the meadow. Most American ladies can't survive without all the conveniences ... like hot showers, running water to brush your teeth ... and how about, literally having a roof over your head. The twinkling stars put us to sleep at night. The coyotes would howl. Sometimes it sounded like a hundred of them at once. Friends dropped in, and would sleep over ... plenty of floor space.

Fire On the Mountain

From time to time my brother Rick lived with us in the tree. Frank stayed up in the meadow a bunch also. It was cool. The rent was right.

CHAPTER 40

"SIGN AFTER SIGN"

Up in the meadow there was quite a collection of humanity. The reason Sandy didn't want any new residents … was because Marcy lived in a tent with her two rambunctious kids, Gustavo from Argentina lived in another tent, there was a run-away teenage boy, who slept under the stars in a sleeping bag, Gustavo's girlfriend was usually found in the mix … and then Little Rick lived in the pump house. The pump house was a small concrete building about eight feet wide and fifteen feet long. At one time it had irrigation pumps inside, but now was empty and abandoned. It was partially hidden on a slope around fifty yards away from Sandy's trailer, and about the same distance from my tree house. Little Rick, who is a very talented primitive artist, converted it into his tiny cave like home … his escape from civilization. He also had a girlfriend or two who would be in camp from time to time. So, in addition to all the traffic that I brought along, the meadow was full of action and interaction, different species of people, campfires, rap-sessions, wild parties, dogs, and of course Kara Jane. I got along great with everyone.

Talking about escapes from civilization, one day I got in a conversation with Gustavo, whom I noticed never left camp at all. Back in the meadow, way down the dirt roads of Topanga Canyon was like another world. You would never guess that millions of people, and a huge metropolis lay within a few minutes … traveling as the crow flies.

Coming down the mountain at night into the San Fernando Valley you can see a vast ocean of lights. It's beautiful really … but those twinkling lights are only a tiny fraction of what actually surrounds the mountains in LA County. Gustavo **never** left our remote hideout, and his girlfriend would bring him whatever he needed. I asked him about that.

He said, "I come from a wealthy family in Argentina. A couple years ago I decided to go to Europe. I traveled all over by myself and had a great time. Then, I decided to go to Asia, so I bought a train ticket east. When I got to Turkey I got robbed. They took almost everything I had including a very expensive camera, and all my money. I eventually was able to call home to my family, and they sent me some more money. It took about two weeks. Finally, I continued my trip on the train, but a few short days later, way inside India … I was robbed again.

This time they beat me up, and really took everything. All my money, my wallet, my backpack with my clothes, and everything I had. I mean everything. I tried to get back on the train, but they wouldn't let me on. I finally jumped on another train, which was jam-packed with people. No one spoke English or Spanish. I traveled all day on that train, and didn't even know which direction or where it was going. They finally discovered I didn't have a ticket and kicked me off the train. It was a completely desolate place where they left me. I didn't have any idea where I was, so I started walking. Wherever I was … it was like the moon.

I was somewhere in the remote countryside of India with just tiny little mud hut type villages. They had no electricity or telephones or anything. It could have been five thousand years ago. The people probably lived exactly the same. I walked and walked. I began to starve, and some villagers finally took me in and fed me. They looked at me like I was from another planet. I would stay awhile, and then walk to the next village. I wandered for over a month, and lost so much weight that I would start to hallucinate. I finally found my way to a larger village, and when I tried to get help, the villagers tied me to a post in the middle of the village by a well. I think they thought I was crazy or on drugs. I was tied right there like a wild animal for several days, and they finally let me go.

Gustavo & Kara

I eventually made it to a city. There were so many people it was incredible. Everywhere you moved, every inch there were people... thousands and thousands of people. It took months of living like a starving rat to get out of India. I flew to Los Angeles, and someone brought me here to Topanga Canyon. I'm going to go back to Argentina, but I can't handle civilization yet. I can't be around a lot of people. I can't even stand to listen to a radio. I have to stay here."

LEONARDO

As mentioned, my friend Frank came up and stayed in the Meadow several times, as well as my brother Rick. They loved it. Life was never dull at the Meadow. I got to know a whole bunch of the Topanga Canyon locals ... old friends and new friends. One of my favorite new friends was a tall crazy Viet Nam vet named Spike. He started teaming up with Marcy. We would take our gals to the beach, and to the OPO, and of course to the Corral ... which was the "out in the boonies" nightclub about a mile down our dirt road (where it met Topanga Canyon Blvd). In Viet Nam, Spike had been wounded, and still had some left over shrapnel in his body. He was able to get several prescriptions for the ever so popular Quaaludes, which on the street are simply called "luds". A couple times I got totaled with Spike. Alcohol and Quaaludes are a deadly combination. Spike found that out about a year or so later. He was involved in a fatal head-on which killed a well known local artist.

While living back in this radical little world in Topanga Canyon, I started having some real unusual dreams at night. I don't remember most of them, but I would wake up in my tree house really shaken and wondering ..."what's it all about?" I would think about all the strange coincidences that had happened ... some of them recently, and some going way back. Was there a pattern? Is some kind of cosmic force, or God, trying to communicate with me? Who and what is God? Or is this all simply coincidence. The Appaloosa horse. The busts. The heads or tails coincidences? And how about the abstract crosses appearing at such a pivotal point ... which, by the way, actually led me here to Topanga. How about Colorado Steve's experience in Boulder, meeting a shorthaired Jesus? I heard on the radio that the hitchhiker who claimed to be Jesus was reported to do his last disappearing act in San Diego. "He made it cross-country! Right on!" It was all too crazy. Maybe those twenty-one hits of acid permanently blew some circuits in my brain!

I knew I wasn't **totally** crazy, because I could function in everyday life. In fact, my pool man friend came up to the meadow, and asked me if I wanted to buy his business. His wife and he had decided to sell their Malibu home and move to Oregon. Ed explained that I could work off the maintenance route by paying him half of the monthly gross for a year, or something like that. It was a good route, and I immediately went into training. For about a month I went with Ed to all his customers. He would pick me up, smoke his second or third joint, and off we'd go cleaning pools. The route was spread out from Malibu to Beverly Hills. I learned to test the chemicals, clean the tile, vacuum, and eventually do magic with a pool net. I enjoyed it ... and figured that maybe someday I could own a shiny red pickup, and a house in Malibu Canyon.

Soon, I was out cleaning the pools on my own. Ed and his wife were planning to look for a house in Oregon the next week. I had a ring full of keys to million dollar homes all over the place. Some of Ed's customers were really famous. I had the key to Aaron Spelling's place, right on the beach in Malibu. I would unlock the gate and go through his garage, past a Rolls Royce, past a refrigerator absolutely filled to capacity with beer and pop, and then to a closed in court yard type swimming pool. I would see his very young wife, and two-year-old kid once in awhile … but I never saw the much older producer of "Mod-Squad". However, one day I shook hands with his next-door neighbor, Lloyd Bridges, as he was getting into a motor home. I had watched dozens of episodes of Sea Hunt as a kid on TV … and I can totally relate to his son … the not so big Leboski … or better known as "The Dude".

As a matter of fact, I had several other stars on the pool route. I took care of Billy Preston's pool up in Topanga, Ed McMahon's pool, which actually turned into his X-wife's pool, and my favorite customer was the movie star Daren McGavin. We had two of his homes, which were located in Pacific Palisades and Beverly Hills. Most people write fan mail to the stars, but one day I had the honor of getting some fan mail from a real celebrity. He cussed out "whoever is doing my pool" in very sarcastic, colorful, and original prose. I will forever keep and value the two page informational letter. I loved watching him on TV also. He stared in the series "Night Stalker" where he played the aggressive reporter tracking down modern day vampires and whatnot. Anyway, the next week after the letter, he gave me a friendly wave from his study. Maybe his shrink helped him through the trauma of his pool man not putting his "customized" plastic skimmer basket, which was an upside down vegetable strainer, in the skimmer properly. Hollywood personalities can be very high maintenance.

I also got to know another member of the Hollywood crowd real well. His house was one of the houses that you could see on the edge of the cliffs as you drive down Pacific Coast Highway. He was a real movie producer and director in a little different category than Aaron Spelling. He made XXX rated porn movies. When I would go to his house I would see Walter Mathow walking a big sheep dog through the neighborhood. I forget the director's name, but he had me do some repairs on his backwash line to his pool filter. While I was talking to him, I mentioned that

I also do a little artwork. I brought him some of my drawings later. He wanted me to paint a marquee for his newest movie. It was titled "The Sex Giant of the Amazon". The concept was to have a real muscular guy with a big bulge, standing like he was royalty, with a blond kneeling beside him on one side, and a brunette kneeling on his other side, both looking up at him with adoration.

He had all the cameras and everything, so I brought Frank and Debbie up to his house to be our models. Frank was about half way in shape compared to the year before, but he was still pretty muscular. I had Debbie pose as one of the ladies … and we'd fake the blond. A few days later I had a couple eight by ten photos given to me, and I started working on the project. I was having a hard time getting started with it, so I put it off. Then, after a couple weeks I started feeling guilty for not getting back to him with something.

One day I was driving down Pacific Coast Highway with Debbie and another friend when I remembered the porn director. It was early evening, and I had been a little excessively drinking. I told Debbie that I was going to pay a visit to my director friend, and put forth a couple of my opinions. She tried to talk me out of it … but no way. I knocked on his door, and he walked out in his front yard to talk to me. I told him … "I tried to put something together for you, but basically it's not happening. As a matter of fact, I don't even want a bunch of old perverts jacking off to my art work."

I went on and on, and was pretty insulting about his business. Probably more along the lines of extremely insulting. The director was half smiling though. For some reason, when I get drunk I often get people laughing. I told him … "I'll clean your pool … but ____ the Sex Giant of the Amazon!" He didn't quit the pool route, which was good.

When I was down visiting Cliff at his new studio a few weeks later, he was starting to **really, really** act strange. For one thing, he wasn't doing any painting to speak of, and most of his students, if not all, had quit. He continued to talk about the Golden Light Theory, and a bunch of other crap. I was so concerned about him that I asked my brother Rick to stay there with Cliff, who was actually living in the studio. The studio had a nice large bathroom with a shower, and was self-contained. Cliff had an extra bed at the end of the building, and for meals they served edible food at the tavern below. Rick is a great welder, and Cliff had told us about a local metal fabricating shop, almost next door to The Glenn Bar. My brother met the owner and got a job there. (Thirty-some years later he still welds in Marina Del Rey.) But at this point, he stayed with Cliff for several weeks in the art studio. I wanted Rick to keep an eye on my friend.

The next few months became so bizarre that I hardly know where to begin. For one thing, I had originally been totally convinced that Cliff's weird behavior was drug related … but after the strange coincidence of him telling me to ask for anything I wanted … and I could have it … and then me asking for an Appaloosa horse … that whole episode with it's own surrounding phenomena, of Topanga Days magic, Alfonso the drunk, Frank at the OPO, and then waking up with a five year old pure-bred Appaloosa … that whole thing kept coming back, over and over, and it was blowing my mind. How could that all be coincidence. I became convinced that there were probably drugs involved, but that something else was going on also. It seemed like some of it was good, and some of it was definitely evil, because Cliff was increasingly losing touch with reality. What is going on?

As I mentioned, I was in addition having strange dreams up in the Canyon at night, and then strange thoughts started popping into my head on a regular basis. One day in the meadow Frank and a bunch of us were sitting around in camp, when Frank told us a story that happened in his childhood. He said … "Back in New York City they had a program for inner city kids to be able to go with a family for the summer out in the country. The family that I was assigned to was a real nice family, and they had a big fancy house. I was about ten years old, and they had two boys about my age, and a sister who was a couple years younger. The one brother really acted like a jerk, and I wanted to beat him up, but I didn't. The other brother and sister were nice.

On one of the days us boys went out in a boat on a little lake. The sister wanted to come along but they wouldn't let her. That afternoon when we got back to the house we found out that the little girl fell down and hit her head. She was in a coma at the hospital. Her father told us that she kept calling my name over and over. It really freaked me out.

I went upstairs to our bedroom and lay down on the bed. There was a TV in the room but it was off. I was thinking about the little girl, and wondering why she was calling my name. It made me feel funny. The TV was just a dark screen, but when I looked at it … a face of an old man with a beard appeared. He was staring at me, and I could see him clear as a bell for a long time. It didn't really scare me that much, and then he disappeared. The little girl woke up the next day, and she was OK."

I asked Frank, "If you saw a picture of that old man in the TV would you recognize him?"

"Absolutely. I will never forget that face."

I told Frank … "Tomorrow, I'm going to show you a picture of that old man."

Exactly when Frank had told us about the old man appearing in the TV, I saw a flash of the self-portrait of Leonardo da Vinci. Something told me that that was probably the man in the TV. It was crazy, but whatever. I was going to see if there was a connection between all of these strange coincidences going on. It was like a spiritual test. I silently said to the atmosphere, and whoever was out there … "If Frank says that, that was Leonardo da Vinci in the TV back when he was a kid … then that means that there is re-incarnation. It **must** mean that there is some incredibly intricate connection between all of our lives and some purpose. (What I really was trying to find out was … who and what is causing all this to happen, or is it all just some mind-boggling coincidences after all.)

The next day the strangeness continued and intensified. I took Frank with me on the pool route. I was sure I could find the self-portrait of Leonardo da Vinci in an art book at a library, but I had no idea where a library was. "Something" told me to go to the supermarket in Pacific Palisades where I would sometimes buy cold cut sandwiches from the deli section. I **absolutely** knew I was supposed to go there. Then, I went to a phone booth and called Ed, who had not yet left to go up north to Oregon. His wife answered. Ed was not at home.

I told his pretty wife ... "Hi Penny. This is Roger ... and listen ... I want you to be part of a minor miracle. I'm going to tell you the answer to something, before it happens."

She said, "What are you talking about? What are you smoking over there Roger?"

I added, "I'm not smoking anything ... and it's a long story, but I need a witness to a little miracle that I think will happen in a few minutes from now. All you need to know is that the answer is "Leonardo da Vinci." Remember that, and remember what day and what time it is. OK?"

She was laughing, and said, "OK, when are you going to tell me what this is all about?"

"I'll explain later. Thanks!"

If I ever told the truth about anything in my life, I'm telling the truth about the next thing that happened. I had **no** idea in the world where a library was anywhere near Topanga. The only library I even vaguely knew of within a hundred miles ... was the L.A. County Library, which was in distant downtown Los Angeles. Nevertheless, I **knew** I was supposed to walk, not drive, from the parking lot. I was also positive we would find a picture of the self-portrait of Leonardo da Vinci from that parking lot. One chance in ten billion. It was mostly single-family homes all around that area. It was not a downtown area with lots of big businesses, and buildings, or anything. I walked back over to Frank and said ... "I called Penny, and told her the answer to who the mystery old man is. Now, we're supposed to walk around the corner of the grocery store over there." I was dead sure, and didn't know why.

Frank grinned as we walked through the grocery store parking lot, and turned the corner of the building. Just like magic ... directly across a residential street was a flagpole with an American flag in front of a small one-story public library! I had never even been on the backside of that market. It was the Twilight Zone. The library just appeared before my eyes! It blew my mind ... but by now it didn't blow my mind.

We walked into the library and I asked the lady to help us. Before long I had a book in my hand with page after page of Leonardo's artwork. Frank was taking all this with a grain of salt. I didn't let him see any of the pictures as I leafed through the book. Finally, I found a full-page picture of the famous self-portrait. I almost showed it to Frank immediately, but then I noticed on the opposite page was a picture of another old man with a beard. This was a painting of a character study done by the artist. I decided to cover that one up with another book. I didn't want to confuse Frank.

I called Frank over and showed him the self-portrait of my favorite artist. He looked at it for a while and said ... "It looks like him, but not exactly. The old man in the TV was different. His hair was shorter, and his eyes were kind of mean looking. Not like his eyes. Let me see the book."

I was holding it up to keep the other book covering the opposite page. I handed him the book, and suddenly Frank started shouting ... "That's the guy. This other picture is the guy! Look at his eyes and hair and everything ... I don't believe it ... but that's him!"

This was crazy. I had heard of people having all kinds of supernatural encounters on TV. This was radical, and way out of the realm of coincidence. And what about Debbie seeing things fly across a room at her boarding school. I never **really** believed that had happened, but she swore it did. I heard about things like the Bermuda Triangle. I tried to understand what was now happening to me. I couldn't tell many people any of this. They'd lock me up. I reasoned to myself ... "OK ... why was the man in the TV someone the artist painted, and not the self-portrait that I saw in a mini-vision?"

Instantly, I knew the answer. I was trying to con God, or whoever was behind all this hocus-pocus, into revealing themselves, in a provable concrete way ... at least prove it to myself. Some of this coincidental stuff was really scary to me. My answer from the unseen world was ... "yes, something is happening here ... but you can't con God."

After that day I became totally, one hundred percent, convinced that God ... whoever or whatever God is ... was for some reason trying to communicate with me. Again, the question was ... "Why?" I started earnestly "talking to the atmosphere". I didn't consider it prayer. I was positive hypocritical religion had nothing to do with this ... because this was **really** happening! I started asking questions, and seeking answers ... and to my continuing amazement, I started getting answers bombarding me from every angle.

A few days later, I told Debbie as we were driving through the mountains down Topanga Canyon Blvd on the way to Joe's Market ... "I've been getting these signs from God or whatever, and it's blowing my mind. And besides that, whatever is going on with Cliff is more than just drugs. I'm positive. I'm getting **sign after sign** myself!"

She said ... "People are going to think you flipped out too, if you don't watch out."

Immediately, as we spoke, I saw an actual homemade sign on a stake by the side of the road. It was on the upcoming curve, and was painted white with neatly printed black letters ... it said ... **"SIGN AFTER SIGN"**.

"Debbie look right ahead there! Read what it says!"

She said ... "Where did that come from? That is really strange!"

The next day I looked for the sign by the road again, but couldn't find it. It had vanished. As we drove along Topanga Canyon Boulevard, I was telling a couple friends about some of my recent experiences. I said, "Right about here is where that sign was. It was there yesterday, but now it's gone."

Debbie, who was very skeptical about everything I had told her, was in the car with us, and she said with a little laugh ... "It really **was** there yesterday ... I saw it too."

Fire On the Mountain

CHAPTER 41

"A SECURITY BREACH"

I had finally concluded that I definitely was experiencing some kind of spiritual or supernatural encounters. The odds were too astronomical to all be coincidental. I kept coming back to the question … "Why? … Why were these things happening?" As I was drawn into this search, I realized that it was pretty unbelievable, and it was best to "keep the mouth shut" for the most part. I told Debbie a lot of what I was thinking, and experiencing, but not everything. Like I said, she was pretty skeptical along with everyone else in the universe. There were several times when I would pinch myself, and check on my own sanity.

I figured that whatever was happening was out of my control, and I would just follow along and let it play out. I instinctively felt it had to have a purpose. I felt different. I had some kind of new energy. For example, one day we walked all the way down the dirt road from the meadow to the paved road. As we were walking along, I **knew** that something was going to happen as soon as we reached the road. I didn't know what it would be, but I started anticipating some kind of event.

As soon as we reached the paved road, I saw a motorcycle come speeding around the curve, and it spun sideways and went down. The rider went flying onto the pavement. Another bike was right behind the first one, and it did the exact same thing … fractions of a second behind the first one. There were two people on the second bike, and now in an instant, three human beings were sliding and rolling down the middle of Topanga Canyon Blvd. along with two spinning motorcycles. I didn't leave my body or anything like some people claim, but something rose up inside of me, and it was like I grabbed a hold of all three of those people, and rolled with them. My spirit was screaming … "Noooooooo!!!" I did not want them to be hurt or killed … I would not let it happen!

It was a miracle. All three of them rolled, and spun around in circles down the road at thirty or forty miles an hour … but, when they finally stopped, they all got up without a speck of blood … just real shaken up. It was another miracle that they didn't get run over by a car, because there were bodies and bikes all over the road … and Topanga Canyon Blvd is very heavily traveled at high speeds. It really felt like I had somehow helped protect those people with sheer will power. I never told anyone that, but that's what I thought.

A day or two later Debbie and I gave a young guy a ride to town. As we drove along I said to the guy … "Your name is David isn't it?"

The kid jerked like I just touched him with a hot electrical wire. He said, "How do you know my name?"

Debbie was shocked too. I just knew his name was David.

It had been a while since I had visited Cliff. I decided to go check on him, as well as my brother. When I got to The Glenn Bar I found Rick inside. He started telling me more weird things about Cliff. Rick said that after work he pretty much stayed in the bar until closing time, because Cliff was acting so strange. Cliff would do things like come into the tavern, order a sandwich, and then start controlling people by spinning little blue pool chalk squares back and forth.

I went upstairs to the studio to see what was going on. Cliff was all excited and happy to see me. He immediately started telling me … "I told you it was happening Rog! I got a hold of a reporter, and then we sent telegrams to all the movie stars! They need to know! Here's one of the telegrams. The dumb ____ers didn't want to send it … but it got sent anyway! This is the place! This is it! We found out that right here is the center of the universe. Isn't it a trip Rog?"

Cliff was laughing and carrying on. Nothing he said made any sense. I looked at the telegram that he handed me. Part of the text was saying … "Dolphins off the pier in Santa Monica … stop … Center of the Universe … 2670 Glencoe Ave, Venice, CA … stop … now is the time … stop … Son of David … stop … " It went on and on like that. It was totally crazy, but the whole thing was funny at the same time. Cliff was acting so happy … in spite of the absolute insanity. What to do?

I spent the night, and the next morning called a hospital and talked to a doctor. He said only the police could make a determination, and help in a situation like I was describing. However, if Cliff came in voluntarily they could put him under observation, but otherwise only the authorities could help. I called the cops, saying my friend needed medical or psychiatric help. They told me emphatically, that unless a crime was being committed, it was not illegal to be crazy. They wouldn't even send anyone to check on Cliff. I finally gave up, and drove back to Topanga Canyon. There are lots of legally crazy people up there ... rock stars, creek-freaks, and lion tamers galore.

I was having a hard time accepting that my friend Cliff was basically gone. Was he ever going to be normal again? I was positive it wasn't just drugs, but how do I help him? I want my friend back ... this is not **even** acceptable!

Every day I would clean my pools, but the little and big signs kept coming. I had a dream and woke up knowing that I was supposed to write a book. That wasn't totally new ... ever since I was eight years old, I talked about writing a book. It seemed to be in me. However, now I knew that all these occurrences were to be documented, and my job was to simply record everything accurately. The thought hit me ... "this story will probably destroy the myth of organized religion." I became so worried about Cliff that I called the doctor at St Johns Hospital in Santa Monica again. He worked in the mental health section, and I told him that I was going to try to get Cliff to come in voluntarily. He gave me directions and instructions. I drove back to Marina Del Rey.

I found Cliff upstairs and said ... "Let's go get a beer down at the bar."

We drank a beer in the crowded tavern. Cliff was talking exactly like he did the last time ... all happy but "crazy as can be". I decided to take it to his level.

"Hey Cliff ... guess what!"

"What???"

"I just got a message in my brain!"

"What is it Rog!"

"The message is saying ... MOVE ... MOVE NOW!"

Cliff thought about half a second and said ..."Holy molly! What the ____ are we waiting for? Let's move!! Dang straight!"

We piled into my car, and Debbie and I drove him straight all right. Straight to St. Johns Hospital. After a brief conversation with the doctor, they locked Cliff up for a 72-hour observation. He told me later that he thought I was taking him to get on a space ship.

The next day I went up to see Cliff in the hospital. He was on the second floor of the totally locked up mental health section. I had to sign in, and as I did, I remembered that I had one little marijuana joint in my shirt pocket. It was too late to turn around and go back to the car, but luckily they didn't do any kind of search. Cliff was glad to see me. He took me to his room and said … "Look out that window. Do you see that line of bushes there with all the flowers? I got them all going. I whipped those ____ing hedges into shape and got everything going! They're perfect now. In here, I'm kind of like a doctor. I do the same thing with the people. It's a trip Rog!"

Then he got real serious, and looked me straight in the eyes and said … "What do you have in your shirt pocket?"

I said … "Why?"

He started smiling and said … "Come on … come on Rog, I know you got something in your shirt pocket. What is it?"

He kept that up and got me laughing. Everything was so crazy.

I said … "Cliff, I don't know why you think I have something in my pocket, but I did forget that I had a joint on me when I came in here."

"Lets smoke that puppy!"

"No way!

Cliff kept it up, and kept it up, and finally said, "Look, you brought me here … the least you can do is turn me on to that one little joint! I'll just smoke it in the bathroom later. OK?"

I finally said to myself … "Whatever trip Cliff is on is not from pot. How did he tune into my shirt pocket anyway??? This is just a little more of the unexplainable. But, I guess one more joint isn't going to make much of a difference."

I told Cliff, "OK. Smoke it later in the bathroom with the fan on. Promise me you won't get caught with it in here."

The next day I came to the hospital again. My friend Gene, the art student, was in the lobby waiting to see Cliff also. He took me aside and said … "Some stupid ____er gave Cliff a joint!"

I said … "How do you know?"

"The doctor told me that Cliff smoked a joint in the bathroom, and then walked down the hall, up to the staff in charge, and shouted ... **"You have a security breach!"**

CHAPTER 42

"THE MIDNIGHT HOUR"

My friend Cliff was in a psych-ward, all kinds of strange things had been happening in my own life, and I could feel the temperature rising. Something was coming to a head. Everything was intensifying. It felt like I was in some kind of battle between good and evil. However, it was a battle that left me with a thousand more questions than answers. At the same time it was exciting. When you become convinced that you are dealing with supernatural powers, whether it is defined as God, or the force, or cosmic consciousness, or ET, or whatever … it got my attention. I was talking. I was talking to the air saying, "What do you want me to do? And besides that … why me?"

I continued to get answers, and I continued to be blown away … that all these things were really happening. The answers and direction came in signs, and dreams, and open doors, and closed doors, and other times things just popping into my head … things that turned out to be one hundred percent true. Like knowing that the kid's name was David. I never had any psychic abilities before. This was coming from somewhere outside of me. In whatever way Cliff was involved or exposed to some of this, it was destroying him. I was sure of that. There was definitely the good, the bad, and the ugly powerfully at work. One other thing was for sure … I want to be on the guy's side wearing the white hat. "Who are you Phantom of the Opera?"

Then this thought took center stage in my mind … "This experience is not happening to everyone. But it is happening to you … big time. What about all the controversy over Jesus? What was the deal with him? He probably experienced something similar to what's happening to you. The problem he had was that he never wrote anything down himself. Other people wrote the story, and as usual they twisted it around. They got the story wrong. You need to write this experience down as it happens ... yourself. It will change the world."

Slowly, I became sure that I was on an important mission. My part was to cooperate and let the powers that be ... run the show. What else could I do anyway?

After the initial 72 hours observation, Cliff was released to his adoptive parents who came in from Arizona. They took him back to their home. I was relieved. The doctors had him on some meds. Toni, his estranged second wife went to see him. She told me that for a couple weeks he started doing real well, eating good and taking his medicine, and then he talked her into bringing him back to California. He came back to his art studio.

While he was gone I met a guy in Topanga, who had a brother in the Manson family. In the past he would visit his brother at the Spawn ranch and whatnot. In my mind, if there was **anything** that represents evil ... it is Charles Manson and his sick "family". I asked my Topanga Canyon friend ... "Do you have anything that belongs to Charles Manson?"

He said, "After the Tate massacre I went up to the ranch and found one of Charlie's rubber boots. The place was tore up, but I know it was his."

"Can I have it? I'm going to fry it, just like I hope Charles Manson is going to fry in hell forever!"

The next day he gave me the boot, and a bunch of us went to a party in the San Fernando Valley at someone's house. I built a big fire of charcoals and wood on a BBQ grill. When it became a flaming hot fire ... I threw Charles Manson in the flame. "It's a preview Charlie."

It smoked like crazy at first. I believed the burning had significance. I was in the mode that coincidence was "here and gone". I expected some kind of connection between me, and Charles Manson, and whoever was in charge. As the boot started burning and melting I looked up at the sky, and there was a line of crows flying overhead. I hate crows. In Ohio when I was a kid, they had a bounty on them, because they destroy the farmer's crops. I tried to shoot one many a time, but they are real smart. I've seen a flock of crows a few times, especially when they attack an owl, but I never saw a spectacle like I was now seeing. The line of crows flying overhead extended all the way from one horizon ... to straight overhead

… to the other horizon. There were thousands of crows. Not black birds. I've seen lines of black birds in huge numbers, but never crows. They were all flying from the north to the south, and the line continued the entire time Manson's boot burned and then some. To me it probably meant that evil was on the move.

Burning Masons's Boot

That night we got totally blasted. As I drove down Topanga Canyon Blvd at one o'clock in the morning and reached the Corral, I whipped my car up the dirt road heading back to the meadow. By now I had driven so many times down this dirt road that I knew every hole, every place to avoid certain dismemberment … and I showed my acquired skills by traversing the entire trek at speeds up to fifty and sixty miles per hour. It was wild, and I did great until I came roaring into the camp.

As you come into the meadow on the right side it is a pretty straight, slightly downhill dirt road. I guess I didn't realize how long it would take to stop, and as I slammed on the brakes the car started sliding on the dirt like ice. We veered out of control to the left and then I saw Marcy's tent coming up fast. We were going to run over it with the kids in it. I was freaking. About ten feet before we hit the tent we heard a huge crunching sound and crash, and the car stopped just short of the tent. My foot almost went through the floorboard I was hitting the brake so hard. A big rock had completely blown out our left front tire ... and stopped us cold. That rock definitely saved our sleeping friend's lives that night.

In the morning I had another shock. Keep in mind that I hadn't heard anything newsworthy about Manson for months, or more like years. Also note that in the meadow, we don't have electricity, or running water, or the LA Times delivered to the door. Well, when I woke up the morning, after I burnt Manson's boot, a stranger came up to the meadow and brought a copy of that morning's newspaper. The headline said ... **"Manson Follower Attempts Assassination of President"**. What a coincidence! Where did it happen ... up north in Seattle. Was it successful ... "no" ... Squeaky had the drop on the president, but forgot to lock and load. She pulled the trigger on President Ford with no cartridge in the chamber.

The thought hit me, "Could what is happening with us conceivably have any repercussions or connections with some of the highest circles of society, and even the government? We probably saved President Ford's life ... or maybe almost got him killed!" Anyway, I told no one my suspicions. But, I knew there must be a spiritual connection, between the forces of good and evil, over the likes of Charles Manson. (The devil couldn't send Manson because he's locked up like a mad dog ... so he sent one of his stupid zombies.) "Keep your mouth shut or get locked up with Cliff somewhere."

Nevertheless, this episode with Manson was one more piece of the puzzle ... one more thing that convinced me that I was in the midst of something mind-boggling, and beyond coincidence. I mean the Guinness Book of Records says that lightning struck one guy six times or something like that ... but where does this stop being coincidence?

Even though I felt like a battle between good and evil was raging on, and that I definitely was not an agent of the dark side ... still my life was getting more and more out of control. The drinking and the drugs and occasional outbursts of violence increased. I got drunk at the Corral and at closing time, as I exited the building, I got in a brief argument with a Topanga local over nothing. I still had my broken arm in a cast, but I attacked him anyway. He turned out to be a semi-pro boxer, and when none of my untrained karate kicks deterred him at all … I was out of breath and knew I was in trouble. I started screaming at him at the top of my lungs, that I was going to blow him away with my 357 Magnum if he didn't "____ off"! (I didn't even own a revolver at the time.) Luckily, Little Rick jumped in between us just at that moment and saved my neck.

I also forgot to mention that shortly before Debbie came back to California, my brother Rick and myself decided to visit some of our friends in San Diego. We had been drinking some brews as usual, but on the drive south I stopped and bought a bottle of whiskey. That was a mistake. We drank the whole bottle using some 7-up as a chaser. By the time I got to Maggie's house I was smoking drunk. Steve wasn't home, but his wife Paula was there. I told her I was going to go find Ernesto in Mexico … did she want to come along? Maggie saw how drunk I was, and tried to talk her daughter out of coming with me … with no luck. Instead, Paula grabbed a bottle of Tequila and we were off.

The Tequila on top of the beer and whiskey was insane. I slammed the gas pedal to the floor on the 8 Freeway, and the old station wagon was pegged. We were going way in excess of 120 miles per hour. Paula and Rick were laughing their heads off, and I was thinking I should have been a racecar driver. I was successfully weaving past the other traffic like they were absolutely sitting still. Mexico was coming up real quick.

Then the party had to have its pooper. I could hear a siren and see flashing lights coming up on me. Here we go! "Oh well!"

I pulled to the side of the freeway only a few miles from the Mexican border and jumped out of my car. The cop was getting out of his car at the same time. I walked up to him with a smile and said … "Give me any mother ____ing test you want!"

For some reason the cop started laughing … "Do you know how long I've been chasing you? Man, I've been chasing you from the other side of National City! Let's see your driver's license."

I told him I lost my wallet with my license in it … which was the truth … and I told him my name was Tom Colbert. He said … "Don't you ever look in your rear view mirror? Didn't you see me back there?"

"When you're going over a hundred miles per hour you need to look ahead for safety!"

He started laughing again, and told me to get in his patrol car. He said ... "You can get in the front with me." I thought that was nice.

He left me in the car and went over to my brother Rick ... "What's your friend's name?"

Rick said ... "I don't know. He just picked me up hitchhiking."

The cop then asked Paula ... "Do you know his name?"

She smiled her pretty smile at the cop and said ... "I just call him sugar."

While the Highway Patrol hauled me off to jail, and a tow truck impounded my car, Paula and Rick went dancing at a nearby club. Cold blooded.

They kept me in jail for the weekend, and I appeared in court on a Monday morning. A public defender interviewed me, and I noticed on his paperwork that they had my name spelled Tom Colviert. I figured they must have run all the computer checks in that name, but I didn't know what to do. I thought I had signed the initial ticket Tom Colbert plain as day. At least I thought I did. When I walked into the courtroom, there was Steve and Paula and Margaret sitting in the crowd. I didn't make eye contact cause it wasn't exactly a laughing matter any more. I needed to play my cards right, or I might have some problems.

When they finally called my case, about the first thing the judge said was ... "How do you spell your last name?"

I said, "C o l v i e r t."

He asked me a bunch of questions about where I lived etc, etc. I lied about everything. The judge then called over the attorneys, and they had a little conference. Then he said ... "We're going to carry this over until ... (such and such) ... a date and in the meantime you are released OR ... (meaning on your own recognizance").

Close call!! I was sure they would never be able to trace any of the charges to me. My Tom Colbert identity would have to go bye-bye. Soon, I had a neat reunion with Maggie and crew. Steve helped me get my station wagon out of hock the next day. He even drove up to Topanga with me and spent a couple days in the tree house. Around the campfire one night he told Sandy and a bunch of us the story of our bust in Mexico, and how I got him out of La Mesa under the worst possible circumstances. He had never thanked me, but the way he told the story, with Kara Jane listening in, was more than enough thanks. It was true ...

I had put my life on the line for Steve, and I would do it again. I really like Steve.

The last night in the tree house Steve said … "Roger, I get vibrations of fire up here. I'm not kidding you … you should get the ____ out of here … cause I'm feeling FIRE big time!"

We crashed in my Topanga Canyon tree house that night way after midnight. I didn't know it, but my whole life was in that late-night mode. It was definitely the mid-night hour. A huge fire would eventually sweep through Topanga Canyon a couple years later. But, the fire on the mountain that Steve felt that night in my tree house … was personally coming after me. I could feel it coming.

CHAPTER 43

"IF THERE'S ANY TRUTH"

I went to see Cliff at his studio in Marina Del Rey, and while I was there, Peter … the so-called Malibu Apostle, called on the phone. I happened to answer the call, and when he said something sarcastic, I told him that I was going to kill him if I found out he gave Cliff any psychedelic drugs. He said the same thing to me as Jill's old boyfriend when I had threatened his life … "I'm going to forget that you said that!" I told Peter he better not.

My brother Rick came up to stay with us again in The Meadow. He is such a good brother. He was planning to stay for a while, because he didn't have anywhere to live right then. It was OK with me. A few days later he went into town and didn't return. He had indicated that he would be back later that afternoon. I wasn't too concerned for a day or two, but then I went into town and made some phone calls. I checked with The Glenn Bar, and I called Ohio, trying not to alarm my mom, but no one had heard from him. About two days later Rick was climbing the ladder to my tree house.

"Where the heck have you been?" … I was so relieved!

"You won't believe what happened to me!" Rick said … "I was in Santa Monica, and went to a bar where they have a bunch of pool tables. I was shooting real good, and a bunch of us were playing for money. I ended up losing big time, and before the night was over I got drunk as a skunk. I was there until way after midnight and then split. I was really wasted and ticked off that I lost so much money.

I walked past this fire alarm on the street. It had a glass window on it. I was so upset that I just punched the glass with my fist. The glass broke and the fire alarm went off … but the lousy thing sprayed a bunch of blue dye all over my hand. I took off running, and finally sat down on a bench. I heard a siren. Pretty soon a cop car drove past. I was thinking … 'that was close'. The cop got around a hundred feet past me, and then stopped, and put it in reverse. I stuck out like a sore thumb with the dye all over my arm. They caught me, and threw me in the drunk-tank at the city jail.

In the morning I was surprised. The police didn't charge me or anything … they just left me go. As I left the jail there was this guy and a chick who started talking to me. They invited me to a house and started talking about God. They really had a good rap. They fixed me some food. They were part of a Unification Church or something like that. At the house there was about twenty of them. I stayed with them for a while. They were really convincing and wanted me to go with them to a ranch up in northern California. I can see how people get brain washed. I'm not kidding you Roger … I almost went with them. You should hear them!

At the house they had a ping-pong table and good food. It was a trip. Then they all got together in a big room, and started singing John Denver songs. You know, "Rocky Mountain High" and a bunch of his songs. That's when I decided … "I got to get the ___ out of here!"

• • •

I continued to check on Cliff from time to time over the next few weeks. Now that he was back from Arizona, he wasn't as happy go lucky as before. He wasn't angry with me, but he wasn't happy that I got him locked up either. That's when he told me … "You tricked me. When you said we're supposed to **move** … I thought you were taking me to a spaceship … not a hospital!"

At first, Cliff seemed like he was recovering. I think he continued to take the meds that the doctor had prescribed for a while, but I'm not sure. I do know he was smoking pot again … just like before. Then one night he really got way out there again. He told me that he saw a cat following him on the power lines … and then the cat turned into a woman and he had sex with her.

He said, "They're filming everything Rog! It's going to have an all original cast, and it's going to open in New York … and it's going to change the world!"

A few days later he started talking about the Golden Light Theory again. He also told me that he saw the three faces of the Antichrist. He said ... "One of the faces was a beautiful man. The other face was an ugly and evil man ... and the third face was a reflection of the first face." What was happening to my buddy?

I got a message to call the doctor at St Johns Hospital. He wanted to talk to me. He told me ... "I have been working with Cliff and his parents, and I want to give you a warning. I've seen several cases like this, and someone usually gets hurt. Most of the time it is the ones closest to the patient who get hurt or even killed. I want to specifically warn you and your girlfriend. You and his parents are the ones who Cliff most often talks about. My advise to you is to bail out. Stay as far away from Cliff Davidson as you can. He's like a walking time bomb. He has been talking about sacrificial robes, and all kinds of craziness with religious connotations. It could possibly be very dangerous for all of you. These people lose complete touch with reality, and have no concept of right or wrong."

I thanked the doctor for the warning, but I was not ready to bail out on my friend. Besides that, I was convinced that there really was something spiritual going on. It was not just a simple case of Cliff going crazy or flipping out on LSD. He needed help ... not abandonment. I asked my brother Rick to stay with Cliff again and keep an eye on him. I was sure that Rick was levelheaded enough to handle Cliff. Basically, I asked him to just crash at the studio. He agreed.

One afternoon while I was there at the studio, Michael the Archangel showed up. I was aware that he had been coming around a lot, especially since Cliff returned from Arizona. He went downstairs to order some food at the Glenn Bar, and I joined him. This was my first chance to talk to him in months. I ordered a beer and told him that I was really concerned about Cliff. He said real sarcastically ... "What are you going to do Roger ... get him locked up again?"

I went off on him in front of a bar full of people ... "Hey Michael ... why don't you explain why you stuck your finger up Alita's six year old son's butt ... you sorry pervert!"

Michael went crazy! He jumped out of his chair and started screaming at me ... "You fool ... you ignorant fool! You don't know what you're dealing with here!"

I jumped off of my barstool along with half a dozen other guys who grabbed both Michael and myself. I started taunting him as people held us apart ... "____ you Michael. Anyone who sticks their finger up a little kids rectum ... is nothing but a lowlife pervert ... and that's what you are ... you sick jerk. You're a pervert and I want you and your uppity friend Peter to stay away from Cliff. I'm going to ____ you up good if I ever catch you around here again!"

Michael continued to scream curses and threats back at me, and to reiterate ... "you don't know what you're dealing with you fool!" I knew he was talking about the spirit world. I was glad that the other patrons had stopped us from fighting. It gave me the perfect opportunity to totally humiliate the degenerate in front of a whole bunch of people ... and besides that, I still had my arm in a cast. It's hard to beat anyone up with a broken arm. I had found that out. I would have given it my best shot, but I didn't have to. Michael stormed out the rear door of The Glenn Bar, and I've never seen him or Peter since.

A BOOK IN A GLOVEBOX

Then came the fateful day when I pulled into the alley beside The Glenn Bar and Cliff's art studio. As I pulled in, I could literally feel evil in the air. It was intense. It was early in the day, maybe noon or one o'clock. Before I even got out of my car I saw my brother Rick walk out of the tavern. I walked over to him.

He said ... "Roger, I'm all freaked out! I couldn't even go to work this morning. Cliff is really gone! He doesn't sleep anymore. Yesterday he was walking around his studio, and then he'd move one of the paintings hanging on the wall a quarter of an inch and stare at it for an hour. Then he would move something else, and do the same thing.

I stayed in the bar until closing time last night. When I went to bed in the studio after two o'clock in the morning he was still up. I finally went to sleep, and then I had this totally weird dream. In the dream I saw President Ford, and then I saw this hand slap him on the forehead with an eyeball. It was an eye like you see on a pyramid. It freaked me out and I woke up!

When I opened my eyes Cliff was standing over me, staring at me, and he was literally reading my mind. I've taken some acid trips, but this was heavier than any of that. He was reading my mind and like trying to take it. I'm not kidding. I split. I'm never going to stay there again. Forget it! His mother and sister are here. They are freaked out too!"

No sooner had Rick told me that story, when one of Cliff's art students came briskly walking to her car, which was parked nearby. I yelled over at her and she waited for me. I asked her where Cliff was. She filled me in on the very latest ... "Cliff has completely lost it! I saw it coming, but it's way out of my league. This morning when I got here he was in the shower. I came back almost an hour later, and he was still in the shower. When I looked in on him, he was holding his fingers up into the shower water! I couldn't believe it! I asked him what the heck was he doing, and he said ... 'I'm fighting the fire that is trying to crucify me!'

Have you talked to your brother? You need to. He is really upset. I'm sorry, but I'm out of here! Cliff is inside The Glenn Bar right now."

Cliff had been eighty-sixed out of the Glenn Bar for making a waitress cry, but today no one was confronting him. When I walked in to find him, he turned his head around and smiled at me. He had the **exact** same smile on his face as Linda Blair had on her face in the movie, when her head spun around in circles in The Exorcist. It was exactly the same! It looked totally demonic. He was eating something, drinking a beer, and talking to himself. I went back outside to try to figure out what to do next.

I went over to my car and got in. I knew I was supposed to do something ... but what? I sat there and tried to assess the situation. My friend is inside the bar, and for all intents and purposes, he looks possessed, he acts possessed, and whatever has a hold of him is definitely destroying him. I had been receiving mind-boggling signs and direction for months, and then I remembered the New Testament Bible that the young Christian girls had given me a couple years back. It was still in my glove box. I had never even opened it one time that I can remember.

I decided to get it out and see if it could address my present situation in any way. I grabbed the blue Bible and said out loud ... **"If there's any truth in here ... show me now!"** I simply opened it up at random and started reading.

The place where I opened was talking about Jesus coming down from a mountain. As he did a man came up to Jesus begging him to help his son. He was saying that his son had a devil, which was causing him to go crazy. It sounded like Cliff ... even worse.

The Bible is a big book. If you think your best friend is sitting in the Glenn Bar with a devil smiling through him … what are the odds that you could pop any book open right to a spot that deals with the very same problem that I was facing? Especially a book as big as the Bible. I had asked for some help … and truth … and I definitely kept reading. It blew my mind. I was sure I was getting supernatural direction. I paid close attention because I had no idea of what to do for Cliff.

In that section that I was reading, it told how his disciples couldn't help the boy, but Jesus got angry and called them "a faithless and perverse generation". He went ahead and delivered the kid completely by himself, and gave him back to his father. The kid was normal and all the people were "amazed". Then a little farther down the page his disciples started arguing about who would be the greatest. They were failing left and right, but still argued about being top dog. It didn't seem like anybody but Jesus was able to help a demon-possessed person. His disciples sounded like a bunch of numb-nuts.

Then, came the part that jumped right off the page and hit me between the eyes. His unfaithful disciples came up to him again complaining … "Master" … we saw a guy casting out demons who is not one of us … and we couldn't stop him. (I'm fast-forwarding and paraphrasing to what I saw in Luke chapter nine.) But the next thing Jesus said was … Don't hinder him … "for he that is not against me is for me."

I read it over several times, and then said to myself … "**I'm not against Jesus**, so according to the Bible that means I'm for him. I'm not one of his disciples, which sounds like I'll have better luck getting rid of devils … like the guy in the Bible. This must be my green light to help Cliff."

Immediately, I knew what to do! I felt totally in charge. I ran up the stairs to the studio. Cliff's elderly mother and sister were there making some phone calls in desperation. I had met his mother a couple times already, and she came over to me crying. She said … "Clifford grabbed a hold of me this morning and said … 'You don't believe a thing I say … do you?' I looked into his eyes and it was not Clifford. I really mean it … it was not my Clifford! I don't know what we're going to do!"

I told her not to worry and that I was going to help. We were going to get him back in the hospital. She told me her daughter had just flown all the way in from Seattle, and was at that moment on the phone with the doctor. I signaled to his sister that I wanted to talk with the doctor also

... and not to hang up. A few minutes later I told the doctor, that I was sure I could bring Cliff back in. He told me ... "You only have one shot at it! We'll be standing by if you can get him here."

Then I called the cops. Before, when I tried to get Cliff in the hospital, the cops wouldn't do anything unless some crime was happening. I told the dispatcher ... "A friend of mine just got out of a mental hospital and is threatening people!" I gave them the address to our location and my name.

In less than five minutes, Cliff's sister told me that police cars were already in the alley. I took off for the door and started running down the steps to catch them before Cliff would see the cops. I wanted to fill the police in on some of the situation before we went into the bar to get Cliff. I got about half way down the stairs when a female cop screamed at me to **"STOP"** ... and she leveled her service revolver directly at me with both her hands on the gun.

I stopped in my tracks, looking down the barrel of a deadly weapon. Women custom agents were bad enough, but this was scary. She said ... "Drop that stick!" As usual, I had my manzanita cane with me, which looked more like a war club than a cane. I couldn't blame the cops for their instantaneous assumption ... the way I was running down the steps toward them with my beard and long hair flying ... and a manzanita war club in tow. I definitely looked more like a nut-house escapee than Cliff.

I dropped my walking stick like a hot potato and told them ... "I'm the one that called you. The person I called about is in the tavern. I came running down here because I wanted to talk to you before you confront the guy. Can I come down there?"

They had me come down the steps, and I gave them a run down on the situation. I finally asked them to let me go get Cliff. I went in the bar and asked Cliff to come with me outside. We walked up to five or six uniformed police, and Cliff says real respectfully ... "What seems to be the problem officers?"

It was the first sane thing that came out of Cliff's mouth for months. He started talking completely normal. He answered all their questions without a problem. It was amazing. The officers were confused.

I said ... "Cliff, what's under your ring? Why don't you take it off and show the police what's under it!"

"Nothing's under it … except my finger."

One of the police said, "Let's see your ring. Take it off please."

When he took the large ring off, they could see the fresh round cigarette burn on his finger.

I told Cliff … "Tell them how you got that cigarette burn."

He said … "I was fighting fire with fire. I do it all the time. You have to fight fire with fire … and I was fighting the fire that was trying to crucify me!"

Well, the cops finally knew that Cliff was out there, but they started debating on what to do. The owner of the bar came out and reinforced some of my story. For a minute I thought they wouldn't do anything, but then the ranking officer asked me … "Did you say that he was in St. Johns hospital? Do you have the number of his doctor so we can talk to him?"

We gave him the phone number, and luckily the doctor was still standing by. When the officer hung up the pay phone, he said … "OK we're taking him in. They want him back at St. Johns."

I had a huge sigh of relief … **"What a rush this has been!"**

CHAPTER 44

"REV"

After Cliff was hauled off to the hospital again, the weirdness continued practically on a daily basis. I started having even more strange dreams, and thoughts, and conclusions about all that had happened. I was now positive that I was supposed to write a book. I continued to keep notes, and reminders, and photos of events. I was also convinced that there is a God at work in all of this, and definitely a devil … or a dark side. I would talk to God and ask questions. I was definitely being led. It seemed that I was led out of drug dealing to Topanga … I was led to the meadow, and to an Appaloosa horse … I was led to help my friend Cliff … and it all seemed to have a common purpose … but what next?

I wasn't sure where Jesus fit in to all of this. There is such a big deal over him. God had used the story that was in my "good luck Bible" of him rescuing the kid … to help me rescue Cliff … at least temporarily. I wasn't against Jesus … therefore I'm for him. Definitely! Everything I had ever heard about Jesus was good. He was for love and peace.

There were about six of us sitting around the camp one mid-afternoon, and we were having a big discussion. Kara Jane was lying in the sun looking like she owned all of North America. I told Sandra a little about Cliff, and the story I had read in the Bible that one day. She said … "I believe in Jesus … all the way."

I told her, "I don't know what I believe, but a lot of stuff is coming down fast! I'm just riding the wave to see where it goes."

Then, I looked up through the branches to the blue sky and yelled real loud … "OK Jesus, if you're really there … what's the deal? Show us what's happening! We want to know!"

Everyone in the camp got completely silent … they all wierded out. Nothing really happened … except that I felt like everyone was stunned. Why? If you yell out, "Hey Buddha are you really there ... or hey Mohammad are you really there ... it doesn't seem to move the needle with people. But, when Jesus comes in the picture, the needle goes way up or way down. I took note of the people's reaction that day. I also remembered Colorado Steve's experience in Boulder. I was seeking.

Everything was starting to make total sense ... little by little. I was on board. It was obvious to me, that I was having a "God experience" and he was revealing himself step by step. I was to be like a newspaper reporter, simply documenting the facts ... and let the chips fall where they may! "Religious institutions ... you are on shaky ground!" (Debbie and Frank were thinking that I was turning into Cliff with a ponytail ... but I didn't care.)

On my faithful pool route, my net was gliding around a beautiful pool, catching every leaf in sight, at this real fancy house. I was meditating on all the latest happenings and God. I was thinking exactly along those lines ... that everything was finally making sense ... and moving in the right direction ... and it was all coming together as perfectly as my new pool net that I had just picked up. By the way, it takes the better part of a year to wear out a deep leaf pool net, but as I emptied the contents over the homeowner's ornamental iron fence (with decorative spikes) ... I punched a big hole in the brand new net.

It really ticked me off ... and then I heard a little voice say ... "You have a hole in your net!" It wasn't audible, but I could hear it in my mind loud and clear. I know it all sounds crazy, but for **months** everything was unfolding in a pattern that was making total sense. Even the bad things made sense ... it was a battle. But this thought wouldn't go away ... and I believed it had significance. My net has a hole in it. A net with a hole in it ... is more or less worthless. "Oh well, how does this apply?"

My brother Rick told me that my mother wanted me to call home in Ohio. When I talked to my mom she told me some real bad news. My Grandpa Ira had died. She said through tears ... "When he knew he was dying Roger, he was so scared that he didn't sleep for several days. He was afraid to go to sleep, because he thought he would wake up in hell. He thought God was going to send him to hell because of all the bad things he did in his life."

My mom continued crying, but I had no answers for her or anyone else. All I felt was that familiar empty feeling when another one you love disappears forever. I was real upset. I was upset with God and everything else. Grandpa Ira had never been afraid of anything. It really bothered me that he was paralyzed with fear as he stared death in the face. How cruel this life can be! Grandpa had his faults but he was a good man ... better than ninety-nine percent of this sick world! A few nights later I destroyed part of my tree house, while cussing out God for the second time in my life. The combination of drugs I took that night almost flipped me out entirely. I didn't care.

The next morning I woke up with a **huge** hangover. I felt bad for all the terrible names I had called God, and for freaking out like I did. I climbed down the ladder to the meadow below and looked for my manzanita walking stick. I was sure it was right here. I had it last night. Then I remembered ... that I had not only cussed out God, but I also cussed out the devil, for about a thousand years, in no uncertain terms. I remembered screaming ... "Stay the ___ away from this tree Satan, (I'm not Satan ... I'm Spike a voice had said) ... or I'll shove this stick up your ___!"

When I still couldn't find my manzanita cane anywhere all morning, I figured with a chuckle, and a halfway sober mind ... "Maybe it's up his ___ ... who knows!"

I walked across part of the meadow to my car and got in. I don't even know why I got in my car. I wasn't going anywhere. I just sat there for a long time thinking about current events and my life. Debbie was still sleeping in the tree house. Pretty soon I said, "OK God ... what do you want me to do next?"

Immediately I saw a business card lying on the floor of the front seat. I picked it up and it said ... "Church of the Unification" and it had an address in Santa Monica. Rick must have dropped it, because it was from the group that had almost kidnapped him to northern California. I figured this must be my next assignment ... "Either they have something for me ... or I will have something for them." It was going to be the next stop on my spiritual journey.

Several days went by before I had a chance to go to Santa Monica. In the meantime, I was talking to Little Rick one morning down at the

Fire On the Mountain

pump house. He was showing me a couple of his paintings. I got on the subject of my other artist friend, Cliff, and I told Little Rick some of his recent behavior. He said … "It sounds like he should talk to Rev. Glenn!"

"Who's Rev. Glenn?"

"He's a country preacher up here in Topanga. He's a cool guy. He'll help anybody. The creek freaks and most of the locals just call him 'Rev'. Maybe you should go tell him about your friend."

The very next morning Debbie and I were at the Center Restaurant, which is the local hot spot … three eggs, hash browns and a cup of coffee for ninety-nine cents … when I saw a heavy set guy playing pool on the one and only pool table. Something told me that he was Rev. Glenn. I had never met him or anything, but one night when I was blind drunk at the OPO, I thought I remembered seeing him reading from a Bible to one of the drunks. It was a brief glimpse in the crowded, noisy, rowdy tavern, but I had that snapshot in my mind.

I put a quarter up to play the next game of pool … but instead he lost and came walking right past me. I said … "Are you Rev. Glenn?"

"Yes."

I said … "I think I have a friend who is possessed by a demon or something."

(I figured that would be a good opening line to a preacher.)

He pretty much surprised me when he responded by saying … "Well why don't you tell me more about it. Have you had breakfast yet?"

His response surprised me, because he didn't raise his eyebrows, or get all sanctimonious or weird in any way … like people at St Marks Lutheran Church back in Ohio might have. Instead, he seemed open to the possibility … but needed a little more input. I gave him a lot more input. We sat down and ordered. I told him the whole story in detail. It took well over an hour. When I got to the part where I was sitting in my car at Cliff's studio, and had gotten the Bible out of my glove box … he interrupted.

He said … "Wait a minute, you missed the most important thing in what the Bible is saying there!"

"I didn't miss a ____ing thing! Believe me … I read it over about three or four times, and at least I know how to read."

He didn't correct my bad language … (I felt like "Oopps".) But then he said ... "Can you find that part you read again? Where was it at?"

I didn't know the chapter and verse, but I knew where it was in my New Testament because I had marked it. I said, "I'll go out to my car and get it."

I came back with my good luck Bible, and looked up the part in question. I now noted that it was in Luke Chapter nine. Everything was exactly as I had remembered it as we read along. It started in verse thirty-seven. When it got to the part about the guy, who was not part of the disciples group, and to the one who was casting out demons ... I became shocked ... because three words appeared that were not there before. Three little words that changed the whole scenario ... back then and now.

The missing words that I didn't see when I had asked "if there's any truth in this book show me now!" ... those three missing words were "in thy name". When you insert those three words into the text it changes everything ... and it definitely would have changed my response that day with Cliff ... especially after the warning that my very life was on the line. I knew my life was on the line. I had read every word in that alley, and I read it over several times. Either my mind was blinded, or those three words were physically not there ... it doesn't matter ... they were not there.

Here's why I got so bent out of shape when I saw those three words. The verse goes like this in the King James ... "And John answered and said, Master, we saw one casting out devils **in thy name**: and we forbad him, because he followeth not with us. And Jesus said unto him, Forbid him not: for he that is not against us is for us."

The day when I was asking for divine help and direction for Cliff, (who I thought was definitely possessed by a demon, or demonic powers) ... everything that had been happening in my life up to then, was leading me to believe that I was in touch with God, and that he was helping me, probably in the same way he helped Jesus thousands of years ago. In the story that I just "bam" ... opened up to ... the disciples of Jesus couldn't cast a demon out ... the only one besides Jesus who had any positive results was the stranger, the one who was not a follower. I got that part. But, he did it "In the name of Jesus". That part was missing. Whatever power had me open to that place in the

Bible wanted me to focus on the next verse where Jesus says … "Don't stop him … he that is not against us is for us." I was not against Jesus or his disciples.

If I would have thought that God wanted me to march into The Glenn Bar, and cast a demon out of Cliff in the name of Jesus … how was that going to happen? I was not a believer, or had any right to use his name. Instead, with those three words missing, it made total sense to me. God had helped someone besides Jesus to rescue people from horrible evil powers … which even his own followers couldn't do … thus I concluded that God was going to help me, help Cliff get free. In my misdirection I instantly knew what to do … call the cops and lie.

I saw the hole in my net. A floodlight snapped on in my mind … "I have been deceived and misled. What was I being deceived about? About Jesus. All the signs, dreams, and thoughts were leading me away from Jesus and religion and Christianity. Why in the world would anyone, or anything with the kind of power to do supernatural miracles and manifestations, like I had experienced … go to such extravagant lengths to deceive me about Jesus Christ?"

The only reason I could come up with was … "it must be true about Jesus! I need to take a second look at this whole thing!"

I asked Rev. Glenn … "Is there somewhere else where we can go and talk?"

"Sure … my church is right around the corner. You can just follow me up there. It's the first drive on the left."

We pulled into the parking lot of the small white country Topanga Community Church, and walked through the front doors. I silently told God … "This is it Jesus … if you are really real, then I'll do whatever … and I mean it!" A few minutes later Glenn took us into his office, and he talked some more to us. He started explaining what it means to be truly born again. This was 1975 and I had never really heard the term "born again".

He explained that to *really* have a relationship with God, you needed to have a spiritual birth. God is eternal and created everything. He created man in his image with a free will. He loves us with a love that is beyond our understanding. He knew ahead of time that at some point we would use our free will to go the other way, like Satan did. Naturally, we followed right along ... but God already had a "master plan" of his own. Before the foundation of the world he decided to become one of his own creation ... to rescue us. God the Son was born into the world through a supernatural birth, and was totally God and totally man. He is the real "Star Man". His mother was human ... his father is God the Father. He was conceived by the Holy Spirit.

My concept of Christianity from my limited Lutheran upbringing was that when we die, God would put us on a big scale ... and if we're a little more bad than good ... then St. Peter would send us off to hell ... however, if the scale tips to the good side ... then it was "home free" in heaven. Rev. Glenn went on to explain the basic truth that we cannot be good enough to get to heaven on our own. Jesus was the only one to live a perfect life as a human ... and then he willingly took all our sins, and rebellion, and imperfections ... and he allowed himself to be judged in our place. The sentence for every murder ever committed, every rape, every theft, every lie, and every big or little sin ... was death on a cross ... a Roman death with real nails, real blood, and unbelievable pain. He didn't astro-project his cells out into the universe and escape the verdict (like the Rocky mountain version of Jesus said he did).

Jesus predicted his crucifixion in advance numerous times to his seemingly dull disciples, and said that after three days he would prove that he was who he claimed to be ... by being raised from the dead by the power of the Spirit of God. It happened, and Glenn said that we have more historical evidence and eyewitness testimony of the resurrection of Christ than any fact in history. An atheist intellectual, who set out to disprove the resurrection, ended up being converted when he looked at the evidence. He wrote a book about it.

The real Gospel message, which Glenn was explaining, and that I was grasping for the first time, was to realize that we needed to be rescued ... that we really are in rebellion to God, doing our own thing ... and that we are full of sin. It was easy for me to admit that I am a terrible sinner. I had made a **huge** mess out of my life. The heart of the Gospel message is ... instead of getting judged when we die, Jesus offers us a new deal right now. The new deal is ... if we receive the risen Christ into our hearts, his death on the cross will pay for all our sins

... and the same Spirit that raised him from the grave will come into our spirit, and cause us to be birthed into the Kingdom of God and his family.

According to the Bible Jesus is the ultimate judge ... and will be judging every single person. But, if we come to him now ... he comes as Savior, not as Judge. We don't have to hope that we earned enough brownie points to make it to heaven. We get forgiven, and born into God's family immediately by receiving what he did for us out of love ... the new birth ... Salvation ... Eternal life! The real thing is so simple that a child can receive it, but so heavy that it takes a lifetime to begin to comprehend. At the same time, I painfully discovered, it can be very cleverly hidden from us, opposed, and resisted by the dark powers. Those powers even twisted the Bible for me ... changing the message completely. It's a favorite trick. In addition to dark schemes and tricks ... don't think the devil doesn't shoot real bullets.

After summing up the Gospel to Debbie and myself, Glenn asked if we would like to receive Christ in our lives and be born again. We both agreed and bowed our heads. We repeated a simple prayer after Glenn, asking God to forgive us, and then receiving Christ in our hearts. It was awesome. I knew that something radical had taken place. I didn't understand much of anything, but felt completely different. What a radical journey we had just embarked on! More radical than all my small time adventures combined. Is this the beginning ... or is it the end? No way Jose ... "God is the same yesterday ... today ... and forever!"

If ever I had ever felt compelled to write a book ... it was now. I had been closely keeping track of events for months, and now I could see that God had been working behind the scenes all along ... probably all my life. For-sure all my life. He's calling each of us! I continued to write in a journal every chance that I had, and I officially began this book with pencil and paper in early October of 1975. I had surrendered to Jesus in late August and wrote the following handwritten forward to this story ...

FORWARD... This book is being begun. By a help I can only have faith so to who will write the last word. Today is October 4th 1975 and I am approximately 1 month old. I pray that every cell in my brain and every move I know and knew of all the Holy Spirit will enable me to put down what has happened however it blows my mind.

Roger Karl Sachs

CHAPTER 45

"UPSIDE DOWN WORLD"

When I walked out of that little church in Topanga Canyon in August of 1975, my whole world had been turned upside down ... or rather I found out later that the world was heading down, and I had been turned right side up. It's a matter of perspective. At the end of the "Good Book" it tells how God is in the process of making a "new heaven and a new earth" ... a perfect one where all this garbage, and warfare, and death will be gone forever. The number one complaint I hear (and previously had myself) ... was how could an all-powerful God create an imperfect world. Well, it turns out he is making one. A perfect universe, but because of love, and free will, there was a big hick-up. But I didn't know any of that detail as I walked back to the Topanga church parking lot with Debbie and Rev. Glenn.

All I knew was ... that something radical had taken place. I knew the devil was real, and now I knew for sure that Jesus was real also. I had run into both of them. The demonic forces had almost taken me out. I could see it clear as a bell now. Here I thought I was being singled out to be a messenger for God, but in reality I was going deeper into alcohol, drugs, immorality, anger, pride, and even the occult. I was an inch away from being killed or labeled insane. That's a for-sure. My next stop on my spiritual journey was to go see the Unification Church group. They are the "Moonies", who according to the TV news, have been charged by parents and former members with brainwashing and kidnapping people. Thank God that Jesus rescued me before they got their tentacles wrapped around my already smoking brain!

I was so hypersensitive to the presence of evil, and the demonic that I asked Rev. Glenn if we could go back into the church from the parking lot, to talk some more. I had some important questions that I just thought of, and I didn't want any evil ears to hear. I was thinking they (demonic forces) wouldn't have access to a church building. How wrong I was! Glenn kind of smiled, and started explaining the real live authority we now have **"in his name"** over all the works of the devil. We are not supposed to be ignorant of the "enemy's devices", but at the same time, we don't have to live in fear that there is a demon behind every bush. I had so much to learn ... but I felt the energizing presence of God cheering me on! It was incredible!

I was a twenty-seven year old baby Christian. Twenty-seven years is a pretty good slug of time, and then of course, I had done an excellent job of messing everything up ... my own life and many others. I definitely had a little reality to face. There were warrants out for my arrest in two or three different names. I had no driver's license, no money, no job. (My pool man friend, had decided to get divorced instead of moving to Oregon, and he took his pool route back.) I still had Mexican drug runners who wanted to kill me. I was years behind on child support ... besides being ridden with guilt over what had I done to poor Nancy and Troy. I was my nerve-shot mother's biggest source of anxiety. And all that's without mentioning how many people I had introduced to drugs, crime, and immorality? It went on and on.

I did a real good job of cooperating with the devil. Could I do better with Jesus? I sensed and prayed that I could, and the sky was the limit ... or rather the universe is the limit. I was going to give it my best shot ... but He was going to have to put Humpty Dumpty back together. I had no idea where to start.

One place to start was that I was still living with my girlfriend in a tree house. I knew that wasn't exactly the way to go ... so I said to Debbie ... "Let's get married." In our relatively short history, I had had such a rocky relationship with Debbie, that I thought she was the last person I would ever try matrimony with ... again. But then, the last thing I ever thought I would become is a **Christian**! I instantly put those two things together, and reasoned that God must have brought us together. She was the one I was with when all this came down. Look what had happened when I planned out my own life. I thought our crazy union had to be a God-thing, and with a little shock Debbie accepted my abrupt proposal.

We continued to live together at the meadow, but for ninety-nine point nine percent of the next couple weeks we stopped having sex, which Debbie thought was stupid ... "because we are getting married anyway." One night while we were in the tree house trying to get to sleep, I heard a bunch of real loud birds just like in an African jungle. Some of them sounded like super loud peacocks if you ever heard how weird they sound. Some of them sounded almost like cats. It was eerie and unnerving. In all the time at the meadow I never heard anything like it. The noises were coming from all directions, and kept getting closer and louder ... it really spooked me. I finally went to sleep, but woke up in the middle of the night with a start. The whole tree seemed to sway upward like something huge had just jumped off. Adrenalin surged through my entire body, and it really scared me. I decided that would be the last night at the tree house. I didn't feel welcome here any more.

In the morning, while I was brushing my teeth by the main camp, Little Rick said, "Did you hear all that racket last night? It sounded like we were in the middle of the Amazon ... that was totally weird!" (I was glad to hear that we weren't the only ones to hear it.)

That very same day, Carolyn, Debbie's friend from New York showed up, and we followed her car out of Topanga to go somewhere in the San Fernando Valley. When we started going down the real steep mountain section just before the Valley, I applied the brakes for an upcoming curve, but my foot went all the way to the floor. My heart about jumped into my throat. The brakes totally failed, and the car was instantly picking up major speed! I tried pumping the brakes with no effect and on the next curve, when no opposing traffic was coming; I drove the car across the road into the uphill side of the embankment. The dirt and brush and everything started slowing us down. For a minute I thought that wasn't even going to stop us ... but finally it did. The whole left front and side of my station wagon was all messed up, but we were alive. Thank God!

I'm not a mechanic at all, but I checked the brake fluid, which was OK, and I pumped the brakes a whole bunch of times. After awhile they started working again. It was weird. Between last night in the tree, and now on the mountain, it felt like something was trying to take us out. In less than 24 hours I almost had two heart attacks. We drove up to the church, and Glenn suggested that we move into the large 50-foot house trailer behind the church. Another couple named David and Gloria, who were also recent converts, were staying there, and this young married couple could also act as chaperons until our upcoming marriage. We moved in immediately.

To live at Topanga Community Church was a trip! God knows I love radical, and this place definitely fit the bill. Not only were there two couples living in the trailer, now that we moved in, but at night there were bodies everywhere on the church property. It was more like a rescue mission than a church. People slept in Glenn's office, and between pews, and in the entryway, and for months Teddy Hamm, one of the most notable creek freaks, camped in the bushes beside the church. Glenn would bring anyone home. He loves everybody. To top it off, Rev. Glenn himself lived in the tiny rooms at the rear of the church with his family of six. It was a zoo.

I was hungry to learn everything, and Glenn started feeding me books to read. He would spend hours and days answering my questions. I was so new that I wasn't even sure if the entire Bible was true. I knew for sure Jesus was alive and real. I thought probably the New Testament was true ... but what about dinosaurs? Doesn't that absolutely disprove the Old Testament? My Aunt Lula had taken me to the Carnegie Museum of Natural History in Pittsburgh as a kid. I had been amazed at the huge skeleton of a tyrannosaurs-rex and other dinosaurs, which were supposed to be scientifically proven to have lived hundreds of millions of years ago. How does that fit into the Bible's account of creation, and about six thousand years of man's history?

Glenn told me to pray and ask God all my hard questions, which I started doing. It was amazing. Practically the day I asked God about dinosaurs ... I turned on the radio while driving my car, and a Christian program was talking about creation versus evolution. In about two minutes, the speaker gave me enough "food for thought" to blow about a hundred holes in many so called scientific proofs. He basically started off by saying that God is eternal, and something has definitely been going on for a very long time ... so no surprise there. However, it takes more faith to believe that some atom or molecule appeared out of nowhere, or out of a big bang, and then defied science itself by going from disorder to order ... and over billions of years mutate into an incredibly complex universe and life itself. That's blind faith and a huge stretch right there.

It takes less faith and has more science to back it up ... that there is a creator. The Bible says God created everything and spoke it into existence. It started with order, but after mankind joined a rebellion started by a host of angelic beings, this present creation along with man, was given a death sentence. Everything is going to disorder, not the other way. People age and die, stars are burning up along with everything else. The Bible doesn't give a timeline on how many millions of years the angels have existed, or what God had going on before He created man, or even this present universe. With God anything is possible.

The broadcaster gave a couple simple possibilities, which made more sense to me than believing that our ancestors slithered out of a slimy mud hole millions of years ago. He said in the Biblical account of creation when God first created Adam and Eve, he commanded them "to be fruitful and multiply and replenish the earth." It was the same command that he gave to Noah after a flood had destroyed the entire population of the world. (There is also tons of evidence of a worldwide flood.) Anyway, there is a theory, and a possibility that there was a pre-Adamic race, and that something was going on before man, making an older earth, which could also include dinosaurs. How can you replenish something if there was nothing there before?

Then there was this little test of logic. The speaker asked ... "If you believe that God created Adam and Eve just like the Bible declares, do you think Adam was a fully grown man, and Eve was a fully grown mature woman ... or do you think they were infants ... or did God somehow create them in fetus form?" He went on to say that most people envision them as mature adults, if for no other reason they seem to immediately communicate with God. This would reveal that God created the first humans with "age-dating factors". If God wanted to place humans, who were one day old, but had age-dating factors of twenty-five year old adults, in the world ... then he could do the same with our planet and our universe. He could have created our world and our universe with age-dating factors just as easily. An all-powerful God can do anything He wants ... except lie ... according to his written Word.

At this point thirty years later, I don't even care exactly how God did it ... I just know He did it. I've heard so much more evidence that supports the Bible that it is overwhelming. You have to be fanatically and stubbornly blind to hold on to the theory of evolution. There is a Creation Science Institute, which digs into the entire subject for anyone with ears to hear. Anyway, God started convincing me that the entire Bible was true, not just the New Testament.

Every question I would throw out there in prayer, I would start getting answers. The supernatural continued ... and continues to this day. It is wonderful. Back in 1975 when I was asking about dinosaurs, I was on a baby-Christian honeymoon experience with God. I slowly started to realize how patient and loving and forgiving he was being with me. I didn't immediately "love Jesus". We grow to love him ... "because He first loved us!" God was so real to me that it didn't take hardly any faith ... but believe me there will come times when he will put our trust to the test. It says "the trial of our faith is more precious than gold". God works every angle.

I was living at the church, but after my pool cleaning went south, I went to work for my art-critic friend Alfonso Costa. He was an excellent builder, (and really was a pretty good artist also). He remodeled homes, and could do cabinets, and masonry, and just about everything ... when he was sober. I really got close to Alfonso. I would go to his house almost daily to feed and work with my horse, Kimo Joe. He paid me cash for working on his construction crew.

From the minute I prayed to ask Christ into my heart, I completely quit all drugs, and stopped drinking as well. I "knew" that God didn't make everyone quit drinking, but that I was supposed to demonstrate to everyone (those that I loved and cared about), the changing power of God. Alcohol had been my main drug of choice, and I severely abused it. I especially love cold beer ... but I grew to love Jesus more. Alfonso and I had scores of in-depth conversations about God ... both when he was sober, and when he was as blasted as the day we squared off at the Topanga Days Art Festival. He really liked me, and he listened ... but didn't listen. He was stuck on, "How could God allow innocent starving children to die?" ("Come on Alfonso ... let's go feed them!")

CHAPTER 46

"THE DREAM"

Living at Topanga Community Church was an adventure in itself. We had a couple sleazy local drug dealers come into the church one early morning, and viciously pull a guy and his girlfriend out of their sleeping bags. A teenage runaway was sleeping in a bag nearby, and when he rolled over to see what the noise was about … the barrel of a gun was staring inches away from his face. The grimy longhaired man told him … "keep your mouth shut and roll back over, or I'll blow your brains out!"

I asked the kid what he did … he said … "I slowly rolled back over, zipped my bag way up over my head … and prayed!"

The dealers thought this other guy and his girlfriend had ripped them off. They took them outside and severely pistol-whipped them. That was just a minor example of the craziness that Glenn dealt with on a daily basis, as he attempted to reach the unique cross-section of people that resided in Topanga Canyon. He has a million stories from his years in the canyon. His congregation was real small on Sunday mornings, and most upstanding residents appreciated his work, but couldn't handle the rescue mission atmosphere. There were many faithful exceptions, and they were real sweethearts who loved Jesus more than anything else. I have many lifelong friends from Topanga Community Church.

One day I felt led to cut some more ties to my past life. I took all my paintings that I felt were so valuable, with the different characters, and creatures, and multi-dimensional effects, and I put them in a wheelbarrow in the church parking lot, poured gas on them and burned them to a crisp. A local witch named Crystal had given Debbie and me a fancy little glass, new-age looking box with golden hinges. I threw that into the fire also. Glenn had been amazed by my little paintings, but didn't tell me to burn them. He agreed that if I felt led to destroy them, then God would honor my act of faith.

The very next time I saw Crystal, which was several weeks later, out of the blue she said ... "What did you do to the little box, where is it?"

I felt bad, because it was a gift, but I told her gently what I had done and my reasons. She went into a fit of anger, almost on the same spot that I had burnt everything, and she started screaming, "You fool ... I knew you were going to do that! That box of light was from Merlin himself!" (She was not nearly as forgiving as Jesus, but then he loves Crystal too.)

I was sleeping in the trailer one night when I had a radical and powerful dream. I can't remember the details, but it totally woke me up ... and I absolutely knew I was supposed to go find Ernesto in Mexico. I lay there in the dark and diligently prayed ... "God if you want me to go find Ernesto you need to give me a confirmation that this is really you!" Eventually I went back to sleep.

The next morning, which was a Sunday morning, I heard real loud voices talking right outside the trailer door. It woke me up. As I listened trying to figure out who the unfamiliar voices were, I realized they were speaking Spanish. I immediately thought this could be a confirmation of sorts to my dream, because I hadn't heard anyone speak Spanish for months and months. I quickly threw some clothes on and went out to see who in the world it could be.

There were two guys outside, and I said hello, and asked "Que Paso?" ... what's happening? It's about the extent of my Spanish.

It turned out that they were traveling with a guest speaker, who was a Hispanic evangelist or something, and he was going to be doing the morning service later that morning. They all had testimonies of coming out of crime and drugs and so on. I mentioned that I had spent a lot of time in Mexico, and had been involved in smuggling and whatnot. The one guy said ... "I know all about that, because I got busted and did time in a Mexican prison."

I said ... "Which prison?"

"La Mesa"

It blew my mind. Again the odds maker in me started calculating the chances that this was another coincidence. It seemed astronomical. I have a dream to go find Ernesto ... then ask God for a confirmation in the middle of the night, (because I didn't think it was the real smart thing to do with warrants, and transportation problems, etc etc). What happens next ... I wake up to Mexico at my doorstep ... along with a guy who did time in La Mesa ... where I had met Ernesto in the first place. It was amazing. It totally blew my mind. My new friend even knew some of the same people that I had met in La Mesa. (In the following thirty years I haven't met anyone like these guys with ties to La Mesa, and similar testimonies as mine and Ernesto's.)

I went to the church service later that morning with Debbie and everyone else, but I personally didn't hear one word the guest preacher was saying. Instead I was thinking and thinking, and then I silently prayed ... "God this is crazy. I lost my drivers license. My car is totally broke down, and I don't have any money. I have these warrants out on me, and people are trying to kill me down there. It's **way too dangerous** for me to go to Mexico right now!"

Immediately on queue ... the very second that I silently said that to God ... the preacher on the platform said into the microphone ... "If God tells you to do something ... . . there is nothing too dangerous ... **just do it!**"

It was the only thing I heard him say the entire morning. It blew what was left of my mind! I lie not ... it was perfectly choreographed. There was no escape now! I was covered with electrically charged goose bumps, and knew for sure that God was sending me to find Ernesto. ("How many confirmations do you need Roger?") I didn't know how it was going to happen, but I knew I was on my way to Mexico!

Since I was going to Mexico, I decided to ask Ernesto to be the best man in my upcoming wedding. I didn't know that my best man was planning to kill me. That was another small detail that came out later. I told Glenn about my dream, and the confirmations that I had received. He was real excited about everything God was doing in our lives. He wrote a letter as my pastor to the border authorities, asking permission for Ernesto to attend my wedding. He would have helped more, but he didn't have an extra car, or extra money either. I actually had a driver's license, but had lost my wallet over a year prior. I couldn't get a duplicate copy from the DMV, because of all my outstanding warrants. I knew I would have to clean up that whole mess ... but one thing at a time!

Right now the question was ... how do I get to Mexico?

Glenn would sometimes ask me to come with him when he was talking to people in the canyon. He always wanted me to meet this person and that person. He knows everyone. A couple times he wanted me to tell my story of coming to God to a particular person, who might relate to my past life. I refused to do it in front of the church, but I usually didn't mind talking to people one on one. There were a lot of people in Topanga Canyon who could relate to my experience with drugs, crime and the occult. Topanga was full of all three departments. The New Age bookstore was practically across the street from the church. Drugs were everywhere, and Uncle Al who is usually found passed out in the bushes, was seen dragging Alfonso across the parking lot by his hair one day. All my friends from the meadow, and even Los Angeles and Malibu were amazed at the radical changes in my life. ("Now he really went off the deep end! He's a Jesus Freak of all things!") However, they couldn't believe that I had no desire to do drugs or to drink. That was a good demonstration for many of my friends. I knew I could drink if I wanted to, but I didn't want to. I was a puzzling topic of conversation, but all of them said they'd come to our wedding.

Within a few days of my dream about Ernesto, Rev. Glenn asked me if I would come and meet a guy who was the lead singer in a rock band. His name was Bob Hite, and his girlfriend had been coming to church. Glenn had been sharing with both of them about God, and he had told Bob a little about me. Glenn said that the rock star, who lived locally was inviting us over to his place for a meal, and he wanted to meet me.

Bob Hite was a great big guy with long hair and a beard to match. He is "The Bear". His band is Canned Heat. I had listened to their music for years, and saw them perform on film with Janis Joplin, and Jimi Hendrix, and that whole early sixties music explosion. Canned Heat was right there in the middle of it all. They played at Monterey and Woodstock. However, presently Bob and his longtime live-in girlfriend were having their ups and downs ... and Glenn felt that God was definitely dealing with them both.

As we pulled up to his house, I noticed an older model green Rolls Royce out in front. I always had wondered as I drove down Topanga Canyon Blvd. who owned that cool looking Rolls. Debbie and I and Glenn had a really awesome full-blown meal with The Bear and his girlfriend Suzanne. It was the first time in my life that I ever had lamb chops. They made us feel real comfortable, and after dinner Bob took us down into the basement of the big two-story house to show us his hobby. He collected jukeboxes and thousands and thousands of records. They were stacked from the floor to the ceiling throughout the entire basement. It was incredible.

Later we went upstairs to his family room, and Bob started asking me some questions. Glenn had planted some seeds of curiosity, and it was easy sharing with him and Suzanne. I don't even know exactly what I said or how much of my experiences I included … I just remember that it was real easy and that Bob was on board. I was learning that sometimes when you share about God … if it's not the right time … whatever you say, just hits the floor and flops around like a suffocating fish out of water. However, when God is into something, and He sets the table … everything can flow like magic, and the air actually sparkles and tingles with life. It is wonderful to be in the presence of God. It's the reason the Jesus Freaks were making bumper stickers saying "Get Hooked On Jesus!" God was definitely in our conversation that evening, and it was fun.

The Bear didn't drop to his knees and repeat the sinner's prayer, but just before we left I told him … "and God is still doing all kinds of radical stuff. He even told me to go to Mexico and find my dealing partner … but I don't even know when I'll be able to get down there."

Bob said … "Why? What's stopping you?"

"I don't have a car right now."

He was sitting across the family room from me, and he threw a set of keys in the air and said … "Here catch! Take my Cadillac. It has a full tank of gas. That'll get you down there and back!"

What a trip! I caught the keys in a one-handed snag, and within that very hour I was driving south down the Interstate toward San Diego … and Mexico … in a rock star's Cadillac. It was almost as cool as the bright green Rolls Royce! Another rock star was riding shotgun … His name is … "The Rock" and "The Bright Morning Star". We were on a mission to capture "The Phantom"! **Right on!**

CHAPTER 47

"THUNDER IN THE SKY"

Ernesto was getting back into shape. He hooked up with one of his former-wrestling partners named Alex, and they named their tag team "The Daltons". He had several other names during his wresting career in addition to "The Phantom". He had been the "X-Man" and "The Chiropractor" and had different names on tag teams. Working out hard and pounding the body into professional wrestling condition took his mind off his other problems. He had agreed to do some dirty work to pay off his drug losses and debts. The time was coming when he knew he would have to pay the piper.

Working as a wrestler probably kept the drug lords at bay also. At least they could see he wasn't a total loser, and was doing his best to make things happen. He had a previous track record of not only moving merchandise, but as being a dependable heavy hitter with a lot of guts. He had collected debts, intimidated and beat people, and even kidnapped at gun point a dangerous man, delivering him in person to one of the drug kingpins who was locked up in La Ocho, the eighth street jail. So far he hadn't killed anyone, but you had to be a little crazy to march into a jail with a gun in your pocket, and a kidnap victim. The man knew he was dead if he alerted the cops. The message from the drug lord to the kidnapped man was … pay up, or this guy will take you for another ride. He paid up.

Ernesto really down deep didn't want to kill anyone … but he was half-heartedly looking for one of the men he was supposed to track down. He considered disappearing down into southern Mexico … but that had never been his style. He was too proud to run. Sometimes the "manyana" thing can work out heavily in someone's favor. Let enough time slide by, and maybe the problem will go away by itself. Nevertheless, he felt the heat every single day, and was real nervous about his future in Tijuana.

Something else very strange had been happening lately. Ernesto planned to go to nearby Mexicali for some business, but no matter how hard he tried ... something would come up and keep him in Tijuana. The next day he would plan to go again, but bingo, something else would unexpectedly keep him in T.J. When this pattern continued for about three weeks straight, Ernesto started wondering why in the world he couldn't get out of T.J. He wasn't really a superstitious man, but maybe there was something, or some reason stopping him from leaving Tijuana. It consciously baffled him ... but whatever.

• • •

As I drove south down the 5 Freeway in Bob Hite's Cadillac, every atom in my body was on high alert. When I made it through Orange and Riverside Counties, and was approaching the outskirts of San Diego, it was getting real late. I thought maybe I would get off the freeway and spend the night at Maggie's place, and then find Ernesto in the morning. The big Cadillac was gliding down the road, making great time, and I said a little prayer … "What to do Lord? Should I keep going on tonight or what?" No sooner had I uttered that question, when I looked up and there was a huge freeway sign which hung all the way across the freeway with … SOUTH … SOUTH … SOUTH … SOUTH … spelled out in huge letters, and a huge arrow pointing straight ahead under each word. I stopped asking questions. It's on!

I remember coming up at high speed over a big rise in the highway, when in the distance all the lights of Tijuana suddenly appeared on the approaching hills and mountainsides that are visible across the border. I actually wondered if I would be coming back alive. It was an eerie feeling, but no time to dwell, because within a few minutes I was at the border checkpoint, and it was time to get the head into the game. Soon, the familiar sights and smells of Tijuana, Mexico descended upon Canned Heat and myself. I started making my way through the madhouse traffic to Connie's house.

I found Ernesto in the late night. He was real surprised to see me, and I'm sure I caught him somewhat off-guard concerning his intentions toward me. He thought I had abandoned him at his lowest point, but now here I was out looking for him. What's the deal? Maybe he should hear me out before resorting to anything else. That was his thinking. It was way after midnight, and I asked if he knew of a sit-down place that still served a cup of coffee. He said … "Where did you get the fancy wheels?"

"It's a long story … hop in and tell me which way to go."

Ernesto directed me to a little restaurant named Ricardos on the corner of 7th and Madero in T.J. I had never been there, but it was a neat little place, and we grabbed a cup of coffee, and had a face to face. It felt like old times sitting across from Ernesto. I started telling him what had happened to me during all the absent months. I told him about the unending coincidences, and other strange things that had happened since our last few deals … had gone from bad to absolutely disastrous. I told him how it all continued in Nashville, and then to San Diego, and about walking away from the last six thousand dollars after seeing the crosses in the window that night. I told him about Alaska, and ending up in Topanga Canyon, and a little about Cliff.

He broke in and said … "You know, I have been trying to leave Tijuana for weeks and I can't. It's really strange."

I said, "Ernesto, listen … I know this sounds weird, but I know for sure that it is Jesus reaching into our lives. I said a prayer and told him I'd do whatever, and everything has changed for me. He's really real, and it's really a heavy duty trip!"

Ernesto looked at me real intent for a little bit and said … "You know what? I believe it!"

Let God strike me dead if I'm lying … but the exact instant that Ernesto uttered those words … "I believe it" … the large windows in the restaurant lit up like flash bulbs as the entire sky exploded with a single bolt of lightning, and a simultaneous earthshaking crack and crash of thunder that shook the whole building down to our very souls … and then it **poured** down rain for about five minutes, and completely stopped.

I lie not … it happened just that way! I was absolutely speechless, and utterly in awe of God. In my mind it was and is to this day … "Thank you God Almighty that you didn't strike me stone dead every time I cussed you out! What an absolute ignorant fool I was in the past!"

I don't think Ernesto said anything. God was doing the talking.

COYOTE

Since Ernesto wasn't going to kill me, I guess it was safe to ask him to be the best man in my wedding. As we drove back to Connie's place he told me that he was being pressured to kill some people, and that he had accepted the job. Now, he wanted to get out of Tijuana for sure. I showed him the letter I had from Rev. Glenn asking permission for him to attend my wedding. We still couldn't get over the bolt of lightning and thunder. It was early October and it hadn't rained for months and months, maybe close to a year … let alone thunder and lightning. Remember the song … "It never rains in Southern California". Almost all our water comes from the Colorado River, not the sky. Ernesto was getting a **crash** course on coincidences.

We finally got a little shut-eye at Connie's house. Later that morning we hit the road again, and tried to get a temporary pass or visa for Ernesto to come to the States. Ernesto directed us to some government building in T.J. where we hoped he could get the necessary permission. We spent most of the day and early evening waiting in lines, and then waiting some more. It was a total drag. In the end some Mexican bureaucrat practically laughed us out of the building ... "You can't get any kind of permit to go to America ... you're a convicted criminal with a prison record ... no way!"

As we drove away in temporary defeat I said ... "OK Ernesto, this is a bunch of crap. We smuggled all kinds of stuff across the border ... hop in the trunk. Let's do this one more time! We tried to play by the rules, but obviously it's not working. I mean, God was real clear about coming down here to find you. I'm sure it wasn't to just say 'Hi and good-by'. I need to get you out of here!"

There are hundreds of full-time entrepreneurs in Mexico who smuggle illegal aliens across the border. It's a very lucrative business. They are called "coyotes" and it's an automatic prison sentence if you are caught bringing illegals to America. Ernesto was not only an illegal, but he was an escaped convict to boot. We found a secluded spot, and within seconds I quickly shut the big Cadillac trunk door over Ernesto. "See ya later compadre". I hopped back in the car and headed for the border. The car felt so quiet. I silently prayed to God as we inched along to the distant Custom Agent working my line of cars.

After an eternity of bumper to bumper, it was finally my turn to drive up to the little booth ... "What is your citizenship? What are you bringing back from Mexico?

"American. I didn't buy anything this time."

"What was the purpose of your visit?"

"I was visiting a friend who lives down here."

The agent walked out of the booth, bent down a little, and looked in the windows. Then he wrote on a little slip, and put it under my windshield wiper blade and said ... "Drive over there to secondary. It's straight ahead and to your left."

(You gotta be kidding! What a drag! What tipped him off? Is it the Cadillac? Is it my long hair? This could definitely be ugly! My heart was doing double time!)

When I pulled into secondary, an agent came directly up to my car

Fire On the Mountain

and looked at the slip on my window. He asked me to get out of the car, and immediately he started to search. He looked in the glove box, and banged on the seats, and did his routine. He was looking for drugs. Pretty soon he said ... "Do you have the trunk key? Open it up."

Here it goes! I numbly put the key in the trunk, and with the pop of the lid ... it was ... "Hello Ernesto!" What a total bummer! The agent immediately called in a couple other uniformed co-workers to help in his discovery. Within minutes we were both taken into custody, and locked up in separate confinement cells upstairs at the border. Busted again.

As they were processing me in, the agent who arrested us asked me a few questions. I told him that I had tried to get a legal permit for my friend, and that it was an emergency. I told him that I was a new Christian, and that I had a letter from my pastor that might help explain things. When I mentioned that I was a Christian the agent looked up at me in utter disgust and contempt. He glared at me almost with hatred in his eyes. The landscape doesn't look good to say the least.

I sat in the little cell for a long time. Eventually the door opened, and I was escorted down a long hall to an office. Inside was an officer sitting behind a desk. He told me to sit down in an adjacent chair. I could see that he had the letter from Rev. Glenn on his desk. They had searched me and taken everything. He started interrogating me. He was real official and professional, but at least he seemed a lot nicer than the agent downstairs. I told him the whole story. I also told him that Ernesto was in a real bad situation, and that I felt it was an emergency ... and I had to help him.

After about a half an hour, the officer asked me ... "Do you know what this represents?" He was pointing to a little fish shaped symbol on his tie.

I told him that I didn't. He said ... "It means that I am a Christian myself. I see from the letter from your pastor that you are brand new in your faith ... but you need to understand something ... God is not in the smuggling business."

I told him ... "I just read part of a book called "The God Smuggler" by Brother Andrew, about smuggling Bibles into China.

He chuckled a little and said ... "OK, but that's a stretch from what you tried to pull. You're real fortunate that I'm the officer in charge tonight. You say your friend has it pretty rough down here in Tijuana? I talked to him. He's not much of a talker."

"It could be a life or death thing for him." ... I answered.

"Well young man, I'm going to turn you both loose, but he's going to have to go back to Mexico. I can't let him into the States. I understand that you want to help your friend, but this is not the way. Believe me. Here's all your things and your keys."

I couldn't believe it! I was free! Ernesto was being released! What a trip! I sincerely thanked the fish man. I'll appreciate that symbol forever! What a nice man! What a total miracle! "Thank you God!"

Soon, I powered up The Bear's Cadillac and was heading back north into the heart of Southern California. The magnitude of the little miracle we had just experienced played through my mind ... "They didn't even run a computer check on us. That's a miracle in itself! I had no I.D. or driver's license. The car is registered to someone else. I told them my real name. We didn't lie about anything! I have warrants. Ernesto is an escaped convict from Lompoc. It's another miracle they didn't even ask us any of that. I would have had to tell them the truth. "God you definitely know how to pull strings! I'm sorry I tried to do things my own way. I didn't even ask you what to do ... I just threw him in the trunk. What a close call! I'm really sorry. I'm trying. What do you want me to do?"

When I finally got back to Topanga, I returned the car with much gratitude, and slept for about twelve hours. I told Glenn everything. His letter had saved our necks. Well, God saved our necks, but He used the letter and put the right guy in charge. I remember another officer that was used in my behalf in Germany. God has been working in my life all along! What an incredible God we have! This whole thing continues to blow my mind. Like I said ... I didn't really love God when I prayed that day to become a Christian. How could I love someone that I just met? It takes time to love someone. But now I'm starting to get the picture! "You really go all the way to rescue us! You even went to a cross ... for the joy that was set before you ... you endured the cross. The joy of rescuing us! I can honestly say that I love you Jesus! It's too much! Thank you."

After I spent time with Debbie and my dog Leo, who fits right in wherever I drag him ... I was wondering what to do next. There is a big

Fire On the Mountain

white cross on the corner of the church property by the parking lot. It sits at the top of a little bluff. A couple of us went up to the meadow, and got the big rock that I crashed into the night that I burned Charlie Manson's boot. It was the same rock that stopped my car from running over the tent with Marcy and her sleeping kids inside. It had saved their lives. We took the rock, and my new friend Big John Schultise placed it at the foot of the cross. As far as I know, it's still there today.

Glenn called me into his office. We were discussing the upcoming wedding with Debbie and myself. It looked like we were going to have quite an event. Lots of my old friends and acquaintances were coming. None of them were Christians, and most of them were still into drugs, and crime, and whatnot. Lot's of my new born-again friends were definitely coming. Even Debbie's father from New York City was flying in. Glenn told me that he had arranged some music, and that several well-known Christian musicians had agreed to participate. Barry McGuire, Keith Green, Wendell Burton, Greg Reed and several others were supposed to be coming. It was going to be a concert.

Glenn also told me that he had an idea about getting Ernesto across the border. He said … "I've gotten to know a congressman and some people on his staff. Why don't we drive over there and pay them a visit?"

Well … a few days before the wedding I showed up at the border again with Ernesto and the following letter …

BARRY M. GOLDWATER, JR.
20TH DISTRICT OF CALIFORNIA

COMMITTEE ON PUBLIC WORKS
AND TRANSPORTATION
COMMITTEE ON SCIENCE AND
TECHNOLOGY

Congress of the United States
House of Representatives
Washington, D.C. 20515

WASHINGTON OFFICE:
LONGWORTH HOUSE OFFICE BUILDING
(202) 225-4461

SAN FERNANDO VALLEY OFFICE:
23241 VENTURA BOULEVARD
WOODLAND HILLS, CALIFORNIA
(213) 883-1233

VENTURA COUNTY OFFICE:
CAMARILLO
(805) 482-7272

SANTA CLARITA VALLEY OFFICE:
(805) 259-6695

October 23, 1975

Officer in Charge
United States Immigration
  and Naturalization Service
United States - Mexico Border Patrol
Chula Vista, California

Dear Sir:

One of my constituents, Mr. Roger Sachs, who resides at 269 Old Topanga Canyon Road, Topanga, California, is presently attempting to assist Mr. Ernesto David Hernandez, of Mariano Arijta 570, Colonia Independencia, Tijuana, B.C., Mexico, in obtaining a temporary permit to enter the United States. Mr. Hernandez wants to participate in Mr. Sach's wedding on October 27, 1975, and will then return to Mexico.

I know that this wedding means a great deal to both of these young men, and any assistance which you could provide to them would be greatly appreciated.

Thank you very much for your help.

Sincerely

BARRY M. GOLDWATER, JR.
Member of Congress

BMG:sb

CHAPTER 48

"AMAZING"

Ernesto and I walked up to the San Ysidro border checkpoint armed with an officially signed letter directly from a United States Congressman. I found out that the pen is definitely more powerful than a trunk. Wouldn't you know that the agent, who worked our line of "walk-thrus", was the same custom agent who had arrested us the previous week? He was the same one who glared at me with fire in his eyes when I mentioned that I was a new Christian. On this next visit of ours, he read the letter from the congressman, and I could see steam start to seep out of his ears. He was trying to hold it in. He sternly told us to wait, and he took the letter somewhere. After we experienced another short wait he returned and stamped a temporary permit allowing Ernesto to enter the USA.

We were respectful to the officer, but his body language was boiling over. ("God, if you can get to hotheads like Ernesto and myself ... then you can also rescue this bitter, angry, and (most probably) deceived custom agent!")

Connie was able to walk across the border, and we picked her up also. I definitely wanted her to attend our wedding. She was family to me all the way. We were off to Topanga! **Unbelievable! ! !** Pretty soon we were shooting up north on the wide, spacious, fully landscaped highways of Southern California, free as a bird ... and here I had always thought that being a Christian would be totally boring.

Finally, the big day in Topanga arrived. I almost got cold feet, because it had been a rocky road with Debbie, and the memories and pain of a failed marriage still filtered through my mind. Besides that, I was definitely not a finished product, and then Debbie still had her own brand of fire. But this is a new day, and anyway everything was in total motion. People from everywhere showed up. My good friend Frank from The

White House, and of course Ernesto, my best man, along with Connie were there. My nameless dealing associate from San Diego attended along with the entire crowd from The Meadow. My good friend Alfonso with his family was there. Spike the Vietnam vet was our head usher. He was totally loaded, but still did a commendable job directing traffic. Little Rick had a small portable tape recorder and was our soundman. Debbie's father gave the bride away, and Carolyn was a bridesmaid. There were Topanga locals, and creek-freaks, and church members crammed into the old wooden pews. Sandy's huge dog kept Leo company and also stood guard in the foyer. It was the only time I ever saw Topanga Community Church completely full.

Glenn had told me about Keith Green for weeks, and soon the wedding turned into a rocking concert. Long before "His Love Broke Through" ... "There is a Redeemer" ... "Create in me a Clean Heart" ... and "A Billion Starving People" were ever recorded and available, the crowd in Topanga Community Church was breaking out in thunderous applause to each song. Keith was pounding on the piano, and taking total charge of the crowd as only he could do. It was great. At one point the wooden sliding cover over the keyboard came slamming shut on the piano, and almost smashed Keith Green's fingers. He let out a gasp as he jerked his fingers out of harm's way. It was a close call. What a bummer that would have been, but thank God, Keith was able to go on to meet the challenges of a worldwide music career. He didn't just "go on" to fame and fortune, he charged forward with a radical contemporary anointing in reckless abandonment to God. It is one of the highest privileges of my life to have been a tiny part of Keith Green's short life. He rocked the world for Jesus with his music.

Barry McGuire was supposed to come to the wedding but didn't make it. However, his guitarist Jerry Melrose was in attendance. Wendell Burton sang several songs. I had seen him in the movie "The Sterile Cuckoo" with Liza Minnelli. The legendary guitarist Al Perkins who worked with everyone from The Rolling Stones to Dolly Parton was also there, although he didn't play. There were three Christian girls who sang really great, and the thunderous applause didn't stop with Keith. The girls sang like angels. It was really awesome. Greg Reid, who came out of the gay lifestyle and the occult, wrote and sang a special song just for the ceremony. Reverend Glenn Adkins, who Ernesto thought was a modern day "Friar Tuck", did a great job preaching to the crowd of thieves and bandits. It was a great wedding. How did all the famous people end up in that little church? I don't know. **It was truly amazing!** Later, we had the reception at Topanga's local American Legion.

Marcy's boys, Spike, Debbie & me, Frank, and my best man Ernesto

Our wedding present from Keith Green was some front row seats at "The Blah-Blah Café" in Hollywood where he was currently performing. We got to know his wife Melody a little, and later would attend jam-packed home meetings in their home in Woodland Hills. I loved being around Keith. I envied his ability to communicate, and his freedom and originality. It was so natural and real. He almost sold me his large van several months down the road, but instead I bought a little trailer to live in. He was so full of life and loved to have fun, even though he was often super-serious and "in your face". We went bowling one night after a meeting with our wives, Melody and Debbie, along with Keith's adopted daughter, and had a great time. Keith wasn't the greatest bowler, but he managed to beat Debbie who was having a tough night on the lanes.

A few days after the wedding Rev. Glenn took Ernesto back to Mexico.

They walked the streets of T.J. for an entire evening. They talked and walked until daybreak. Glenn gave Ernesto several books to read. One was "The Cross and the Switchblade" by Nicky Cruz. Ernesto read them all. He really liked Rev. Glenn, and had never met anyone like him ... so sincere ... so concerned ... so giving. He was trying to absorb everything that was happening with all this "God-stuff". Over the next couple weeks Ernesto visited a bunch of Christian churches in Tijuana. It was quite disappointing, because every pastor who he talked to recommended some other church for Ernesto. He finally gave up. No one wanted to help "his-kind" of people. Pretty soon he started dealing again.

I also had my hands full back in Topanga. I bought a tiny 18-foot trailer for Debbie and I to live in. We made payments. We parked it on Alfonso's property right next to Kimo Joe's pasture. I worked on Alfonso's crew, but quit when I found out that it was completely illegal for me to work for an unlicensed contractor, even if I declared my wages and paid taxes on the cash he paid me. It really offended him when I quit. He told me ... "You have your morals, and I have mine."

What kind of example was I to be, if I went from one kind of crime to another? I also decided, since I was temporarily out of work, that it was time for me to turn myself in on my outstanding warrants. I had no idea of how much time I would get, but I wanted a clean start to my new life. A couple of the charges were real serious, and might even bring prison time. I called the San Diego police department, and checked to see if they still had warrants on me, and on two of the aliases that I had skipped out on. I specifically asked if they had a warrant on Tom Colbert or Tom Colviert. They told me on the phone that they had them on the computer, and told me to "come on in." (Here it goes!)

Debbie wasn't crazy about the possibility of me doing extended jail or prison time, but was nevertheless supportive of my decision to turn myself in. Rev. Glenn and his wife Frankie, and Alfonso and his wife Rita assured me that they would keep a close eye on her, and not to worry. Glenn wrote me another letter to the authorities backing up my reasons for turning myself in. I still have a copy. He really went to bat for me.

A young flute playing hippy named Charlie, who I had been witnessing to, decided to accompany me on my journey. We hitched to San Diego and then to Tijuana, because I wanted to say good-by to Ernesto and Connie, before that dreaded moment when I would be confined behind iron bars again … for who knows how long. It's a weird feeling when you actually step out and face up to so many uncertainties … but I knew that God was definitely with me. That was the one and only "for-certain".

Ernesto wasn't doing so hot. I could tell that he was up to no good. Nevertheless, we shared some great homemade flour tortillas, refried beans, and fresh super-sizzling hot sauce at Connie's familiar kitchen table. Connie thought I was a little crazy for turning myself in. As we wandered around T.J. my hippy friend remarked, "This is great … you can just throw your trash anywhere!" And then it was time to go to jail.

Soon, I was saying good-by to Charlie in downtown San Diego, and I walked into the busy police department. I told an officer … "I want to turn myself in. I have some warrants, and I want to clear everything up. I recently became a Christian and I want a new start."

They interviewed me in a small room. I told them **everything**. I told them about getting involved in drugs, and dealing, and getting caught in Mexico. I told them all the alias' that I had ever used, and about the hundred mile per hour chase down the five freeway, giving false information to a police officer, skipping out on my own recognizance, being sought by a detective on other drug and domestic charges, going to jail under an alias, and everything that I could think of. It was a Friday and they processed me into San Diego County Jail. It was a trip.

At one point they put me in a large bay with about twenty other prisoners. I got talking to a couple guys, and of course my favorite subject came up … a brand new life in Jesus. They were listening and asking questions. When people ask questions, it means they're not bored or disinterested. I like it when people ask questions. One spooky looking prisoner was walking around the bay back and forth. He was listening to our conversation intently. At one point I said to the guys … "I found out that the devil is real." The spooky guy came flying over to our table, got right in my face, and screamed … "____ the devil! He's a punk! The devil has a pencil pecker!"

I started laughing because the guy was so bizarre. He got a smile on his face when I started laughing, and then he started laughing. He said … "Yeah that's right! The ____ing devil ain't nothing!" … and then he walked away again. (You never know what you're going to run into in a local jail cell. What's the world coming to?)

The guy might not have been impressed much with the devil, but the devil must have been real fond of him. Too bad I was such a new Christian, because I would have loved to see what would have happened if I had mustered up the boldness to say ... "In the mighty name of Jesus Christ come out of him!" That would have been a treat. In the Bible Jesus delivered a guy with over a thousand demons. It's no big deal for him.

I spent the weekend in the San Diego jail, and on Monday they took me out and drove me to a courthouse in Chula Vista. It was the exact same courtroom where I had been released under the name Tom Colviert. That was one of the most serious set of charges, and I was expecting the worst on that one for sure. I also knew that when I was in jail in Mexico, the FBI had interviewed me, and the DEA had been close to catching up with some of our activities. Maybe a judge, knowing some background, would throw the book at me even on some of these lesser charges. I had also just finished my probation for the drug bust in Malibu. My mind was churning around with some of those thoughts, and like I said, I was expecting bad news. At the same time I had seriously handed it all to God. It was too heavy for me ... and whatever happened ... happened. Jail is not the end of the world anyway.

Pretty soon I was ushered into a room with an officer, and he had me sit down. He said ... "Over the weekend we ran every computer check on you there is. We ran it on all the other names you gave us also, and we did it several times. The only thing that came up is a warrant in San Diego for your dog being off a leash. The judge has sentenced you to three days in jail ... time served ... and you are free to go."

What! I couldn't believe it! God must be in control of the police computers ... **when he wants to**. I was totally shocked ... and so thankful! How could nothing show up on any records? I had entirely forgot about Leo being picked up by the dogcatcher years back. I had bailed him out of the dog pound and signed a citation I guess. I don't even remember ... and had no idea there was a warrant. Anyway, I'll do three days for man's best friend. ("Leo, I hate to say this after all we've been through ... but Jesus is my best friend!")

How cool! God loves to blow my mind! I love it too! **HE IS ABSOLUTELY AMAZING!**

TOPANGA COMMUNITY CHURCH

Rev. Glenn D. Adkins
Pastor

269 Old Topanga Cyn Rd.
Topanga, Calif. 90290
Phone: 455-1843

June 16, 1976

To Whom It May Concern:

This letter is in regards to Roger Sachs. It has been my privilege to see a continued spiritual growth and maturing in Roger's life since I first met him. In my own ministry I work with many people who are addicted to alcohol and drugs. Since Roger has become a Christian, he has been dedicated in helping others overcome their alcohol and drug related problems. He is very serious about his commitment to Christ and his fellowman. Roger is truly trying to establish a new life and also do his best to clear up all the wrongs that he can.

He and his new wife, Debra, have lived in the community for the past year, and he has been avidly studying the books of my library to further his knowledge in his new found faith. It would be my recommendation that Roger receive all the breaks possible so he can continue his studies and preparation he is receiving at this time. I have faith that Roger's life will become a blessing for our society.

If any other information is desired, please feel free to call any time. Thank you.

In Christ's Service,

Rev. Glenn D. Adkins

Rev. Glenn D. Adkins
Pastor
Topanga Community Church

GDA/ds

Rev Glenn, me, Ernesto, Blank, Spike ... looking back ... Alfonso and Little Rick
(Hugging Consuelo in the bottom photo)

CHAPTER 49

"THE VINEYARD"

I had cleared up one mess hanging over my head, but had many to go. Now that I didn't have any outstanding warrants I was able to go to the DMV and get a duplicate copy of my driver's license. I was still way behind on child support in Ohio. That was a big one. I would send money whenever I could. I actually owed money to the state back there, because my X-wife was getting some kind of assistance. I also wanted to get all that caught up. It would take time or a miracle. I started claiming zero exemptions on my payroll, which would produce a refund at the end of the year. The state of Ohio confiscated my refund checks for about a decade. That was one way I started to climb out of the hole with them. The money comes easy when you are working for the devil, (but then he robs it all back). It comes much slower when you earn it with honest sweat … but then God blesses you little by little in countless ways.

After I quit working for Alfonso, I went to the Employment Office in Santa Monica and registered for work with them. Because of the fact that I had been recently convicted of a drug possession charge, and had successfully completed the diversion program, (which was basically the AA program) … all that made me eligible for a special job program. The state would pay half my salary to an employer for six months, or something like that. Soon, Eddie Egan & Associates in Beverly Hills hired me. This family owned business was the most exclusive flooring company probably in the world. I think my starting wage was less than four bucks an hour. I worked in their shop as an apprentice to their shop manager, Ted Krulivech, who is the neatest refugee that Yugoslavia ever produced. He was a working fool, and a gold mine for Eddie Egan & Associates. I could write two books about his life, and his brother (who ended up leading the underground resistance against the Nazi's in World War II).

I loved working for Ted ... but it was a drag hitchhiking to work every morning from Topanga Canyon.

I think I worked there for the better part of a year until I was offered a job at a pool maintenance company. I had purchased an old six-cylinder Ford van and was mobile again! When I left Eddie Egan & Associates, I hated leaving Ted and our lively conversations about life, and God, and mean nuns who smacked his little knuckles with a ruler long-long ago. That was enough religion for him. I loved listening to his dramatically expressed, broken English, well-seasoned stories. I hope I was able to plant a seed or two ... like for example Ted ... Jesus is not a nun! People blame God for everything!

Between Rev. Glenn and Keith Green, I was drawn to attend a home church meeting on Mulholland Drive up in the Hollywood Hills. The young blond-haired pastor was named Ken Gulliksen, and the minute I heard him speak I felt the presence of God in such a special way that I can't describe it. I **knew** everything he was saying was straight from the heart of God. The big fancy house was jam-packed with young people, and when they sang worship songs led by Keith Green and Ken, it was like heaven-touched earth. Ken had been a part of the Jesus People explosion that had recently happened at Calvary Chapel in Costa Mesa. He had a young family with a couple kids, but God told him to leave his secure position at Calvary Chapel, and start a brand new work up in L.A. It started as a Bible study, with no salary and no security, and grew into a budding church. He named it "The Vineyard". When I first attended, The Vineyard was about a year old. I loved everything about it.

The thought hit me immediately ... "all these people are experiencing God in about the same way as I am. It's incredible! I'm not the Lone Ranger after all!" I had felt the wonderful presence of the Holy Spirit ever since I asked Jesus into my heart, but at the same time didn't relate to a lot of what I saw in church. I love Glenn to death, but he comes from a hard-core Pentecostal background, which I couldn't fully embrace, (although I probably needed that initial injection) ... but this group of Christians was so down to earth, relaxed, and tuned-in to where we live and breath, that it totally blew me away. The Gospel and the Bible came alive in ways I never imagined. I started dragging people to church ... and they were getting born again left and right.

I had made several trips down to find Ernesto again. Sometimes he would actually hide from me. No matter how difficult he could be ... I was constantly reminded of the thunder and lightening that punctuated our confession of Christ that one super radical night in T.J. Presently, he was doing so many drugs that he turned yellow and even his eyebrows and eyelashes fell off. He looked really-really strange with no eyelashes and facial hair. He was drinking turtle blood every day trying to regain his health.

One night I found him drunk as a skunk, and we went over to Connie's place. His elderly Uncle Henry was there, and Ernesto started crying like a baby, and asking his uncle what he should do. I had never seen him cry, but Uncle Henry was no help for his drunken tears. Ernesto was in a war of his own, but didn't want to give it up. Several months later he was back on top of the world, dealing big time again, living with two teenage runaway girls from Guadalajara, and spending money like water. I got mad at him for about the first time ever, and told him ... "The next time I see you, you're not going to have anything to your name. Watch and see!"

Later he told me ... "When you told me that, I thought you was crazy. I had everything going my way. I knew something was going on, but I didn't think religion was for me. I laughed when you got mad ... but the next time you came to Tijuana, I was **completely** broke, and the only place I had to stay was at my aunt's house ... and her house was so full that the only place left to sleep was under Connie's kitchen table. It came true what you said."

Back in America the Vineyard outgrew the Mulhulond Drive house, and we started meeting at a Methodist Church in the San Fernando Valley. Pretty soon Ken had that church building packed out with hundreds and hundreds of people. Every week his sermons were so anointed that I couldn't get enough. This guy had such a genuine, and healthy, and loving way about him. It drew people to Christ like a magnet. It amazed me. He knew the Bible inside and out, and I became totally convinced that Ken Gulliksen was what a real Christian should look like. I never got to know him personally very well, because the hundreds grew to thousands over the next few years. I saw the incredible demands that a successful leader has upon his personal life, as he tries to be there for everyone. It's impossible, and I was never offended that I was not in on the "inner circle". I was happy to be in on the Jesus circle. You know ... the circle of life. He's the real Lion King!

One night we had a concert at church. Keith Green absolutely blew the place up. After him Randy Stonehill did the same. The talent that flowed in and out of the Vineyard was off the charts. During the concert Keith shared a lot of personal testimony between songs, which was really on-target, and then he said ... "the Lord is healing a canker sore on the left side of someone's mouth". It was the first time I heard a healing called out in a meeting. Keith quickly jumped into the next song, and I wondered if someone actually got healed. Weeks later in a service at distant Topanga Community Church, Glenn was asking if anyone had something they'd like to share ... about what God was doing lately. A real pretty girl was visiting the church and she said ... "I went to a concert recently, and Keith Green said God was healing a canker sore on the left side of someone's mouth. I was shocked because I had a terrible canker sore on the left side of my mouth ... and when he said that ... suddenly the sore was completely gone! I was stunned but didn't say anything. I felt bad that I didn't tell anyone, but I am now. Jesus healed that sore!"

The Vineyard grew so much that Ken went to two services. I would go to both of them most of the time. That's how much I loved it! For a long time Keith would lead the worship, and then Kelly Willard led for a while, and then Chuck Girard led the weekly worship for months. (He is the lead singer from the most popular ever contemporary Christian group, "Lovesong"). Our normal services were like mini-concerts with guest speakers and guest musicians. I heard Norman Grub speak there one Sunday shortly before he died. He was Rees Howell's son-in-law and wrote "The Intercessor". We're talking history. One day I got to church about forty-five minutes early for some reason. I sat in the back of the church with only around four other people in the whole huge building. They were getting the sound and equipment set up. A pretty gal was testing the mic, and then she started singing this incredible song all the way through. She sang "You light up my life" and it was Debbie Boone. The song had just topped out the secular charts that week, and I got a private rendition perfectly performed from start to finish. What a trip! God is good and he definitely is the Light of the World!

I ordered the tapes of every service, and had an extra set mailed to my mother back in Ohio. Thirty years later she tells me she still listens to Ken on some of those early Vineyard tapes from 1976 and 77 and on. "God is the same yesterday, today and forever". (Ken is showing a little wear and tear.)

For a while The Vineyard was like the children of Israel in the Bible wondering around from place to place. We moved again and met for a short time on the UCLA campus. Then we met at the beach at Lifeguard Station #14, which was between Malibu and Santa Monica on the beautiful Pacific Ocean. It was great and never rained on us once. The crowd started at around a couple hundred and grew to around fifteen hundred. The same thing happened every time Ken moved the church. When Ken decided to go back indoors, Hal Lindsey took over the congregation at the beach. He had just written the popular book "The Late Great Planet Earth".

Ken's first assistant pastor, Brent Rhue, started a Vineyard in Lancaster, and then Bill Dwyer took over the congregation in the San Fernando Valley. Ken moved to a location in downtown Santa Monica, and built another thriving congregation there, right next to a Mormon church. (I got interested in what they believe, and it would blow your mind to hear the true documented history of the Mormon Church, and discover what they actually teach. In my honest desire to see us all delivered from hell, I shutter at the fate of so many people trapped in false religions and cults like the Mormons and Jehovah Witnesses. If the devil can't take us out by drugs, sex, and rock and roll … he'll keep us away from the real Jesus with power, pride, or other gods. (It's the same story over and over. Golden calves or golden angels blowing a horn to hell.)

Anyway, by the late seventies there were six Vineyards beaming a spotlight on the one and only true living Word of God. How can we miss him? It clearly says … "In the beginning was the Word, and the Word was with God and the word was God" … "He was in the world, and the world was made by him, and the world knew him not. He came unto his own, and his own received him not.

But as many as received him, to them he gave the power to become the sons of God, even to them that believe on his name:
Which were *born*, not of blood, nor of the will of the flesh, nor of the will of man, but of God.

And the Word was made flesh, and dwelt among us, and we beheld his glory, the glory as of the only begotten of the Father, full of grace and truth."

If we can grab a hold of the truth in those few verses of the Gospel of John, then we will have won ninety-nine point nine percent of the battle. Jesus is God. (Not "a" God like the Jehovah Witnesses cleverly insert.) He is the creator. He gives life. The darkness in this world rejects him … but as many as receive him … they experience a spiritual birth. They get born-again.

I'm getting ahead of the story a little, but I have come to discover that there are lots of good Christian churches around the world, besides the early Vineyard. Nevertheless, I am so grateful to God to have had the privilege of participating in, and witnessing the birth of such a significant work. Much later Ken would invite John Wimber to come out from under the Calvary umbrella of churches, and come into The Vineyard. John was having a little trouble explaining the phenomena that occurred at his church on Mothers Day 1980.

Many people think that John Wimber started The Vineyard but that is not true. I had moved to Orange County in 1978, and was actually attending Calvary Chapel Yorba Linda when the merge happened in the 80s. I had also attended Calvary Chapel Costa Mesa for almost three years prior to that, and benefited much from the teaching ministry of Chuck Smith. So God gave me a front row seat to the whole thing. Not only did I get a front row seat, but I also became close friends with the controversial hippy-evangelist, missionary, Lonnie Frisbee. (And who said Christianity was boring?) He is the mysterious unnamed "young man" in John Wimber's books, who kick-started both the Calvary Chapel and Vineyard Church's phenomenal growth and success. During the Jesus People Revival Lonnie's photo had been plastered all over Life and Time magazines. How could this one little guy stir up so many pots ??? But that's another story. One that needs to be accurately told for the Glory of God! Lord willing it will be.

CHAPTER 50

"CITY OF REFUGE"

Ernesto was continuing to have his share of problems in Mexico. He found himself back in La Ocho on a serious charge of dealing a quantity of heroin. He knew this could produce some serious down time … and he was dreading another long stretch in La Mesa. From inside the jail he finally cried out to God, and promised him he would quit dealing if he got him out of this mess. To Ernesto's amazement everyone who was involved got convicted except him. The first time that he was sent to La Mesa he was totally innocent of the charges, but this time he was guilty as sin … and walked. It absolutely stunned him. However, like so many jailhouse commitments, when he was released his religion lasted about a heartbeat on the street. On the other hand, he was getting real tired, and was starting to think about what to do with the rest of his life. He was wrestling again … only this time with God!

One thing that had changed for sure was that he was falling in love with one of the young runaways from Guadalajara. Her name was Bertha and even though he was sixteen years older, he was absolutely crazy about her. After Bertha ran away from home, thousands of miles inside of Mexico, she was heading for America, and had made it as far as Tijuana. There, as so many do, she found herself completely broke, homeless, and at the mercy of a cruel poverty stricken world and the elements. She came to the door of Ernesto's sister's apartment, carrying a Bible, and asking for work and shelter. The slim sixteen year old was not a Christian, but carried the Bible to try to indicate what kind of girl she was. When Ernesto saw her, he told his sister Dora … "Hire her!"

witnessing to my partner in Tijuana

Soon Ernesto wooed her into his camp, and showered her with the fruit of his illicit business dealings. She was impressed with the money, and with Ernesto, and the security. One day I came to T.J. to look for Ernesto again, and we all went downtown shopping. He had just completed a big deal and his pockets were lined with money. I saw him buy Bertha and her girlfriend practically everything they looked at. A street photographer took a photo of us. Bertha is hanging onto Ernesto. Next to him is the other runaway girl and myself. The other two guys on the left of Ernesto were two of his workers. The overlaid pictures are mug shots of Ernesto and one of myself. This collage came off a little bio pamphlet. Anyway, Ernie even curled his hair for his new heartthrob.

About six months after this picture was taken, and after the close call in La Ocho, I was out looking for Ernesto again. He had been working at a nightclub called "The Crazy Horse" as a bouncer, and was trying to phase out of dealing. After work he took me to the shack that he rented way-way up in the steep hills south of downtown Tijuana. It was a remote dark desolate area. Ernesto said that people dump bodies up there all the time. The little wooden house was practically at the top and on an endless slope. Rickety stilts supported it. It had no heat, and that night was really-really cold. It was late February 1977. As we talked inside Bertha kept a blanket around her to keep warm. She stayed real quiet in the dimly lit house and hardly made eye contact. The wind was howling outside and as we talked the big rugs on the floor started jumping up and down in various places. Ernesto smiled and said ... "We have central air-conditioning." The wind was blowing up through the cracks in the floor under the rugs making it bulge, and jump all over the room. It was a trip.

Bertha was now about seven months pregnant. She spoke absolutely no English and looked cold and scared. Ernesto was telling me that he would like to get out of Tijuana, but he didn't know where to go. I told him I would try to help him, because I heard about a Christian ranch way down below Ensenada. I said I would check it out for him as soon as I could. However, I had to split late that night and head back to Topanga, because I had to go to work the next morning. I got back around three o'clock in the morning, and had to be to work at 7:30 AM at Eddie Egan and Associates. God definitely had to recharge my batteries.

The soonest I could get back down to Mexico was a couple weeks later. Someone had given me some real sketchy directions to the aforementioned Christian ranch in San Vicente Guerro. I had never been past Ensenada, and this ranch was in a small village several hours farther south in Baja. Rev. Glenn's brother, John drove me down there since I hadn't purchased my van yet. I was still hitchhiking and using borrowed vehicles. John wanted to check into importing paintings from Mexico, and he agreed to drive me to find the Christian ranch, if I helped connect him with some Mexican outlets for artwork. I had my good friend Richardo, Ernesto's brother, work on the project for us. I had known Richard from the beginning, but Ernesto never allowed his young brother to be involved in any of our drug related business. That was good. Richard was presently a valued employee at the Conquistador Hotel, and straight as an arrow.

Everything went great for John in Tijuana. We met all kinds of artists, and dealers, and wholesalers, but a day later, when we finally arrived in the tiny village down south, the small dirt road leading to the ranch was completely flooded. We couldn't get through. There was a huge run off from melting snow in the distant mountains, which was causing a torrent of clear cold water. We tried to find a way past the washed out road, and soon we saw a couple buildings that looked like an old motel, and some kind of auditorium. We decided to pull in and ask directions. John could speak a little Spanish, and was planning to go to Medical school in Mexico City or something like that.

It turned out that the place we stumbled onto was a Christian orphanage. It was great. What a neat discovery, (and coincidence)! The flowing water just led us straight to the orphanage. I met the directors, Rick and Kay, who were a couple from the mid-western United States. They had about eighty kids in the orphanage, and had been down there for something like five years. They even knew Ken Gulliksen. They had three young kids of their own, all with blond hair and fair skin, running around like crazy with all the cute little dark skinned children. The kids were all jabbering away in Spanish. Rick said they went on leave to their home in the States last year, and his mother got real upset that she couldn't even communicate ... "with my own grandchildren!" The kids spoke absolutely no English! It was cool.

We spent some time at the orphanage, (and over the next couple years I made multiple trips to visit, help on building projects, and introduce people to Mexico missions). However, on this first trip, I eventually found the elusive ranch we were looking for, and decided it wasn't a good fit at all for Ernesto. There were some problems, which don't need to be discussed. I was all bummed that a door was not opening for Ernesto and Bertha to get out of Tijuana.

We drove all the way back to America, and to Topanga Community Church. I told Glenn about the disappointing results concerning the ranch. He told me ... "You know what, someone came up to the church this weekend, and left a handwritten paper. I don't even know who it was. But it talks about a place of refuge in Mexico, and has a little map and everything. Let me go get it. Maybe it's from the Lord for Ernesto."

Glenn went and found the paper. Here it is at the end of this chapter.

Where did it come from? No one knew ... not even Glenn. The next weekend I was off and running. I followed the map and drove down to the remote village of Guadalupe (where some people had a vision of Mary), and found Chaplain Quinones. He didn't worship Mary, but did have a big place, with a dorm, and a Bible school, and a whole program geared to X-convicts and drug offenders. I taped most of our conversation on my little portable Hitachi tape recorder, and told him all about Ernesto. He shared his entire story about being on death row in San Quentin, where he was miraculously saved and set free (with the help of a praying and determined mother). He mentioned he was going to T.J. soon. I practically begged him to find my friend. He said he'd try. I gave him directions as best I could to the remote hillside location outside of TJ. A couple weeks later he did, with much difficulty, find Ernesto and Bertha at their shack. However, Ernesto took a bus to Guadalupe, stayed the day, and then decided against taking his pregnant girlfriend to the re-hab program. I had tried.

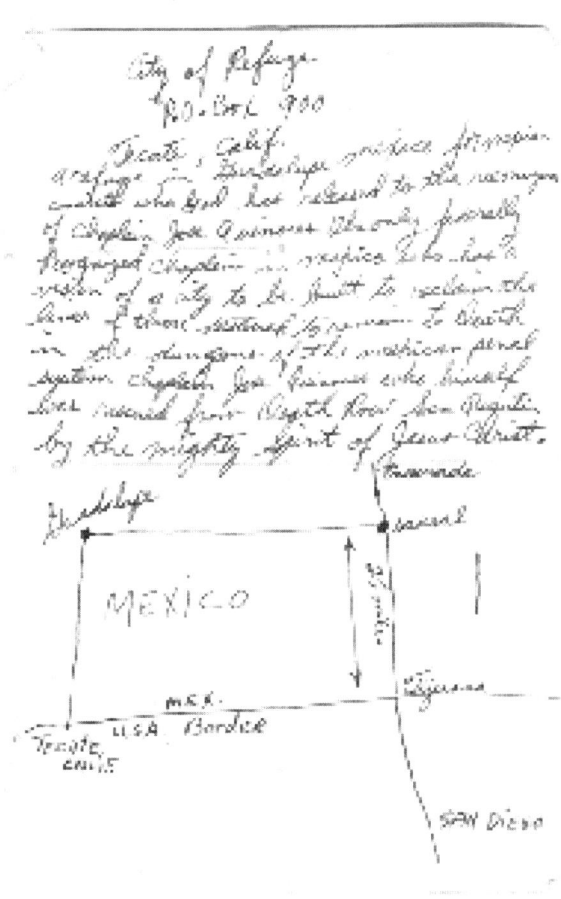

CHAPTER 51

"REAL MEXICAN PANCHOS"

While Debbie and I were living in Topanga Canyon, I would hitchhike every day to work at my job with Eddie Egan & Associates. The retail store was in Beverly Hills, but the shop where I worked alongside my friend Ted, was in Culver City, a neighboring town. All of Los Angeles County is really one huge unending city ... but very diverse with it's millions of people, palm trees, and "occasional" blue skies. When you hitch the same route every day, down Topanga Canyon Blvd to the PCH, and then up the Santa Monica Freeway, you start to get regulars who would swing out of the multiple lines of cars and pick me up. This one gal named Judy would give me a ride to work, sometimes daily. I had a couple regulars on the trek back also.

I got to know Judy pretty well. She drove to work all the way from Thousand Oaks, which was about forty miles from Topanga, and then she had another twenty-five or thirty miles yet to go. Soon, she knew much of my life story and I knew a lot about her. She talked about her career, and was excited about a house in Thousand Oaks that she had just bought. She was maybe a few years older than me in her early thirties. When I told her that Debbie was pregnant she was all happy for me. One morning on our drive to work Judy said ... "Why don't you and your wife move in my house with me. I'm all by myself in a big place. I could use the company, and with a baby coming, a little trailer might be kind of tough for you guys. I'm serious ... I think it would be great."

What a neat gal! Debbie was real happy about Judy's offer. I was very appreciative, but sad to move out of Topanga. I love Topanga Canyon and always will. I went back constantly to work and care for Kimo Joe.

We recently adopted a new dog named Onimy, and she made the move to T.O. with us. She was a purebred Malamute. We had lost Leo because a young psychedelic gal, (and total space-cadet) from Seattle, who stayed at the church for a couple weeks, had hitchhiked out of Topanga Canyon with my incredible four year old Golden Retriever. I am still absolutely heartsick about that. My young Malamute pup was easing the pain. She was a beauty also. We all quickly adjusted to our new place, with a big kitchen and our own bedroom. Judy was so easy-going and an animal lover herself. In the back yard she even had a full-grown raccoon in a huge cage.

About a week after we moved to Thousand Oaks, I saw a "For Sale" sign on an old Ford van parked near Judy's house. That's when I purchased the van I mentioned earlier. I was never so thankful for a vehicle in my entire life. It was old, had a million miles on it, but the faithful six cylinder was good on gas, had lots of room inside, and I loved her. That vehicle effectively ended my hitchhiking career for the rest of my life … (with one dramatic exception in Africa a few light years down the road).

Anyway, we started attending a nearby church named Newbury Park Foursquare Church. The pastor, Wayne Jennings, was a close friend of Glenns, and he became one of the father figures of my early Christian experience. He had been a large contractor back east, before going into the ministry and was such a neat man. He owned some acreage and allowed me to build a corral for Kimo Joe. I rented a horse trailer and moved Kimo to Newbury Park. The congregation put their arms around Debbie and myself even though Debbie was not really a happy camper during this period. I went to Lamaze classes with her. She was rapidly growing as the months clicked by and motherhood approached.

One early Sunday morning I got a message that Ernesto had called Topanga looking for me. He wanted to go to The City of Refuge in Guadalupe. Could I come down to Mexico and help him? I knew it was important that I go even though I had work the next day. Ernesto had never asked me for anything, so I knew it was serious. Debbie and I went to church that morning, and toward the end of the service Pastor Jennings asked if anyone had a prayer request. I finally spoke up in church and asked everyone to pray for Ernesto, and for me also, that I would have enough time and gas to go get him. It shocked me when people came up after the service, and started handing me tens and twenties. I really wasn't asking them for money, but it was such an encouragement. I had more than enough for the journey.

From Thousand Oaks to Mexico is a pretty good run. By the time I finally hit the road and made it all the way to Tijuana, it was around suppertime. I found Ernesto and Bertha up in the desolate hills like before. Almost two months had passed since my last visit, and Bertha was definitely huge with child. To me she looked like she was ready to deliver any second. Ernesto filled me in on all the latest news. Apparently, God was winning the wrestling match.

Two recent major events had pushed Ernesto over the edge. One happened while he was on duty at The Crazy Horse. It's kind of a long story but here are the highlights. Ernesto was called to assist with a disruptive and violent man, who didn't want to wait to get into the nightclub. Ernesto confronted him and ended up injuring the man's arm. The guy left the club parking lot and came back with a gun. He pointed it right in Ernesto's face and pulled the trigger. It misfired three times. Ernesto was able to get the gun away from him, and they called the cops. When the cops got there, they took him away, but soon let the guy go because he was the son of some high-level government official. The guy came back again with an automatic weapon, and opened fire inside the club. Ernesto was next door at a restaurant when he heard the shots and saw the owner of the club running toward him. They both hid in a ditch. The young thug shot the place up breaking bottles and putting holes everywhere but he didn't shoot at the people. He was looking for Ernesto. He swore he was going to kill the owner also, as well as Ernesto.

The other incident happened a couple weeks later when Ernesto got a ride home by three guys. As they were driving up in the darkened hills, (with absolutely no street lights), someone in the car hit Ernesto in the back of the head with something. He didn't see it coming at all. It opened a pretty good gash in his skull. Ernesto threw open the moving car door and hit the ground running. As he ran into the shadowy blackness trying to get away, he could **clearly** hear men running right behind him. He finally decided to wheel around and fight … but when he did … there was no one there. Nothing but eerie silence. It totally blew his mind. Where did they go? It freaked him out! Bertha later cleaned up his blood soaked hair and scalp. The next day Ernesto called Topanga trying to find me. It was getting way too crazy for him.

After spending a little time in their breezy shack that late Sunday afternoon, I began helping Ernesto and Bertha pack up their few belongings. It was early April 1977 and absolutely frigid that evening in Tijuana. I had completely forgot to bring a jacket or a warm sweater in my rush to get out of Thousand Oaks. Not like me at all. I like to travel prepared.

Bertha said something to me in Spanish, and I asked Ernesto what she said, "She wants you to put on a poncho. You look cold. Here put this on." He threw me a well worn folded up poncho. I don't think I had ever put one on in my life. It was really colorful, and soft, and thank God ... warm! It's basically a blanket with a hole in the middle. Ernesto and Bertha both already had their own ponchos on ... and suddenly I had the feeling that there must be a hidden camera somewhere filming all this. It was classic. Bertha's multi-colored poncho was extended way out.

Pretty soon, we were completely loaded up and my van was on the toll road heading toward Ensenada. Adios dark spooky hills! It was by now pitch black outside. About a half an hour into our trip Bertha started having severe pains. "Oh God, please don't let her go into labor now!" I thought for sure that she was. A few minutes later my old Ford started to cough and spit, and my prayers accelerated ... to desperate! "This cannot happen in the name of Jesus!"

The van stopped missing, and young Bertha stopped moaning. "Thank God!" I found the turn-off to Guadalupe and started heading inland. Eventually we found the dirt road leading into the village, and to the re-hab ministry. Everything looked very different in the darkness, but I was pretty sure we were on the right road. Soon, we came up to a small church filled with people and we decided that we should stop for directions. I pulled the van over and killed the engine.

If anything in my life has been classic, the next few minutes definitely were. Are we still filming? I hope in heaven they have holograms, or time travel, or some way to catch this scene again. I felt the presence of God before we even opened the door to the church. As we walked inside, several of the peasant-looking people turned and stared at the three visitors coming in from the very cold darkness. Under my colorful poncho I felt completely grafted into the picture. Ernesto looked like Pancho Villa, and shy little Bertha was right by his side looking very young and very pregnant. The preacher was going full blast in Spanish. It was the man we were looking for, the director of The City of Refuge, who was the guest preacher. We walked in just as he was giving an impassioned alter call to come forward to receive Jesus Christ.

Not more than a few brief minutes after we entered the church, Ernesto and Bertha joined a small crowd of people going forward to completely commit their lives to Christ. It was perfect timing. We didn't even have to wade through a long sermon to get to the good part. It was bam-bam-bam. My heart felt like it was on fire as I watched Ernesto and the rest of the people kneeling at the altar. It was awesome. God was there. Soon that little church erupted into fast paced celebration type worship ... en Espanol! I didn't understand a word, but understood it all. When Jesus told us the story about the lost coin in the Gospel of Luke he added ... "Likewise, I say to you, there is joy in the presence of the angels of God over one sinner who repents."

About two weeks later I took Connie down to see her born-again nephew. I picked her up in T.J. early in the day, and drove all the way to Guadalupe that morning. As we drove down the dirt road toward The City of Refuge, I thought I saw Ernesto and some other people walking beside the road. I said ... "Connie I think we just passed Ernesto."

I stopped the van and waited for the people to walk up. As they got pretty close I said, "Yeah, that's him."

Connie looked right at the people walking up and said ... "Where's Ernesto?"

She was looking right straight at her infamous nephew, and didn't recognize him. In a second Ernesto was at the window of the van, and Connie was laughing her head off. She told Ernesto ... "Oh my God, I can't believe it. You look young or something. I didn't believe it was you!"

Ernesto got in the van and said with a smile ... "What's happening Rogelio? (That's how Mexicans pronounce Roger.) How are you Connie? So if I don't look like me, who do I look like?"

Connie was laughing and said ... "I didn't recognize you when Roger said it was you. You look ten years younger. Before, you always had a lot of lines on your face, and you looked angry and hard. But now the lines are gone! You look peaceful. I still can't believe it's you!"

"It's the Lord, Connie," Ernesto explained.

We had a great visit. Ernesto and Bertha stayed at The City of Refuge.

The ministry had a two-year Bible school as well as a strict discipleship program. They were married on Thanksgiving Day 1977 seven months after arriving. Ernesto and Bertha both agreed to live separately, even though they were married, during their time of schooling and preparation. Ernesto immediately felt called by God to reach out to prisoners, and people trapped into similar lifestyles of drugs, crime and alcohol abuse like his old life.

In addition to his physical appearance, the change in Ernesto was absolutely unbelievable. I believed it one hundred percent, but then almost couldn't believe it. When you pray for someone for a long time, and then God radically answers your prayers … it still blows your mind. At least it did mine in Ernesto's case. From one of the most proud, self-willed, wild, power-hungry individuals that I ever knew, he now completely humbled himself, and was willing to mop floors or do whatever. He diligently studied at the Bible school, and treated Bertha with the utmost respect.

I tried to talk him out of living separately a couple times, but he finally told me, "Before in my life sex was something I took … something that didn't mean anything. I was never faithful to anyone, and I used women. Now, we both agree that we want to have God in our marriage, and we want to use this time to learn all we can. We will have our whole lives to be married when we leave this place. The director's wife is going to raise our kid while we are here. I want Bertha to feel special. We take walks and even hold hands like we are dating. I think the Lord is pleased."

I shut my mouth after that speech. By the way, most American women might absolutely shudder when they think about Bertha's child-birthing experience. Exactly 15 days after Ernesto and Bertha arrived in Guadalupe, her time suddenly arrived to deliver. Naturally the director and his wife were out of town that day, so they had no vehicle available. As her labor pains increased, Ernesto **slowly** walked her down the dusty dirt roads over a mile and a half to try to find the one and only doctor's house. The small house was equipped with two beds, which served as the clinic for the whole village. About half way there Bertha's water broke. She was screaming at Ernesto. When they finally made it to the house, the doctor was not at home.

The doctor was out on a call at a ranch, but his wife was home. She was in the last stages of a pregnancy herself. Ernesto and the doctor's pregnant wife delivered the seven pound eight ounce baby. Ernesto told me ... "The wife of the doctor almost fainted. It was too much for her. She handed me the baby and it was hot ... hot like a loaf of bread coming out of the oven. It was a girl, and I held her while she cut the cord."

Ernesto and Bertha named the tiny little girl Berenice Hernandez. She was born on April 19th, 1977. God replaced the agony of childbirth with "joy that a child is born". Ernesto was **instantly** transformed in Bertha's eyes from the most evil, vile, stupid man in the world ... to a loving father.

Seven months later when Ernesto and Bertha were married, no one had enough money to prepare a special meal or a reception to celebrate the occasion. The City of Refuge itself operated on a shoestring. However, some Americans unexpectedly arrived at the ministry with a whole feast, because it was Thanksgiving Day. Even though Turkey Day is a totally American holiday, on that November day in Mexico it doubled as a gift from heaven for the newlyweds. The loving coincidences have never stopped.

CHAPTER 52

"AN APACHE AND A MISSION"

My Apache Indian friend, Henry Garcia was a very special person in my life. Several months after I became a Christian, I remembered the old Indian that I had helped find a new apartment. It had been years, and I wondered if he still lived at the same place. He had gently witnessed to me about Christ **with his life**, when I was running full blast in the opposite direction. I wanted to go back and tell him what had happened to me.

I drove to L.A. and knocked on his door. Some lady opened the little, tiny, two- inch window on the door, and said something in Spanish. I asked for Henry, and pretty soon I heard his voice say through the closed door ... "Yes, can I help you."

"Henry this is Roger Sachs. I don't know if you remember me, but you helped me put a new ceiling up at my place years ago."

The door flew open and Henry said ... "Sure I remember you! Come in - come in! It has been a long time. How are you? I want you to meet my wife Anita. Since I saw you last I got married again. Sit down! What's been going on with you?"

"Well Henry, I always remembered that you were a Christian, and I just wanted to look you up, and tell you that I asked Jesus into my heart recently. I am a Christian now."

Henry started to say something, but then got all choked up, and he started crying. He cried for a long time, and couldn't talk at all. I felt the presence of God fill the apartment. It was awesome. I almost started crying.

I ended up spending the whole evening there. He had Anita fix us a great Mexican meal, after he whipped away the tears in a slightly embarrassed way. She is from southern Mexico, and didn't speak a word of English, but just like with Bertha, we clicked real good in no time. I told Henry about Ernesto and my desire to help him, and Henry told me that he did missionary work in Mexico for over forty years. He and some other missionaries helped start a whole bunch of churches.

Henry said ... "I stopped making trips to Mexico when I had my stroke and couldn't drive anymore, but then the Lord sent me a partner, and for years he drove, and we continued doing whatever we could to serve the Lord in Mexico. As you might remember, my father was Apache, but my mother is Mexican. I have a great heart for the Mexican people, but then my missionary friend died, and I haven't been able to do anything for years now. I was thinking that maybe the good Lord is finished with me ... but maybe he wants me to help you with your friend Ernesto. We could go and check on some of the people that I know also, and who knows what God might have in mind."

"That would be great Henry!"

We started making plans, and from early in my Christian life we started working together. Over the next few years we made all kinds of trips down south. I also took him to my church The Vineyard Christian Fellowship, and even made an appointment with pastor Ken Gulliksen. Henry and I both shared about Ernesto's needs when he was going to Bible school in Guadalupe. Ken was so respectful to Henry. He commented that it was such a privilege to meet someone who was serving Christ on the mission field long before we were born, or even thought of. That was true.

One evening at Henry and Anita's nifty corner apartment, he told me the story about his father. He said ... "Apache men didn't interact with the children that much, and my father was very, very reserved and quiet. To us he seemed mean. He was also the Indian Marshall on the reservation. He was respected by everyone, but could be very ruthless. He was the judge, jury, and executioner on the reservation.

One time some men robbed a government payroll, and my father and a band of his men caught them. He hung the men right there. The payroll was all in gold coins, and he hid it. He drew a map to find it again, but never went back. My mother still has that map.

During that time in the late eighteen hundreds and early nineteen hundreds there was the Apache Indians in Mexico who are a cousin tribe. They are called the Jica Indians. (Henry pronounced them the "Yacki" Indians, and is actually the Jicarilla branch of the Apache Indians). They would come across the border, steal cattle and horses, and rob the ranchers. My father and his warriors would chase them and kill them. He even went into Mexico, and killed them in their own land. They knew who my father was, and they hated him. Most of his life he was the enemy of the Yacki Indians.

There was a Christian missionary man who came to the reservation, and he talked to my father many times. Finally one day my father prayed with him, and became a Christian. My mother became a Christian also. Then my father felt that God wanted him to go back to the Yacki Indians, and tell them about Jesus. He thought they might kill him, but they didn't. In fact, he lived with them for long periods of time in Mexico. He became a missionary to the people he persecuted. We were left alone many times, and didn't know if we would ever see him alive again.

He did come home, but when I was just a teenager, he had an accident and was killed. He was thrown from a horse. That was the beginning of a lot of problems for my family, when he got killed. But, I think the Lord put the call on my life to become a missionary like my father. Brother, the Lord works in mysterious ways. Like the good book says in Isaiah … 'For my thoughts are not your thoughts, neither are your ways my ways, saith the Lord. For as the heavens are higher than the earth, so are my ways higher than your ways, and my thoughts than your thoughts.'"

Henry continued … "In fact, I was not that serious about God for much of my life, and was more or less angry and bitter about many things. During World War II when I was shot on the aircraft carrier by a German warplane, they flew me to a hospital in Italy. They didn't expect me to live, and I knew I was dying. Let me tell you Brother Roger, that I cried out to God and promised him … that if he would heal me I would serve him the rest of my life. Do you know from that minute on I started to live again. God completely healed me … and I have kept my promise to this day. We have a wonderful Lord, and he has been very faithful.

The Lord has been with us all these years. My mother is 104 years old now, and still works at a clinic **way** down south in Baja, Mexico. She lives in a little house next to the clinic. She cleans up and takes care of the place for some Christian doctors in San Diego. They fly her in a little airplane to see us every so often. The Lord is very good."

(I knew the Lord had the call of missions on my life also. My Apache Indian friend, Henry Garcia became my first missionary partner. It was an honor to serve with him, and really cool. We worked and traveled together for about a decade until he moved down to Mexico with Anita, and we lost touch. He would be over a hundred years old now if he is still living ... which is very possible because his mother lived to be 107. God bless you Henry and Anita!)

• • •

CHAPTER 53

"TROUBLE IN PARADISE"

Does everything go super-smooth after becoming a born-again Christian? It didn't for me. I was absolutely thrilled to be experiencing a completely new life ... a life that was about exactly the opposite of my previous one. It was a huge adventure that was producing positive new results. From the moment I asked Christ into my heart, things changed forever. The only problem was, that everything didn't become perfect immediately. I might have Jesus in my life, but I was a far shot from being truly "Christ-like", which should be the goal of every Christian. We all fail, and the best thing we can do is admit our part in the deal. We can then humbly ask God to forgive us.

I had done that with my past life, but to my greater disappointment I continued to fail in many ways. Debbie had gone along with the initial conversion to Christ for my sake. She prayed the prayer right along with Glenn and myself. Many months later she said that she truly asked Jesus into her life, and I was surprised, because I thought she already had. I knew that we both still had a lot of baggage that we brought into the marriage, and it was going to be a challenge. But, I also believed that God was going to keep doing miracles for us. I definitely wanted us to have a happy marriage.

One of the initial problems was that Debbie felt I married her because God told me to marry her ... not because I wanted to. That was a hard one for me to answer to, because it was true in many ways, but not the whole truth. I did honestly love Debbie, and want the best for her. I appreciated all that she was offering of her life to me, and I was fully committed to her through thick and thin. At the same time, I did solidly believe that our relationship had the supernatural stamp of God on it. We had had so many highs and lows coming out of the drug world, along with our dysfunctional family backgrounds ... that (prior to becoming a Christian) I would have never given us much of a chance at marriage. That was also true. But that equation of certain defeat changed when I felt God had brought us together.

No matter how I framed it, she still didn't feel like I truly loved her. From my perspective, when someone is consistently throwing negatives at you, it is hard to show love even when you want to. I wasn't mature enough to love her unconditionally like Jesus does us. Debbie is one of the most intelligent, sensitive, and creative people I ever met. At the same time she is just as headstrong and stubborn as me. I hate to say it, but in our past relationship before we got married, whenever we butted heads, I would absolutely control the situation ... or be gone. I treated her terrible during those times, and didn't really care if she liked it or not. I wanted peace in the camp or get out. It was the only way I could deal with her. She responded to that kind of treatment with a couple years of chasing after me. It's a pattern in many relationships. She seemed to love it, and could not take no for an answer.

Now that we were married in a Christian marriage, and I was really trying ... I couldn't use that previous brand of conflict-resolution, and I was pretty miserable when we bickered. We both had tempers, but now I didn't win so easily. She wrote me a letter one time and said ... "I want the old Roger back ... the Roger who lived for the moment!" (The truth is, if that Roger were still around we wouldn't have lasted ten minutes as husband and wife.)

Nevertheless, I continued to diligently try to make our marriage work, and Debbie did too. She really just wanted me to love her and put her number one, but I was failing to meet that basic need in her life. I don't recommend that the first thing a person does after coming out of the drug culture and crime ... is to get married as a baby-Christian. We got hit with all kinds of obstacles. One was finances. Debbie came from a pretty wealthy New York Jewish background. Her divorced mother was furious about our marriage, and wrote ... "I will never speak to your father again for flying out there and giving some semblance of legitimacy to this marriage!"

In addition to pressures from home, for most of our past relationship I either had a lot of money from dealing drugs, or a lot of free time to live in tree houses, or hitch cross-country. Now I was working and

Fire On the Mountain

making three dollars and something an hour. It was hard. Debbie got a job also and commuted to L.A. She was also trying. Her mother wrote and ridiculed our financial situation, and offered Debbie lucrative alternatives if she moved back to New York. I didn't want anything to do with it. When she learned that Debbie was pregnant she totally blew a cork, and said in another letter ... "Why didn't you do something about this pregnancy? If you get pregnant again I'll come out there myself with a meat hook!"

In spite of these pressures and others we still plugged away and had some good times mixed in. Debbie liked Ernesto and I took her to Mexico many times. We also both love San Diego, would stop in at Maggie's house a few times, and make the rounds in Ocean Beach. One day while we were driving on the freeway in San Diego, I mentioned something about Paula, Steve's wife. Debbie said ... "I hate to say it, but I think Paula is an evil person."

I said, "She definitely can be, but that's not really Paula. Down deep I think she is like a little girl. What she really needs is love."

Exactly when I said that, a car in the next lane had a customized license plate that said ... "FOR SURE'.

I told Debbie ... "Look at that license plate next to us ... What Paula needs is love ... . . FOR SURE!"

I didn't make too big a deal of it, but it fit perfectly, and I had been attending coincidental graduate school for years now. I guess Debbie just thought I was borderline crazy. She is a very quiet person and often hard to read. But, that was the first license plate that I thought might contain a little exclamation point from God. After all, he was answering my prayers and questions in all kinds of ways. If he wants to communicate through the Bible, or through a preacher, or radio program, or through an angel, or donkey, I guess he can use anything ... even customized license plates. The real question is ... "Does God really interact with us in an everyday way ... where the rubber meets the road!"

Anyway, over the months ahead I would see numerous coincidental license plates that perfectly fit the situation, or prayer, or thought. I spend a lot of time driving in total solitude. A divinely placed license plate at seventy plus miles per hour can quickly break up the boredom. At the same time I didn't run my life by these little "signs". Many of them were humorous and confirmational like the first one. Most Christians would not necessarily think you're crazy if you said that God answered your prayer with a Scripture verse or maybe even a dream ... but when I mentioned that God gave me a license plate, they would crack up ... and definitely give the high eyebrow. I stopped mentioning my little Morris Code with heaven ... but I told God ... "your way **is** the highway ... keep it coming any way you want!"

Well, our own beautiful baby girl was born on January 29th, 1977 in Tarzana, California and she was perfect. I also had something very special happen on the way home from the hospital that early morning after her birth, which I'll share in a bit. When my baby daughter Denielle was only a few months old, I reluctantly agreed to take up her grandmothers' offer, and move to Manhattan, New York. Supposedly, my mother-in-law promised even more things, like buying us a loft, connecting me with a job, and a high paying position for Debbie in her company. I really-really didn't want to leave California, but was willing to give New York City a try for the sake of my family.

Debbie went ahead first, and a couple months later I followed. I had to wind up affairs in California. Things like making provision for my horse Kimo Jo, and my dog, which just had eight incredible puppies. My female Alaskan malamute had a date with a huge Saint Bernard on a visit to the City of Refuge in Mexico. What a neat mixture. Each pup was totally unique and **huge**. I found homes for a couple of the pups. Rev. Glenn kept the rest, including Onimy, and found homes for them after I left. My friend Big John Schultise went partners with me on my stallion, and we moved him back to Topanga Canyon from Newbury Park near Thousand Oaks. I parked my old Ford van at a friend's place, and boarded a jet to the Big Apple.

My previous stay in Flushing, New York in the borough of Queens didn't turn out so hot. This move didn't do a whole lot better. I made my way directly from the airport to the 55th floor of the Empire State Building to meet with Debbie at her mother's firm. It was great at first, however, there was no loft, no job connections ... and I daily took a graffiti covered subway to a job I found in Brooklyn selling imported frame moldings to art galleries and frame shops all over New York City. Her mother did pull some political strings, and was able to get Debbie's name moved up to the top of a seven-month list for a government subsidized fancy apartment. She got in, in about a week instead of seven months. The apartment was way up high in a modern building, located right in Manhattan, overlooking one of the rivers that caught on fire. I actually liked the job I found, but hated the herds of people on every sidewalk, the continuous honking horns, and concrete piled into the sky. It's totally unnatural to stack up that many people in such a small place. The whole city reminds me of a glorified La Mesa.

After about two months, a blowup with Debbie, and an "appointment" with her mother ... I informed them all ... "If Debbie wants to be married to me, then she needs to come back to California. Thanks for the help ... but no thanks."

The subject of my religious commitment was the hot topic, and her mother told me in our meeting, "It doesn't bother me that President Carter talks to God. It bothers me that he claims that God talks back!" She continued, "And then there is this business about the devil and demons ... there is no such thing!"

I told her I used to believe the same way, but was proved otherwise. She didn't want to hear anything, but offered to pay my way back to California. I declined her offer. My Apache Indian friend wired me bus money to Ohio. The day I attempted to leave New York City a huge ice storm hit and all transportation was **totally** shut down. I remember walking around the paralyzed metropolis in a freezing snowstorm, praying to God for wisdom and direction. I stopped on a nearby bridge and felt so confused with mixed emotions. Was I doing the right thing? I could see the Empire State Building where Debbie worked a short distance away, and in the distance I could see the Twin Towers. At that moment, it seemed like my whole life was a storm. "God ... what to do?"

The weather broke, and once again a Greyhound bus attempted to deliver me from the huge concrete jungle. This time it was successful. Good-by New York City. I was definitely sad, but finally confident that I was making the right move. In Ohio, I stayed awhile, but soon my X-wife Nancy had me served with legal papers and I was thrown in the Sandusky County Jail for back child support. "Holy cow!" When it rains ... it pours ... or turns to freezing windblown sleet!

The judge gave me ten days. I submitted to the whole ordeal, because I deserved it and more. It was weird when the young jailer who walked me up an ancient looking set of jailhouse steps to the cellblock, turned out to be one of my old schoolmates from Ross High. Some kids grow up to be good guys, or maybe even cops ... and then there are the bad apples. I realized that God forgave me for everything in my past ... but there are still consequences. I was continuing to "pay up" ... to reap what I had sown. I reminded myself ... "If you would have been caught for half of the things you did, you would probably be in prison until your seventy-years old. Ten days is nothing."

There were about twelve or so guys locked up with me, and they had an on-going euchre tournament happening every day. I love playing cards. I jumped right in and had a great time. I didn't get preachy with my fellow misfits, but when I silently prayed over my meals, they started asking questions. It was cool. In my spare time I wrote up a business plan to start a pool maintenance company in California to give to my dad. Frito-Lay had just bought out his independent distributorship after a five-year-long legal battle with them. He was looking to do something new. I got real close to the guy who bunked in my cell and drew a pencil portrait for him, which he really liked. I signed it "JC loves you". He told me that a farmer would be coming the next day. He said ... "He comes in here and does like a Bible study every week. They say he's been coming in here for years."

Sure enough, the next day the farmer showed up with his Bible and interrupted our euchre game. I really respected him for what he was trying to do. You could tell he was sincere, and also really tell that he was a farmer, with his big hands and farmer tan like my grandpa. (My grandpa's face was as brown as my Apache friend, but his mostly bald-head was as white as a Caucasian baby's butt, from wearing his hat all day on the tractor. There was a perfectly straight line across his forehead between the two colors.) One of the other prisoners said to the farmer concerning me ... "You don't need to get this new guy converted, he already talks to God."

The farmer looked over at me and asked my name. "I'm Roger Sachs."

He looked surprised and said, "Sachs ... who is your father? I know all of the Sachs family."

"Carl Sachs is my dad."

He thought a second, and then in his steady deliberate way he said ...

"I guess I don't know him. I know Howard and Bill and Don."

I told him ... "They are my uncles. My dad was the youngest in the family and quit farming, so that's probably why you don't know him. So you come in to the jail and share the Bible? That's neat."

"Yes, for years now, every week. I do what I can." (God has his servants everywhere!)

As the middle-aged farmer talked with me he mentioned a wild friend of mine from Fremont that committed suicide. After my own rebellious journey led me to the cross of Christ, I always planned to write this particular friend a letter, or somehow communicate the kinship and connecting feelings I had toward him. Jesus has a special love for the lambs that stray away from the flock and get lost. He left the ninety-nine to find the one. I was real lost but he found me. I wanted Jesus to find and rescue all my friends, and family, and relatives who might have taken a wrong turn, or been trapped by the sneaky tricks and lies of the enemy camp.

I never got around to writing that letter, or tracking Jason down by phone, and I was shocked to hear the news that he committed suicide. What a tragedy. I am heartsick. I am also so sick of all forms of procrastination in my own life! I wanted to talk to him ... but now it's too late. The message of Christ is too important to put off. It's my motivation for this book ... for my life. Who knows how much time each of us has left? How many people do you know ... that are gone? I still have hope for my friend, and know in my heart that suicide is not the unforgivable sin. Remember, I came close in that department too, and have great empathy. Only God knows exactly what was going on with Jason, and only he has the ultimate power over each of our souls and destinations. All you hard-core theologians ... "get a life!"

In the midst of sorting out my own troubles, I still had so many questions for God. A jail cell is a good place to pray. My number one argument against Christianity had been, that I could not believe that God would send all non-Christians to hell forever point blank. I will probably get a lot of flak from religious folk, but I don't think it is as clear-cut as my childhood preacher had declared ... holding up his Bible. What about all the billions of people who lived before Jesus came to earth to rescue us? What about all the aborted babies? What about a lot of things? There are theories, but no real solid answers that I can see. They say that the three days Jesus was in the grave he separated the sheep from the goats ... that's one interpretation of several scriptures. There are lots of other scriptures that talk about the subject ... which in my mind offers "reasonable doubt" about the destination of unbelievers. The Bible warns that no scripture is of a "private interpretation". We need to look at the whole counsel of God.

What I do believe is that God left the subject a little foggy on purpose, because he don't want us to focus on any other way to get into his family or his Kingdom than through his Son and the radical, costly, unbelievable sacrifice on the cross. But the Bible talks about a person in Romans who never heard the Gospel ... that God writes his law upon his conscious ... and will judge him accordingly. It talks about Jesus being the judge ... and about "those who were **judged** worthy" to enter into his Kingdom. It is not all that clear cut about who makes it to heaven. **Jesus also says things like ... "Marvel not at this: for the hour is coming, in the which all that are in the graves shall hear his voice, and shall come forth; they that have done good, unto the resurrection of life; and they that have done evil, unto the resurrection of damnation. I can of mine own self do nothing: as I hear, I judge: and my judgment is just; because I seek not mine own will, but the will of the Father which hath sent me."**

What is totally clear-cut to me is that Jesus is God the Son who became a man. He took our judgment on a cross, and if we receive him and the free gift of salvation ... we get born again, and are **"passed" from judgment to life.** We no longer get judged for salvation because he took our place. He took our judgment. The Bible is also clear that he is either going to be our savior, or our judge. It says that "all judgment" has been given to him. This is where my common sense kicks in. From everything I have learned of Jesus, and everything I have experienced since receiving him ... I have learned to trust him. Jesus is without flaw, and I believe he is going to be totally fair with each and every living soul ... including my friend Jason ... not according to people's version of fair and loving and just ... but His version.

He has numbered every hair on our head according to the Bible. It says his thoughts toward us are more than the sand at Malibu or the stars in the sky. I don't know what has happened to all the unbelievers who ever lived, or ever will ... but I can't say for sure they are all in hell. I totally don't believe that. I'm trusting the King of Kings with their souls. He is the judge, not any of us. Nevertheless, I sure wouldn't have wanted to be judged for my life. Thank God he has taken away my sins "as far as the east is from the west". I know for sure ... that every born again believer is going to rule and reign forever with Christ in an eternal Kingdom. Don't play Russian roulette with eternity ... by trusting or hoping in your own goodness, or anything besides Jesus!

• • •

I did my ten days. As a matter of fact, when they came to release me from the cellblock, I didn't want to go. Our euchre tournament had become real exciting. But, freedom is better than winning a card game. From my short stay in Ohio, my mother gave me her secret "nest-egg" to start over in California. I was totally broke. She told me she prayed about it, and had total peace that I take the money. What a blessing! It was enough to fly back to California, and get me started in the swimming pool business. Eventually, years later I went from my own maintenance company to obtaining a C-53 state contractors license, and then building fancy custom gunite swimming pools. My dad even sold his properties in Ohio and went partners with me in California in 1979. My handwritten business plan that detailed the pool maintenance business had caught a big fish. Some good things can still be written up in a jail cell. (At the end of this chapter is a newspaper photo of a big fish my dad caught in Florida).

Many good things were happening, but some heartbreaking things also. Prior to my parents moving out west, Debbie came back to California and we gave it another try. I had previously rented us a really neat little house in Santa Ana about two miles from Disneyland. I had moved from Topanga to Orange County to work for a couple pool contractors, putting my time in to qualify for the state exam. That was my goal. I was making a little over five bucks an hour working as a pool plumber. We attended church at Calvary Chapel Costa Mesa. Everything was going pretty good for a year or so, but not really. We got some marriage counseling. However, before long with the encouragement of her mother, Debbie decided to call it quits ... and it was Thomas Tears time. That was the name of my first lawyer who helped me represent myself "in-pro-per". He was all I could afford.

By the time Denielle Marie Sachs was approaching three years old, Debbie had filed for divorce, taken Denielle out of state back to New York, and we were in the midst of a nasty custody battle. Her mother actually hired a famous Century City lawyer, who had just won the Lee Marvin palimony case. Back in New York Debbie went to work in her mother's public relations firm again. In the legal papers her "side" characterized me as being "an alleged drug smuggler, college-dropout, sometimes pool maintenance person, who had a religious experience and personality change, and now claims that God speaks to him on the license plates of cars on the Los Angeles freeways." (Hey, what can I say ... sometimes the truth is a little bizarre.)

Nevertheless, I eventually won custody in California, when the court ordered us both to get psychiatric evaluations. Debbie again fled the state with Denielle, instead of getting the evaluation. I won the case but lost my daughter. A slime ball lawyer back in New York filed for custody in that state, twisting even the court record of the judge's ruling in California ... and I didn't see my daughter again for over seventeen years. I hired a lawyer in New York, but couldn't fight them from California. I was already about bankrupt. Each state has it's own laws, and don't recognize any other state's family law. It's a crummy system.

I was completely robbed of Denielle's entire childhood, and she was robbed of a father. On top of that she has been poisoned against me, told all sorts of half-truths, and is to this day afraid of me. The one time I saw her as an adult, she mentioned that she has seen the court papers (from her mother's side) accusing me of all kinds of things ... some true, and some absolute lies and distortions, but she has never to this day seen or heard both sides. The judge that the New York lawyer tried to paint as an "Orange County super-conservative WASP" (white - Anglo-Saxon - protestant) ... is actually a Jewish judge who is very fair and competent. Divorce is such an absolute disaster. Everyone loses ... especially the kids. I have great empathy now for the people caught up in heart wrenching custody battles, kidnappings, and other battles over the children of divorce. I can only pray for my little girl, and can't force myself on her. The few days I saw her when I flew her out here after seventeen years, ended in her saying ... "This is a mistake."

Sometimes there is definitely trouble in paradise. It is one of the most hurtful things in my life to have lost my daughter. She is a beautiful young woman now ... and I continue to pray for her. Thank God that He has taken care of her through the years. I know Debbie loves Denielle, and I'm grateful for that. I am tempted to "state my case" in much more detail, and try to come out a late winner, but I have already lost this battle. My only comfort is that God knows every bit of the truth, and I can only trust him. I do believe and trust his promise that "all things work together for good to those who love God and are called according to his purposes." Somehow this will work out for good.

My parents actually moved to California a few weeks after Debbie returned to New York for good. My dad had contemplated the move out here for a long time, and had finally sold the house in Ohio and made the plunge. Too bad they missed having a closer relationship with their granddaughter by just a couple weeks. My mother is such a loving person, and my dad is a very loving grouch. It might have even helped our marriage having their support ... but who knows ... only God.

My dad and his big fish

CHAPTER 54

"THE FBI LIED"

When Ernesto and Bertha left the City of Refuge they returned to Tijuana. It was 1979. Ernesto had spent two years preparing himself to reach out to the lost and hurting, and was determined to do just that regardless of the obstacles. There were a lot of them. Right after graduating from the Bible School, the whole ministry folded. It was a shock. Somehow they were surviving, even though their mentor from the City of Refuge was no longer in the picture, as had been originally designed. The director told them ... "You're on your own."

They found a cheap, cheap apartment, and began their life living together as husband and wife, along with little two-year-old Beronica. Apache Henry and myself would chip in with as much as we could, but I was just making wages, and Henry survived on his social security retirement. Ernesto took a lot of flack from almost every direction for not immediately going out and finding a normal job. He was positive his job was to serve God full time ... living by faith.

He began by simply walking the streets. One day a huge, muscular man walked up to him and said ... "Do you remember me?"

Ernesto did remember him, because he had badly beaten the man up over some drug related business years ago. At the time the guy was about nineteen years old, but he had grown up considerably.

He told Ernesto ... "I have been waiting a long time to run into you again. I'm not afraid of you any more."

Ernesto replied ... "I'm not afraid of you either. In fact, I'm not the same because God has set me free, and delivered me from fear. Before, I had to keep up an image, and never show weakness, but the truth is I was always afraid. Jesus is my strength now."

The guy looked at Ernesto for a while, and said ... "I heard you were around again, and that you had religion. I didn't believe it, but maybe you're for real. I'm happy for you. I'll see you around."

Ernesto started going back inside La Mesa to visit Johnny and other friends. He witnessed, started a Bible study, and stood tall for Christ, shoulder to shoulder with some of the most dangerous criminals in the world. I had been visiting John myself on a pretty regular basis while Ernesto was in Bible school. Sometimes Ernesto and I became like a "good cop … bad cop" spiritual tag team. Ernesto would usually play the bad cop, telling his former friends that they need to … "turn or burn". I would soften the blows with the additional truth of God's incredible grace, patience, forgiveness, and loving kindness. Both aspects are true.

Johnny was doing a long stretch in La Mesa, and I got the bright idea of putting some of the prisoners to work making Christian art and handcrafts. There was a lot of talent inside La Mesa. I figured it would be a combination of honest enterprise, and a good Christian witness. Johnny got real excited and before long he had all kinds of things going. He even had me working with the dangerous new Cavo after Fitch got killed, because he controlled the furniture factory inside the prison. John found a couple artistic cons who made us JESUS belt buckles out of beautifully carved abalone shell, cast in resin and hand polished. I sold lots of those, but they took a long time to produce. We made framed scripture verses that were colorful hand weavings. They also made lots of hand carved frames and other products for us.

It was a good deal and fun. In addition to business, John would take us all over La Mesa to people who needed prayer. He really cares about people, and is a human communication devise. He surprised me, and told me that he had prayed to receive Jesus with an X-con turned preacher named Nick Cadina years ago in a prison in the States. John said … "But I get side tracked too easy. I need to be around people like you and Ernesto. When I get out of here maybe I can help you guys. I know a lot of people. I'd also like you to talk to one of my brothers. He lives in Lake Elsinore, and I worry a lot about him!" (I did spend major time with his brother, Ernest, bringing him into the prison to visit John, and sharing Christ to the best of my ability. Ernest sadly died a few years back, but I'm confident he is with Jesus.)

Apache Henry came in the prison with me, and helped us minister to the needs. He prayed for an old pot farmer who had both of his legs amputated. The man looked like death warmed over laying in his caraca. La Mesa blew Henry's mind. It blew everyone's mind. I took my dad inside the prison a couple times. Johnny had a little tiny restaurant among his other prison endeavors, and my dad was amused by his hustling personality. John fixed us a great lunch and a strong cup of coffee.

Together, my dad and I talked my mom into visiting La Mesa with us. As my little mid-western mother was getting processed in, with the backdrop of a clamoring mob of raggedy prisoners behind the iron gates, the guard asked her name. She was so petrified that she told me later … "I couldn't even remember my name. He asked me in Spanish first, but I didn't know what he was saying. Then he said in English, 'What is your name?' I stood there with my mouth hanging open, and couldn't even say my name! I was never so scared in my whole life! Your friend Johnny is funny and very charming … but I'll never go back to that place. Forget it!"

Inside the prison I became friends with a young guy, who was the resident Catholic nun's runner. This nun is an American lady who made La Mesa her life work after raising six kids. She has become very well known for her work in the notorious prison. I admired her courage, but was a little confused when I heard she also had the cigarette concession for the whole prison. How did that fit? Her runner would do errands for her, and his name was Louis.

One day I asked Louis, (who is from L.A. and speaks perfect English), what he was doing time for in La Mesa. He told me … "I would come to Mexico, and we had some real good drug connections. The Federalies finally busted me by myself with some drugs, but the way it all happened, they knew I had to be with someone else. They took me to a building and tortured me. I wouldn't tell them who my connection was, or who was with me. They knew I was lying. It was my brother who was with me. No way was I going to turn in my brother. They did all kinds of things to me, but finally they took a pair of pliers and pulled off one of my nipples. Then they did the other one."

Louis pulled up his shirt to show me his chest. He had two healed up slits where his nipples used to be. It still makes me cringe and hurt like crazy to just think about it. I would always go look for Louis amongst the maze of thousands of prisoners, and we became friends. I was even more surprised that he had absolutely no concept of what a born again Christian experience was all about. What did the nun talk about all those years? I explained that it's not simply going to church and trying to be good. It's about personally receiving Jesus into our hearts and giving him our lives. It's about asking for forgiveness and making a trade with God. He took the sentence for us ... we get His life. When you realize that's the real scoop ... it's a no brainer. However, we can't earn God's salvation like so many religious people try to do. I asked if he ever sincerely said a prayer and asked Christ into his life. He told me ... "Not really."

In the middle of La Mesa one day Louis prayed to receive Christ. He was already a handsome young guy in his mid-twenties ... but now he glowed. About a year later he asked if I could come down the next week because he was getting released after something like six years inside. I drove down and had the privilege of driving him back to America. It was a Sunday and on the drive up north, I asked if he wanted to catch our Sunday evening service at my church, which at the time was Calvary Chapel Yorba Linda. I told him that after church I would drive him the rest of the way to L.A. He agreed, and we ended up getting in another long conversation about God and the Bible on the way to church.

We finally made it to the "church in a gymnasium". At the evening service that night the pastor John Wimber preached exactly what we had just talked about in the car ... **exactly**. He even used the same scriptures that I had mentioned to Louis, and my friend thought that I must have known what he was going to preach about that evening ... but believe me I was as shocked as Louis. Shocked and filled with joy when the Holy Spirit does stuff like that! Everything was the same. It's so cool.

AGENT AIKEN

I got to know the guy in charge of the prison ministry at Calvary Chapel Costa Mesa. His name is Rodney Lewis, and I told him about Ernesto. Almost immediately he said ... "It sounds really neat what God is doing with you guys, but how can your friend have any kind of lasting ministry when he is an escaped convict here in the States? He needs to clear his name, before God is going to bless his ministry. I'm positive about that. Do you think he's open to turning himself in?"

"I don't know. Why don't we go down and deliver that message to him. Maybe it's the right time for him to get squared away legally on this side of the border. I know he wants to do God's will ... all the way ... so let's go see what he says."

The next weekend we headed for T.J. and found Ernesto. I introduced Rodney and after a few basic pleasantries, he laid the hard news on my friend. Ernesto got real serious, and said ... "If the Lord wants me to pay my time to the States, then I have to do it."

We left Ernesto, and on the way back to the border, as we drove through poverty on the left, and poverty on the right, Rodney said to me ... "Before we came today I doubted if your partner would turn himself in on an escape. He might do some serious time ... like his original sentence plus a few years. I was really surprised the way he responded. He didn't bat an eye when he figured it was a message from the Lord. If he keeps that kind of heart, the Lord is going to use Ernesto big time."

Within days of that weekend my dad and I were doing a repair job on one of the pools on our pool route, when the homeowner invited us to stay for the evening meal. During the meal one thing led to another, and I asked the man of the house what he did for a living. He said that he worked for the FBI. His name is George Aiken, and he had been an FBI agent for over twenty years. I mentioned that I was now a Christian, but that I had been on the other side of his fence prior to that. His wife was a really sweet lady, who had fixed us this awesome meal, and she started asking me a hundred questions. She practically drug out my whole story. My dad had never even heard most of the things I had done, or the details of my conversion, so it was revelation time for him, as well as for the Aiken family.

It turned out that they were super committed Christians themselves. George was even a deacon in his church. When I told him about Ernesto wanting to turn himself in for escaping from Lompoc, he said ... "Why don't I go down to Mexico with you and meet Ernesto. I can probably help a little, or at least make sure he gets in front of the right people over here. He might have a problem at the border, which I can help with. I can't guarantee any help with his sentence, but sometimes every little bit helps." (What a coincidence that God would send us a Christian FBI agent!)

On the drive to Tijuana I asked George what it was like on some of his dangerous cases. He told me, "I've been on some pretty scary busts, with some dangerous characters, but the most respect I have is for the every day black and white police officer. They drive around in marked cars, wearing a uniform, which really is like a huge target for every nut or psychopath running around out there. When we take someone down, it is often after six months of surveillance with a five-man team. We know everything about the guy, including his X mother-in-law's favorite color. We know every move he makes, and we pick our time, and move in with maximum force.

The regular police never know what they're up against from moment to moment. I have a ton of respect for them. It's just like the police officer patrolling Ocean Beach recently, when a nut rode up to his patrol car on a bicycle, and shot him in the face. The officer probably thought the guy was asking for directions, before he pulled the gun out and shot him point blank in the head. It happens all the time ... things like that, and the young officers usually have a wife and two or three young kids left behind. It's no wonder that some police get cynical after awhile, and might use excessive force when the adrenalin gets pumping.

I remember this one particular case that I worked, when we went after a really well organized murderous bunch of criminals. It took months of surveillance. Finally we busted down their door on a second story apartment, and took them all into custody. They had all kinds of firepower inside, but we did it so fast that they never had a chance to get to their weapons. I was fine during the whole operation, but after it was all over I went out to the bushes and heaved my guts out. That happened to me a couple times over my twenty years."

We made it to Mexico, and George really liked Ernesto. He was struck with Ernesto's humility and commitment to serve God. He looked around and saw the poverty, and conditions that Ernesto and his young family were living in. It really moved him and he told me ... "I'll set things up for Ernesto to come in, and we'll do whatever we can to help him. It's an awesome thing to see what God can do in a person's life. When I bring him across the border, let's give him a week or so before we actually take him into custody. I'd like you and Ernesto to come share at my church, and tell your story. Can you guys do that?"

I didn't want to, and told George ... "I'm terrible at public speaking. It scares me more than witnessing to a caraca full of cutthroat murderers in La Mesa. I don't know why. I think I need a little more healing or something, but anyway I'm no good at it. My heart starts beating a hundred miles per hour, my hands sweat, and one time I went totally blank at my church in Thousand Oaks. I swore I'd never do that again! I want to do anything and everything for God, but I don't think public speaking is my gift."

A week or so later, Ernesto said his good-bys to Bertha and little Beronica, and met George and another FBI agent at the border. They came directly to my parent's home in Tustin, and Ernesto and I had a neat week of freedom together. George finally talked us into coming to his church that Sunday and told me ... "Most everyone is afraid of public speaking, but our pastor is a great interviewer. You won't have to prepare anything, and you and Ernesto can come up together, and just answer his questions. **It will be easy.**"

We both agreed, but it still wasn't easy. The FBI lied. Ernesto didn't have any trouble. He was a little nervous, but I about had another panic attack. My face turned red, my brain stopped working, and I guess I made a little bit of sense answering his questions into the microphone. My parents and a bunch of friends and family were all there along with hundreds of other people. When it was over, I was super angry with myself for agreeing in the first place ... and for the next decade would avoid public speaking like the plague. "What can I say? Sorry Lord!"

CHAPTER 55

"ANIMAL"

When FBI agent George Aiken finally took Ernesto in, George thought some of his connections in the criminal justice world would be able to help, but immediately Ernesto was lost in the system. They shipped him off to LA County jail first, where he was just a number with no special treatment. He was another illegal alien with a record and a violent past. In fact, Ernesto later told us that during the thirteen days he was in LA County, he was treated worse than any prison or jail that he was ever in. He finally was sent to Terminal Island Federal Penitentiary. It was unclear how long his sentence was to be. After I found out where they sent him, I filled out the paperwork to get on his visitor's list. I was glad it was Terminal Island, because it was less than an hour away for me. I was able to visit almost every Friday.

I'll never forget the first time I drove across the big bridge in Long Beach to Terminal Island. I was by myself and finally found the large modern prison. It was nothing like La Mesa. "T.I." was state of the art … La Mesa was "controlled insanity". I parked my pickup truck in the parking lot. There was a van that pulled in a couple spaces from me and several men got out. This one huge guy about six-foot-six yelled over at me … "Hey, what does that sticker on your window mean?"

I had a bumper sticker on my rear window that said "JESUS LIVES". I told the guy it meant that I was a Christian.

He said … "What are you doing here?"

"I came to visit a friend of mine."

The man walked over and introduced himself … "I'm Jim Tucker and do you see all those stickers on the back of my van? I guess that probably makes me one of you Jesus nuts too. We are going in to the Chapel service, and this is my team. This guy over here is Ernie Hollands, and his criminal nickname was "The Cockroach". He's giving his testimony tonight. I did about twenty-seven years inside some of these institutions, and they just called me "ANIMAL". You won't be able to get into the chapel service unless we get you clearance, but here's my card. We have a chapter inside called "Convicts for Christ" and I'll keep an eye out for your friend. What's his name? Is he saved? Come see me at our ministry in Fullerton. I have an office and a thrift store at the address on the card."

Little did I know but for the next twenty-four years, I would work off and on with this huge man who everyone called "Big Jim". That first evening at the prison I visited with Ernesto inside the T.I. locked down visiting area, and showed him the card Big Jim gave me. There were some infamous inmates in the room that evening with their visits. I saw the doctor who supposedly killed his wife. His case had made T.V. coverage for months. The multi-millionaire Delorian guy was there also with some of his family and lawyer types. His case had made international news. I told Ernesto about the Convicts for Christ deal that was inside the prison. As the days and weeks flew by, Ernesto plugged right in with the "Convicts for Christ" chapter, and he also became lifelong friends with Jim Tucker.

Right after Ernesto was sent to Terminal Island Federal Penitentiary, I went back to Tijuana to visit Johnny in La Mesa, and to check on Ernesto's wife, Bertha. That's when I found out that Bertha was pregnant again. Ernesto flipped out and was real upset when he found out. He would have never turned himself in while she was pregnant or with a newborn. God worked it out so that he didn't find out ahead of time, and then God worked out another total miracle. Ernesto was released after six and a half months in Terminal Island, which is unheard of for an escapee. His second child with Bertha, little Ernesto David Hernandez was born on Nov 3, 1980 only two months after his release.

Ernesto was finally a free man on both sides of the border, and as our work with prisoners and re-hab ministry developed, with the help of God and radical friends like Big Jim Tucker, he was granted a passport and visa, which is also unheard of for a deported felon. Not only does Ernesto have a free pass to America, but also today he is part of the San Diego Chaplain's association. In Mexico he has a 40-acre re-hab ranch and a program inside La Mesa as well as in the new prison near

Tecate. He and his team are inside the huge new concrete facility five days a week. He has worked inside La Mesa for over twenty years. In fact, Ernesto became so effective in prison work that the warden at San Quentin asked Ernesto to come to America, to help stop a war that was breaking out between two Mexican factions inside that prison. The Mexican American prisoners were pitted against the south of the border Mexican nationals.

They put Ernesto on closed circuit TV, and he told me he don't even remember what he said after he left the prison. However, whatever he said worked so well that they used the video in other prisons to stop violence. The warden at San Quentin showed his appreciation by having a car completely remodeled inside the prison workshop. They rebuilt the motor, reupholstered the inside, and completely repainted the car. The aging car was as good as new, and then they presented it to Ernesto for his ministry work in Mexico. What an incredible change in one person's life. Ernesto was a minor plague to two nations in the past ... but now he was stopping riots in high-tech maximum-security prisons. That bolt of lightning out of the sky was no coincidence. God has his ways, and timing, and chosen vessels.

While Nixon was still president I helped Johnny get included on the recently enacted prisoner exchange program. He had several years in La Mesa left on his Mexican sentence. For a long time he didn't want to apply for the transfer to America, because John thought he would probably get extradited to Nevada on some old crimes, and might actually get more time than he was doing in La Mesa. However, he finally decided to take the risk. Miraculously, the American authorities totally released him after a few days in a San Diego jail cell. It blew his mind. He hopped on a bus, and a couple hours later called me up from a phone booth in downtown Santa Ana.

"Hey Roger ... Guess where I am?"

"Did they send you to Vegas? What's going on?"

"No ... they cut me loose. I can't believe it. I'm in downtown Santa Ana. Can you come pick me up?"

I was totally shocked. Immediately I jumped in my truck and within a few minutes picked up a smiling Johnny Moustache. At the time Big Jim Tucker had put me in charge of one of his half way houses, and I brought Johnny into the home, which we had named Freedom Manor.

It was great. I wanted John to stay out of trouble so bad. Jim also spent some personal time with the little X-convict. Johnny is about half the size of Big Jim, but the one thing they had in common was decades of incarceration in about every maximum-security prison in California.

Nevertheless, Johnny only stayed with us for less than a week, and he was back into the wind and up to no good. Unfortunately, he had run into some of his old friends. Sometimes it can be **very** disappointing working with long-term offenders ... but at the same time, God uses every kind word, every bit of friendship, and especially every bit of truth that's shared in love from his Word, the Bible. The scriptures say ... "The Word of God never returns void." It always has an impact, one way or the other. (I didn't see Johnny again for a couple years, but he keeps popping up in my life until this very day. He did a couple more stretches in prison, but is now married to a wonderful lady named Ernistina, and they live in Tecate, Mexico. He is off parole and doing real good ... thank God.)

They wrote a book about Big Jim Tucker named "Three Gates To Hell". He has one of the most radical, heartbreaking, and ultimately victorious stories ever told. No one thought a person like Big Jim could ever change ... but God has his ways. The book is good in many ways, but after I got to know Jim real well he told me ... "My wife doesn't even like the book."

Jim Tucker

I asked him ... "Why not?"

He explained ... "Well the ministry that published it, thought that people were not quite ready for all that happened with me. They told the basic story of my life. In fact the book did good. They say that thousands and thousands of copies were distributed or sold, but Virginia says they watered it down so much that ... 'it's not even Jim'. She don't like it, and besides that, I owe the publisher about six thousand dollars right now for copies that I give out in prisons and juvenile halls. The people I'm trying to help don't have any money!"

I worked with Big Jim for years and years. I learned so much about prison ministry, and re-hab, and not giving up on people. I saw the struggles he had to keep a large ministry going. I saw the sacrifices he made, and the cost it had to his family and his health. I saw his huge heart, and no-nonsense approach to everything. I respect him more than I can say. I saw his uneducated vocabulary, and childlike faith literally stun huge crowds at conventions. I also saw him stun and completely disarm a couple prisoners in the tiny passages of La Mesa prison in Mexico. He poured his heart out no matter where the Lord took him. He was booked for speaking engagements sometimes a year in advance. I witnessed the fruit of thousands of lives changed by this man's life.

Big Jim just died last year and I miss my friend terribly. Ernesto and I were with his family in the intensive care when he took his final breath. Big Jim was the first person I ever saw die, and leave this world as we held his hand … and I pray it's the last. Even Jesus wept, when he felt the human emotions that accompany the death of a friend … and this was when he knew he was going to physically raise Lazareth from the grave that very same hour. I know we will see Jim again soon enough … but it still hurts.

After Ernesto was released from Terminal Island, Jim's ministry, New Life Crusade, ordained him, and kick-started Ernesto's ministry in Mexico. Jim put me on his board of directors here in the States. We owe so much to this man. For the last several years of his life we worked closer than ever. Ernesto and I would drive to Riverside, California, pick Jim up, and have a special breakfast at his favorite Denny's restaurant each month like clockwork. He told us one morning at our big round breakfast table … "You know, everyone talks about the so called 'jailhouse conversion' … and how it lasts about the blink of an eye when we hit the streets. Well the three of us can show what success is. Jesus was not only able to catch us … **but he has been able to keep us** … which probably takes a bigger miracle! I have thirty-five years in Christ, and you two are catching up quick. That's real success!"

About a year before Jim died, we spent some very special personal times with another friend of ours who has dedicated his life to rescuing prisoners. His name is Frank Pica, and he was sent to prison forty some years ago. He had been part of a New York mafia family … and you don't quit the mafia. However, Frank got "born again" in prison, and Jesus not only opened the spiritual prison doors, but also gave him favor with his mafia associates. Miraculously they let him walk after his release. They told him … "You have always been a good soldier Frank. You did your time and kept your mouth shut. Now, we don't want to hear anymore about you … or your God … just disappear."

The whole story is another incredible testimony, which Frank is very tight-lipped about. He subsequently got as far away as he could from New York, and came to California. Years after moving here he was asked to join a ministry team to share with some prisoners. It was a one-time thing theoretically. However, after that first visit, the leaders informed him that it was their last day, and they felt Frank was supposed to take over the ministry. He was totally shocked and apprehensive.

Frank prayed for divine guidance and direction. God gave a green light, and for decades now Frank has developed a tremendously effective prison ministry throughout the West Coast. He has and still is leading hundreds and hundreds of souls to Christ almost single-handedly. While most citizens are fading into early retirement, this elderly "Christian soldier" is waging war on the enemy with all that he has left. It is inspiring! Outside of the prisons he as a re-hab ranch, sober-living houses, and a very effective program right here in Riverside County. He is doing a tremendous job. Jim Tucker not only wanted to help Ernesto more … but he also wanted to help Frank. The scripture is so very true … "the harvest is plentiful but the laborers are few."

Big Jim and I talked about Charles Tex Watson getting saved in prison. I vividly remember my co-worker at Adhor Farms telling me about the bloody scene that he witnessed on his milk route. I was very skeptical about Watson's conversion, and asked about his alleged conversion. Jim was convinced that he is a "for real" Christian. It was hard for me to imagine that God could forgive someone who committed crimes as horrible as this Manson family killer … but apparently he did. It should, in the final analysis, encourage everyone … that **if** we sincerely repent and turn to him … he can forgive anything. Many people believe they are too far gone to come to God. It's a lie of the devil. Charles Tex Watson and Carla Faye Tucker are both famous examples of the incredible transforming power of the cross. They are forgiven, but still have to face the consequences of their terrible crimes. Watson will never see daylight outside of prison walls … and the **glowing** Carla Faye was denied a stay of execution, by the then Governor George Bush. I strongly support the death penalty, and can't really fault President Bush on his decision ... but in Carla's case I would have commuted her sentence to life in prison without the possibility of parole. In the days before her execution she shined for Jesus ... and when the time came, she faced death with courage and incredible faith in her Savior. It was sobering, inspiring, convicting, and heart wrenching all at the same time.

Jim Tucker was such a huge blessing in our lives. He told me that the ministry that published his book gave him the rights back. He said ... "Why don't we re-do the book, because it's out of print now, and we'll put some feet to Ernesto's ministry and the ranch in Mexico.
Jim knew I had to finish this book first, but I told him ... "OK, but let's un-water down your story and tell it like it really was."
Jim heartily agreed, and he gave me the original manuscript to "Three Gates To Hell". It's sitting in a box in my file cabinet right now ... patiently waiting. Lord willing, I want to completely re-do, or at least re-name his story simply ... "ANIMAL".

Ernesto, Big Jim, Roger & my son John (in front)

CHAPTER 56

"SECOND CHANCES"

Probably the very best thing that can happen to anyone is to get a second chance. Some of us need seventy times seven chances. I've met a lot of people who messed their life up more than I had, but nevertheless, I did a pretty good job on my own. Between drug and alcohol abuse, dealing and legal problems, relationship breakdowns, family problems, guilt, anger, and suicide attempts ... I think I covered all the bases for screwing up. I had successfully failed at two marriages. In addition, I'm sure that my absence from the home had severely damaged my oldest children to say the least. Every kid deserves two loving parents. My two oldest never knew what that would be like, although Nancy, my first wife remarried. Unfortunately, her new husband had a terrible relationship with my son Troy, and the new stepfather hated me with a passion. There is nothing good about divorce ... especially for the kids.

I got a phone call from a young girl in Ohio when my son was sixteen years old. She said ... "Troy is in the hospital right now, but he is going to be OK. The kids at school found out he is gay, and he tried to commit suicide. They pumped out his stomach, and he wanted me to call, and tell you that he is coming to live with you in California." I spent years praying and trying to make up for my failures with my son. He is such a gifted and excellent person. He came to California and lived with me a couple times over the years, starting with that time when he was sixteen, but he has been in and out of the gay lifestyle most of his life, and almost died of AIDS several years back. Thank God some new medications have brought his T-cells back up to where they should be. We almost lost him. I have seen close up what the homosexual world has to offer its victims.

As I mentioned, my daughter in New York City is equally heartbreaking to me, although she is healthy and hopefully happy. She graduated from NYU and is smart as a whip. The last time I talked to Denielle on the phone was right after 911. For a couple days I didn't know if she was one of the victims in the Twin Towers. It was scary. I was so relieved when she finally answered her phone. She said her office was not that close to the towers, and also that she had taken a job in New Zealand. That was the last contact I've had with her, and now I don't even have a good phone number. I'm continuing to trust God with her life. Until a miracle happens, which I pray it will ... that's all I can do. There are so many broken families everywhere. It is so sad. Thank God he forgave me for my part in the breakdown. Without His forgiveness I don't think I could have handled the guilt.

In the aftermath of two divorces I stayed single for a long-long time. Enough was enough. From the time of my split with Debbie, it was about five years, which seemed like an eternity. I didn't even date for most of those years, which were right in the prime of life, the late twenties and early thirties. Instead, I threw myself into missionary work, and discovered that God can make the most of every season of our lives. During that time I worked with my Apache friend, Ernesto, and Big Jim Tucker. A single person can have one of the most rewarding lives **ever** serving God. I saw that firsthand, and experienced it in wonderful ways. Nevertheless, in the long haul I didn't feel called to a single life forever. At the same time I knew I needed a lot of healing and re-wiring, before I could ever truly be marriage material.

Then I met a beautiful gal at my church named Roxanne, and God gave me another chance to have a family. We were married on November 20th, 1983. Ten months later on my birthday, which is September 24th, my second son, John David Sachs was born. What a birthday present and total joy he has been! I am three years older than my wife, and then lo and behold ... exactly three years after John was born, (this time on Roxanne's birthday, July 20[th)], God sent us a beautiful baby girl. Her name is Jenna Marie Sachs, and of course she is **perfect**. How cool to have our children born on our birthdays! I also had the privilege of raising my stepson Nathan Barker from the time he was eleven years old. What a talented, sensitive and gifted kid he turned out to be. God out of his mercy gave me another chance. A loving family is a snapshot of what God wants to have with each of us ... no matter how many bombs have exploded in the past. I love my family more than I can ever express.

We have been married for well over twenty years now. Even our new marriage has been tested many times. To my knowledge no marriage goes unchallenged by the forces and pressures of life, and hell itself. Nevertheless, God has matured us enough to weather the storms, grow, and learn to appreciate the countless blessings. Roxanne graduated with a degree in fine art from U. C. Riverside, and taught elementary school for twenty-three years. Recently she retired from teaching to pursue her art, and loves being a Plein-Air artist. I plan to resurrect my own art career, Lord willing, pretty soon myself. Watching Roxanne has totally inspired me. Years ago as a new Christian I heard God say clear as a bell … "I want you to write and paint." What a coincidence that he would bring me a wife who loves the Lord with all her heart and is a super talented artist.

Not only did most everything change for me personally in a very positive way after my encounter with God in 1975, but also other good things began to be added to my life. Lots of second chances. Lots of new friendships and opportunities. God opens doors and closes doors, and starts directing our lives … as much as we let him. Another huge blessing was some news that I learned from my mother. My Grandpa Ira had prayed with a Christian minister to receive Christ the day he died. Grandpa knew he was dying and for three days was afraid to go to sleep. He was sure he was going to wake up in hell. He had terror in his eyes, but my mom said after he prayed she saw a peace come over her father. My mom was holding his hand and told him ... "Just let go dad, it's going to be alright." At the very end ... Grandpa Ira surrendered to Jesus! You don't know how much that means to me. (I cussed God out for nothing.)

As a rebellious teenager I said I hated my dad ... but another great blessing Jesus has done in my life was to heal our relationship. We became partners in business as well as father and son ... and friends. My dad is seventy-six now, and still going strong. I love both my parents immensely. They are both total gold. I'll never forget the late evening I came home from a mission trip to Mexico, and my dad and his best friend, Dick Ohms, (my childhood Sunday school teacher's husband) were smiling at me from ear to ear. My mom said ... "Guess what we did this evening".
"What?"
"Your dad and Dick both got baptized at church!"
Even though Jessie Ohms was one of the most dedicated and loving Christians in my life, (and in the world), her husband never wanted anything to do with Church or religion. Well, that all changed when he received Jesus personally that evening, and symbolically sealed his conversion in the waters of baptism. It's about a relationship with God, not Churchianity ... and Dick excitedly told me all about it. Dick said ... "I never thought it would be like this, and I know I'm just a baby and brand new (he was in his sixties) ... but now I want to learn everything! God has been so good to us and thank God Almighty for his patience with me!" (My dad didn't say anything. He just kept smiling from ear to ear.)

EXPLOITS

I've been jumping back and forth through time a little bit in this story, (and someday I bet we can do it in person), but probably one of the biggest adventures of my life began in England in 1990. It was the beginning of a new phase of missionary work among other things. My wife and I joined a team from our church and we went on a ministry trip to London. I was thrilled to be on the trip, but was also in a hard place personally ... feeling the winds of change hitting ... but not knowing what to do. We spent eleven days there in England and had a totally radical experience.

On the last day in England I went on a long walk to seriously talk with God. I had been a beleiver for 15 years but I felt confused ... especially about my business and my future in general. The economy was getting real bad, and anyway I wanted to be free to do more ministry and missionary work. At the same time I had a huge overhead, young kids, employees, a store, and two partners ... one being my father. What to do Lord?

My Apache friend, Henry Garcia, and two Christian business associates had started a missionary non-profit ministry with me, back in 1982, which we named Freedom Crusade, but I hardly had time to develop it. We did manage to make monthly trips to help Ernesto in Mexico. I took countless teams and caravans of trucks filled with clothes, and food, and lumber down there. Ernesto had been donated a forty acre property outside of Tecate, Mexico and we helped him build a thriving re-hab ranch from scratch. We even planted a small church in Tecate. That was a total blessing, but I also sensed some major changes coming for our family personally. Nevertheless, I didn't understand it.

As I walked along a narrow sidewalk in High Wickham, a town just outside of London ... going up and down some small hills, I point blank asked God again ... "What the heck do you want me to do?"

This time I finally heard Him speak. It was one word. It wasn't audible, but it might as well have been. He simply said ... "Exploits!"

It actually made me laugh, because it seemed so remote and far off to do exploits for God. I remembered reading something about exploits in the Bible, but didn't remember where. As soon as I could I grabbed a concordance, and started reading in the prophecies of Daniel about a time when many "will fall by sword and by flame, by captivity and by plunder, for many days". It also says about that future time ... "but the people that do know their God shall be strong, and do exploits." Daniel was talking about a time yet to come at the end of the age when evil will sweep over the earth ... just like it's doing right now. It's time for us to rise up and walk in the power of the Spirit of God. It's our calling and destiny **if** you have Christ in your heart.

When we get born again we get a second chance at everything. It's a miracle how God rescued me. He is definitely in the miracle business. I've heard hundreds of stories just as dramatic as mine, and even more radical, of how God came to the rescue. I'm positive I would be dead by now the way I was heading. As I look back over my new life in Christ, I can see where God did lots of small exploits with us, and a few big ones. I believe in my heart there is much more to come ... and it's all of our jobs to simply be available. It is so exciting to walk with Jesus. It's so blessed to have a clean slate and **second chances**. We need them. "Thank You God!"

As I was writing this chapter about second chances I just received a letter from my son in Cleveland, Ohio. It is perfect timing, (of course), and his letter means the world to me. It is a real long letter telling me all about the things that God is presently doing in Troy's life, and how he is using him daily. He is so excited. He has been totally involved with an AA program for going on a year now, and with his permission I want to share a portion of what he wrote ...

Dad,

Today is November 17th of 2005, which I never would have believed I would live to see. It's 10 PM. I've just left a meeting at the World Famous Angle. I went with my sponsor in AA, Jeff Boone, who has helped me learn how to finally communicate my feelings in a way that is helpful, with honesty, unselfishness, love and purity. That, in and of itself, is a miracle.

At the Angle a man named Kevin, sober for 2 years, told his story (lead). Dad, I can't tell you how amazing and wonderful it is to me to see how God reaches out to people. Kevin was another perfect example. He showed so much gratitude that God has allowed him to see all the love and beauty that was already surrounding him, but that he didn't see.

My thoughts drifted to so many things God, "Jesus", has done for me, that I should be grateful for. I've been clean and sober for only 10 ½ months and already have had countless miracles. So, to save time, paper, and not to mention strength in my hand, I'll start with just this last Tuesday.

(Troy started writing over three pages outlining all the things that happened in just one day. My hero, Jack Bauer ... is not the only one who stays busy for 24 hours at a time. Here are a couple highlights to Troy's letter.) ...

I found myself wanting so badly to lie down and sleep as 10:30 PM rolled around. However, Jesus called me to duty. I received a phone call from a

20-year-old boy I met several months ago, but haven't seen since. When I met him we were at an audition for a movie being filmed here in Cleveland. His name is Greg and it didn't take long to realize we knew some people in common. After the auditions Greg and I went to a coffee house (Barista) where I shared with him my story about HIV. He listened with awe that I had gone through so much. He asked for my phone number, which I gave to him, and apparently he held onto it till now.

When he called he was very upset. He proceeded to tell me he had been crying for 3 days. He just found out he is positive. The first question he asked me was, "How do you stay so healthy looking and happy?" I explained that I have a higher power in my life that helps me realize I need to be grateful for what I have today. This sparked a whole series of questions that lasted till 4AM. But how happy I felt that God trusted in me to want to help this boy.

I don't have a J.O.B. so I thought it would be OK to sleep in late Wednesday morning. Yet, again, Jesus called me to duty. My phone rang about 9 o'clock. It was a woman we call Max. Her last name is Maxwell. She had great concern for another friend of mine named Bill. He has been a real inspiration and a friend in AA. Not only does he have great spirituality, but he is also very funny. Especially when you get him to tell you about the sober white-water rafting trip he went on. I tell you his story makes me laugh through tears.

Max said no one has heard from him for days, and that she was at his apartment building. His car was there, but he wasn't answering. We ran through a list of possibilities, like maybe he's using again, but it just didn't sound like Bill. So, I gave her Roger's number since I knew Roger had an extra set of keys to Bill's place.

It wasn't even an hour later that I learned my friend Bill had passed away. He was 36 years old. He had a hemorrhaged esophagus and died in his bathroom on Saturday. He lay there for four days. God has kept us strong and banded us together. I secretary a meeting on Wednesday nights, which I turned into a candle light meeting about 3 weeks ago. It is a discussion group and the Spirit of God flowed in that room last night like I've never seen before in this group. So moving and so loving. Bill always loved that meeting and he was with us last night, in our hearts.

Troy then told about Jeff and himself trying to help a young newly sober guy named Jason along his path … and then I'll include the end of

Troy's letter ...

Jason said he has tried praying but it just feels strange to him. Jeff told him it is because he is new at it and its normal. Jeff told him to just keep doing it, even if it feels weird or sounds funny, that eventually he would get better at it. I chimed in with a line from the AA Big Book. "It's better to act your way into thinking, than to think your way into acting." Jason turned to me and asked me how I pray. Right away your voice came in my head, Dad. You told me once to just talk to him (Jesus) as if he is sitting right next to me, as if he were a friend ...

After leaving Jason back at the Keating Center, Jeff asked me how I was dong on my ninth step: Make direct amends to those we had harmed, except when to do so would injure them or others. In particular he referenced you.

You see, I have been "thinking" about this for almost 3 months now. I have made many amends with other people, and have many more to do. But, what to do with you? How could I find a way to help you understand that I am changing? That I see how wrong I was to blame you for not being the "Dad" that "I" wanted. For not loving my mother the way I thought you should. For thinking you should have protected me from Roy. I was so wrong to be so frustrated with you and your Jesus Freak Prayers.

Most of all Dad, how can I tell you that I'm grateful to have had you in my life. That even though we have had long periods of time apart, you have touched my life. It makes me happy to know you have a wife and kids who love you and need you. They have all been so very kind to me, and I love them for that.

This week is not unusual to me. It is an example how God has been moving through my life, how the changes have been daunting. I believe in part due to your prayers for me, and I thank you.

Love Always and Forever,
Troy Melvin Sachs

Above: Roger and Roxanne
Below: Roger, John and Jenna in England, 1994

CHAPTER 57

"REBEL WITH A CAUSE"

When I began this story I wasn't sure if I could cram everything into one book, but I really, really tried. With all my heart I want to take people from where I was ... to where God, out of his mercy, has taken us. I wrote and wrote and wrote ... but it is impossible to compress the next thirty years into a few final chapters with any kind of clarity. I thought I had experienced a radical life before ... but it was nothing. Absolutely nothing. Real life starts the microsecond that our spirit unites with the all-powerful, all-present, Spirit of the living God. The Holy Spirit is just as real as Jesus ... and just as much God. I have come to love the Spirit of God as much as Jesus and the Father. I especially love His presence and seeing Him **move**. It is the best! When I was fishing for salmon in the mouth of the Colombia River and saw the most spectacular sunrise of my life ... I concluded that it was worth living to experience that one breathtaking scene out in the Pacific Ocean. However, I want to declare with all sincerity that a three second touch of the Holy Spirit can be more mind-boggling than a million light shows ... and in the last three decades it has been non-stop with the One who will never leave us or forsake us. It's not all fireworks ... but it's wonderful to experience the "peace that passes all understanding". I want to share a little about one of the most radical highlights of my walk with God.

Along with the peace that passes understanding ... there also came the time when my Christian experience slowed down, and I went through a long dry time. It lasted about a year. One day I sincerely complained ... "God, you know how much I love you and how much I appreciate everything ... but I want to mention that things have gotten pretty boring. When I worked for the devil, at least he kept it exciting. Can you **please** bring a little action and excitement into the picture again?" Shortly after dropping that request into the suggestion box, God opened the door for our London trip ... and then he sent another unique, and radical person into my personal life. This person was the most gifted, unpredictable, controversial, and anointed person I ever met. It was Lonnie Frisbee.

At the Docklands Conference in London I spotted Lonnie walking through the crowd. There must have been around ten thousand people at the conference. It was huge. I hadn't seen him for about seven years. He was not a part of the ministry team, but he suddenly showed up in England on his own at this much publicized conference. (I had previously heard the rumor that Lonnie had a falling out with John Wimber, however, I didn't know any of the details).

After Lonnie spoke at our church on the now famous "Mothers Day 1980", he was invited to go on staff full time. For about three years he ministered regularly at the Vineyard. It was wonderful, and he led the way for a huge "signs and wonders", missionary, and church planting push that literally went around the world. It's documented history. He was the catylist. Amazing and miraculous things **happened** when he ministered. He had prayed for me one time back at Canyon High School in Yorba Linda, and I wanted to write about the life-changing experience and healing that accompanied his prayer. When I saw him in the crowd ... instantly I "knew" I was supposed to go talk to him. I had never personally talked to him in my life.

I was way up high in the auditorium with my wife and friends, and I left my seat and made my way down to where I saw Lonnie walking through part of the crowd. It was during a break time and I had a long way to catch up to him. He turned around as I finally walked up, and said to me, "Colorado right?" Lonnie then said ... "I felt bonded with you years ago, but it got short-circuited!"

His comment stopped me in my tracks. I felt the presence of God as I approached Lonnie, but didn't know what to say. The only time we could have had any kind of bond was during that short prayer time in the midst of hundreds of people. Was he confusing me with someone else? Nevertheless, somehow in my heart I knew it was true. I did feel a connection to Lonnie. Finally, I asked him where he was living now, and that I'd like to talk to him sometime back in the States. I told him I was working on a book and did missionary work in Mexico. I gave him my business card to my construction company in Moreno Valley. He told me he had just moved back to California and he took my card. Our whole conversation lasted only a few minutes.

When I returned to America from our short trip to England in 1990, I put my house up for sale, but the recession had hit so strong that nothing was selling. I was desperately trying to figure out how I was going to do "exploits" for God. A couple weeks after readjusting my brain back to the everyday business grind, my office manager, who was at the time my very organized sister-in-law, said ... "You have a call on hold from a Lonnie Frisbee."

I quickly answered the phone and Lonnie said ... "The Holy Spirit is having me clean up some of the things from the England trip. You said you'd like to get together, and I'm sorry it took so long for me to get back to you. Why don't you come down to my place in Poway? Let's see what the Lord is up to."

A couple days later I cleared my schedule in the middle of the week, and drove about fifty miles south to the rural community of Poway in San Diego County. I was pretty excited because of everything that I heard about Lonnie Frisbee over the years. As mentioned before, his picture had been plastered all over Time and Look Magazine, when the Jesus People revival hit Southern California in the early seventies. People from all over the world had made claims that they encountered the power of God at one of Lonnie's meetings, or when he prayed for them in a McDonalds restaurant, or in Africa, or wherever. He was totally bold, and totally wild. People got saved left and right, and people got healed and delivered also. The stories I heard seemed to be unending and almost unbelievable. I vividly remembered the radical healing I experienced when he prayed for me back at Yorba Linda about 1980. My original hopes for meeting with Lonnie Frisbee was to get his permission to write about that encounter, and anything else that he might share. Those hopes looked real positive as I drove down the 15 Freeway.

I also had heard about some of the controversies that surrounded his life, and the rumor that Lonnie was gay. I had no idea of what was fact or fiction ... but something wasn't adding up. One thing was for sure, I personally never felt so close to God, as I had in the frequent meetings that he did at Canyon High School. God's presence was even more intense when he prayed for me, and then again when I briefly talked with him in London. I knew there had to be more to the story than meets the eye. I prayed all the way down the highway, and then I heard a peaceful little voice speak to me. The first thing I heard was … "Let him do most of the talking. Do you see the bumper sticker on that car?" (It said "REBEL WITH A CAUSE") "That is my son Lonnie!"

 I lie not, God was clearly speaking to me.

The Holy Spirit was filling my pickup truck as I drove to meet with Lonnie. It was amazing. When the presence of God shows up in a powerful way, I feel this rush of joy that floods my whole being. It's better than better. It makes me laugh, and permanently smile, and feel so very much alive. I love everything about God. Then he told me … "I want you to give Lonnie a message from the Body of Christ … from you the believers. The message is … 'we want you, but we don't need you'."

Only a couple times did I ever feel confident enough that God actually spoke something to me for someone else … and then confident enough to go and share it with them. This was a little spooky, but I still felt the peace and excitement … so lead on Lord. I found my exit and found my way to John Rutkay's house where Lonnie was living. As I drove in the driveway, Lonnie and a gal named GiGi were unloading a bunch of groceries from a car. Lonnie gave me a quick hug, introduced me to GiGi, and then I helped them carry in the groceries, which were mostly vegetables from a market in San Diego.

I didn't have to worry about letting Lonnie do most of the talking. He can talk-talk- talk, and everything he said was interesting, and funny, and then bam- bam - bam … in an instant, the conversation could become totally anointed and from another dimension. God's dimension. But, it all happened so naturally; that you feel like you must be in Palestine, and that Jesus is right there in our midst … pouring himself out. He was! It was really cool spending the day with Lonnie and Gi Gi. It was more than cool.

Lonnie is a very talented artist. He showed me his paintings, which were all over the house and in the garage. When we went into the garage he had a flashlight, which he quickly flickered back and forth like a strobe light on a huge poster hanging high on the wall. The poster was a blown up photo from Time magazine in which you could see thousands of people at a mass baptism in the ocean at Corona Del Mar. Lonnie laughed and turned off the flashlight. He drug out several of his favorite paintings from a stack and showed them to me. He had some sculptures and leather masks also.

At one point during the day he turned to me and unexpectantly said ... "I see you like a little banty rooster walking across the barnyard all by yourself. Most people don't have the ability to walk alone, but you can walk alone. I see whitewater ministry and controlled danger." Lonnie went on for about five minutes reading my life before he hardly knew a single thing about me. I don't even remember the rest of what he shared, but I think I have it written down somewhere. It doesn't matter. It was encouraging and very supernatural. The presence of God was so strong ... it was incredible.

He asked me about my ministry work in Mexico, and I told him that I

Fire On the Mountain

was taking a team to the ranch in Tecate that very next Saturday. He said ... "Why don't you stop here on your way to Mexico, and I'll cook the team breakfast this Saturday. What time do you usually pass Poway, and how many are on the team?"

"That would be awesome. There is about eight or nine of us this time."

I spent most of that day at the house, and eventually shared a little about coming out of the drug trafficking world, and everything that God did. Lonnie said ... "It all fits together. I need to take you to my church. I'm not in the Vineyard order any longer, and now I go to a church called Set Free. The pastor there rides a Harley with a license plate, which says "BikerPas". You're going to meet a lot of kindred spirits there. **THOUSANDS** are coming to Christ through that ministry! They are running to the altar, and all the churches around them can't figure it out! I haven't seen that happen since the Jesus People days!"

It was such a cool day. Lonnie knew that I had been in the Vineyard from the beginning, and I could tell he was still stinging from some hurts, and politics, and whatnot. He had more than a few unkind remarks about certain individuals, and he could be very entertaining in his assassinations ... but I could feel the bitterness. I knew it was time for me to deliver the message that I heard from the Lord. I knew in an instant that he was a sidelined giant, and needed some restoration. He needed a second chance just like the rest of us. I told him the message I received ... "Lonnie, the Body of Christ wants you ... but we don't need you."

He looked at me for quite awhile and in a soft voice said ... "I've always loved the Bride."

That was kind of how the first day of our friendship happened. I took my team down there the next Saturday and filmed everything. Lonnie and I started working together, and I helped him prepare for a mission trip to Brazil ... his sixteenth to that nation. I tried to be a peacemaker between him and John Wimber, but the Vineyard didn't want my help. We started doing a series of mission meetings, and I videotaped everything. It was awesome. Lonnie was working on a book already, and when months later the ghostwriter suddenly quit because of personal problems ... Lonnie gave the project to me.

For the better part of three years I became a close part of Lonnie

Frisbee's life. He told me everything about everything in his life, in his ministry, and in his heart. He had a huge burden for my son Troy back in Ohio. He prayed for him and wrote him a letter condemning the homosexual world ... but not condemning Troy. I usually spent a couple days a week or more with Lon. We had one of our very best ministry trips out of California to Colorado. (Colorado right? Yeah Lonnie ... it was right on!) He said that he felt the presence of God in our series of meetings was the most anointed of his whole ministry. That shocked me when he said that. He didn't care if it was thirty people or thirty thousand. He definitely is the most unique, and gifted person I ever met. I know why God put such a powerful miraculous mantle on Lonnie ... it's because man looks on the outward appearance ... but God looks at the heart.

Some of his inner-circle cronies got real upset when Lonnie gave me his autobiography to write. They wanted this well known connected guy to do it, and they told Lonnie concerning me ... "the guy is a total unknown ... he has never written anything but a few newsletters!"

Lonnie **screamed** back at them like only he can do ... " **I don't care if the book comes out 'See Dick run!' At least I know he loves me and won't do me in!"**

He was a trip. As many now know Lonnie died of AIDS on March 12th, 1993 when he was only forty-three years old. Many are trying to label him a point-blank homosexual, but Lonnie himself refused to be labeled in that camp. He told me ... "I will own up to all of my sins and failures, **but I never lived the gay lifestyle!"**

In 1994 Roxanne and I and the kids disentangled ourselves from society and went on a missionary journey, which took us around the world. It was truly awesome, and I feel we actually did do exploits for God ... or rather he did them through us. In many ways, my friend Lonnie paved the way for us, because of all the contacts and relationships that originated with him. I miss him terribly ... but most of all I miss the anointing God placed on him. According to Lonnie, that anointing is available to all of us ... if we get desperate enough for God! He said the day of the superstar is over, and "God wants to pour his Spirit out on all believers!" Many voices are now saying the same thing.

"Thank you Jesus. You definitely answered my prayer and took the boredom out of my walk. You continue to take messed up lives and make them a blessing! Tell Lonnie we love him!

CHAPTER 58

"TO OPRAH FROM LONNIE"

So many other things have happened that it's hard to know what to focus on, but I wanted this story to be an accurate and truthful account of how God invaded my life, and many of those around me. At the end of the Gospel of John it says that **if** he, (the eyewitness), told everything that Jesus did, "even the world itself could not contain the books that could be written." I can fully relate to that conclusion. God has done **so** many incredible things just in my short life that it is almost unbelievable … but in my opinion absolutely totally impossible to be random coincidence. He has demonstrated his reality to me over and over and over. It has become the main message of my life … "Jesus is real!" He took a mixed up, dope-dealing hippy, and turned my world upside down. He supplies the missing piece of the puzzle. It's what everyone is searching for down deep. At least it was for me … and then we should keep in mind what a terrible price he paid to ransom us from the jaws of hell.

People get all hyped up on TV because Nostradamus made some vague prophecies five hundred years ago in France. Some of them appear to have come true … big deal. The Bible has made hundreds and hundreds of prophecies for **thousands** of years, and they all have come true like clockwork. Most of them are directly or indirectly about Jesus himself and have been fulfilled already, but many are about the end of an age, and they are unfolding right before our eyes. None of the prophecies of the Bible have been proven false. The devil and the powers of darkness work overtime trying to conceal that truth.

All you "would-be authors" out there, including myself … just try to write a book that will predict the future without error for thousands of years … a book that will reveal God, his nature, and his master plan for his entire creation … and then make it a book that will stand up to every criticism and assault over centuries of time from thousands of so called atheistic intellectuals, tricky filmmakers, and godless ACLU lawyers. That's what the Bible has done, and continues to do. It stands up. No one can silence its message. The Romans couldn't. The communists couldn't. No one can. It is a supernatural spiritual book. It is the all time best seller, and millions, and millions, and millions of people have testified that it changed their lives, and brought them into a personal relationship with the Son of the Living God.

While I was working closely with Lonnie Frisbee on his autobiography, he called me up one morning and wanted me to drive into Orange County, so that we could meet with a friend of his named Jack Simms. Lonnie wanted Jack to do the chapter in his book relating to the Vineyard Christian Fellowship, and the ensuing worldwide church movement. He told me … "Jack was right there for the whole thing!"

I had never met this man, but was very impressed by Jack Simms. He had a cameraman lined up with professional video equipment and the whole nine yards. I could immediately tell that Jack Simms was very intelligent, connected, and tuned in. I was always amazed at the huge spectrum, and variety of friends and associates that were a part of Lonnie's life … from skid-row bums, to talk show hosts and authors like Rich Buehler.

On the drive over to Fullerton to do this film session at Jack's place, Lonnie started discussing how he wanted the film to serve a dual purpose. He told me … "I went into a restaurant with your friends Darrel and Evie Ballman about a week ago. The restaurant was jam-packed, and we had to wait quite awhile to get a table. While standing in the crowded entryway I could see a TV high up in the lounge area. When I happened to look up at the TV, Oprah Winfrey was talking. She was talking about broken people, and sexually abused and exploited children. **Instantly**, the Holy Spirit electrified me with his presence! My entire body was filled with the precious presence of God from the top of my head to the tips of my toes! It was the power of God on me, and I knew in that moment that I was somehow connected to Oprah! I think we're supposed to write her a letter, or maybe send her a film clip from the film we're going to shoot this morning. Maybe the Lord wants me to go on her program. He showed me her heart for the people."

We shot hours and hours of film that day and the next, and I recorded the audio on my little Sony tape recorder as back up. Lonnie addressed Oprah during the entire film. Jack Simms promised that he would make copies for me after he converted them to VHS. He also volunteered to edit a few minutes of the film to send along with the letter that Lonnie wanted to dictate to Oprah. With the help of another special friend, Maurine Gore, we managed to type out a rough draft of the letter to Oprah … but then Lonnie started going downhill in his health, and the warfare over his life intensified. Even our close relationship was tested. He made a last trip to Africa and came back very, very sick. As I mentioned before, AIDS ultimately claimed his life at age 43.

Jack Simms never gave me copies of the film, and then with a huge shock I learned that he was killed in a freak accident. He was flying in a private jet with the owner of one of the huge fast food chains here in America, which was landing at John Wayne airport. I was later told that this wealthy businessman was a committed Christian, and was helping Jack do a film about Lonnie. Apparently the small private jet got caught in the wake of a commercial jet and was thrown to the ground. It was on TV and in all the newspapers.

Years and years have gone by. I felt led by God to put everything that Lonnie and I had in process on hold, even though I have a notarized contract giving me complete authorization to finish and release his autobiography, and any future biographical work. We had compiled volumes of written material, audio, and video. We laid out his entire book. It is a treasure chest of God's love, power and reality. Maurine Gore who was working closely with Lonnie and myself on several projects including the Oprah letter, went back to Africa after Lonnie's death to work with AIDS children. She spent years in Africa. She did an incredible job ministering to the helpless.

I lost track of Maurine for a long time, but on a ministry trip of our own in 1994, I tried to look her up in Cape Town, South Africa. After all the years of separation I missed her by only a couple days. She had just returned to the States. We finally reconnected by telephone here in California, and Maurine invited me to join her on a new upcoming trip back to Africa. I was real excited about the possibility. When I called a few months later I received another huge shock. Her son told me that his mom couldn't come to the phone because she is in heaven. "What!" I had just talked to her and she sounded great on the phone. Nevertheless, a defeated cancer came back with a vengeance and quickly took her out. She is with Lonnie and Jesus, who she loves so much … but how sad for us down here, and for all the children in Africa. So now, that means that all of the original players in this communication to Oprah about sexually abused children, and broken people are dead except for me.

In all these years I don't think anyone else ever sent Oprah the letter Lonnie wanted to send. The film we shot with Jack Simms is still in hiding. However, I feel led to finally get Lonnie's connection to Oprah out there. Lonnie's story of victimization is powerful, and after publishing his autobiography, (which is a mindblower in itself), he wanted us to write another book aimed at rescuing sexually broken people. We laid the groundwork for it and I want to see it through. It is too long and premature to put the letter to Oprah in here at the end of this book, but in Lonnie's autobiography I am going to include it … Lord willing. At this late date I feel it will accomplish more that way and get the most exposure. It's really for everyone.

Many people have claimed that Lonnie was like Samson in the Bible … a powerful servant of God, mightily used, but who fell morally … and it cost him his eyes, and his life. I think it is very true. Samson was used to defeat multitudes of God's enemies, and Lonnie led thousands of people to Christ, blazed a way to missions, and introduced the gifts of the Holy Spirit to a generation of believers. Like Samson, he unfortunately fell morally for a period of time, and it cost him his life. Lonnie even had eye surgery and was nearly blind before he died. However, Samson repented and it says in the Bible that God used him one last time … and … "in his death he took out more of the enemy, than in his entire life."

Like in the case with Samson, I am totally convinced that God is **yet** to do a greater work in Lonnie's death than in his entire ministry! I believe that. To reach more people and touch more lives than he already did is monumental. Lonnie even predicted it, and it's a radical concept. It drives me to do my part. It is definitely a tall order, but he wanted every aspect of his entire life to count all the way … even his death. There is definitely spiritual warfare surrounding this whole subject of Lonnie Frisbee. That in itself is a positive signal. Nothing comes easy. The cross wasn't easy. The main thing that Lonnie wanted ... was to rescue people for his Savior and friend Jesus ... and Oprah if this happens to find its way to you ... I hope the purposes of God when the Holy Spirit fell on Lonnie in the restaurant ... will all be fulfilled according to His perfect will and in His perfect timing. I pray in the name of Jesus that the Spirit of God will fall on you and every reader with power and His loving touch. That will make Lon happy. This is a little advance notice that a letter is on the way from beyond the grave!

"All to thee ... my precious Savior

I surrender all !!!"

CHAPTER 59

"CUSTOM PLATES"

How could one simple prayer in Topanga Canyon change my life for the last thirty years so dramatically? Other people have turned over a new leaf from time to time, and had life changing experiences. I can't deny that. Tom Cruise and John Travolta are hooked on Scientology. (Very expensive to say the least.) Shirley McClain is vigorously pushing reincarnation and whatnot. Donald Trump's god seems to be money ... big time. Osama Bin Laden and millions of Muslims are willing to die and kill for Allah. It goes on and on. Politics and religion is the real "Neverending Story" and is the ultimate debate for mankind. I was never so presumptuous in the past to claim that I knew the truth. However, that all changed when I prayed with Rev. Glenn to receive Jesus Christ into my life in August of 1975. The man who claimed to be the truth did exactly what he said he would. He willingly laid his life down and picked it back up ... and when I surrendered he came into my heart, and caused my spirit to be born again. People can debate religion forever, but I know what happened to me.

Jesus not only claimed to be providing us eternal life, (and as some critics label it, "pie in the sky" after we're dead), but he also said ... "I come to give you life and life more abundantly". I found out that the image of Christians that is painted by Hollywood, and other major liberal medias is a shameless lie. They portray the Christian life as boring, hypocritical, narrow minded, ignorant, sadistic and pitiful. Some Christians do fall into those categories ... but an honest survey of everyone who has put their faith and lives into the hands of The Son of God would paint another picture altogether. To truly walk in a loving relationship with God is the greatest adventure anyone could take. Eternal life is just frosting on the cake. I would not trade one minute of my new life. I especially would not trade places with any of the people I mentioned for all their fame and money and power. In fact, I greatly fear for them and sincerely pray that they will meet the risen Christ for themselves some day.

I was labeled a real nutcase and religious fanatic, because of my claim that God spoke to me multiple times on custom license plates while driving on the highways and byways of America. As this story comes to a close, I want to include the most dramatic occurrence of this freeway madness. It is also associated with my long lost daughter, which has significance to me ... and gives me hope.

Back when I was a relatively new Christian, and while things were going pretty good between my wife Debbie and myself ... we had just moved from Topanga Canyon to Thousand Oaks and were eagerly awaiting the soon arrival of our baby. Debbie was very, very pregnant, and one night while we visited Westwood, her water broke in Ships Restaurant near the UCLA campus. We piled into my old Ford van and rushed to the hospital in Tarzana, which is in the San Fernando Valley.

I was right in the delivery room, because I had taken the Lamaze classes with Debbie, and now it was definitely D-Day. Her time had arrived and she was huffing and puffing, and I was doing my best to be a breathing coach ... in a very ineffective way. Childbirth is radical. Debbie was in labor a long time. We arrived at the hospital before midnight, but our perfect little baby girl wasn't born until about six o'clock the next morning. It was amazing.

Finally, I could break away and go home to get some sleep. Our new baby who we named Denielle was wrapped up in blankets along with her tiny little wristband. She was sleeping like an angel next to a bunch of other babies behind a glass wall. Debbie was finally sleeping also, and I cranked up my old van and hit the freeway. Thousand Oaks is about a half hour drive from Tarzana.

As I was driving along the Ventura Freeway I felt like a million dollars. I was so excited to have a daughter. It was such a rush to have been a part of Denielle's entry into this world. I started to pray and thank God for her and for her safe delivery. Debbie was totally amazing, and thank God I'm a man. I felt the presence of God next to me like he was riding shotgun. It was tangible, and real, peaceful, and powerful. I started talking to Jesus like he was my best friend. If we know it or not ... he is our best friend. It was like I didn't have to think of what to say to him or anything ... just talk, talk, talk as we drove along. It was so cool.

At one point of the drive I saw a license plate that related to what I was saying to God, and a little confusion injected itself into my van. I didn't know if it was truly a message from God or not. I was super tired and it made me a little upset. I boldly turned to my friend and said ... "God this is ridiculous! People think I'm absolutely crazy when I say that you talk to me on license plates. I'm not going to pay any attention to another license plate for the rest of my life ... unless you clearly show me that it's you on the next license plate that I see!" I really meant it, and the ball was in his court.

There were no vehicles in sight close enough to read their plates as I zoomed along the freeway at seventy miles per hour. It was well past seven in the morning by now and totally light outside. I looked in my side mirror and saw a little yellow car in the next lane. I decided to slow down a little and let it pass me so I could read the license plate. I was in the fast lane, and as the car caught up with me I could see that a pretty blond girl was driving. She inched past me, and soon I could see the rear bumper of her Chevy Vega. Right in the middle was the license plate, which read ... "ITS ME".

My entire body was electrified with giant goose bumps. The license plate frame had the Christian fish symbol to add a clarifying exclamation mark! The presence of God had been with me all morning, but now it was wonderfully magnified a trillion times. I totally love it! Why can't it be like this every second of every day? His presence is beyond explanation.

I stayed behind the Vega for miles and miles ... reading that license plate ... all the way to Thousand Oaks praising God the entire time. What else could I do??? He is indescribable and totally incredible! Lo and behold the little yellow car got off the freeway at the same exit as mine. (Another huge coincidence). She pulled into a gas station, and I followed her like a magnet. As the young pretty blond got out of her car, I walked over and said ... "Why did you put that on your license plate?"

She said ... "I don't know ... why?"

"I see the fish symbol ... are you a Christian?"

She replied, "Well ... I'm a little backslid right now, but yes I am a

Christian."

I told her ... It's a long story, but God just used your car and your license plate to do a little miracle for me. You got off at my exit and I just wanted to ask you about it. Why did you put "ITS ME"?"

"I don't know ... I just did. So what happened?", she asked.

"My wife just had a baby and I've been up all night, but God bless you. God really used your car, but it's too hard to explain right now. You'll read about it. I'm working on a book and it will definitely be in it."

She looked at me intently and said, "You're not going to tell me, are you?"

I headed back to my van, but told her ... "Believe me, you'll read about it! God bless you!"

I figured she'd be reading this story in a matter of months. I had no idea it would take thirty years ... but I'm trusting that God has kept her in his loving hands all these years.

That was back on January 29th, 1977 ... on my daughter's birthday. The headline in the newspaper that morning reported that the Hollywood actor, Freddie Prince committed suicide. He was the young star of the very popular "Chico and The Man". How totally sad! One person enters the world, and another leaves it. How important it is for us to broadcast the news that Jesus is the answer, and nothing else can rescue you! Ron Hubbard can't help when the lights go out. Mohammad's bones are still in a grave. Buddha has exactly the same problem. Every other religious leader in history has nothing but theories about how to earn our way up to heaven.

Jesus did exactly the opposite. Instead of teaching us how to work our way to heaven and into oneness with The Force, he came down from heaven himself to reveal God ... and do for us what we couldn't do for ourselves. He was innocent of any crime, but convicted for our sins. He willingly took our place of judgment. He was executed like a common criminal and put in a grave. The big difference between him and all the others is that his bones are not to be found. He rose from the grave, and it is such a widely documented fact of history. Read "The Case For Easter" by Lee Strobel. He is one of the atheists who became a believer when he researched the evidence. As I mentioned previously there is more eyewitness testimony, historical evidence, and overwhelming circumstantial evidence for the reality of Jesus, and his resurrection, than any other ancient historical fact. Put that together with the hundreds of Biblical prophecies that have all come to pass concerning the Jewish Messiah ... and his reality becomes indisputable. The prophecies have come absolutely true ... in perfect timing.

Neo is not the One. The Big Bang didn't create you through billions of years of impossible mutations. Jesus is the One. He is the Alpha and Omega, the first and the last ... the living Word of God who became flesh and dwelt among us ... "the only begotten of the Father." Open your heart and ask him in. It takes sincerity and humility to recognize that we need a savior. But what do we have to lose except our stubborn pride and hell. If you're not sure about Jesus like I was ... honestly ask him if he is real. He will show you just like he has revealed himself to millions of others. He'll do the same for any hungry heart. "Ask and you will receive ... knock and the door will be opened." If you need proof that he's real, he'll provide it. He never lets us down. But when he does show you ... then do your part and receive him! It's all about getting spiritually born into the family of God by repenting and receiving the free gift of salvation. It's the Gospel.

I was a sincere unbeliever and totally anti-Christian, and anti-any-religion. It took the series of amazing coincidences to convince me that something supernatural was going on. The path led me to the cross, and when I saw that I was wrong about my previous assumptions, and had been deceived and heading for ultimate destruction ... I turned my life over to God and his Son. It was the best move I ever made, or ever will.

In part of the Lord's Prayer (which is really the disciple's prayer) ... Jesus taught us to pray ... "Our Father who art in heaven, hallowed be thy name. Thy Kingdom come, thy will be done, on earth as it is in heaven". That familiar petition is in process. The Kingdom of God is coming to earth! According to the Bible, God is going to create a new heaven and a new earth. It tells us to "Look up" ... the night is well spent and it's later than we think! He has outlined the real "Master Plan" in the Bible, and then supernaturally backs it up with the entire trinity ... Father, Son and wonderful Holy Spirit. I thought I had a workable master plan for my life, but it was stupid, and shallow, and totally a dead end. It was ... "Let's beat the system and get rich selling cannabis ... or die trying!"

How ignorant! Thank God he had mercy on me. It is so much wiser to give ourselves over to God, and his will for our lives. He is the one who created life as well as the billions of stars, which are light years apart. We cannot comprehend a God with that kind of power ... but that's who we are interacting with here ... the absolute God of the universe.

I want to also mention that the ways of the world can be very, very inviting. Let's not kid ourselves ... sin can be fun, among other things. Drugs can be fun. Sleeping around with multiple partners can be intoxicating. Lots of money can quickly open up a million different worlds. Power and prestige feel real good. My life was captivating in a few of these ways. I know what it feels like to have people I respect "kiss-up" because I have something they want. The problem is that there is a spiritual world. There is a God and a Devil ... a heaven and a hell ... a right and a wrong way ... along with this gigantic battle for our souls. For sure, sin does have short-term rewards, but then it turns around and enslaves us. It's a counterfeit with eternal consequences. It destroys us with heartache, broken lives, disease, divorce, and ultimately death. The "ways of the world" are cleverly designed to keep us away from God and real life. However, the mighty God of the Bible has his own ways, and He sets us free when we turn to him. His Son is ... "The Way, The Truth, and The Life."

Because I really liked to gamble and shoot craps in Vegas, I often think about the odds for things to happen. I hear the odds for winning the Mega Lotto is something like a hundred and eighty million to one. When I think about all that has happened leading up to my decision to receive Christ, as just being random coincidence ... I'm positive the odds for that being true are more astronomical than for winning the Mega Lotto. The odds for all this to be coincidence are off the scale. The odds for that license plate saying "ITS ME" after I emphatically asked God to show me if it was him on the next car on the freeway ... for that to be coincidence is also off the scale. It is literally impossible to be coincidence ... and since I've been on this journey with Jesus he has proved himself faithful a million times over.

How many coincidental things have happened in your life? Could there be a pattern unfolding? Is God trying to get through to you? Do you want him to get through to you? Do you feel a battle raging away? Is it pointing toward Christ or away from him? Have any sincere Christians crossed your path at important junctures? The Holy Spirit pursues us, and calls us, and interacts with us in a million ways. Press in and find out for sure what's happening.

After we receive Christ and yield to His will, our lives become more and more rewarding. I want to personally declare that God is definitely good! In 1994 I closed my pool construction company down, my wife retired from her teaching career, and we went overseas. It was an awesome time. John and Jenna were ten and seven years old, and Roxanne home schooled them for the next two years. We went to England first for four months, and then to South Africa, Namibia, and New Zealand. It was a great adventure and we lived by faith, which was another sub-adventure in itself. It is mind boggling how God took care of us, and especially the kids ... each step of the way on our journey. It was truly a blessed trip around the world. It could be a sequel. We left L.A. flying east to London and eventually returned to L.A. from Auckland, New Zealand. We circled the globe and it was better than the Amazing Race.

My old friends and acquaintances from my past can discard everything I say about God, but they can't deny that something happened to me that completely changed my life. No one can convince me that it didn't happen ... because it happened. Our testimony belongs to us and is a powerful tool. Jesus says ... "By the word of your testimony and your love for one another ... they will know that I live." I wrote up my own personal tract titled "BUSTED", while I was in England. It is a very condensed version of this story ... and at the end of it I included an invitation to receive Christ. I want to close this book with the last page of that little testimony.

• • •

Today is D-Day, June 6th, 1994, and fifty years ago exactly the greatest military offensive in history was launched against Hitler and his evil empire. Thousands of young Allied soldiers paid the ultimate price to obtain the liberation of Europe and the world. They were the finest sons of Great Britain, America, Canada, Australia and many other nations.

Jesus also paid the ultimate price with his blood ... and he conquered death itself ... our last enemy. He obtained the victory for each one of us. He gave his life as a ransom for all, including those brave soldiers. He is the King of Kings and Lord of Lords. He is God's Son and the Captain of our Salvation. Turn to Him and be delivered from this evil and perverse generation ... for He comes to judge the quick and the dead.

Father, I pray for each person reading these words. I pray that the Holy Spirit will touch them and guide them to Jesus. By your power, in the name of Jesus, birth them into your family and into your Kingdom. We come against all the forces of hell, that would keep people away from Jesus, and in His name we rebuke you. Release these people. We loose salvation to every hungry heart right now ... and we thank you Jesus for everything. We can't even comprehend all you've done and all you are ... but we worship you ... and pray all this in Your Name.

For those of you who are ready to surrender your life to God ... I want you to pray with me just like I prayed with Rev. Glenn. I want the Holy Spirit to fall on you with his loving touch! He has been there all your life ... calling those who are open and ordained for eternal life. Jesus says, "Today is the day of your salvation". Don't wait for tomorrow. He wants you just like you are, and remember, "tomorrow may never come". This simple prayer will change your life forever. It did mine.

• • •

Heavenly Father ... Please forgive me for all my sins. I want to know you personally. I want to experience the complete forgiveness you offer me. I turn away from everything that separates me from you. I am sorry for all my failures and sins. I give you my life. I receive your Son Jesus into my heart. I want to be born again. I want the Holy Spirit to come into my spirit and perform the greatest miracle of all ... to grant me eternal life in the family of God. Let that same power that raised Jesus from the grave, flow through my body right now. I exercise the measure of faith you've placed in me, and I confess with my mouth that Jesus is Lord, and I believe in my heart that God raised him from the dead. Thank you Jesus for taking my place on the cross. I receive that gift. I receive you. I will live for you to the best of my ability with all my heart.

Fire On the Mountain

Thank you God. FILL ME WITH YOUR LOVE in the name of Jesus Christ my Lord!

AMEN

THE ANGELS ROCK!

Tecate team to La Mesa

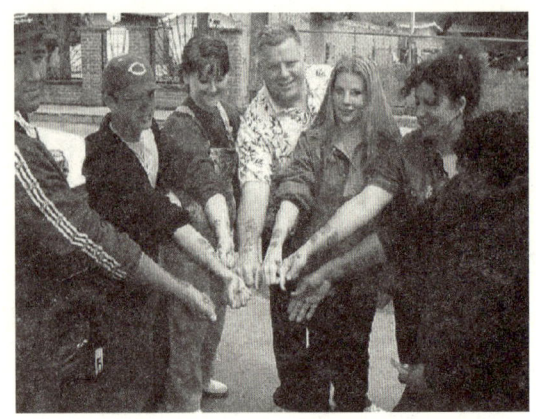

Ernesto

England in 1994

NAMIBIA, AFRICA

Moses looked up and saw … "Fire on the Mountain!"

God is a consuming fire and he spoke out of the burning bush … He is speaking now … "Come to my Son and live!"

BLESSINGS!

Postscript

Just before I leaped off my branch suspended over the Grand Canyon, I bounced this manuscript off several of my friends, relatives, and acquaintances. I wanted, and still want feedback. Does everything flow? Does the message come across? I don't just want a popular book ... I want souls added to God's family. I'd like to see multitudes delivered from the jaws of hell ... but then again, if one person reads this story and receives Christ ... it will be a huge success.

People in general seem to live in perpetual denial, and I'd like to remind everyone that ... we are all dying, and facing the same destination ... a cold, silent grave in a box, or maybe a fancy urn. But, out of his incredible love Jesus gave us the real "alternative life-style". The grave is not the end. Instead of eons of suffering in hell ... he offers us eternal life ... that's the alternative!

Listen to this mind boggling truth from the all-time, best-selling book in history, and please let it sink in ... "Eye has not seen, nor ear heard, nor has entered into the heart of man, the things which God has prepared for those who love Him. But God has revealed them to us through His Spirit." That is a radical declaration from God Almighty concerning his plans for those of us who trust him. The Bible clearly outlines an incredible everlasting "Master Plan" in which we are invited to partake.!

My good friend Ed Warth called me up long distance from Colorado, and said ... "I just finished reading your manuscript." (He was the first one.) Ed continued ... "I have a couple people I'd like to give it to. Would that be all right? I think they would really relate to your story, and get the Gospel at the same time. I really got into it myself. It was better than TV. I want more!"

That was so encouraging to hear, and exactly the reaction I am shooting for. My pastor (David Spoon) says that people will get emotionally involved when they read this story. I like that too. God gave us emotions. These are good signs to me that it was worth thirty plus years of waiting, working, and dreaming. I don't know if I've become all that I hoped for, when as a brand new Christian in 1975, I wrote the first handwritten forward to this book … stating that … "This book is being begun by a baby. I can only have faith as to who will write the last word." Well, the "last word" is fast approaching kid. God has taken me a million miles, but as I think about it … I need to constantly go back to that special "first love". I had it all then … I had Jesus. We need an eternal honeymoon with our Savior … and none of us have "arrived" until we meet him face to face. That's when we'll finally be like HIM! What an ultimate trip that will be!

The best thing I heard my friend Ed say was … "I want more!" Well, as I mentioned, I feel this book is a basic introduction to some of what God has done, and "is doing". Like I've stressed over and over, the most important thing for everyone … is to make that decision for Christ and get born again. It is square one. Nevertheless, there is much more to God, and his plans for us, than simply getting birthed. He doesn't just leave us as helpless little newborns wallowing around in our messy afterbirth forever. He has a plan, and a job for each of us. I feel what God has done for me, and through me … is totally radical, and off the chart. But, in comparison to some of things he has done through many of his other kids … it is kindergarten stuff. Consider the life of James Finney, Smith Wigglesworth, Rees Howells, Corey Ten Boom, Kathryn Kuhlman or Billy Graham. They are some of the more recent heroes of the faith.

Here's another encouraging scripture that I made reference to … "For you see your calling, brethren, how that not many wise men after the flesh, not many mighty, not many noble, are called: But God has chosen the foolish things of the world to confound the wise; and God has chosen the weak things of the world to confound the things which are mighty; And base things of the world, and things which are despised, has God chosen, yes and things which are not, to bring to nought things that are: That no flesh should glory in his presence." (That means, among other things, that we are all eligible, in spite of our many limitations … to be used by God.)

I want to note that I caught a little backlash for including some bad language in the first edition of this story. The last thing I want to do is to grieve God, or alienate a whole bunch of people. At the same time I want to reflect as much reality as possible, both in my past life ... and especially in the here and now. I didn't want to sugarcoat anything, and have tried very hard to be as honest and transparent as possible. The world I came out of was pretty raw, and there are a whole bunch of people still there. They are the ones I'm hoping to reach among others. I prayed a lot about the matter, and feel that to some people the story might not ring completely true if I change all the language, and try to completely sanitize it. I also got a bunch of counsel and input from people that I respect ... and believe that in this one particular case ... God is giving a green light. However, in this printing here I edited out, and changed most of the offensive language to try to reach out to everyone. So, if someone gets a hold of an unedited copy of this testimony, and are offended by the language ... please forgive me.

I am chomping at the bit to release the story directly from Lonnie Frisbee that we worked so hard on. In his prime, this little hippy only weighed about 130 pounds, with size five shoes ... but I believe he was a super heavyweight in God's eyes. Jesus definitely gets all the glory for what he did through Lonnie's life. That is Lonnie's heart all the way! He lived for his Savior, and he died in His arms. I honestly think I knew him better than anyone on this planet. He came back from a missionary journey to South America in 1991 and told me ... "Roger, God showed me in Brazil that you are my Jonathan."

It was an honor to be his friend ... to be his Jonathan. Lonnie is not finished with us yet. He has been dead for over a decade now, but is going to speak to the entire world directly from the heart ... by the power and anointing of the Holy Spirit of God. That's how he always operated.

There is more coming Ed! Believe me!

Love ... Roger

P.S. S. For anyone who wants to get involved with Christian missions, or help with mission projects ... you can reach us at Freedom Crusade, P.O. Box 5667, Santa Maria, CA 93456. We are developing a web site at www.freedomcrusadeinfo. My e-mail address is: sachs948@msn.com and freedomcrusade8@gmail.com. With a little vision, and a chosen rag-tag anointed army ... we can do "exploits" beyond our wildest dreams. I'm sure of it. The manual says ... "Taste and see that the Lord is good!"

I would like to take a team back to England, Africa, and New Zealand ... ASAP ... Lord willing! We will always be heading for Mexico ... laboring with my friend Ernesto as much as possible. God Bless ... RS

Acknowledgements

A whole lot of people are so important to me, and helped in this project. My parents, Carl and Polly Sachs not only brought me into this world, but we spent hours taping, and re-visiting family history. It was fun, and those tapes are treasures, which I will always safeguard. Ernesto Hernandez is a main character in my life, and has patiently spent years contributing to the details of this true story. His son, Ernie, just finished law school in Mexico … and was also a great help. Big Jim Tucker, and Lonnie Frisbee have flown away … but they are both great inspirations and partners.

There are tons of people, who did a little … and did a lot. I never realized what a big project a book could turn into. Aunt Lula planted seeds in my life. Jessie Ohms, the Chaplain in Germany, the girls on the bus in Ohio, Henry Garcia … and so many others watered those seeds. When the time was right, Rev. Glenn Adkins harvested a soul for the Kingdom of God. Glenn and I meet, and talk on the phone on a regular basis. He is in the final stages of a book, and we are helping each other. It's exciting.

As a brand new Christian I prayed for a lovely Jewish lady on my pool maintenance route in Beverly Hills. She came out to tell me something about her pool, but was in so much physical pain that she had to sit down. I hesitantly asked if I could pray for her, but instead she asked me to tell her "exactly" … why did I decide to become a Christian. (God had been setting her up.) I told her the whole story in detail. With tears she prayed to receive her Messiah. It was very dramatic. The next week on my pool route she told me her pain was gone. How cool! Because she was in a writer's group, I gave her three chapters of this book in 1975 for her to "brutally critique". That's what she told me she was going to do. Her name is Birdie Abrams, and she was probably around my age back then.

I am presently fifty-eight ... so that means she needs some good genes to still be with us. Anyway, she wrote me saying that the style "works for you" and that the book would be a hit ... and would help a multitude of people. Her encouragement propelled me forward for all these years. It was probably the most significant early indicator to me ... that I was on the right track ... and to "keep going". However, I completely lost track of Birdie, but "God bless you Mrs. Abrams ... wherever you are!"

My good friend, former pastor, lawyer, bowling partner, Charlie Wear played a significant role in my life, and in this book. He sent us the money to return from the mission field back here to California. (We had survived on less than $500 a month while overseas.) He encouraged me to get writing again, when this project had been sitting on the shelf for over a decade. When we arrived back in California, he actually filled our refrigerator with food, and gave me several thousand dollars, (no-strings-attached), to write for a couple months in a row back in 1997. I finished about a third of this book during that general period ... before I was quickly conformed into a full-time working class construction hero again. It's all good. Charlie also loved Lonnie, and came to all our meetings back in the old days ... when he needed a little help. Charlie is radical.

Back in 1982, Apache Henry helped me start our small missionary ministry along with two Christian swimming pool maintenance friends, Richard Davis and Mike Oldham. All the people who have helped in our ministry efforts over the years, have directly or indirectly contributed to this book including ... Ben & Irene Cowenburg, Robert Nickolaus, Bob and Debbie Sirignano, Chuck and Karen Mantyla, my anointed friend Jill Austin, Ian & Jane McCormack, Tom Chapman, Daryl & Evie Ballman, Greg & Diana Riegelman, Maurine Gore, Pastor Phil Agular and Set Free, Richard & Janet Wecki in England, Mike Polk in Africa, Ed & Julie Warth, Steve Macy, Frank Pica, my good friend Ron Pfiffer, Pastor David Spoon, my radical Kiwi friend Craig Bloor ... and many others. Two people who I will be eternally grateful to are Ken and Dianne Pursley. They served with us in the local church for years, and literally kept us alive on the mission field ... with packages, ATM bank transfers, telephone calls, and prayer. They additionally let my family of four live with them twice ... before and after our trip around the world. I wrote much of this book in their home. They are truly giving, loving servants of Jesus, and we continue to serve together in Freedom Crusade.

Everyone should be the most thankful for his or her family. My eighteen-year-old daughter Jenna has helped me do some editing. My sister-in-law, Linda Kucera has helped me with more extensive editing. Linda is tough and sharp ... a good combo. My brother Randy and his wife Kathy have had some great input. I really appreciate it.

My son John is so genuine, and such a committed young Christian ... that I am blown away. He is preparing for the mission field at a Christian University, and has a tremendous burden for the Islamic people. He went to London with a team from his college two years ago, and reached out to the large Muslim community there. He just returned from another missionary trip to Thailand, and absolutely loves the people. John and I compare notes, and pray for each other. It's great. My other son Troy agreed to let me share his recent letter, and is always such an encouragement. I love my entire family, including my parents, brothers, absent daughter Denielle, step-son Nathan, and extended family, so much that words don't exactly make it ... don't even come close to what I feel. I can't express how grateful I am for them.

To top off my list of acknowledgements, I am so thankful for my wife Roxanne, who has made a million sacrifices for the kids and myself ... and for my crazy dreams, visions, and ministry callings. She knows about "counting the cost" spiritually, physically, financially, and emotionally. We found out what it feels like to "pick up our cross and follow Jesus". It's wonderful, but has a price tag. When you go after souls ... there will also be intense spiritual warfare. We have learned the importance of staying "in-tune" ... and staying close to Jesus, and to each other. Nothing is too hard for God! Roxanne and I have been in the "School of the Holy Spirit" for a long time, and I thank God for such a gifted, determined, sincere, loving, and courageous wife.

At the end of the day ... Jesus is the winner! He conquered the grave, and wins the prize. Believe it or not, the Bible declares that we are his prize, and his inheritance. How humbling! He must really love us! Thank God!!!